LETTERS OF GEORGE GISSING

From a photograph by Messrs. Elliott & Fry.

George Gissing.
May 1901.

LETTERS OF GEORGE GISSING

To Members of his Family

COLLECTED AND ARRANGED

BY

ALGERNON AND ELLEN GISSING

WITH A PREFACE BY HIS SON
A PORTRAIT IN PHOTOGRAVURE
AND A FACSIMILE LETTER

HASKELL HOUSE PUBLISHERS LTD.
Publishers of Scarce Scholarly Books
NEW YORK. N. Y. 10012
1970

First Published 1927

HASKELL HOUSE PUBLISHERS Ltd.
Publishers of Scarce Scholarly Books
280 LAFAYETTE STREET
NEW YORK. N. Y. 10012

Library of Congress Catalog Card Number: 77-130257

Standard Book Number 8383-1158-X

INDEXED IN BCh³

Printed in the United States of America

PREFACE

"FOOLISHLY arrogant as I was," wrote my father in *The Private Papers of Henry Ryecroft*, " I used to judge the worth of a person by his intellectual power and attainment. I could see no good where there was no logic, no charm where there was no learning. Now I think that one has to distinguish between two forms of intelligence, that of the brain, and that of the heart, and I have come to regard the second as by far the more important." These words will not infrequently be recalled to the minds of all who read the letters included in this volume. A book similar in character to that from which the above extract has been taken was contemplated by the author towards the end of his life ; but death came before it could be written. In it were to be set forth his ideas as further modified by experience. He realised that there was need of another work in which his gradually changing view of things might find expression ; and it is indeed unfortunate that such a project was never carried out, for we know comparatively little of his mental development in later days. The letters assuredly reveal some change of attitude, yet of his inner thoughts we are but rarely given a glimpse ; and we cannot but regret that we have not been allowed some more definite knowledge of his maturer judgments.

At the beginning of his career my father suffered a great loss in the untimely death of William, a younger brother of great promise, who, had he lived longer, might have been the means of directing the course of his life into smoother channels. Yet he faced the struggle with unflinching courage and with a determination such as but few have ever shown.

The letters have been allowed to speak almost entirely for themselves, with which object in view as little as possible from an outside source has been introduced. Here and there have been inserted extracts from the diary; but this is done chiefly with the idea of furnishing such details of his movements and occupations as are not contained in the letters. The entries are, as a rule, short and hurried ; they were intended either to recall to the writer's mind the principal events of each day, or in a few words to summon up before his vision certain impressive scenes which he had looked upon during his travels on the Continent. Except in the case of his foreign travel there are but few detailed descriptions or expressions of opinion; consequently the entries contain little that would be of interest to the public. The diary is written in a minute but perfectly legible handwriting ; and on some of the pages, illustrative of his travels abroad, are to be found careful sketches which shew that he possessed much undeveloped power, especially in the representation of landscape.

In a letter printed near the end of this volume my father wrote the following words : " I hope my *Ryecroft* will be out as a volume early in the year. . . . On the whole I suspect it is the best thing I have done, or am likely to do ; the thing most likely to last when all my other futile work has followed my futile life." And again, in *Henry Ryecroft*, he gives expression to a similar feeling of disappointment in the retrospect of his earlier work : " There was a time—it seems further away than childhood—when I took up my pen with eagerness ; if my hand trembled it was with hope. But a hope that fooled me, for never a page of my writing deserved to live. I can say that now without bitterness. It was youthful error, and only the force of circumstance prolonged it." Such words I believe to have been written in all sincerity, yet their truth is by no means established. For, in so far as his work was uninfluenced by the mere desire of fame ; in so far as it was intended to benefit the human race, and was undertaken in the spirit of humility ; thus far precisely is his condemnation of himself unjust.

ALFRED C. GISSING.

RICHMOND, SURREY,
May 1926.

CONTENTS

EDITOR'S NOTE

Portions have necessarily been omitted from many of the letters. Except in those cases where a definite theme has been broken into, these omissions have not been indicated by dots.

I

EARLY LETTERS (1868-1877)

WRITTEN during school holidays from Monkshouse, near Bamburgh, on the Northumberland coast. Age 10½. Spelling and punctuation retained.

MONKSHOUSE
27th (June, 1868)

DEAR FATHER

On Thursday we put the line to catch the fish into the sea and on Friday morning when the tide was down we went and got the line in and there was five flat fish and the biggest mother said would wey above two pounds we had them for tea and they would have been beautiful only they were rather underdone. The line being entangled mother undid it for us and laid it out on the sands and when we went back after dinner of course no line could be found but it turned out the Thorpes had been their and had taken it and very coolly baited it and put it into the sea. I suppose we shall have to wait till monday till we get it because we can't go out to-day.

They all went out yesterday and got a lot of shells which they store up in a drawer and I think by when we come back we shall have about enough to stock the house.

I asked Willie if he had anything to say to you and he said that I was to say he was very well but as soon as I had put it down he began to cry and said that now he'd nothing to put in his letter but at last he made it up all right and he encloses his letter in this evelope. Mother hopes that you have got the key this morning. We all send our best love and are all well.

I am

Your affectionate son

GEORGE R. GISSING.

SEASCALE,
Jan. 17*th* (1869 ?)
(Plainly written Jan., but surely a mistake for June.)

DEAR FATHER

I was very glad to receive your letter to-night. I did not go to Gosforth this morning as mother said I had better not go.

All the lichens I find are on stones and I can hardly get them off without breaking. Today we found a large sea mouse which we put in the bottle. The sketch I send you is Gosforth church you do not see the ground, but that first piece is the wall. This morning it was very misty at first but it all cleared off and we have had a grand day, we could not see the Isle of Man however but we saw a ship pass by for Whitehaven. I am very glad Willie is enjoying himself. Tonight the sunset on the hills was splendid, just the colour that it is on the framed pictures in the drawing room. Tomorrow if it is fine Mr. Tyson is going to drive us to Wast Water. We have kept the star fish and it has dried well but is so very brittle that I don't know how we shall get it home. We have seen St. Bees here splendidly today and it has been very rough on the sea. The foam after the sea went down lay in huge masses all up the shore and kept blowing about and when you put your hand in, it was as hot as fire. Algie is now writing to Willie and mother has just told him to put something in the letter so he said " O ! yes I'll put a P.S." and now he has been so grieved because he has to put " Your affectionate brother " and has not room for a P.S.

I am very sorry that you are so badly off about the weather at Wakefield for it is so different with us. I should just like you to be dropped down here I can think how you would fudge in the hedges for you would no doubt find lots of things. The only thing I am afraid of is that you will burst out laughing when you see what we have brought. The other day as I was walking over the periwinkle stone I performed the exploit of nearly tumbling off one stone into a deep pool, and just as I was recovering my equilibrium I fell headlong into another but it only ended in getting rather wet.

Today as a wave had come up rather farther than mother expected she fell and I went after her and she fancied at first she had put her arm out. I can fancy you can picture us all rolling together on the sands.

We all send our very kind love to everyone and we are jolly.

I am

Your affectionate son

G. R. GISSING.

P.S.—Just off to Wast Water so cannot send drawing till tomorrow.

To his brother, nine years old, at Seascale alone in the winter for his health. If Jan. of the preceding letter is correct it must belong to 1870. The advancement in style may support this, so possibly George and his mother had joined the invalid for a week or two in the new year.

Dec. 28 (1869).

DEAR ALGIE,

According to your request I give you a few hints about sketching from Nature, and I hope you will find them useful at Seascale. When you begin, stand up, and partly close your eyes. By doing this, you see, you will get the principal features in the landscape which are always wanted first.

By principal features of course I mean the largest and principal objects, such as mountains etc. Then sketch out on your paper, what you see when like this. Of course you will see no small objects such as gates and posts, but you do not want this yet. Sketch the outline very lightly indeed, as you will often have to rub it out and correct it.

When you have done this, open your eyes, and *then* put in the gates, posts, fields etc. Of course you have heard of such a thing as perspective. This means that you must make the mountains farthest off lighter than those nearer to you, and the outline and shading of a gate near to you must be darker, and also *larger* than one far off. You must particularly remember to make things far off *smaller* than one near, for this is the great merit of a drawing.

If you try colours, do not make them flaring as nothing looks worse. It shows such bad taste and ignorance. Of course the colours of things far off must be lighter than things nearer.

I am sure, Algie, that you will sketch as well as you can and either send them in letters or bring them when you come home, for I shall copy them and make paintings of them, and you will come in for your share.

I am
Your aff^{te} brother
GEORGE R. GISSING.

The following is a diary which lasted for seven days, written by George when two months under thirteen. It is on three sides of a foolscap sheet, and as the fourth side is blank the effort was evidently abandoned.

DIARY.

September. 1870.

10*th.   Saturday.*

This morning no fresh War news. Germans still reported to be marching on Paris. According to expectations Algie began his turn of mumps this morning, which I have happily got over. A nice row those three :—Algie, Willie, and Maggie, kick up in that nursery ! Not much illness among them. Today I invented, and intend to construct, a little model of a locomotive engine, working by steam, also a model of a Roman trireme, the oars moving by steam. I have read J. Eastmead's lecture upon Gladstone's book *Juventus Mundi.* I wish much I could have heard the lecture delivered, but I happened to be at the School of Art that night. The late winds have blown a tremendous lot of apples off the trees. I gathered them this afternoon.   I hope I shall soon begin my oil-painting again.   The last thing I did was a landscape for mother.   I am doing at the School of Art now a copy in black chalk of a cast from Westmacott's *Bluebell.*

I read a little book today of Willie's called *The First Paper Maker* which shows that the wasp was the first to invent this substance, with which it built its nest.

11th.   *Sunday.*

Went to church in the morning.   The boys and Maggie no better.   Had a jolly desert.   Drew a little in the afternoon. Today I heard a very good thing.   An Irishman was complaining about a hard sentence given to some prisoners " Why " he said " out of thirty who were sentenced to penal servitude for life only fourteen survived."

12th.   *Monday.*

Went to school.   Ward who blew his face up with Sodium and Poppleton who fell off a pear tree have not come yet.   I hope they will tomorrow.   The boys are still getting on with mumps.   The Prussians are still approaching Paris.   Nothing else of consequence.   This afternoon went to the School of Art, and brought home my picture which is very nearly finished. Tonight I prepared a study of a picture to be done in pencil " Orpheus playing."   Father gave me a long round tin to hold drawing paper, and the three volumes of trees he has.

13th.   *Tuesday.*

Jefferson came to school this morning.   We went to the garden before breakfast and got some potatoes and pears.   The boys no better.   Got on with my picture.

14th.   *Wednesday.*

Went to the School of Art this afternoon and finished the " Bluebell."   Banks is doing a landscape in sepia.   Mr. Smith is going to give me some competition work to do next.   Boys a little better, Willie gets down to dinner now.   Do a bit to my

picture.   After tea I went to the garden and got the biggest
basket full of pears, *off the ground*.   We have filled this before
off the ground, and there is about twice as much on the tree
yet.   I carried that basket up, full all by myself.   I took a few
pears to Mrs. Sweeting who gave me a shilling this of course
went to my paints.

15*th.   Thursday.*

This morning is Willie's birthday.   I gave him a lead pencil
as a present.   Father has given us a very nice little book.   It
is called *That's it, or Plain Teaching*.   It is profusely illustrated
having upwards of 1,200 illustrations.   It is a book by the
author of *The Reason Why* which I have.   I began to do
latin verses today for the first time.   Ward and Poppleton
have'nt come to school yet.   Maggie is much wuᵣse today
being very sick.   Doctor Wood has been.   We had a grand
mince pie for dinner instead of a plum pudding.   Willie has
not received any other present.   I give the following extract
from *That's it* because I think it a fact worthy of attention.
" The number of eggs deposited by certain of the oviparous
species of fish is enormous.   The sole lays 100,000.   The
carp 200,000.   The Tench 400,000.   The mackerel 500,000.
The flounder 1,300,000.   The cod 8,500,000.   The salmon
20,000,000."   p. 93.

On the same page it tells us that those Mermaids' purses I
have seen at the sea side are the eggs of the dog fish.

16*th.   Friday.*

This afternoon had holiday at school.   Maggie still very
poorly.   The boys better.   Drew a good bit today.

17*th.   Saturday.*

Maggie a little better.   No war news.   Sargeant came and
we had a drill in the midst of drizzling rain.   There was one
thing I learnt in my science this morning which I think
interesting.   " When the halo is seen round the moon it is a
sign of rain.   Because when this is the case the moon is seen

through partially condensed vapour. The larger the halo the nearer the vapour and the greater the probability of rain." Finished my picture of 'Orpheus' to my satisfaction. Orpheus is sitting playing on a lyre. In front of him runs a little stream, falling over stones. A fish jumps out of the water. Beyond him is a stag in a listening attitude. Behind him is a tree on which squirrel is seated. In the distance is a stag running up. Beyond the stream is a wild boar and a fox. About him are large trees. A lion is behind him and a rabbit down by his side also a tiger. This afternoon it rained, but I, Willie, and Nellie went to the garden.

His father died in December 1870, and early in the next year the three brothers were sent to boarding school, whence, at the age of 13½, George writes the following to his sister of four years old.

Lindow Grove
Alderley Edge, Cheshire.
April 3rd, 1871.

My Dear Little Sister,

I write for Algie and Willie as well as myself wishing you very many happy returns of the day.

I hope you will like the new house you are going to and will be as comfortable as you were in the old one, though I am afraid we shall never like it as much, as dear Father lived with us in the other. Tell little Madge (sister of 7½ years) that I wish her to get on to be able to read well, and she may look at my books as often as she likes. Indeed I should be glad if you would take the simplest you can find and tell Madge to get to read some tale out of it well by midsummer. We are all very happy here but we shall be very glad to see you all when the holidays come.

I am afraid you will not be able to have a plum pudding because dear Mother is so busy but you will get something tomorrow I think which I could not send off today. I have directed this letter to our old house, but I hope it will find you in good time. I shall soon know the address of the new one.

I shall have some drawings to send you very soon now. I must end up now as it is time for post.

With love to all

I am

Your affectionate brother

G. R. GISSING.

$14\frac{1}{2}$ years old.

LINDOW GROVE SCHOOL

May 5, 1872.

MY DEAR MOTHER,

I am afraid that you will be wondering what has become of me it is such a time since you heard last. The Science Examinations came off last week. I am glad I have been up for them, for they belong to the same lot as my Drawing Examinations and Father often used to say he should like me to go for them. But now I have to work in earnest for my great exam, the Oxford. If I pass that I don't care. I shall work as hard as ever I can for I know you would like me to pass well. This is in about three weeks, so that I have but very little time. After that I shall have a thorough rest. We shall all be with you in about six weeks. How the time does go ! I never knew a half go so quickly in my life, I suppose it is having so many exams. If I pass all I go up for, I shall have passed five this half.

Last Wednesday was May Day, and what do you think ? About 7 miles off there is a very old town called Knutsford where they keep up the *May Queen.* Several of us started at 12 and walked there. We got there in good time. There was a long procession of little boys dressed up as soldiers, next followed a car, all decked with flowers, on which was seated the May Queen in the middle, and round her several little children dressed up with flowers, etc. After them followed little boys each carrying a thing to represent the different trades. We saw the May Queen crowned beneath the May Pole. There

were thousands of people there, as it was a glorious day.   We
walked back, got back at 6, and were seated in the exam. room
at 7 where we sat till 10, so it was a hard day's work.

With best love, I remain
Your affectionate son
G. R. Gissing.

Lindow Grove
April 19th, 1873.

My Dear Mother,

  I have to write you a very long letter today, which I
hope will interest you.   Last Sunday Mr. Wood, who was at
Colwyn (where he has his new house) sent a letter inviting me
to go over.   So I went by train, and got there about 7 o'clock
in the evening.   The next morning, Monday, Georgie Wood
and I set off and walked, first to Llandudno.   You can imagine
how I enjoyed going to this place, which we hear so much about.
It is a beautiful crescent of houses situated on a glorious bay,
between Little and Great Orme's Head.   We passed on and
walked quite round the Great Orme's Head, by some rocks
which I have only seen equalled at Flambro' Head, a place which
I think you have heard of.   As soon as we get round this Head,
we come upon the river Conway, which just there flows into the
sea.   Well, we walked about 4 miles down the side of the
river, till we came opposite to Conway, when we crossed by the
celebrated Conway suspension bridge.   We saw Conway Castle,
and all the beauties of the place.   Conway, viewed from the
opposite side of the river, is, I believe, the most picturesque town
I ever saw.   It is built on the side of a hill, and backed by the
tremendous Welsh Mountains.   The castle too is glorious.
I remember there are several large pictures of it in that large
scrap book at home, which I have often looked at and wished
I could go there.   We had some lunch at Conway, and passed
on along the sea shore, at the foot of some glorious mountains.
We passed a place called Penmaenmawr, and saw the mountain
of the same name, one of the highest in Wales.   Here we got

our first glimpse of Anglesey which is a long, rather low, island. We next came to a village called Llanfairfechan, where Georgie took the train back to Colwyn   I went on, and passed through some of the most splendid scenery I ever saw.   On the left was a never ceasing panorama of huge mountains, and glorious glens, and on the right the sea, with Anglesey and Puffin Island in the distance.   At last I came to Bangor, went and saw the celebrated tubular bridge over the Menai Straits, and took train for Colwyn at 7.15.   Bangor is a long-stretching place, with only one street, about 1 mile and a half in length.   Being Easter Monday the place was crammed, and passing up the street and in a full carriage to Colwyn I didn't hear one single word of English spoken—all were Welsh.   This day I thoroughly enjoyed.   The day before I came Mr. Wood and the boys had been up Snowdon, a treat for which, I am sorry to say, I was too late.   On Tuesday, as school began again on that day Mr. Wood etc. had to go back, but he proposed that I should walk back to Alderley, and as I was willing, on Tuesday afternoon about 3 o'clock I set off.   I walked along the coast through Llandulas, and Abergele (where the fearful railway accident was), then turned inland to St. Asaph.   This place is the smallest *city* in England.   It is a little village, gloriously situated on the side of a hill, at the bottom of which a river flows, and the *Cathedral* is a rather large village church.   I should very much have liked to go inside but had not time.   I then walked on and climbed a very high hill, from the top of which I had the last glimpse of the sea.   The sun was just setting, and the scene was magnificent.   I could see the Ocean for miles round. Colwyn Bay and the Great Orme's Head in one direction, and the long stretch of coast in the other.   I passed on and as it was getting dark it began to thunder and lighten tremendously it sounded amongst those hills.   At last I came to a little village called Caerwys and found an inn, where there was one person who could speak English.   Here I put up for the night, and glorious it was.   I had ham and eggs for tea, ham and eggs for breakfast, with splendid milk.   Then after tea I sat by a large fire and listened to old farmers talking Welsh.   I had breakfast at 7 and set off at 8. I passed through the villages of Halkin, Northop, and Hawarden, in the last of which was a very swell wedding going on, and the whole place was decorated. Shortly after passing this place I got into Cheshire, and then the country changed from gloriously hilly to disgustingly flat. I passed through Chester, and on to a place called Kelsall, where I put up for the night; had ham and eggs for tea, ham and eggs for breakfast, and a good bed. Here of course I had not the pleasure of the Welsh. Next morning, Thursday, I set off at 8 o'clock, and walked through Northwich, the salt-mine place, Knutsford, and got to Alderley at 1 o'clock. So I had been one whole day and two halves. The distance I reckon about 67 miles.

Now you see one of my wild walking ideas has been realised at last ; and rarely I enjoyed it. You know I had never been in North Wales before. All the days were glorious, and a little rain every night just freshened everything up. When I come home again I hope to have the pleasure of going over this with you on a map.

With love to all

I remain

Your affectionate son

G. R. GISSING.

MANCHESTER (1876).

DEAR LITTLE NELL,

Very many thanks for your letter which I received this morning, and for the French one I had the other day. Both I liked much. I am so glad you like your French ; you cannot do better than go on and work at it as hard as possible. At Christmas we will try and read some little French book together, that will be very nice.

I suppose I seem to you to be a tremendous age now. [He was 18½]. It does not seem so long however since I was only as old as you are, and you will be at my age before you know it almost. The time goes so quickly that we cannot afford to

waste a single minute, and I only wish I could have two or three
years back again to make better use of them.   Nothing makes
one more comfortable than to think that no time has been
wasted, and I am sure you have not wasted much yet.

I hope you will not mind my writing such a short letter.
I am just waiting for tea to come in; and after tea I have to
rush out to a committee meeting, and then back again to work,
so that I really can hardly find time for anything.   However
I hope soon to see you all, and then we shall get a little talk
together.

Your affectionate brother
GEORGE.

On leaving Manchester this year he went to America, and
the following letter to his brother William is the earliest that
has been preserved.   George was now a month under nineteen.

71 BARTLETT ST.
BOSTON, MASS. U.S.
Oct. 5th, '76

DEAR WILL,

I suppose you will be thinking it was about time that
I wrote again; so as it is Saturday night, and we have just
finished dinner, and I have a horrible cold, I may as well employ
myself for half an hour or so in a conversation with you across
the Atlantic.   By the bye, you can have no idea what the
Atlantic is unless you have crossed it.   Of course there are
always lots of vessels going between America and Europe and
yet there is so much room that we only saw about half a dozen
during the whole voyage.   Then the waves are something
glorious.   There is always a long swell, so long that our
steamer, which you know would be by no means small, did not
fill up the space between the crests of two waves.   One or two
days it was decidedly rough; it was impossible to stand on deck
without holding by a rope, and the waves were then so high
that we never could see farther round us than the distance of
about three waves, and very often could see nothing beyond one.

I woke up in my berth one night, and found myself being knocked from one side to the other like a sort of shuttlecock and the basins, etc. were all dancing jigs over the cabin. I am happy to say I was not once sick. I asked mother to let you see the last letter I wrote her, so there will be no need of telling you all my novel experiences over again. There are more blacks here than I expected to see. At the Restaurants the waiters are nearly always blacks. I have been on the steam-cars only once yet. Each car is very much larger than yours in England. It will hold about fifty people. They sit across the car, and each one has an arm-chair to himself. In the corner of every car is a large stove where a fire can be made. There is only one class, and that very much better than 1st class in England. Our democratic notions do not allow of division into classes. As the train goes along you can walk right from one end to the other if you want, and fellows walk up and down selling refreshments, papers, and books. We call Railway Stations here Depôts. They carry democratic notions here to a great extent. It is quite a common thing for a workman to go up and slap his master on the back and ask him how he is. Worse than that, no servant-girl will think of cleaning boots, so we have to have them blacked in the streets, and the result is that the Americans have almost always dirty boots on. One polish a week is the most anyone ever thinks of. I used to be greatly puzzled at meals; there are so many kinds of vegetables always. Thus we nearly always have at dinner, squash, white potatoes, sweet potatoes, tomatoes, green corn, cauliflowers and turnips, and you are expected to eat them all together. The different kinds of bread is something astounding. We have white bread, brown bread, graham bread and corn bread, all very sweet, and you take a piece of each on your plate all at once. Fruit is tremendously plentiful and cheap. You get grapes for 10c. (5d.) a pound, and peaches at the same price. Apples have been sold in New York at 3c. (1½d.) a bushel. You can get a lobster here for 10c. which would cost 2s. 6d. in England. Water-melons and bananas swarm, and cranberries are plentiful. We eat cranberries with our meat.

I have got a splendid boarding-house. There are about ten other people in the house, all very pleasant. Of course we all take meals together, and excellent meals they are too. Meat and potatoes we always have for breakfast. The price for room and board is 10 dollars a week. I am sorry to say I have got nothing to do yet, but I hope to have very soon. My principal friend here is Mr. Garrison. He knows the editor of the *Atlantic Monthly*—one of our best periodicals—very well, and thinks he can perhaps get me a place on its staff in some capacity. I have just written an essay on Burns and Heine as song-writers, and it is going to be shown to the editor.

This time is rather exciting here. It is the year of the Presidential elections and everybody talks of nothing else, except I should say, the Centennial Exhibition which has had as many as 280,000 paid admissions a day. All the young men in Boston parade the town with bands and torches. The effect is very pretty. At the head ride officers on horses. As I write I can hear one of the bands just approaching. The sole object is to get up excitement about the election. We have two parties here, Republican and Democratic. The former is the party which carried the anti-slavery movement and has its chief strength in the North; the latter the old slave-holding party and is strongest in the South. The Republican candidate for the Presidency is Mr. Hayes and I think he will get in. The elections are in November.

I am doing a good deal at German just now. I have translated a great part of Heine's poems into verse, and I think it would be worth while to go on and translate the whole and then publish it. If I do I think I shall publish it in England, and then I shall ask you and Alg. to see to the business, proofs, etc. for me. I suppose you would do that. But of course it would be some time before I could do all, he has a great deal of prose. Have you read any of his verse? If not, ask Mr. Wood to lend you the *Buch der Lieder*; you will find it simple and very delightful. I remember though that his is a favourite copy and he might not like to lend it; perhaps you will be able to buy it soon. I think it is pretty cheap. I hope to hear very soon that you have more leisure; you were not troubled with that commodity when I saw you last.   I hope Alg. is flourishing. Tell him to be sure to let me know what he does in reading, etc. and do you the same.

I do not see much of the ocean.   Our harbour is so many miles round that it is a long way to the open sea.   I went in a steamer the other day across the harbour and a little way down the coast to a place called the Nantasket Beach.   The waves were rolling up splendidly, as I have not seen them on the shore for a long time.   I took a few sketches.

With love and best wishes

Your affectionate brother

G. R. G.

To his youngest brother still at school at Alderley Edge.

71 BARTLETT STREET,
BOSTON, MASS. U.S.
Nov. 13, 1876.

DEAR ALG.

Many thanks for your letter.   Please thank Will for his.   Both were very good and gave me great pleasure.   I have sent this letter to mother, and she will send it on to you.   Ask her to let you see the letter I have written to her; it has some information in it.

So you like Boswell; I felt sure you would.   He is immensely amusing.   Another very amusing book about Dr. Johnson is Mrs. Piozzi's *Anecdotes* (she was Mrs. Thrale), if you should ever come across it.   I am doing a little writing for newspapers and periodicals.   Ask mother to let you see the newspaper I sent her.   Do you hear anything of the little girls?   I should like to hear how they get on, *de temps en temps.*   You say you fear you will have to leave off German.   Of course it mustn't interfere with your examination, but I would not drop it if it can be possibly kept up *ever so little.*   I have been reading a great deal of German lately, and now I can get on very well without a dictionary.   I have read a lot of Goethe and some German novels lately.   The latter I read as if they were English.   I have long wished to get to that.   Haben Sie *Daniel Deronda* gelesen ?   It is George Eliot's last novel, you know, and has created a tremendous sensation.   Read it at your first opportunity.   It is very good.

   It was the election here nearly a week ago (see mother's letter) but this country is so vast that the returns have not come in from all the States yet, and things are rather uncertain. . . . Tuesday night was a tremendous sensation.   At one of the telegraph offices they had what we call a Stereopticon.   It is something like a magic lantern, and with it they threw the returns as they were telegraphed in, on the side of a house where the crowd could read them.   The intervals they filled up with portraits of the candidates, and comic cartoons.   It was very good fun, though it rained cats and dogs.   Last Friday the Centennial Exhibition at Philadelphia closed.   For the last month there have been over 150,000 visitors every day. I am very sorry I could not go, but it would have cost about £5. It takes from 7 o'clock at night to 9 o'clock in the morning to get to Philadelphia.   The newspaper consumption in this country is something astounding, though they are much dearer than in England.   On election day 232,000 copies of the *Boston Herald* were printed (about ten editions) in weight altogether 14 tons!   Pretty fair that.   I guess an ordinary English paper doesn't often run so.   We have just had a wonderful invention here called the " Telephone " by which people can speak to each other at the distance of several miles. They even talk of its superseding the telegraph, for they do not yet know all its capabilities.

   Do you keep quite well ?   I am in splendid health.

   We have some reading aloud in our family here every day. This morning I have been reading some of *Vanity Fair* to them; very enjoyable.   We have a glorious public library here.   It is free to all to use and I can assure you it is excellently patronised; for here, you know, everybody reads.   There are very few books that one would be at all likely to want that it does not contain.

Altogether Boston is a splendid place. I should be very sorry ever to leave it for good. I have just been writing some "Sketches of Life in a Manufacturing Town." I have sent them to one of the magazines, but have not heard yet whether they are accepted. I suppose things go on with you very much in the old style. I hope some day you will be able to take a trip over here. It is really a very trifling matter. You meet comparatively few people here who have not been in Europe. Everybody goes, even the servants, and they think nothing of it. One thing we get here that you have in England, and that is— barrel organs. They play just the same tunes and are very abundant. There are a great many Chinese here, and they are chiefly washermen. As you walk down the street you see a sign like this—" Hop ting, Chinese Laundry," and other names equally beautiful. But the great place for Chinese is San Francisco. There they abound. I must go to California as soon as possible. You can get across for 20 dollars and it only takes you a week. Fancy a week in the cars! But they are different from your cars. Each one holds about 50. There is only one class, and that is better than English First Class. What we call the Palace Cars are fitted up just like a large dining room, and you eat and drink and go to bed at your ease. Every car, too, has a fire place in it. More news soon.

Yours affectionately

G. R. G.

To illustrate some of the circumstances of George Gissing's life up to the end of 1879 several letters written to him by his brother William are introduced. This brother, two years younger, died in the spring of 1880 at the age of twenty, and the value which Gissing attached to his letters is shewn in the fact that he preserved every one of them. Unfortunately the letters written by George to William have not been found, with the exception of one from America here given and three in 1880 to be given presently. This brother, now 17, having left school and obtained a clerkship in a bank in Manchester, writes to his brother in America.

WITHINGTON,
Jan. 17, 1877.

DEAR GEORGE,

I have just received from mother your letter to her. I am very glad you are settled now, though I hardly expected from your previous letters that it would be as a master ; nevertheless I am very glad to hear it, as there seems to me to be something in the quiet routine of teaching which is very pleasing —having none of that hardening influence which business has, and which even I, I fear, begin to feel already; for ordinary business can produce very little satisfaction, generally having only for its foundation that mean money-making spirit which is the bane of the world—no music, no poetry, no love in it, only one everlasting stubborn fight—but let me use the paper to better purpose.

*   *   *   *   *

It doesn't answer for long working nearly 15 hours a day, and it *is* work too, I can assure you.

I have nothing to tell you about music except that I get no practice at all nowadays, but hope to shortly again.   I become more convinced every day that very few people know what real music is.   They enjoy it but only as one would enjoy hearing beautiful poetry in an unknown language.   They can tell that it is fine but do not understand its meaning.   I think no man can exactly describe the effect of music on the soul (for I believe it is the soul that it does affect).   I have often tried to express it but never can, there are several points to be thought of concerning it.   To take two points: 1. Different harmonies produce different effects on the same subjects whilst in the same condition (moral condition or state of mind), or 2. The same harmonies produce different effects on the same subject according to the different condition he is in.   But in the first of these assertions we find grave music does not always produce a corresponding effect, and the same with light music.   But the most predominant effect of music is, I think, to produce an indefinite longing, which passes into a sweet calmness, faintly tinged with melancholy or rather sadness, perhaps produced by the abatement of the bliss felt for the time, but leaving permanently within a feeling which makes us kinder to all around us, and better fits us for the duties we have to perform.

When this reaches you I presume you will be quite settled down, therefore I send you my best wishes for success and prosperity.

Your affectionate brother
WILLIAM W. GISSING.

To his brother Algernon at School.

BOX 331
WALTHAM, MASS.
Jan. 28, 1877.

You will have heard by this time that I have, at last, got a place. In every respect I am much pleased with it. I have classes in German, French and English ($800), and all are very orderly, attentive and interesting. I daresay you have some general idea of our public school system here. We have three kinds—Primary, Grammar and High Schools, and I am first assistant teacher in one of the last. All the schools are free, and boys and girls attend the same classes. The perfect order that prevails and the respect with which the masters are treated is delightful. I never saw anything like it in England. Waltham is a small town (10,000) situated in a most beautiful hilly district. It is noted for its watch factory, the largest in America. It is only ten miles from Boston, so that I get into town at least once a week.

Last Friday our term ended, and we are now having a week's vacation. To end up we had a public viva-voce examination, and a good many people were there.

I was very pleased with all your letters; they were good and interesting. Do not fail to let me hear how you get on and what is doing generally. We are in a considerable difficulty (politically) here at present. You know the election for President was held last year, and no decision has yet been arrived at as to who is elected.   There has been so much corruption in the South, particularly in Florida, S. Carolina and Louisiana where the whites oppress the black voters terribly, that the returns sent from the several States cannot at all be relied upon. Congress is at present considering a special bill for the counting of the votes for President, and we hope it will pass and things be arranged amicably ; some people even fear a civil war again. In that case it would be something like the state of affairs in 1860, except that the blacks in the South would now be free and would do all they could to support the Republicans.   At one time things were in a fearful state in New Orleans.   There two men were elected Governors at once, one Republican and the other Democratic.   One of them got into the State House and was besieged there by the other with troops!   Fancy such things happening.   They are, however, rather quieter by this time.

This is one of the severest winters that has been known here for years.   Ice has been thick on the ground since the beginning of December, and though there is often a very hot sun, it does not melt.   No wheel-carriages are used here now; they are all sleighs.   We have all to wear a kind of galoshes that we call rubbers, to prevent us falling down as we walk.   The thermometer is every day at zero and when I go out in a morning the breath freezes on my face.   We have to be very careful not to get our ears frozen.   On Mount Washington (N. Hamp.) the thermometer was one day at 47 below zero!   The snow in New York State has been so bad that 8,000 railway cars were blocked and could not move on for about a week.   This is rather tremendous, isn't it ?   You heard, I suppose, about the Brooklyn fire.   Last Friday there was another tremendous affair in Boston, though fortunately only two people were killed. In an oil manufactory 1,500 barrels of kerosene blew up at once! You may think what an explosion it was when I tell you, that a few minutes after that, one barrel blew up by itself and sent a man six feet into the air.

The other night we formed a sleigh party at the school, and had a real good time.   All the teachers went and about thirty

scholars.   We started at half past seven in the evening, went to
a town called Brighton, where we dismounted and played games,
etc., in a large hotel, then came back again and got home at
half past twelve.   You have nothing of that kind in England.
You know it couldn't be done with a lot of English school boys,
but here you always treat your scholars like gentlemen and they
respect you.

I see from the papers that Niagara is nearly blocked with ice.
It must be fearfully cold in Canada.   I have got a very comfortable place to live in.   It is not a regular boarding house,
but simply a private family—I live like one of them.   I pay
8 dollars a week including washing, so that putting my salary
and my private teaching together I can live very comfortably
indeed.   Everybody tells me that they are very much pleased
with my teaching, so that is satisfactory.   When I first came
here I had the newspaper reporter come to see me, wanting to
know where I came from and where I had studied.   A High
School teacher is an important person here.

I hope Will still gets on well and likes his work.   Are the
little girls all right ?   I hope they get on with their French.
I can tell you I am very glad now that I did so much French
and German; it is being useful to me.   I hope you all keep quite
well.   I suppose by what I hear from England that you are
having rather a bad time there, continued rain and that sort of
thing.   I guess I'd rather have our cold than that.   I thoroughly
enjoy our weather, and do not suffer in the slightest.   Everyone
is astonished at me.   Do you read the magazines at all ?   I take
in a magazine called the *Eclectic*.   As the name implies it
consists of a selection of all the best articles from English
periodicals.   So I manage to keep *au courant*.   I don't know
when you will get this letter, the boats are so long going in this
weather.   Love to all.

II

RETURN FROM AMERICA TO PUBLICATION OF *WORKERS IN THE DAWN* (1877-1880)

In the autumn of 1877 Gissing returned to England and, under the same unsettled circumstances, entered upon his London life. He was now married. In the course of a characteristic letter to him, dated October 18 of this year, his brother William, still in Manchester, says:

This morning I received a letter from Mother in which she says she has heard from you. I wish it had been to say that you had found some employment. . . . Once get permanent employment, and then the ship can again resume a straight course, having been a little delayed and turned about by fogs and cross-currents, but now the mist has risen. . . . Please let me know of your arrangements. Anything however small which I can ever do shall never be withheld.

1 St. Paul's Place
Withington
Oct. 30, 1877.

My Dear George,

Many thanks for your last letter, safely received from Mother. It contained so much that I do not even yet feel equal to answering it as it deserves, but am unwilling to delay longer. . . . Your present employment has come at the right moment, giving us just what we wanted—time to look vigorously round for a permanency. That is the thing. . . .

And now we will turn to your questions. Subjects for essays, say you ? Ay, plenty, but of such a nature as, I fear, not to be

palpable to you.   No two minds run in the same groove, so
let us all make due allowance, let us all show due admiration.
You see my mind is not developed.   I think a great deal, I have
ideas, but I cannot as yet catch, condense and transmit to paper
a true exposition of my opinions.

Here they are, and others there are which may afterwards
come to mind.   [Then follow ten subjects amongst which are :]

6. The higher education of women discussed.

7. The important quarrels of nations are settled by international arbitration :—some reasons why the matter is arbi-
trated *after* 50,000 strong useful men have been killed in
preference to *before*.

9. The difference, if any, between the effect of music and that
of poetry on the human mind.

10. The characters of Dickens and Thackeray compared,
and how far the character of a writer may be gathered from his
works.

" Very unsatisfactory these " you will say, " in fact no half
dozen pages of foolscap to be extracted from them altogether."
You are probably right.   " Allowance " please in my case.

It often, I assure you, requires more time than that taken in
drinking a cup of tea to wash off the hardening effect of one's
contact with the world.   Then my time is short.   I walk both
to and from town every day when the weather at all admits it.
That is two hours of the day ; not lost though, for I can observe
and think during that time.   During the hours of business,
business receives my whole and devoted attention (as it necessarily must if I wish to do anything).

*   *   *   *   *

I get home as a rule by half past six.   My bed time is a
quarter past ten (rising at six).   Now, look, here is a nice time
from 6.30 to 10.15 for study, etc. with these disadvantages,
tea and supper intervening; three unintellectual people in the
same room, who regard reading as unsociability and it is condemned accordingly: Miss C. favours us with her tales about
her servants ; Mr. C. profusely (if not stopped short unanimously) with the prices and merits of coals and the rearing of

pigs, but still I read a little.   Recently one or two of Smiles'
books, Bacon's *Essays*, Carlyle, at long intervals a novel.

*   *   *   *   *

From the same :

Nov. 21, 1877.

My Dear George,

Allow me to express my fervent hope that you may
spend very many happier birthdays than to-morrow.

One score of years.

We must turn our heads a moment.   Leave our hopeful
looking forward to review the ground already passed.   Perchance we shall see some points in the distance which will bring
to mind old resolutions and experiences, materially assisting us
in our difficult clamber up the hill; quite a new supply of
walking-sticks!

We can see all behind us, but the road in front gives a sudden
bend, hiding everything.   It is fortunate, for all our attention
must be given to passing the present rough, awkward bit of
ground.   It is hard for me to be travelling the same path with
you and not able to assist you.   But I will assist you; by
encouragement, by example, by anything and everything in my
power.   We, as men living in this noble world, have only one
course to pursue—a straight one of open truth.   This takes
away half our difficulties.   We never have to calculate and
change our policy; we never have regrets for the failure of that
policy.   If this do not help to bring us means of life, it will at
any rate at the end bring us a consolation most certain.   We
have tried to do nothing unworthy of a *man*.   We must lead,
we will not be led.   Men shall meet us, and leave us, meeting
another shall say, " We have just spoken to a true man."

How fine these words sound!   Will they bring us a loaf for
tomorrow ?

If my words are worthless this question will shatter them.
If they are sound we can view the two together, the ideal and
the material.   *I* can do so.   My own words stimulate me ;
they determine me, urge me on, producing in me a resolute

happiness, looking for the first chance which will bring me that loaf.

How earnestly I hope that you will quickly obtain some congenial labour.

A few words as to my own movements.   New lodgings next Monday with the hope of spending less money.   I will let you know how I get on.   This is no hasty step, of course.   I have found out all that I can about the woman who keeps them, and am satisfied.   I quite intend to be comfortable, so of course I shall be.   I shall, I hope, get some music and reading.

Another twelve months I feel sure will better all of us.

Much love from your affectionate brother
WILLIAM W. GISSING.

From the same :

Jany. 20, 1878.

MY DEAR GEORGE,

I received a note from Alg. yesterday reminding me how long it is since I wrote to you.

I was considerably disturbed by changing my lodgings but I have secured my chief object. . . . .

For the last three weeks it has generally been after one when I have got to bed and then off at eight in the morning, so that for the next few weeks I intend to be out as much as I can and get plenty of sleep, etc.   I have reason to believe that I must be very careful with myself.   So you see that, except to let you know that I was all right, I have had little to write about, but hope soon to commence a better correspondence, telling you all my own little experiences—anything that will at once cheer and encourage you.   My one desire is that you may as soon as possible resume your true place in life.   Your mind cannot live amongst its present surroundings, it must rise far above them.   And besides, the duty you owe to your fellow men will urge you on; we do not live for ourselves but for others.   That is a poor life which only lives for self.   Your knowledge must be given out and extended over as great an area as possible.

So we must carefully consider what will promote this continual advance and suit our actions accordingly. I do not know what you are doing at present beyond preparing that B.A. candidate.

*   *   *   *   *

Your affectionate brother
WILLIAM W. GISSING.

The following letter to his younger brother gives some intimation of what he was doing by its reference to his first long novel, of which they had talked during that brother's recent visit to him in London. (Never published and title forgotten.)

22 COLVILLE PLACE,
Jan. 30, 1878.

I snatch the first spare moment which presents itself to fulfil my promise with regard to library-cataloguing. What say you to something of the following description?

[Then follows a detailed classification of all literature.]

In the meantime, could you do me a favour. I want all the Chemistry and Natural Philosophy that is required for Matriculation squeezed into the narrowest compass possible. If you still have your notes I should think it would not take you long to do this. I mean, you know, notes to be made on all the *essential* points—such as all the necessary formulæ, etc. Could you do this within a few weeks?

Feb. 2.

P.S.—I am glad to say I have begun to have lessons again with my pupil, and still more rejoiced to add that the *Translation* project is not wholly abandoned. If they can secure a publisher I think I am pretty sure of the work. I shall see on Monday what your position is, and let you know at once; possibly I shall not post this till then. Am getting on well with my novel, which progresses at the rate of about 12pp. (foolscap) a day.

[Added in pencil.]

BURLINGTON HOUSE.

Rejoice, old fellow! You have taken a *first class*. Many congratulations.

To the same :

22 COLVILLE PLACE
Feb. 12, 1878.

I have been very far from well these last few days, and do not, I am sorry to say, feel much improvement as yet. This has prevented me from writing you some of the letters I promised, but I hope soon to be able to let you have a few lines on the general principles of study.

The novel does not get on as well as I could wish—in fact I feel unequal to almost any effort just at present. The sickening political news has a great deal to do with it, I believe. Do you read the papers ? If so you will see that the Porte has refused admission for English vessels to the Straits, and tonight the papers tell us that the Russians are occupying Constantinople and a squadron has been sent to the Mediterranean. I used to be strongly pro-Russian, but really there seems to be such underhand work on that as well as the other side that one gets disgusted. It is sickening to hear all this twaddle, however, about " British interests," as if it was more to our interest to kill several thousands of Englishmen and involve half the population in ruin and beggary than to stop for a generation or two the progress of the Slavonic races which is ultimately inevitable! To me it appears that all we need bother about at present is the keeping open the Suez Canal and that interest does not appear to be threatened. France, Germany and Austria form considerable wedges between us and Russia, I think. If Russia chooses to cut off the supply of corn, etc. from Odessa— well, she looses a good customer and we go elsewhere for a market. Gladstone, I think, still holds on to the right course. You see he held out to the last against the £6,000,000. If only we could kick old L. out of Constantinople, and put Gladstone in Beaconsfield's place, we might have some chance of steering clear yet.

Please to drop a line to Will (or perhaps you will see him soon) and tell him I will write as soon as possible. What does he anticipate with regard to the war ? Ten to one we shall all be food for powder before the business comes to the end. . . .

I cannot write more at present as my head is bothering me a good deal. You shall hear again soon.

Feb. 28, 1878.

To Algernon,

Today is a red-letter day in my calendar, for I have seen no less a person than *Alfred Tennyson.* One of his sons has, today, been married to a daughter of Frederick Locker, the poet, at Westminster Abbey, and in expectation of seeing Alfred, I was present at the ceremony. There were numbers of grand people there (including the Princess Beatrice). Amongst them I recognised Herbert Spencer and Henry Irving, the actor. Alfred was unmistakable. I knew him in a moment. He wore precisely the same cape-coat which you see in his portraits. His son was remarkably like him.

*   *   *   *   *

I am getting on with my novel which I hope to be drawing to a conclusion in a little more than a month.

*   *   *   *   *

You may have seen in the papers an account of the riotous meeting in Hyde Park last Sunday. I was there. There must have been hard upon 100,000 people there, but owing to some hired blackguards of the government faction, nothing could be done. War still appears to be imminent. Have you seen the proposed treaty of peace between Russia and Turkey? Turkey will retain nothing in Europe save Constantinople. Austria is making vigorous preparations for war, and we, as you know perhaps, have even decided on the commander to lead our forces.

Alfred T. has a poem in the March *Nineteenth Century.*

William writes on March 8, 1878:

Many thanks for your kind letter of the 1st inst. I read with sorrow your last sentence " I am almost despairing." Pray let me cancel it. It frequently happens that when our affairs look at their very worst something turns up close to us, of which we had not the least suspicion. Let us then hope that you may quickly be gladdened by some good fortune.

It is very bad only having one room. You of course do everything possible to keep it fresh. Do you consider it best to remain in London ?

After you have finished with your Matriculation candidate and should nothing else turn up, if you continue writing, could not publishers be solicited by letter, supposing you came to live anywhere else ? But I suppose your Museum ticket is invaluable; you absolutely could not get on without it, as elsewhere the books you require would not be within your reach. I wish you would confide more to me, for you of course know that it is no idle curiosity which makes me mention it but only a sincere desire to help you, if I possibly can in any way. The bold thought which struck me was: could you come up here and join me ? but you would require some small income from some source or other, as with all my economy I cannot do without help from home which galls me terribly, knowing the heavy strain lately placed upon Mother.

To his brother Algernon :

May 2, 1878.

It was very annoying that you had such very bad weather for your tramp. . . . I was glad you did not miss Haworth. I suppose you climbed the almost perpendicular street and saw the little parsonage where *Jane Eyre* first saw the light. I admire your pluck in trudging along a day through the rain. I once did the same thing in N. Wales. I think that such a walk is not after all so wholly unenjoyable as some stay-at-homes imagine. There is always *nature*, and that is interesting in every aspect. When I am out on a bleak wintry night, I can always find one pleasure at least in the situation, and that is in the images from various novelists and poets which surrounding sights and sounds recall. I should think your wild day on the moors must have brought vividly before your mind several passages from Jane Eyre, and the passages in Dickens are innumerable which a wretched night in London summons to the thoughts.

*   *   *   *   *

I have been busy this week, for M. has lost his clerk temporarily and I have been acting in that capacity, for the sum of one guinea. The hours are tremendous, *from ten to ten*. However I feel much better than for some time. On account of this extra work I have not been able to get on with your notes, but I will recur to them on the first opportunity. I know you have quite enough to keep working at. Don't forget Captain Cuttle " When found, make a note of."

Novel progresses though slowly.

Great excitement here on Eastern crisis. Confound it! I wish they would let us have peace and quietness. You know, I suppose, that the Paris Exhibition opened yesterday. I understand that, with the exception of the British portion, it was not half complete. How I should like to run over! Mais hèlas! C'est impossible.

More before long. At present χαίρε.

To the same brother on May 22, 1878:

*   *   *   *   *

My memory is very treacherous. Did I tell you that I have got another pupil ? He lives near Temple Bar. I give him 3 hours a week, from 8-9 a.m. in Latin only. The remuneration is wretched, 4s. for the 3 hours each week. But all's fish, etc. The novel progresses, and will I trust soon be finished, now that I have some time to myself. . . . .

Could you by any possibility procure me legal counsel on the following points ? A man intends to shoot one person, but under an error shoots another instead: what punishment would he receive ? Don't be alarmed at the nature of the question; it merely has its rise in fictitious exigencies. Moreover, a man is being tried for murder and during the trial another gives himself up as the real murderer. How would legal proceedings be conducted ? Enter into minutiæ, if possible, when you have time.

Do you keep a journal of your reading ? It is very interesting to do so and make slight critical notes. I have not had much time for reading lately, and now I am grinding up Cicero's *De Officiis* which is the book my new pupil has. I have just been glancing through Dicken's *Uncommercial Traveller,* a capital series of essays—and reading some French novels by Eugène Sue and Henri Murger. Thank Heaven, the French is just as easy as English to me. I would give something for a good set of German books, for I have absolutely none.

En attendant une réponse à toutes mes questions.

Je reste

à jamais votre

G. R. G.

On June 16, 1878, *William writes :*

I was glad to hear you had another pupil. I should think he congratulates himself on the bargain. There is, however, one good point about it, he may bring others, and let us hope more profitable ones.

It must be very interesting examining the holes of London, as long as you don't catch a fever. . . . .

Is the novel nearly ended ? I should think the anxiety to dispose of it advantageously must be immense after so much labour. Little change occurs here, but I hope my next letter will be more interesting.

To his brother Algernon :

July 24, 1878.

In your last you said nothing of Will. Is he better ? The publishers respectfully decline the honour of publishing my novel. Just what I anticipated. The next must be better.

* * * * *

How do you progress with work ? I have not been able to get an hour at the Museum for a long time, though the work I am doing is not remunerative. It is working off little jobs for M. at the office, and most of my time is fribbled away at it. I would give a trifle to be able to get into some regular position, so as to be able to go to bed at night and clearly know where the dinner was coming from next day.

Do you see Tennyson has a new volume of *lyrical* poems coming out ? I am delighted to hear it. . . . .

Have you heard anything of your own holiday ? I hope you will get one of some kind. I have given up all hope of anything but starvation and wretchedness.

On August 14, 1878, *William writes :*

Cannot the novel be sold ? I fear they are overstocked. I think your idea of a foreign tutorship is very practical. It is this influence that bothers us again. I will make all inquiries I can. I know one or two Germans but no Frenchmen. Let me know your wishes, and at any rate I will do my best, even if nothing come of it. But something may turn up between us both. I must now close. I will try and see one German gentleman tomorrow.

It may be here mentioned that a sum of about five hundred pounds, George Gissing's share of a trust fund which had been thrown into Chancery on his father's death, would be payable to him on his attaining his majority. This would occur on the 22nd of the present month, a fact which would sufficiently

account for the renewed buoyancy of succeeding letters.   He
had now removed to 31 Gower Place, and from that address
on November 9 he writes to his brother Algernon:

"Dear to the vulgar as Lord Mayor's Day."   That
functionary's office seems now-a-days to be of no very great
importance.   The name makes one think of the old French
maires du palais, who, from being simply the head of the king's
household, grew to be the actual head of the State, and then,
in the person of Pepin, got possession of the crown.   The Lord
Mayor's show seems an extraordinary relic of the past, lingering
on after all its significance has departed.   Strange to say, we
always preserve those usages longest which have least to
recommend them.

What a scandalous condition England is in with regard to
public libraries.   You know that the last Public Library Act was
permissive merely, and, as such, of little practical use.   There
is not a town of the least pretensions in the States, which has not
its excellent Free Library. . . . It is a disgrace that London
possesses nothing to compare with all this.   Have they taken
any steps towards it in Wakefield?   It was proposed to bring
the Act in force in Hackney a short time ago, but a majority
voted against it.   One worthy sage opined that the inhabitants
of Hackney were not so illiterate as to need such factitious aids
to learning as public libraries.

＊   ＊   ＊   ＊   ＊

Your system of walks is interesting, and I only wish I could
accompany you.   I had no idea that the division into "Wapen-
takes" still actually exists.   Let Mother know that I am anxious
to hear how she gets on.   I do hope she will take care of herself
during the winter.   Many thanks for your long letter.

On Nov. 12, 1878, *William writes:*

＊   ＊   ＊   ＊   ＊

I hope your conviction with regard to your true sphere of
work is right.   Our two dispositions differ so.   I am so fond
of hard facts, you know.   I would merely say this in connexion

with your intention. Keep your two natures wide apart.
That one which loves to build an imaginary world, filling it
with ideal scenes and characters, and that one (and the one which
is to guide you through life), which looks upon the realities of
life with a clear unerring eye, estimating everything at its right
value, and acting accordingly; for I really believe in writing
fiction there is a danger of losing a just apprehension of practical
affairs.

To Algernon :

31 GOWER PLACE,
Nov. 15, 1878.

I have just sent off to Will about 300 pp. of the novel I have
on hand.   He has promised to read and criticize. . . .

What do you think of an advertisement like this ?

" SPECIAL NOTICE TO THE WORKING CLASSES, by whom I
live.   We have entirely removed from —— to ——.   For
about 16 weeks our trade has gradually increased.   Customers
approve the change.   We are the Originators of the Working-
man's and Middle-class Boot Stores.   Our greatest want is
gratitude to you.   It stimulates us to do our utmost.   We find
our neighbours make all sorts of statements about us.   Perhaps
it amuses them, and reminds us of the words of an ancient poet:

> Who hath not seen the snarling cur
> Snap at the Newfoundland ? "

Is not this prime ?   Who is the *ancient* poet who speaks in
such marvellous metre of Newfoundlands ?   I suspect, *parva
componere magnis,* that this ancient poet falls under the same head
as the old plays from which Scott drew headings for his chapters.

Would you believe it, I have three pupils in Latin, all above
twenty-one, and each of them finds the most insuperable difficulty in understanding that mysterious trinity of concords:
(1) that a verb must agree with its Nom.   (2) that a transitive
verb governs Acc. case.   (3) that adj. must agree with its
noun.   After several weeks of steady perseverance, one of

them is at length acquiring a dim perception of the meaning of No. 1! Surely these, like Sir Toby Belch, have a most weak *pia mater*.

Talking of *Twelfth Night*, do you see that Phelps is dead, dead at 72 ? " I knew him, Horatio; a fellow of infinite jest, of most excellent fancy." That is, I knew him on the stage. Let me see. I saw him at Manchester in Malvolio, Justice Shallow, Bottom, and Sir Peter Teazle, in School for Scandal. In each and all he was perfection, an excellent proof of which is, that whenever I take up a Shakespeare and read those parts, I fancy I hear and see the man before me, his every look and inflection of voice. His Malvolio was glorious. "Some are born great, some achieve greatness, some have greatness thrust upon them." How he spoke those words! Then Bottom's soliloquy when he wakes after the ass's head has been removed! " Methought I was—and methought I had—but man is but a born fool if he will offer to say what methought I had "—" I will get Peter Quince to make a ballad of the dream, and it shall be called Bottom's dream, because it hath no bottom." Alas! He was advertised to play Cardinal Wolsey at Drury Lane next month, and I would have gone to see him, had it cost me my dinner for a week. We have none left like him. He had the interest of the legitimate drama at heart, and I can imagine with what scorn he thought of the trash which now occupies our boards. He had lived to see the days when " Our Boys " could run for 1,500 nights, and " Pink Dominoes " bid fair to run still longer. Had he not lived long enough ?

You know what abundance of material for poetry and drama is contained in the mediaeval history of the Italian Republics. I have just rooted out what I think will prove a good subject from that source. I think of trying a play on it, when I finish my novel.

At last they have finished the inquiry on the "Princess Alice" affair. They seem to divide the blame pretty equally between her and the " Bywell Castle." The jury sat all night, smoking and drinking ale and wine. Don't you think a jury should be deprived of such excitants as the latter two ? I should think it would at once hasten the verdict and ensure its being weighed by clear brains.

A story is told in last night's paper.   A man travelling in the Hebrides found from the visitor's book at an hotel that Tennyson was in the house.   He said to the landlord " I should think you congratulate yourself on having such a great poet lodging with you."   " Poet!" cried the landlord.   " He who has my best bedroom a poet!   Why, I thought he was a gentleman!" Is it not characteristic of the age?

On Nov. 21, from Rose Cottage, Wilmslow, William writes:

Let me first congratulate you heartily upon having attained manhood, and secondly, may there be many happy years of life in store for you.   Your prospects have materially brightened since I wrote to you on this day last year.   Plans are formed, and we have something definite to look forward to.   It remains to realize all our hopes.   It seems to me very strange that you are only 21.   I am only 19 and Alg. 18.

Your MS. I acknowledge to be bulkier than I expected, but it is not large enough to frighten me.   I will read on as quickly as I can.   I think it is very wise not to leave England until after winter.

In a week or two we will settle everything definitely about your visit.   We have ample accommodation here, and I think you will say I am a lucky fellow to have such a place found for me.   One thing alone troubles me—when am I to talk to and see you?   Every night I shall be at the Bank till 10.30 not getting home till midnight, and off again by the first train. However, we shall not commence the "Balance" until after Christmas Day, so if you come a few days before, we shall be all right. . . . Again many happy returns.

A few days later William says:

As I have not been in town for a little time, I have not been able to find out about the Free Libraries.   It is indeed disgraceful that there should be none in London.   But I must

comment on your remark—" for a man living in my quarter
of London who has an evening to spend by himself and cannot
afford to go to an entertainment there is absolutely and literally
no resource but the gin-shop." I do not know whether you
mean *only* the most ignorant and vicious of the people, or others
as well, but I cannot recognize such an ever-restless, excitement-
seeking element in our people ; if it exist, I think its victims
could not be reclaimed by the quiet pleasures of library or
reading-room. I fear my high ideal of man must be brought
much lower. I am sorry to think his mind contains not enough
self-support to last him a few hours, without rushing in despera-
tion to seek the nearest means to drown temporarily all
consciousness of being.

To Algernon :

31 GOWER PLACE,
Dec. 5, 1878.

I heard from Will the other day, and he appeared to make
light of the return of bad symptoms. I only hope he may be
justified in doing so, but I should very much fear—from what
Fowler said—that he is not. He told me he was going to see
a Manchester doctor; I am waiting anxiously to hear what
opinion the latter expressed.

The Queen's speech is in the evening papers: short, but as
it appears to me, not very satisfactory. " I have taken the
earliest opportunity of calling you together, and making to you
the communication required by law." Indeed! Some might
have the hardihood to suggest that " Law " required a sum-
moning of Parliament before war had been irresponsibly rushed
into. But we live in days when the spirit of the Stuarts is
commencing to stalk our island in a manner calculated to make
us " fools of nature most horribly to shake our dispositions."—
What a state they are in in Berlin! I am afraid I must not
think of going there, as I had half hoped to be able. If things
do not alter they will soon have a state of affairs most un-
pleasantly resembling the Parisian Commune. Badly as we are

off in England under the present mis-Government, we can hardly imagine ourselves submitting to measures such as those employed against the Socialists.

Have you any present use for your Greek Lexicon? I presume not. I wish I could have it, together with some Greek author. If you are not using it, could you bring it me in January? I have got a sudden wish to take up my Greek again, which I have dropped now for nearly three years. That is too bad, you know; one ought to be able to read Greek at least as well as German, considering what a vast influence the Greeks are exerting upon the literary artists of the present day. It is almost like a second Renaissance. Did it ever strike you, how a return to the Greeks in the region of Art has accompanied a return to Nature in the region of Science? During the last two centuries the Greeks were little, if at all, read in England (read, I mean, as they *ought* to be read, to exert influence upon English writers), and I need not tell you how barren those ages were in a scientific point of view, as compared with the present. Are not both correlative portions of the same movement? The Greeks were nothing if not precise and clearly defined in their ideas, dealing little in mysticism; and what is our modern scientific movement but the expression of a wish to escape from the fetters of a mystic interpretation of nature, and define our knowledge in precise and clear-cut shapes. There may be nothing in this idea; there may be much. Suppose you send it to Will, and ask him what he thinks?

Do you think mother is really improving? And the girls? Does their teaching seem really to benefit them? Do they get ideas?

Dec. 8.

What is the exact date of your examination? I am glad you appear quite decided to come up.... Will writes me a letter containing some sadly conservative principles. I am afraid he is among society distinguished for anything rather than advanced views. He is quite savage on the subject of socialists and

communists. I suspect you are rather more liberal in your
tendencies; is it not so ?

Have a care lest you work *too* hard. Be sure and tell me
the exact date on which you contemplate coming up.

To Algernon :

Dec. 10, 1878.

Delighted with the cutting about Will which you forward.
I consider the exploit uncommonly clever. Has he said anything to you about my novel ?

The lodging would decidedly *not* be like the last. I must
have been crazy when I put you into such a hole; but then I
had got used to it myself, you see, and had forgotten what a
decent room was like.

*   *   *   *   *

I rejoice to say I have another pupil: this makes four. He
is a Greek, who speaks and writes English perfectly well, but
wants lessons in the elegancies of English composition. I visit
him three hours a week. He lives in most luxuriously furnished
apartments in Paddington.

To Algernon :

70 Huntley Street,
Bedford Square,
Jan. 19, 1879.

Last Friday night, according to agreement, I went with
Bertz to the Lyceum, and we enjoyed ourselves immensely.
He had tea with us here before we went, and supper on returning.

You say you have read the " Shorter Parliaments " article in
Nineteenth Century. There is also an article on " Atheism
and the Church " well worth looking at. You ask for the
liberal papers. The truth is we have no *thorough-going* weekly.
The *Spectator* and the *Saturday* are, of course, excellent from
a *literary* point of view, and the former is the more liberal of

the two ; but neither is bold enough to advocate principles at all worthy of advanced thinkers. These and the *Athenæum* (I am afraid you cannot see the *Academy*) I should advise you to glance through *without fail* each week. Never mind the political part, just read the reviews and the occasional essays. Some of the monthlies are a little better. The *Nineteenth Century* and the *Fortnightly* lead the way, both opening their pages to even the most pronounced theories, providing they be competently expounded. Articles by Frederic Harrison, Richard Congreve, Swinburne, and Matthew Arnold, you should never miss. The *Nineteenth Century* is particularly catholic, it admits opinions of all colours. The *Contemporary* I should advise you to look at (if possible) principally for the summary of current events, etc. at the end. It is liberal, but as a rule rather heavy. All the other monthlies are devoted to a popular form of literature, and are far from advanced.

I have seen an advertisement of a new (6d.) monthly called the *Liberal*. I have not seen the January No. but the list of articles in it is good, and if well conducted it ought to be more advanced than any paper we have. I must look after it. By next post I will send you a copy of today's *Dispatch*. The leaders in it always repay careful reading. It is absolutely *radical*. I only wish you could see the *Echo* regularly. As regards opinions that is the best paper in London. There seems to me to be room both for a first class weekly and a daily, both to be *extreme* but not shallow. Bradlaugh publishes a paper called the *National Reformer*. I have never seen it, but I believe it is very crude. The man has not depth enough, though he is on the right path.

I would give anything if you could get a *Comte*. But I fear it would not be easy to find a second hand one ; I must find out what the price is. It is a book that should be read very slowly and digested well. By the bye, see if they have any of Herbert Spencer's books in the Mechanics' Institute Library. He is perhaps our greatest living philosopher.

I have got an idea which I fancy is by no means a bad one. It is, in short, to give *public readings*. I might begin in the suburbs, and if moderately successful hire a more central hall afterwards. You see, it would be a step in the direction of lecturing, which is a great aim of mine. What do you think of the plan ?

Love to mother and girls. Hope mother will write again soon.

To the same :

Jan. 26, 1879.

The " Verax " you mention is the editor of the *Manchester Examiner,* Dunkley by name. He has come into note in consequence of the publication of a series of letters on " The Crown and the Constitution " written in deprecation of the attempts just now being made by my Lord Beaconsfield & Co. to aggrandize the power of the Crown at the expense of the Parliament, to imperialize the government in short. They are, I believe—for I have not seen them—very well written. I was glad you have at all events an occasional breeze of liberalism to stir your not over-bracing atmosphere. I am afraid, however, it goes no further than in politics.

How convinced I am growing that we must base our thoughts and action upon a sound substratum of facts! We must know our histories—the history of deeds and the history of the thoughts which were at the root of them. Without such sound knowledge, and the mental growth consequent upon its acquirement we are not competent to *speak,* however great the impulse within us may be to do so. We are liable at any moment to a rebuff from one who—though his views are not really so sound as our own—can be apparently supported by the citation of undeniable facts. I have planned out for myself a course of reading which I shall pursue, I trust, with increasing firmness. I shall go through all the great standard works on general History: *e.g.* Thirlwall's *Greece,* Arnold's and Niebuhr's *Rome,* Hallam, Guizot, Buckle, Gibbon, etc. etc., and read, by the side of this, works on Philosophy. When these *general* studies have sufficiently prepared my mind, I can proceed to the *special* investigation of those points which are particularly attractive to me, *e.g.* Church history, schemes of education, etc.

If I succeed in my scheme of delivering lectures, one of my first will be entitled " Intellectual Emancipation." It will review at length the present situation of our but moderately educated classes with regard to the highest thought and effort of the age. It will urge upon them the casting away of worn-out dogmas, and by the establishment of a wise scheme of national education, ensure the enlightenment of the succeeding generation. I think, too, I could write a lecture on Temperance, though I leave you to consider whether it would greatly resemble the ordinary utterances delivered from the platform upon that subject.

I think a great deal of good work could be done by a lecture upon the principal religions which the world has seen. People are so desperately impressed with the Jingoish idea that their own religion is the only decent one which has ever existed, and that all nations holding others are to be classed together as Heathens. A little light on this point might not come amiss to some of them.

Comte used to say, even till the end of his life, that he should live to preach in Notre Dame! Like most other optimistic philosophers he was too sanguine. And is there not an excuse for him? When one has pierced so deeply into the secret of history and gained so clear an insight into the future of the human race as Comte had, it is hardly possible to help believing that others will at once, and for ever, be convinced by our clear proofs and statements. We are too apt to forget the deplorable state of the intellect of 999 out of every 1,000 men, that utter absence of receptivity, that absolute lack of formulative power which renders the assault of a new idea as little effective as that of a cannon-ball against a feather bed.

It is a fact, regrettable though it be, that scarcely one man in ten thousand is capable of original thought. This we must bear in mind in all schemes of social improvement. No material advance will ever be effected if we do not take for our earliest watchword—popular education. If *we* can prepare the soil, I fear we must be content to leave the sowing to our sons; yes, even to our grandsons. The people must be taught that they

have minds, that their intellectual part is not a mere aerial harp
for the empty currents of ecclesiastical wind to play meaningless
tunes upon. But what labour will be needed before such a
preparation can be brought about !

The establishment of a complete system of education, supple-
mented by a thorough network of free libraries, is the first
thing to be aimed at. To that end we have a destructive task
to perform ; we must destroy the State-Church, and do our
utmost to weaken its hold upon the popular mind. By hacking
away here, and ploughing there, surely the field will at length
be got into something like a state fit for the sower.

Be sure and let me know how you get on. I have taken up
Curtius' *History of Greece* (5 large vols.) and have got to the
commencement of the Persian Wars. At the same time,
according to my plan, I am reading Strauss's work on *The Old
and the New Faith*—a grand book. Work steadily ahead at
your Hallam, etc., and if you have any time I would recommend
Gibbon. The period he treats of is at the root of our modern
civilization. By looking back into the old world, and forward
into the new, it embraces a most significant extent of time, and
is rife with lessons. You have several good editions of Gibbon.

William writes :

WILMSLOW
March 14, 1879.

Many thanks for yours of the 7th. It was my turn to write
as I did not consider that apologetic note I sent worthy of the
name letter. Teaching and walking from place to place con-
sume all but a small fraction of day time now.

How do you get through so much work ? I waste an hour
over about two chapters of Cicero's *De amicitia*, and feel, of
course, great contempt for myself at the end. How, I repeat,
do you get through so much work ? and on lentils, too ! No,
I say, that won't do. I know all about lentils; they are, of
course, nutritious (rather *less* so than oatmeal) but you must
supplement them with other food. The waste of nerve force

now going on in your body from hard work is in *excess* of the food supplied to renew it, but not sufficiently so to cause you present inconvenience. Before long the results will be terribly disastrous, for the weakness gradually induced will prostrate both body and mind. Now, for you, it is most important that your thinking powers should be active, clear and strong, which cannot be with an empty stomach, for the mental and physical forces are indissolubly connected. I pray you discard lentils.

What I have written is not mere *gab* " ut aiunt," but deserves attention. I know your reply to all this, and indeed it grieves me to the heart, " Give me the means and I will eat." Oh, George, don't despair, spend as much as you can upon food. I am doing my best here and be assured that the moment I have a surplus of income, however small, it will go to help a brother rather than to the Bank. Take breath and continue the struggle as cheerfully as possible. But whither do your steps lead ? I confess I cannot yet see. You are gaining immense stores of knowledge, almost, I fear, at the expense of life; but what about *means* of life, which disagreeable subject we must face. People will not pay you for *being* learned, but they will if you make them more so. Moreover it is no satisfaction to get knowledge for the sake of keeping it yourself; it must be circulated either in lectures or books.

Have you cleared much by your lecture, and your short articles ? It is a start at any rate.

I am

Your affectionate brother,

WILLIAM W. GISSING.

To Algernon :

March 23, 1879.

Just a line. Last night I lectured at Paddington on " Faith and Reason." It was an immense success! I spoke (not read) for an hour and a half, and at the end received the enthusiastic thanks of the meeting. The chairman offered to propose me for a lecture at another and much larger club, where they have

a hall that will seat 800.   I think it likely I shall lecture there
in a few weeks and my subject would be "The State Church
from a Rationalist's point of view."   If you are writing to Will
please tell him this. . . .

*In the course of a letter dated April 4 of this year his brother
William says :*

The paper you sent me is very curious, and the first of the
kind I have seen.   I saw a notice of a lecture by Bradlaugh,
but saw nothing of Mrs. Besant.   You surely do not think with
that crew, or do I know nothing about them ?   I don't know
where you have got to, or how you have got there, but there is
evidently an immense distance between us.

Whether I am far behind, I can't say; or whether you have
got off the road, led by an ignis fatuus—a false, delusive argument, which has left you up to the neck in a foul bog of
uncertainty—I can't say.

To Algernon at Broadway in Worcestershire :

Aug. 5, 1879.

We have had such very fine weather lately that it has tempted
us out a little into the open air.   One day last week we had a
glorious walk.   We went by train to Richmond, walked thence
through the Park, past the Star and Garter, all the way down to
Kingston, then crossed the river, and back up the other side,
through Strawberry Hill and Twickenham (where we saw
Pope's Villa), to Richmond again.   This was very grand.
Whereabouts in Kingston is M.'s place ?   We wondered when
we were there.   Did you ever go to Twickenham and about
that region ?   I think I never saw such flowers as those in the
gardens all about there.   It was like fire in places.   I think if
ever I am *en état de* afford a villa I shall take one in that district.

Another day we went to Kew, and another to Hampstead
Heath.   There are gloriously fine views from parts of Hampstead.   We saw quite a number of painters at work on different
scenes.   Yesterday, it being Bank Holiday, we carefully shunned

the country.   However, I was glad it was a fine day, for I dare-say millions of people were out in pursuit of pleasure.

I see from the papers that there are steamers leave London for Ipswich or Yarmouth daily, returning next day.   In September there is such a trip to Ipswich and back at a low price, and I seriously think we shall go.   We might go on Saturday and return on the Monday.   It would be quite a little voyage, and no doubt very enjoyable.   Yarmouth of course would be nearly twice as far, and so still better; but the expense runs a trifle high.   I only wish you were here to go with us.

I have just got through my mortgage chapter this morning, which makes the 21st of the novel [*Workers in the Dawn*]. I think I have worked things in pretty well, and made a diabolical scoundrel of the fellow who insists on selling up poor Mr. Tollady.   The poor old chap has just been found dead in an arm-chair (probably heart-disease), and I am going to give him an impressive burial in Highgate Cemetery tomorrow, if all goes well.   Never mind; Mr. John Waghorn will come to a bad end yet.

I suffer intolerably from indigestion.   I suppose you don't know any specific ?

I only hope we shall some day be able to get to Stratford together.   I should enjoy it hugely, as you can imagine.   At present I have three weeks or a month's hard work before me, in which I hope to finish my novel.   I did nothing all last week. I have previously worked for 4 weeks without a break, and when I sat down last Monday (but one) morning, I couldn't write a word.   My brain was positively dried up!   Now I feel able to go at it again famously.

To the same :

38 EDWARD STREET,
Aug. 13, 1879.

Thanks for letter received this morning.   You have indeed been having a splendid turn; it must have done you good.   But I certainly think you are right in the determination to settle

down to law for a while.   You see, bread-work is absolutely
necessary.   I often feel I should like a day off from my fiction-
writing, but I say to myself that it is bread-work, and stick
bravely to the desk.

Two good bargains today.   Imprimis—the *first* edition of
Scott's *Quentin Durward* 1823, 3 vols. in excellent condition,
price *one shilling* (published at 10s. a vol.).   Secondly—the
14th edition of *Paradise Lost*, 1730, " Printed for Jacob
Tonson, in the Strand."   This contains some fourteen or
fifteen illustrations of a most fearful and wonderful description.
Price 1s. 6d.

I must get down to Wakefield as soon as my book comes out.
When will that be ?   I hope before Xmas, or very shortly after
at latest.   Ten days' work will complete it.   It will make a
volume about the size of " Shirley " in your edition.

To the same :

38 EDWARD STREET,
Aug. 20, 1879.

Many thanks for the photos.   I hope nobody will miss them
particularly.   They will be a great delight to me.   It is an
extraordinary thing, but certainly five nights in every week
I dream of that eternally moving mountain of water.   I suppose
it made an immense impression on me.

Good news.   I have just finished my 28th chapter.   I
calculate that I shall put the finishing touch by the 3rd of
September!   Not so much longer, you see.

I wish I had been able to see either you or Will this summer:
but I suppose I must wait till spring, 1880.   By the by, 1900
isn't so far off, is it ?   One may reasonably hope to see Jan. 1st
1900, I think.   That year ought to be fertile in great things.
Victor Hugo says that in the 20th century there will be no such
thing as war, that all countries will amalgamate into one, that
governments will be unneeded, etc. etc.   *Peut être !*

No doubt you work ahead at the law.   I find there is
always a vast satisfaction in a holiday after a period of fierce

application; much better than half work and half holiday always.

I hope old Will has come back better from his holiday.

To the same :

Sep. 22, 1879.

I am sorry to say I have been rather slow at novel lately. A number of things seem to have occurred to prevent my working.

On Saturday night I squeezed into the gallery at the Lyceum to see Irving in "The Bells," a melodrama which exhibits some of his most powerful acting. It was his first appearance in London since his return from the Mediterranean. The play was fearful, a perfectly horrible story. He is going to play Shylock for the first time soon. We must certainly try to go.

This morning it is glorious weather, finer than we have had it for many weeks. I suppose it will be the last of the sunshine. But I shall not be sorry when the winter comes. The long evenings are a great blessing; one gets so much work done.

I have promised to give an evening of readings and recitations at a club in Chelsea, at Mercier's request. I hope it won't come off just yet. I *must* finish my novel.

I have just finished reading through once more Vasari's *Lives of the Italian Artists*—a vastly interesting book.

In the course of a letter of October 12 *his brother William says :*

Your novel will now be nearly finished, I expect. It must be published and bring you money, money . . . .

You will easily see with what pains I am trying to tack together a letter whose parts have no substance in them. But everything seems in statu quo, except my " high spirits " which apparently attracted Mother's attention—they, after fluctuating with great rapidity, have, at last, settled down low, low, low. And yet there is a touch of cheerfulness somewhere if I could find anything or anyone in this great, round, miserable world to call it out.

Can't you send me some good news soon ? How are things ?

And from the same writer on October 22 :

I consider it your plain *duty*—if such an abstraction mean anything, which I know it does—to tell M. he must alter the time for his work. And for this reason. You will then keep well and be better fitted for all your own work, and the *bread* work will be got through much more lightly. We expect it from you, otherwise you lead us to think you do not consider your life worth 2½d. which, if you look forward, then survey your knowledge and power, will be an obviously small remuneration for it.

But what next ? I shall ever regard you in error until you change this opinion—that the only reason for existence is that the sum of happiness should exceed the sum of misery. I feel sure they are not well-weighed words, or written in a moment of trouble, hastily. I think the only reason for existence is that each should advance the world one point or more, in some particular. With this in view, I think everything will work round it, even the grievous question of how to live; for with the desire to get money (and so become happier and more influential) comes more aptitude in changing employments or following up any with cheerfulness and pleasure. All should examine the cause of their misery before deciding not to live. Perhaps I may be writing ignorantly and weakly, but these thoughts are forced out by your remarks.

The novel, *Workers in the Dawn*, was at last finished ; originally it was under another title, as is seen in the following letter to his brother Algernon.

Nov. 3, 1879.

I have been very remiss in my correspondence of late, chiefly, I fancy, for lack of subject matter, as you say. I am, however, happy to be able to inform you that the novel is to all intents and purposes *finished !* It consists of 46 chapters, of some 450 MS. pp., and will I fear, make three good volumes. I say *fear*, because I suppose publishers rather hesitate about a book by an unknown author when its printing comes very expensive. The title is to be *Far, Far Away*—a somewhat singular name, but which, I think, conveys the *idea* of the book, which is very greatly directed to social problems, principally the condition and prospects of the poorest classes. In an early chapter occurs the incident of a band of little children singing the popular hymn—" There is a happy land, far, far away!" and hence the title, the suggestiveness of which you will of course see.

I have read it aloud to Bertz, and the task took me four long days—say, of nine hours each, so you can imagine it is not short. I have just a little polishing to do, and one chapter to rewrite; but I hope to despatch it to Messrs. Chatto and Windus at the end of this week.

I have got a new pupil, or rather correspondent, for whom I am correcting a translation of a German novel for publication. I charge 1s. per 12 printed pages—small. Each 12 takes me about 2 hours.

It gets terribly cold here. I go to M. each morning still, getting up at five so as to be with him at seven. For the last six mornings I have had the walk in vain, being always told he was engaged. Is it not a trifle too strong ?

Excuse the scribble. The pen is bad, and the hand and head in a hurry. Bertz's opinion of the novel is enthusiastic in the extreme, and he is generally very coolly critical. He was immensely interested to the end, and protests it is impossible not to find a publisher.

Let me hear how work goes on. I buy a cheap book occasionally, but cash, cash, cash! Bertz, however, assures me I am on the eve of a change of fortune. So be it!

To the same :

Nov. 5, 1879.

By the bye, I have a glimmering of a good idea for a play, but I need legal help for its development. It originates thus. I read in this evening's *Echo* that Vera Sassoulitch, the celebrated Russian Socialist, has just had £60,000 left her by will, but she cannot obtain it except by personal application, and she happens to be a fugitive from Russia, under sentence—I think—of death. If not claimed in five years it goes to the State.   Now here, to begin with, you will see a good dramatic situation; but I suppose the law is not the same in all countries, and I could not venture to lay my scene in Russia.   But suppose something like the following.   A man commits a murder and succeeds in escaping justice and lives in hiding.   Shortly after the coroner's inquest has fixed the guilt upon him, a large estate reverts to him (never mind how).   Now how would the law deal with a case like this in England ?   I conclude that to claim it he must turn up somewhere or other, and of course this would involve arrest. Well, my drama would proceed thus.   The man has committed the crime under some very (morally) excusable circumstances, and is by no means a bad man.   He hears (in hiding) of the estate falling to him, and is suddenly possessed with the desire of appropriating it; not for himself, but in order to be able to enrich some other person in whom he is much interested.   He turns up, claims the property, is at once arrested, tried and condemned.   Now would it be in the man's power, under such circumstances, to make a will like any other man and leave the property as he desired ?—I think you will see there is the kernel of a good exciting drama here, eh ?   It might be ingeniously complicated by making the criminal be supposed (owing to certain arrangements of his own) dead.   Please let me have your comments on this affair.   If I can screw it into shape I might be tempted to set to work on it at once.

To the same :

5 HANOVER STREET,
ISLINGTON, N.
Dec. 21, 1879.

Will has not said anything to me about publishers having made up their lists for the year.   Do you take this to mean *literally* for this year—or for some arbitrary publishers' year, extending goodness knows how far the other side of January ?   I should suppose the former ; at least it is to be hoped so.   I have heard nothing as yet.   I have thought of stirring them up a little, but I fear it would be vain to write to them before the 1st of January.   Of course this is the busiest time with them.   It is quite possible they have not yet looked at my MS.

I am studying German literature pretty closely at present. I think I may perhaps make it a specialty some day.   It is not too much studied in England.   In consequence of my acquaintance with Bertz I hear very much of German life and occasionally see German socialists who are living in London, also read socialist newspapers, etc.   You have not the remotest idea of the fearful system of tyranny at present ruling throughout the German Empire.   Freedom of speech and of the press has long since ceased.   Let me give you an instance of barbarous tyranny, which you will scarcely credit.   A German labourer received some sort of injury from another German whose name was Lehmann.   Well, to revenge himself, he chalked up somewhere or other—" Der alte Lehmann ist ein Lump," " Old Lehmann is a blackguard!"   Now, as it happens, *Lehmann* is a popular nickname for the Emperor; and, on this account, the man has been sentenced to a heavy term of imprisonment for chalking up that phrase.   Can you believe such a thing has happened in the 19th century ?   Instances of suicide in the army from intolerable cruelty and oppression are of every-day occurrence. Of course there will be a fearful revolution sooner or later. It is only a matter of time, and I, for one, should be heartily glad to hear of its outbreak.   Most probably the deaths of old William and Bismarck, which cannot be far off, will bring some decisive change.

To the same :

Jan. 2, 1880.

We only sat up to see the old year out and the new in, and following Father's immemorial practice, I read Tennyson's appropriate poem aloud;   then we threw up the window and listened to the bells which sounded finely on a south-west wind. It was a wonderfully warm night, but a little cloudy.

I regret to tell you that Chatto & Windus have returned my

MS. They write a polite letter, regretting that their hands are very full for a long time to come. Never mind; I might have expected it. You see if they *had* accepted it, it would have been a piece of quite extraordinary good luck, something I could scarcely look for, bearing in mind the precedents of other young unknown authors. I immediately sent it off again, however, to Smith & Elder, having changed the title. *Far, Far Away*, after all, appeared to me a trifle sentimental, and perhaps not too impressive. The title now is *Workers in the Dawn*, a much more apt one. Pray tell me what you think of it. It is a novel, you must know, of social questions, and the principal characters are earnest young people striving for improvement in, as it were, the dawn of a new phase of our civilization. I am rather fond of this new name, and, as regards the novel itself, I feel desperately certain that, sooner or later, it *must* find a publisher.

At present I have gone desperately to work on a few short stories and novelettes, which I mean to sow broadcast among magazines and papers hoping that *some* at least may take root. I have tonight finished a horrible story—"Cain and Abel," the writing of which has made me shiver. It is rather in Poe's style, be it said. It is a tale of two brothers. The elder is christened Abel, after his father; and the younger through a curious circumstance receives the name of Cain. The name haunts him like a Fate, and he ends as the convicted murderer of his brother Abel. Rather horrible this, eh ? But I assure you it is dreadfully effective.

With every good wish for the New Year, *and* for the new decade.

To his sister Margaret, whose age was seventeen.

Jan. 13, 1880.

I seem to have had your letter lying a long time open, in the drawer of my desk, on purpose that I might be reminded to answer it, but my hands are so full of work just now that I really haven't been able to find time. I am now screwing in a few minutes between eleven and midnight.

I am very sorry that you have lost your best teacher; it appears to me that when one is being taught, so much depends on one's becoming accustomed to the ways of one's teacher. It is just as in studying from a book.   A girl who devotes herself to studying *one* special history of England thoroughly, will generally learn much more than another who skips from book to book, reading a bit here and a bit there.   I am glad you liked the teacher's habit of giving you etymological explanations.

Etymology used to be one of my very favourite studies; there is nothing I liked better than tracing the various meanings of an English word from its use in Anglo-Saxon down to modern days.   I wish you could somehow get hold of Marsh's *Lectures on the English Language.*   If your tastes are at all like mine in this respect, you would revel in these books.   There are two series, I don't think they are very dear.

By all means, if you can manage it, get the Clarendon Press edition of Shakespeare's plays, one by one; and study the notes, which are admirable and thorough.   A woman is a mere duffer if she is not able to read Shakespeare with perfect intelligence of his vocabulary.   I should advise you to pay the same attention to Chaucer too, but, of course, you will not have time for everything at once.

Perhaps on the whole it is good for you to go in for the Cambridge.   Such test examinations do one good by giving a special tendency to one's study.   There is nothing worse than desultory reading, without any definite object.   Always say to yourself, now I will confine my reading to certain subjects—pretty nearly—till I have a good idea of it   Then, in reading English Poetry—of which I devoutly hope and trust you read a good deal—don't skip from Chaucer to Tennyson, and from Shakespeare to Crabbe; but read all the principal authors of one period taking for your guide a book like the little Stopford Brooke primer.

So you have read *Shirley*.   It is, on the whole, certainly Charlotte Brontë's best book.   She seems happier in it than in the others, though she was miserable enough, at times, while writing it.   I think perhaps Caroline Helstone is a better drawn character than Shirley herself, though the latter is very delightful. You speak of Forster's *Dickens*. Do you know there is a single volume edition just issued ? Dickens' letters, too, have just been published by his sister-in-law and eldest daughter. I have not seen them yet, but they must be delicious reading. It was a curious fact that Mrs. Dickens died a few hours after the publication of the book, in last December. I know the house where she lived during the last years.

I wish I could see you all now and then. Perhaps I might be able to manage it for a day during the summer. I shall if I possibly can.

The weather here is simply, flatly, plain-speakingly, emphatically, undeniably, unimpeachably, desperately—beastly! Every morning it is pitch dark, till 11 o'clock. Sometimes we never have any daylight. In my study I generally have to burn a lamp all day long. Do you know there are men in London who go the rounds of the streets with a cart selling paraffin oil ? I often think they must rub their hands over weather such as this. I never see one and hear him shouting " Ile—Ile— Paraffin—I-i-i-i-ile!" without being disposed to rush at him, break his tins and scatter his petroleum about the streets.

I enclose you a cutting from a paper which may amuse you. Dickens could not even write the shortest note without some admirable fun in it. What a man he was!

In the course of a letter dated Jan. 24 of this year, his brother William writes :

I consider that the greatest advantage is to be derived from reticence—not eternal. We are constantly changing. If therefore we change certain opinions, we have not to regret the publishing of our previous notions. If we suffer no change in certain opinions, and a *necessity occurs* for making them known, then out with them; ten to one they will be more mature and appear at a more suitable time than when we first formed them.

Ply them with short tales, you may win the day yet. If the battle goes against us it will then be time to talk about another occupation.   That literature is your path there can be no doubt, but there is wanted a comfortable income to back you up. Seriously, could you not without great mental pain turn to any profession or trade that you know of?

To Algernon :

Jan. 25, 1880.

You will think I have altogether forgotten you, but it is merely want of leisure which has hindered me from writing. I have been perpetually at my desk, morning and evening, yet I am sorry to say that I have still no result to report.

Workers in the Dawn has now been declined by three publishers.   Smith & Elder write anent it, " It possesses a great deal of graphic power and some humour, but in our opinion it is very deficient in dramatic interest.   As a series of scenes the book is good, but as a continued tale it fails to meet the requirements of the reader of fiction."

Yes, but for " the reader of fiction " I did not write, nor do I expect to please that worthy abstraction.   My novel is only deficient in dramatic interest in the sense in which all the best novels are deficient.   It is not sensational in plot, since its object is to depict real life.

I next sent it to Sampson, Low & Co., and they also favoured me with a criticism, which is somewhat amusing: " *Workers in the Dawn*," they say, " is undoubtedly very ably written, that is our reader's opinion; but we are sorry to say he does not recommend it to us, on account of its rationalistic tendency, and certain details of a profligate character.   We do not believe in fiction being the proper vehicle for conveying doctrinal opinions, for one reason that most readers will not read them. We should have been glad to have taken the work but for these reasons."

Of course this criticism is foolish.   It is not *I* who propagate a doctrine, but the characters whose lives I tell.   Because I choose to take my subject from a sphere hitherto unused of novelists, shall I therefore be accused of making fiction the vehicle of doctrinal opinions ? As to the " profligate incidents," I don't understand what they mean.

But you see the novel cannot be without merit and significance. I feel sure I shall find a publisher, and that, when published, the work will attract attention. It is now in the hands of Kegan Paul & Co. They have acknowledged receipt of it, and promised to give it " an early and careful consideration." No one hitherto has done this. Paul & Co. are very liberal, and I cannot help nourishing some sort of faint hope.

I am now setting to work at another long novel. At present I intend to make only one volume, but it is very uncertain whether I can keep it within these bounds. Yes, I *do* feel sure that fiction is my forte; every day more sure of it. You see that Sampson Low says the novel is " undoubtedly very ably written." For history I have not the necessary knowledge, and certainly not the necessary leisure. No, you will see that I shall force my way into the army of novelists, be my position there that of a private or of a general.

To the same :

Feb. 7, 1880.

Many thanks for your last, which contained valuable information. *Workers in the Dawn* is still in the hands of C. Kegan Paul & Co. I suppose the result will be the same as hitherto, but still there is always hope.

In the meantime I write hard at small tales, of which I have several in the hands of Magazine editors. If none of these are taken, I shall be *au désespoir*. Then I must very seriously begin to think of some business or other, even if it be the position of draper's clerk. Yet, if ever literature was a man's vocation it is certainly mine. I feel that no amount of discouragement will make me cease writing; indeed I cannot conceive of my life otherwise than as being spent in scribbling. I have written now for so long that it has become second nature. I don't think I have ever told you how well I got on in America. Whilst in Chicago I wrote a story every week (three columns) for the leading daily paper, for each of which I was paid 18 dollars, *i.e.* more than £3. Then I had a sketch (about 6pp.) in a very good monthly called *Appleton's Journal*, for which I received 45 dollars, *i.e.* £9. The latter, by the bye, was a story, the scene of which was the Farne Islands, and was chiefly descriptive. It was mentioned by several papers as the best article of the number. Well, the battle shall go on sternly till the beginning of July, and if by that time I have earned nothing—well, I must look out for the draper's clerkship. There is nothing else for me.

Last Saturday week we had the worst day and night known in London for very long. After nine at night the street lamps were perfectly useless. You could scarcely see the light even when standing directly under them. I had to go to Bertz that night, and in returning I was more than two hours making three miles, for I had *absolutely* and *literally* to grope with my stick, like a blind man, all the way. No 'buses dared to run, and the few cabs and carts which continued to voyage, did so with the driver walking at the horses' head, with a lantern in his hand. Boys made an admirable trade with links and lanterns, which were, however, of little use. I had to give such a boy a penny to be taken over King's Cross. I should *never* have found my way into the right street, though I am as familiar with the place as with my own study. Another night it was nearly as bad and I took a lantern.

The next two letters, written on the same day, show that during this month of February the MS. of *Workers in the Dawn* had been returned by Messrs. Kegan Paul, but no reference to the terms in which they declined it has been preserved. The author now despairing of acceptance by publishers at their own risk, yet resolved that the book should see the light, formed the bold project of publishing at his own cost. For this purpose he signed an agreement with Messrs. Remington & Co., under which the author was to pay them £100 in three instalments during the course of the printing of the book, and after publication receive two-thirds of the profits of sale as shown by ordinary half yearly accounts. This defiance of Charles Lamb's elementary principles of publishing was cautiously never disclosed to either of his brothers, a significant fact in one so instinctively candid. Yet from the exultation of his announcement the author had evidently deceived himself into believing the arrangement to be an advantageous one. It may be noted that Gissing is now three months over the age of 22.

To his brother William :

Feb. 26, 1880.

DEAR WILL,

Write this a red day in your private calendar; for today, at twelve o' the clock, Hal, I signed an agreement with Messrs. Remington & Co. for the publication of *Workers in the Dawn.* Yes, it is really to see the light; it will be published either at the end of next month, or the beginning of April, in three vols. price one guinea. Don't be frightened at the figure; you shall of course have a presentation copy *de la part de Monsieur l'auteur.* The terms are these. First of all the advertising expenses (about £20) are to be deducted from produce of sale, after which I have two-thirds of all profits. Not bad, is it ?

Do not entertain great hopes from the financial results; for I know very well that the book cannot be popular, like Dickens, or Miss Braddon, or Mrs. Henry Wood. There is much of desperate seriousness in it, and it must be accepted by intellectual people, if it all. The settlements are to be twice a year, 30th June and 31st December; but I fear there will be little to show in June. The publisher tells me his reader's opinion of the book is high: but of course one cannot reckon on that, as the opinions of so many other readers have been desperately *low.* I have sent all this news to Alg., who no doubt will be pleased.

By the bye, when you send me a literary contribution, let it be written in a good bold hand. I have learnt by sad experience that this is indispensable with editors, *et hoc genus omne.*

By all means keep up your spirits. I myself am in desperate exaltation just now, perhaps foolishly so. Never mind, it helps me on with my work. I shall of course begin a new novel at once, and it will be of a far more popular character. If it is successful, of course it will throw back its success on the first work. Surely I must soon derive some profit from my labour.

Of Campanology I grieve to say I know nothing; I cannot even find the term in my encyclopaedia. But under the head of *Bell*, I find " Eight bells, which form an octave or diatonic scale, make the most perfect peal. The variety of *changes* or permutations of order that can be rung on a peal, increases enormously with the number of bells; 3 bells allow 6 changes; 4 bells 24; 12 bells give as many as 479,001,600 changes." In short, I suppose one would work the thing out by the algebraic rule of Permutations and Combinations ?

I know that an authority on Campanology—which is still studied—is a celebrated London clergyman, the Rev. H. Haweis. If I got you his address would you care to write to him and ask him for information ? Let me know. I half believe he has a book on the subject. I will look when next I go to Museum.

I have been working hard all day getting ready my first volume for the press, whither it goes at once. It will be a tremendous work, the correction of proofs; yet not so unpleasant.

Alg. writes in good spirits, and so shall I for the next month or so, I think. Of course you will write at once and let me have your sympathy in these eventful times!

Keep up your spirits. Patience does everything.

Affectionately, dear Will,

G. R. GISSING

To Algernon :

5 HANOVER STREET,
ISLINGTON, N.
Feb. 26, 1880.

At last I have obtained a publisher for my novel. . . .

I am sure this news will rejoice you. Shall you tell mother about it ? I don't quite know how she will take the matter, for I much fear the *opinions* of the book will by no means please her.   I forgot to say that it will be published in three volumes at one guinea.

I have this evening been preparing the first volume for the press, whither it will go immediately.   The correcting of proofs will be a serious but a pleasant labour.   Of course I shall begin a second novel at once and write *con furore*.

On Feb. 27 William writes :

Alg. is a lucky fellow to look forward to a visit to you shortly. I would give anything to be able to, and to have five or ten pounds to spare when I get there.   I am seriously in want of some musical works which I can't possibly get yet.   Last time I was with you, you remember, we picked up a good deal of cheap music at some shop or other.

The other evening I was out and met a lady who had studied music under Sir Julius Benedict.   I felt most interested in what probably she did not know herself, namely, she seemed to bring very near to me several great men.   Thus, her master Sir Julius Benedict studied under *Weber* and *Hummel,* while Weber studied under *Michael Haydn* and the Abbè *Vogler ;* and Hummel under *Albrechtsberger* and *Mozart.*

I am as delighted as you can be to hear the good news and congratulate you most heartily; I am glad to hear of signing agreements.

March 11, 1880.

Dear Will,

I am ashamed to look at your fine long letter of the 27th ult., and think it is still unanswered.   I have been very busy of late.   This morning I have sent back the second batch of proof-sheets, completing the first three chapters.   Remington wanted me to reduce the book, seeing that it would be vastly longer than the average novel of the day; but I told him that this would be impossible save by re-writing it, and so the printing goes ahead.

I get on with my new work, the name of which I scarcely yet know.   I hope to finish it by the end of May.

Indeed I heartily wish it were possible for you to come up at Easter, but I suppose financial considerations sternly forbid it. Alg. might be able to get you some music. At all events we will certainly try. The pupil of Sir J. Benedict and the associations clinging to her must have been very interesting. Some of the names you mention are unknown to me, though doubtless they ought not to be. I would give a trifle to have you playing frequently in my neighbourhood, so that I might form my taste and learn at all events the elements of musical criticism.

My book is sure of a certain number of friends in the critical world, inasmuch as it will assuredly have violent enemies. One or two of our weeklies, *e.g.* the *Athenaeum* and *Academy*, give very reasonable critiques of the new novels each week, and I hope for decent handling. Yet it is amusing to see how often these two papers flatly contradict each other in their verdicts.

Some of the publishers' advertising tricks are curious. You know it is usual to extract passages from favourable reviews, and insert them in advertisements. A few weeks ago I read a review of a new novel by Ouida, written in a fiercely ironical vein, and behold! shortly after I came across a few passages from the same review inserted—perhaps innocently—as laudatory criticism.

Thanks for the interesting papers, which I herewith return. Haweis is a very popular preacher just now, orthodox, but still very liberal and sensible. His church in Marylebone is crowded to suffocation every Sunday. His wife has written a book telling ladies how to dress on £15 a year!

I have good walks now-a-days. Bertz has gone to live at Tottenham, some six miles from here, and I walk out to him twice a week, when we spend the evening together. Finding it impracticable to live on the results of teaching and what little German newspaper work he could get, he has realized a little capital he possessed and means to do nothing but study for some years, with the view of taking some academical position when he returns to Germany.

Shall you pay heavily for your organ lessons? I have no

doubt they will be very useful to you.   Kind wishes from both of us.

Affectionately, dear Will,

GEORGE R. G.

To Algernon :

March 11, 1880.

I open the drawer in my desk, and find two of your fine long letters looking me reproachfully in the face—all the more so since that of the 23rd February asks for information of a kind I could easily have obtained.   I promise that I will speedily pay a visit to the Museum on your account, and send you an interesting letter.   I have been there several times lately, but always for the purpose of getting up medical information *re* apoplexy and paralysis, matters I have to deal with in my new novel.

I should certainly advise you to take up A.S. and early English. I bitterly regret that so many of my fine English books are left in America, whence it appears I shall never recover them. Yet I have here two A.S. grammars.   Shall I send them, or will it be time enough in April ?   They would not cost much to forward. . . . . Work, work, that's all.   Even novel-writing is not too leisurely work, so one do it well.

You speak of returning home from the office " furiously ravenous."   Have you ever been conscious, when so fearfully hungry, of an unusual lucidity of thought, an extreme enthusiasm for work of every description ?   I have frequently felt this, but of course it only lasts as long as the hunger is kept within *tolerable* bounds.

I have no doubt at all of being able to get you a reader's ticket for the Museum.   No doubt I shall have acquaintances then.

I have a good deal of walking now-a-days, as my friend Bertz has changed his residence to Tottenham, whither I march twice a week.   It is a walk of some six miles.   I get there at 6.30 in the evening, remain chatting till 10.30 and catch an 11 train back into town. We have had such perfectly glorious weather lately that this walk is most enjoyable. I fear the summer warmth and sunshine won't last long; it is too good for March.

I am delighted to hear you are so well. Poor old Bigler used to tell me a tale of an old professor of his who used to repeat the axiom—" La santé est une grande partie de la science!" and I daresay it was a true one. It is a grand thing to be well. I rejoice to say I seldom have much the matter with me. My work is very regular, and no doubt that accounts for much. As a rule now, I rise at 6.45, walk from 7 to 8, pondering the chapter of the day, which I write from 9 to 2, five hours, you see; about as much writing as one can do well in a day. I find that I always invent best in walking; *solvitur ambulando.*

You see Parliament dissolves on 28th inst. Pray let me know anything you hear about Summers' candidature for Ashton.

To the same :

March 20, 1880.

We both look forward to seeing you with immense satisfaction. I very much hope you will make shift to stay over the Sunday. Is there no train back on Sunday evening ? . . .

I am very glad that you feel a growing interest in Early English. It was once my study of studies, and I hope yet to be able to devote much time to it. But you must at the same time determine to look up early *German* literature. The *Nibelungen Lied* and other old metrical romances are glorious reading, and throw, of course, much light on the English poems. I *particularly* wish you to take up German. I am glad to say that I now read it almost as easily as English, and I do not suffer a week to pass without getting through some Goethe or Lessing, or other German classic. Seriously think of German. Even if you have not time to go at it very strongly just yet, you might certainly refresh your knowledge of the Grammar with some hour or so weekly.

Lately I have been reading Burns a good deal. It surprises

one to find how many of the Scotticisms are pure old English. Thus Burns has *nieve* = fist, and you remember how Bottom says, " Give me your *neif*, good Master Mustard-Seed," and so on, to a great extent.   At present I am going in for a course of Wordsworth, whose fame " doth daily greater grow," and will I fancy do so for many a year to come.   Wordsworth pretty well studied, I shall pass on to Chaucer, whom I have in the excellent Aldine edition, the best extant.   Really one ought to have Chaucer at one's fingers' ends, if only for his influence on one's English style.

Of my new novel I have written 8 chapters—about half the first volume.   I progress but slowly, for on reading the proofs of *Workers in the Dawn* I am dissatisfied with much, and see how greatly I might have improved my work, had I taken more time over it.   Now I spend hour after hour in thinking of my characters and making their very forms, looks, tones absolutely vivid before my mental eye.   By the bye, can you and Will excogitate for me a title ?

The subject of the novel is the dissipation of illusions, the destruction of ideals, in short the failure of a number of people to gain ends they have set up for their lives, or, if they *do* gain them, their failure to find the enjoyment they expected.   I have thought of *Will-o-the-Wisps*, but on second thoughts I suppose that ought to be *Wills-o-the-Wisp*, and that is awkward. Try and think of something for me.

Again—could you persuade Will to write me a description of Stockport, as seen from the railway viaduct ?   Some of the scenes of my novel will be in Stockport, some in Macclesfield and neighbourhood.   I do not, of course, want a topographical article on the town, but a half humorous, half serious description, which I could make use of.   Don't let him trouble much about it.   A couple of note pages would suffice.

I shall be very glad to hear the Easter adventures, and particularly glad to have them from your own mouth in the course of a fortnight or so.

March 27, 1880.

Dear Will,

Just a line, which must not arrogate unto itself the name of letter.   I was very glad to hear that you would have Alg. at Easter.   If your weather is like ours, you will rarely enjoy yourselves.   An account of your adventures in the form adopted last year would be by no means disagreeable to me.   But I have already laid upon you several tasks *per* Alg.; and must not over-burden.

The loss of four pupils is somewhat serious; I presume all in the same house ?   Were it not for the pecuniary loss involved, I should of course congratulate you on the diminution of galley-like labour.   I used to groan horribly in the spirit over my own wretched pupils; but truly your case is worse.   I had only to drive into them *hic, haec, hoc,* or *du, de la, des,* or the like, and their blunderings could only distress my patience. But in the teaching of music, a numskull's fumbling about the keys must injure one's sensibilities.   Fancy a dunderheaded creature strumming out daily one of the *Lieder,* with every other note false.   Heavens!   I should be afraid of losing the delicacy of my ear.

Curious, when one thinks of it, that this particular one of the Arts should be popularly conceived within the reach of every Philistine, whereas it is recognized as regards the others that they require very special qualifications.   It seems to me it would be more excusable to have every child taught drawing, irrespective of natural qualifications, than music; for though they never become artists yet we know how eye, hand, and sentiment *ought* to profit by the practice.   But I fail to see what benefit a blockhead derives from five-finger exercises.

Of course we must remember that so many sentiments besides love of art are at work in this matter of music-learning. To play is to make an exhibition of *personal* dexterity, very much resembling, in the majority of cases, the skill of which Blondin boasts.   Then again, there are the *social* purposes wherein the facility in strumming is of avail.   Moreover, the *tuneful* part of man's nature seems to be one more eagerly demanding satisfaction than those parts ministered to by painting, or sculpture, or literature; and thus we tolerate a bungler on the piano where we should kick a man out of the room who pestered us with vile sketches, or the perpetual caterwaul of sesquipedalian verses.   In *my* republic I would have every child taught the rudiments of music, drawing, prose and verse composition, but by teachers who were capable of very quickly deciding whether it was any use pursuing the instruction in one or any of the subjects.   Thus those who had talent would be encouraged on their way, whilst the dunderheads would receive a very salutary check reminding them that they were guilty of profanity in invading precincts open only to the high-priests of Humanity.

Did it ever occur to you to study Philosophy of any kind ? I wish you could get a peep into that world.   I suppose you know the names of Spinoza, Kant, Schopenhauer, etc ?   I hardly know whether such studies would be in your line, but I wish they were.

I very much hope you will be able to fulfil your project of coming up to London before the end of the year.   In fact it is a sure thing that you are *rusting* at Wilmslow.   I wish to goodness you could somehow exchange locality.   I should advise you to think very seriously over matters when you get your money.   Perhaps you have plans.   I hope so.

In my searches for music with Alg., I will duly beware of Messrs. ———.   I hope you are really, as you say, in excellent health; but with your rural habits of life a good walk ought not to knock you up.   That looks bad.   Don't overdo it with Alg.   *He* is an able-bodied individual, to whom twenty miles with a *brass* at the end are as nothing.

By the bye, if you ever run short of literature to your taste, don't fail to let me know, and I will send you a book or two. They would cost very little.   It must be doleful to sit and look round in vain for a book to suit one's humour.   One cannot always extract savoury juice from a treatise on Counterpoint and Fugue, or lighten one's melancholy hours by a perusal of the law of Landlord and Tenant—interesting as these works may be at the proper time.

I began with the intention of writing a page, and I have scribbled more than a sheet. Well, perhaps this *may* pass for a letter, after all. But I will take up the pen again speedily, perhaps to send a few more idle speculations on music and music-teaching.

Affectionately, dear Will,

G. R. G.

The Easter holidays referred to fulfilled all hopes. In strolling through the green Cheshire lanes and fieldpaths William seemed full of life, but barely a month later he died suddenly when little over the age of twenty. In the course of a letter to his surviving brother shortly afterwards, George writes:

Very many thanks for the books you sent. Mine was just what I should have desired, especially as it was one of Will's prizes. His merits were, though, not such as men are in the habit of rewarding much with prizes and the like; his universal kindness and good will could be felt, indeed, by all who came in contact with him, but their value was too great to be represented by " rewards of merit."

At present it is a constant subject of grave thought with me, to what species of study I shall especially devote myself. To be a mere dilettante in everything by no means accords with my humour, and as one cannot be omnivorous it is a very serious question, what especial branch I should take up with the view of effecting something real.

Of course, this has nothing to do with my novel writing: *that* I shall pursue always, inasmuch as I feel a special aptitude for it, and it will, it is to be hoped, prove my material staff in life. The study of which I speak is to be taken up for my own satisfaction, for the sake of developing my manhood as far as in me lies. He is but a poor fellow, as I am sure you will grant, who studies with no object save mere bread-winning. Of course that cannot be neglected; in *your* case, for instance, I should say the bread-winning aspect of study is at present the most important.   But, alas! I am older than you; *my* bread-winning education is as complete as it will ever be, and I must sternly face the fact that only a short time may remain to me in which to develope what intellect I have.   " The night cometh when no man *can* work " is a good sentence to have ever before one's eyes.

For, though I myself look forward to no future world where the negligences of this may be made up for, I do not on that account say, " let us eat and drink for to-morrow we die."   The immortality of man consists in this reflection—that not a word we utter, not a thought we think, not a battle we win, not a temptation we yield to, but has, and *must* have, influence upon those living in contact with us, and from them, like the circles spreading in a pool, extends to the whole future human race. Therefore is it of vast importance to me whether I set an example of an ignorant and foolish man, or of one bent upon using his faculties to the utmost.

Unfortunately, the subject I have most desire to master is nothing less than the laws of the universe—in other words the science of all sciences.   I want to know what are the laws which govern the evolution of species on the earth, physically considered, and then to know the laws by which the mind of man is governed; for it is evident that the science of Psychology will soon become as definite as that of Physiology.   But all this pre-supposes boundless learning; I can never hope to satisfy myself.   But shall I on this account renounce study altogether? Just as well make up my mind not to eat at all because I cannot procure the dearest luxuries for my table.   I have thought, then, of something like this.   I must get hold, by degrees, of some of the best books on Natural Science—*general* works, which treat of the *laws* more than the minutiæ.   Then I must get some excellent history of Philosophy, and master the current of thought from the beginning of Indian wisdom—in its large phases.   And whilst all this is going on, I must read diligently every kind of work distinctly bearing on human history.

Well, these are only aspirations—and fine ones, you will say, for a man who has not a penny of income.   But I sincerely hope my book will bring me something.   I think it will be out next week.   If I get nothing from it, and cannot hope for anything from the next—well I must look out for a handicraft, and hope to have a few stray hours in the week which I can devote to higher thoughts.

May 9, 1880.

DEAR SISTERS,

As Alg. has let me know your address in the country, I must not neglect to send you a word or two, whilst you are, I hope, enjoying the green woods and fields and the blue sky in this delightful spring weather.   Since I wrote last to you we have all suffered a sad loss; dear Will was a brother whom we shall long miss and can never forget.   But we know very well that it would not have pleased him to think of us saddening our short days with useless grief—he, who always thought so little of himself, and was so anxious for the comfort and happiness of others.   Rather, we must be glad that we *once* had him with us, and always keep him in our minds as an example to live by.

I hope you are enjoying yourselves in the country; how I wish I could be there too, away for a short time from these dark streets.   I had a pleasant walk the other day with a friend of mine.   We went right out to Epping Forest, which is some twelve miles from London, and where, you will remember, lies the scene of " Barnaby Rudge."   There is an inn called " The Maypole," but the sight of it grievously disappointed us; it was nothing but a hideous " gin-palace " built the other day.

Write, both of you, whenever you have time and let me know what you do in school-work and general reading.   I heard from Alg. that one of you, I won't say which, was rather disposed to overwork herself for certain examinations.   This is, of course, out of the question; no examination in the world is worth the sacrifice of one's health, remember that!

I am very glad to hear that Mother will follow you to Broadway [Worcestershire].   The change will do her good ; no doubt it will.   Remember when you are all together at home how much poor Mother has had to suffer, and be careful, as I know you are, to help her in every way. Depend upon it, there is nothing like forgetting ourself and working for the good of others. It is the only way to be happy.

With much love, dear girls,
Ever affectionately,

GEORGE.

To his brother :

May 16, 1880.

In arrogating to myself exclusive reason in the philosophical questions, I only meant that I side with the very vast majority of thinkers who have lived in the present century, the vast majority of the men who have influenced the world. But remember, one of my principles is that *absolute* truth is—at present at least—unattainable, and I do not *condemn* those who think otherwise, merely differ from them. Herein you are unjust to me. Yet again, in a matter like this, the burden of proof certainly rests upon the supernaturalists.

An agnostic, like myself—*i.e.* one who says of things beyond his senses he knows and can know nothing—is justified in refusing to be converted by those who, you will surely grant me, are convinced merely by their *sentiments*. Establish your dogmas on a scientific basis, in clear relation with the hierarchy of human knowledge, and we ungrudgingly grant them a place in our system. But, as I say, to convert you is not my object. I only wished you to sympathize with me and believe *I* was genuinely convinced. Above all, *condemnation* of opponents, *as long as they confine themselves to intellectual regions*, is a word out of my vocabulary.

To the same :

May 30, 1880.

I was glad to hear you received my three formidable volumes so speedily. I shall be very curious to hear your detailed criticism. Much of the book I can hardly expect you to approve, and I feel you will think the tendency very gloomy. Well, that is owing to my temperament, and the special mood in which it was written. If you knew much of my daily life you would wonder that I write at all, to say nothing of writing cheerfully. But in that book, I have, so to speak, *written off* a whole period of my existence. My next book will be very different. I have passed beyond the stage at which it was possible for me to write just such a book as *Workers*.

The chest affection lasted only for a few days, and is now, I am glad to say, departed, leaving, as I think, no traces. It must have been a slight cold on the lungs.

The first volume of my new novel I have read to Bertz, who thinks it an improvement on *Workers*. Now that the plastering community (I think I told you the house has been painted, papered, etc. from top to bottom), have well nigh departed, I hope soon to get to work again, and to give, perhaps, six weeks to each of the other volumes—very possibly less. The book will have much more chance of popularity.

I fancy my own health is—as you put it—rather *horsish* than otherwise. It is seldom I have anything at all alarming the matter. I always *feel* the energy of health, and indeed, considering my haphazard manner of dealing with the matter, it would much surprise me to hear that I had not more than an average constitution. Two days in the week, you know, I walk out to Bertz, but other days I have seldom inclination to wander on a vague constitutional about the streets. The two evenings, however, are precious to me; it is on the walk out and back that most of my happy ideas come to me. If I am puzzling long about some knotty point, I generally conclude by putting it off to one of those evenings, when I am sure to have the matter settled *ambulando*.

I suppose Nelly has no examination in view? The matter of girls' examinations depends entirely upon what is likely to be the girl's future life. If a girl is to be made a teacher it is certainly right that she should pass examinations; but, as a mere feature in education, I see little good to be effected by these tests. A girl's education should be of a very general and liberal character, adapted rather to expand the intelligence as a whole than to impart very thorough knowledge on any subject. General reading is what I should advise a girl to undertake; and that reading should certainly *not* lie in the direction of the Higher Mathematics or Political Economy.

So you fear you will have no summer holiday. I shall, of course, have no holiday of any kind, for I have never before been in such mind for productive work. By holiday, of course, I mean cessation from writing; a change of scene I should hail with delight, were it only possible. Very much depends on these next two or three weeks. I think the reviews of *Workers* will certainly begin next Saturday, and, should they be favourable, I may, of course, hope for some profit from the book. If I am ignored I must think very seriously of some mechanical day-labour.

     *   *   *   *   *

To the same :

June 8, 1880.

In view of the very kind efforts being made by some of your Wakefield friends to procure a circulation for *Workers in the Dawn*, I think it is better that I should send you a few lines (relative to the book) which I should like you to show to any interested in the matter. The book in the first place is not a novel in the generally-accepted sense of the word, but a very strong (possibly *too* plain spoken) attack upon certain features of our present religious and social life which to *me* appear highly condemnable. First and foremost, I attack the criminal negligence of governments which spend their time over matters of relatively no importance, to the neglect of the terrible social evils which should have been long since sternly grappled with. Herein I am a mouthpiece of the advanced Radical party. As regards religious matters, I plainly seek to show the nobility of a faith dispensing with all we are accustomed to call religion, and having for its only creed a belief in the possibility of intellectual and moral progress. Hence it follows that I attack (somewhat savagely) the modern development of Ritualism, which, of course, is the absolute antithesis of my faith.

In doing all this, I have been obliged to touch upon matters which will be only sufferable to those who read the book in as serious a spirit as mine when I wrote it. It is *not* a book for women and children, but for thinking and struggling *men*. If readers can put faith in the desperate sincerity of the author, they will not be disgusted with the book; otherwise it is far better they should not read it.

I write this in order to relieve you personally from any unpleasantness which may ensue upon the introduction of my book to Wakefield, and you would do me a service if you could show this to such as have manifested the least interest in the matter. I fear it is the fate of many men to incur odium by their opinions, but the odium is only cast by those who cannot realize the sincerity of minds differently constituted from their own.

To the same :

June 15, 1880.

Very many thanks for the card. . . . .

The *Athenaeum* knows very little indeed of the spirit of my book, and his knowledge of the letter may be gauged by his twice calling poor old Tollady a " bookseller." Then what in the name of conscience does the fellow mean by calling Gresham a " Skimpolean cynic " ? I imagine the likeness between him and Harold Skimpole, in *Bleak House*, is something which it requires special critical acumen to discover. Yet Bertz and I agree that it is rather an attractive review. Above all, the critic does me the justice of believing in my sincerity, and even says that the book may do good. I believe it will. But he treats it too much as if it were a mere polemical pamphlet, and not a *work of art*, as which, of course, I desire it to be judged. We shall see what other reviewers have to say. Such a long review in the *Athenaeum* is rather a compliment.

I am very glad you are using my open letter. It is a most shocking thing that *genuine* writing, let it express what opinions

it may, should be offensive to anyone.   This is a relic of the
Middle Ages.

*   *   *   *   *

Does Mother seem better for her change? Alas! my
chance of anything of the kind seems of the slightest.   Well,
I suppose my body and brain will hold out a few more years,
till what Thackeray called "the great, big, stupid Public"
can be a little impressed and made to relax their purse-strings
for the support of one who would fain enlighten as well as
amuse them.

ISLINGTON, N.
June 20, 1880.

DEAR SISTERS,

I have owed you a letter so very long that I am almost
afraid you will tear up these few lines in disgust without reading
them.   "Oh, it's from that fellow, George!"   Nellie will
cry out.   "Throw it into the fire, and let's show him we don't
care whether he writes or not!"   Nevertheless I will go on
scribbling, and say that I hope you, Madge, have come back
like a giant refreshed with wine, and that you, Nellie, have
been a brave little housewife this long time—keeping accounts
with desperate accuracy.   You must both of you write to me
before long; from Madge I shall expect a volume descriptive of
her travels in barbarous lands.

I can tell you a story which will give you a little amusement.
The other day a friend of mine was walking by the side of a
river, where there were some boys bathing.   One of these
boys was at a little distance from the others, and my friend
noticing something curious about him, soon saw that he was on
the point of being drowned.   Without waiting to throw away
his hat and take off his gloves, at once he jumped into the river
and succeeded in swimming to land with the half-drowned boy!
I should like to have seen him as he walked home; he must
have looked remarkably like a water-rat on its hind legs.

Now that Madge does not go to school, of course she will
have more time for quiet reading.   I hope she will choose one
or two good books (such as Macaulay) and read them slowly

and carefully.　I should also advise her to do a little *every* day at French; that is very important.

Write, both of you, as soon as possible to your affectionate brother

GEORGE.

June 25, 1880.

DEAR MADGE,

Nellie menaces me with her most severe indignation if ever I dare to address two persons at the same time again; so today I have sat down to write separate and *most private* letters to each of you.　First of all your portrait pleases me very much, except that there is a peculiar little pinch in the corner of the mouth which makes one imagine you might have just swallowed a very sharp drop of vinegar.　I have wanted your portraits for a long time, and it rejoices me to be able to put them in my album.

By the by, do you keep a diary ?　If not, I should certainly advise you to do so, now that you have more time to spare. Put in it all the main events of each day, and, at the same time, every book you read, with remarks upon them.　Likewise jot down special thoughts that come into your head.　To say nothing of the pleasure it gives you to look over such a book in future days, you benefit much by the careful thought it necessitates, thoughts about yourself as well as other things and other people. I have found it a very good exercise to try to *learn* myself, asking myself whenever I do a thing of some importance—Why do I do this ?　Would it be better to leave it undone ? and so on.

I am glad you like *The Antiquary*.　It is a capital book, all the better that it depends for its interest on fine character-drawing, rather than upon mere exciting incident.　Don't read *too* many novels, but try to know all the best; you should get hold of Jane Austen's novels, they are very healthy.

I was glad to hear you are so much better; health must be kept up whatever goes.

Affectionately, dear Madge,

GEORGE.

To his brother :

July 23, 1880.

I told you I sent a copy of *Workers* to Frederic Harrison. I now send you a copy of his letter. Good Heavens, I fear it is too strong! But he promises glorious help.

Why don't you write ? I begin to be rather uneasy about you. Let me hear soon.

Copy of Mr. Frederic Harrison's letter.

38 WESTBOURNE TERRACE, W.
July 22, 1880.

MY DEAR SIR,

There can be no doubt as to the power of your book. It will take rank amongst the works of great rank of these years. I have not yet finished it, and I cannot yet make up my mind as to its place as a work of true art. It belongs to a school of which I know nothing, and which I hold at arm's length, at least I think so. I am no critic, and very rarely read a modern romance, and I especially hate the so-called realism of Zola. But your painting of dark life seems to me as good as his, and to have a better social purpose—at least I hope so. I am, as I say, very little experienced in judging fiction, and I make no pretensions to judge at all work so full of power both in imagination and in expression as your story. It has most deeply stirred and impressed me by its creative energy. And I cannot wait till I have read it cooly, and felt it as a whole, before I write to you. It kept me out of bed a large part of last night—I took it up after my work—and that is what very few books have done for many years.

There cannot be the smallest doubt about its power, and power of almost every kind that fiction admits. But as you ask my opinion I will be frank. I do not pretend to offer either advice or criticism, your work is far above anything I could do in that way, if I wished. And I do not wish. But I will tell

you what I feel about it—as yet—before finishing it.   I am
not sure that the social and moral aim is sufficiently sincere, or
rather sufficiently strong, to justify the deliberate painting of so
much brutality.   Perhaps it is.   I have not yet read enough
to see what your moral and social aim exactly is.   I am the
last person who ought to pretend to judge such a book, for I
loathe books of the " Assommoir " class and never open them,
nor indeed modern fiction except on rare occasions.   Your
book therefore goes against all my sympathies in art, so that
my admiration for its imaginative power is wrung from me.
Whether prostitutes, thieves, and debauchees talk as you make
them talk in the night-houses of the Haymarket, I do not know,
nor wish to know.   It is possible that they are introduced to
good purpose.   I will try to see it.

But I will not trouble you further with my present half-
instructed feeling.   That is a personal matter with me, and
cannot be of any value.   I think I know enough of romances
to say this—that you may be sure of your book eventually
proving a literary success.   There are scenes, I am sure, which
can hold their ground with the first things in modern fiction.
The circulating libraries will be very shy of it.   I do not think
girls ought to read it at all.   But men of insight will very soon
discover its power.   I will myself take care that one or two such
read it, and I will urge my own opinion on the editor of more
than one literary review.   I never presume to "review" books,
as the picking out of scraps, and the saying of smart things about
them, is called.   And if I did review the book publicly, I
might say many things which the author would not like.   But
you may be quite sure of this—your book cannot be lost sight of.
Do not be in a hurry.   Books like that are not often written in
England, though they sometimes are in France.   You will be
neglected for a few months, abused for two or three, and in six
have a distinct (but not altogether tranquil) reputation.   Such
is the opinion of an avowed ignoramus in these matters.

If after this letter, which I have not sought to make pleasant,
you care to make any further communication to me, I shall
on my side be very willing to know more of you.   I am one of

those Goths, fanatics, or prigs, as we are sometimes called, who think much less of artistic or literary power, than of the objects for which it is used, the principles with which it is associated, and the character of those who possess the gifts of the angry fairy.   I have written enough to show you that anything you choose to tell me of yourself, your views and aims, will deeply interest me.   I write from the country, and I am going next week to another part of the country.   I shall return to London in August, and I shall like to meet you there, if you care to meet me after this frank letter of mine.

I am, yours very truly,
FREDERIC HARRISON.

P.S.—To show you that I do not write in any unfriendly way I will repeat to you three criticisms or remarks made on the book by my wife, whose judgment in fiction I trust far more than my own.

1. There is enough stuff in the book to make six novels.

2. The finer type of London workman has never been so truly drawn.

3. Where are the "Workers in the Dawn"?

You had better regard what I have said as premature till I know more of your work and of you.

To his brother :

July 29, 1880.

I send the enclosed cutting, because you may not have time to see the *Daily News* of today.   It is calculated to draw attention, though why he should call my style "illiterate" I confess I know not.

Frederic Harrison has written to eight literary friends about my book, five of these being the editors of good papers.   Surely there will be some result.   I shall see him when he returns to town in August.

Rejoice to hear that you are so busy.   Don't bother yourself to write much, but let me hear you are alive now and then.

I suppose this practical work is all profitable towards your examination ?

Am toiling at my new work, but don't get on as well as I hoped.   I have been writing at it too quickly.

To the same :

Aug. 20, 1880.

Your letter from the hostelry hight " Hare and Hounds " [at Embleton, Northumberland], has given me the utmost delight.   You don't say much about the weather, but seem to have had it glorious.   It almost pains me to read about such a delightful tramp.   I imagine you enjoy yourself a little.

I, too, have had my travels since I wrote last, but they have been confined to the regions of drawing-rooms and editors' offices.   I have dined twice with Frederic Harrison, who is doing very much for my book.   Then he introduced me to John Morley, who has asked me to write both for the *Pall Mall Gazette* and the *Fortnightly*.   For the former I have a definite order for three or four articles which will be ready in about a week.

Summers called to see me last week.   He has seen many reviews of my book which I have not.   He has got a copy taken by the Reform Club.

By the bye, Morley has made Matthew Arnold read it. All this town talk must sound strangely, like echoes from a far-off land, in your Northumbrian retreat.   At this moment I have a pile of half a dozen German pamphlets on Socialism which I must read today.   So you must excuse more.   We must write at greater length when you return.

All this sounded hopeful enough, and no doubt in many cases would have meant that the tide had actually turned. But temperament, no less than harassing domestic circumstances, robbed Gissing of all material advantage from this unbounded kindness of Mr. Frederic Harrison.   It is idle to speculate on what the young author might have done had he been personally free to battle with poverty only. Certainly, Sam Johnson himself could not live and work on less. But, as it was, Gissing had for ever to lament bitterly that he was incapable of journalistic work, and no less of congenial social life if he was to apply himself to literary work at all. So depression again soon overtook him, as the following extracts from letters to his brother at this time sufficiently testify.

Remington horrifies me by saying that only 29 copies are sold. . . . I have done nothing of late in the way of journalism. I positively have not the necessary peace of mind; and the gradual exhaustion of my resources is becoming a very serious subject of consideration. I fear the book is having no sale at all. Yet you will see it *will* have, some day.

The *Spectator* was unjust in many respects, most outrageously so, however, in saying that in describing the life of Mr. Gresham, Mr. Norman, Mr. Waghorn, and the well-to-do people, I was describing something I had never seen. *All* the reviewers take me for a working-man, I fancy, tho' a careful reading of my book would show such a supposition to be grossly absurd. Why, it is the *other* kind of life that I have had to make a study of—the low, not the middle-class life. And, say what they like, *all* my well-to-do characters are natural enough. But they will not confess the likeness. They are willing enough to admit that I have drawn blackguards well when those blackguards are of the poorer classes; the existence of blackguards elsewhere they won't recognize. " O Scribes and Pharisees, hypocrites ! "

*   *   *   *   *

The worst of it is I ought now to be exerting myself very seriously to find some fixed kind of occupation. I fear I must give up hopes of the book bringing anything in, and my position is getting somewhat ambiguous. But what kind of work am I fit for ? They won't take me in a business office, for I know nothing of such things; and the things I *could* do are only to be obtained by special interest. I assure you the outlook is about as gloomy as it well could be.   It is impossible to think of literary work in my present state of mind.

Oct. 3, 1880.

DEAR NELLIE,

Whenever I begin to reply to one of your letters I labour under the painful impression of having to discharge a debt with much accrued interest—an experience I hope may never befall you in the literal sense.

Your trip to Ilkley must have been very enjoyable.   It was good of you to bear in mind my advice regarding sketching. Of course you will preserve the sketches you made, even though you deem " nasty " an appropriate epithet to apply to them. I shall demand to see them some day, I hope.

I send this letter to the new house, where I imagine you are now settled.   Of course I shall form all sorts of ideas of the place's appearance.   Is it six or seven stories high ?   Are there four or five parlours on the ground floor ?   Is the orchard at the back likely to pay the rent in apples and pears ?   And do you suppose the peach crop on the walls will be good next year ?

In any case, I am convinced it is a vast improvement.   You who have had only one change of home in your whole life cannot imagine what it means to look back upon some five and forty removals—" flittings," as I think they are called.   No, you have had a happier time of it, and I trust will be equally comfortable as long as you live.

Angry, when I heard you were moving so soon after my visit ?   I should just think I was.   Indeed I tore out my hair to such a dreadful extent, that I am now almost bald—think of that!

Ever affectionately, dear sister,
GEORGE.

On Nov. 3, *he writes to his brother :*

Many thanks for your sympathizing letter.   The matter of occupation is as much a puzzle to myself as to you; I only know that *some* must be obtained. It gives me pleasure to hear you speak with a little more hope as regards my literary prospects; I myself think that a second book would go far to get me some sort of a name. Certainly I have struck out a path for myself in fiction, for one cannot, of course, compare my methods and aims with those of Dickens. I mean to bring home to people the ghastly condition (material, mental, and moral) of our poor classes, to show the hideous injustice of our whole system of society, to give light upon the plan of altering it, and, above all, to preach an enthusiasm for just and high *ideals* in this age of unmitigated egotism and " shop." I shall never write a book which does not keep all these ends in view.

III

WORKERS IN THE DAWN TO DEMOS (1880-1886)

To his brother :

Nov. 11, 1880.

At the last moment I hasten to send you a note on Ireland, remembering that to-morrow comes your debate.   It was the general opinion of the Positivists that Home-rule *ought* to be granted, unless the government is prepared with some very striking measure for a solution of the land difficulties.   One speaker feared lest a separation between England and Ireland might lead to the latter allying with some Continental power, and making war on England, especially considering Ireland's intense Catholicism and feeling of nationality.   In any case, and whatever measure is to be proposed, it is the duty of the government to put some end to the scandalous insecurity of life and limb.   Harrison himself said that, without wishing to seem cynical, he almost hoped that the difficulties would accumulate for a few years, so that they might end in a most tremendous outbreak, and thus bring about a truly *social* revolution.   For we must remember that the behaviour of the great Irish landlords in *permitting* such dreadful want and suffering on their estates, stamps them as social sinners of the worst kind, and points to a radical revolution in our ideas of property.   The possession of land is only a sacred *trust*, no man *can* " own " land like he owns his watch, for instance, seeing that land is not a human production made for the individual, but the common and indispensable basis of life.

Other countries besides England and Ireland have been in

close proximity yet unable really to unite, *e.g.* Spain and Portugal, Russia and Poland.   Of course the selfish politicians urge that Ireland is too useful to be relinquished.   Such arguments ought not to be listened to for a moment.

Do you read the letters on " Disturbed Ireland " in the *Daily News* ?

I shall miss the post if I write more.

At Harrison's the other night I met Ellis, the great authority on early English pronunciation and dialects.   I expect you know him ?

To the same :

Nov. 18, 1880.

What should you think of writings of mine being published in St. Petersburg?   I was astounded this morning to receive a letter from Professor Beesly (of University College), saying that he had been requested by Tourgéneff (the great Russian novelist), to find someone who would supply a quarterly article of some thirty pages on the political, social and literary affairs of England to a periodical published in Petersburg, and called *Le Messager de l'Europe*.   Beesly thought of me.   My articles would of course be translated, and I should receive £8 for each!   I have written to say I should be glad of the work.   Probably I shall hear from the editor of the *Messager*.   This is not bad news— what say you ?

Also I am glad to tell you that Frederic Harrison is busy in finding me pupils.   Better still, he hints that he shall very soon want a tutor for his own sons, and thinks I might supply the place.   Ye gods! this would be grand.

You see I am slowly obtaining a footing among people worth knowing.   Of course I cannot foresee how matters will go, especially the St. Petersburg business ; but—

> " He either fears his fate too much,
>   Or his deserts arc small,
>   Who dare not put it to the touch,
>   To win or lose it all."

I suppose I shall have to become frightfully learned in politics—especially Irish matters—for my Petersburg articles. I shall be bound to take in more papers, I fear, and yet don't see how I can possibly afford them.

To the same :

Nov. 22, 1880.

I am not sure that I quite understand the subject of your debate for next Friday. For indeed no one could say that physical courage is as much thought of now as in any previous period of our history. But I daresay they mean what you suggest—also, I hope, they have an eye to the so-called "athletic feats" which people now rave so much about in certain circles. Certainly there never was a time before when people walked round a sand-strewn circle for six successive days, till they drop from exhaustion, as they are constantly doing now at the Agricultural Hall in London; and probably no other age ever saw a Dr. Tanner. Our age, in fact, is thoroughly empty, mean, wind-baggish, and the mass of people care so little to find employment in intellectual matters that they are driven to all manner of wild physical excesses for the sake of excitement. Also remember the *betting* element in these disgusting scenes. Compare all this with the state of affairs in Greece, where the aim of all was to procure "a healthy mind in a healthy body." All were athletic, but only to *supplement*, not to *extinguish*, their intellectual activity—most likely their glorious intellects were greatly due to their perfection of bodily health. I wish you could get an idea out of all this for a five minutes' speech, for it is a capital subject. I would confine my remarks to *social* features. I might mention also the brutal way in which so-called open-air "sports" are now carried on, to the utter disregard of *human* suffering—for this also belongs to the preponderance of physical exertion. I find, *e.g.*, in a recent newspaper, that in County Cork there are some sixteen packs of hounds, and at least £20,000 a year is spent on these and horses. Now these sportsmen have done nothing at all to relieve the dreadful human suffering prevalent in their neighbourhood!

I cannot possibly write more now, for I have just heard that my Petersburg article must be sent off by the 20th December. This is dreadful, and will involve a fearful consumption of both ends of the candle.

In a letter of December 5 to his brother he speaks of having been engaged for two hours every morning in teaching the two sons of Mr. Frederic Harrison, and continues:—I have also got two evening pupils at present. Both are likely to go on for some time. So things look brighter just now.

Amid all this, I feel very seriously that I must be getting on with my new novel. One can't live for ever on the reputation of a first book, and my novels will always be the backbone of my literary existence. It is at present my hope to publish again just before Xmas 1881; that is the best time of the year.

And again to the same on Dec. 21:

Time has been at a premium with me of late; I seem to struggle perpetually with arrears of work. Yet despite every morning being occupied at Mr. Harrison's (I only get back at 2 p.m.) and every evening in the week save Sunday being claimed either by a pupil or by Bertz, I still manage to write a few pages of my novel now and then. It is all the harder to do this, seeing that for composition I absolutely require a period of mental and bodily peace to *precede* the actual writing. Yet I know very well that this alone is my true work, and it shall not be sacrificed to whatever exigencies.

I rejoice to say that Mr. Harrison has urgently requested me to continue teaching the boys after Xmas—most probably for a long time to come. Mrs. Harrison, moreover, promises to get me another family in the same neighbourhood very shortly, for the afternoons.

I have not actually begun to pen my Russian article yet; but must do so immediately after Xmas Day. I am waiting with much curiosity for the steps to be taken by Government on the re-assembling of Parliament. I fear there will be blood and thunder work in Ireland yet.

I was delighted at your reference to the London sojourn next year. Do you anticipate coming in April or so? Those will be fine times, though doubtless we shall both have our hands too full to permit of very much social enjoyment. If I do really obtain teaching in another family for the afternoons, I shall certainly give up my evening pupils; for the time will be of much more value to me than the money.

To the same :

Jan. 13, 1881.

Only just a line—for I have once more good news. I have to-day given the first lesson to the children of Vernon Lushington, Q.C., and late Secretary to the Admiralty. There are four girls; I give them an hour twice a week. With the Harrisons I recommenced last Monday, and things go very smoothly. Doubtless I shall have other pupils before long.

Remington shows no sign of sending in a Xmas account. Certainly my book is finding some readers, for Mudie puts it in his selected list for the new year.

On Monday next I send my article to St. Petersburg, and shall rejoice to have it off my hands. It has cost me immense trouble. I don't think the next will be as difficult.

To the same :

Jan. 16, 1881.

I sit down to write to you in vast relief of mind, having just signed, sealed, and prepared for delivery my Petersburg article. It makes 36 pp. of large octavo MS., and has cost no little trouble, I assure you. Happily, the division on Parnell's Amendment took place on Friday night, so that I was able to bring my report up to a definite period. It goes to-morrow morning for the land of Nihilism. I have dealt very fully with the Irish question, then with the English Agricultural depression, Fawcett's Post Office reforms, the so-called " crisis " in the English Church, and " Endymion," the last coming in for not a little severe criticism, as you may imagine.

I am reading just now Carlyle's *Latter-day Pamphlets,* which have admirable ideas on parliamentary institutions, etc. It is here that he uses his famous expression for the British Public— " twenty seven millions, mostly fools."

The weather is unutterable. I have never known such cold, save in Massachusetts.

You have not said much lately about progress of work. I presume you peg away through legal authorities. I am just reading Sir James Mackintosh's *History of England*—very clear and useful. Also I am reading a translation of Michelet's *History of the Roman Republic.* I get more and more towards historical reading. It is my ambition to write a historical novel one of these days, the subject to be Greek history at the time of the end of the Peloponnesian War. But it would require immense work.

Please tell girls they shall have a line before the end of the week, as I am comparatively free now. (To-morrow, by the bye, I shall have six hours' teaching, with walks of some eight miles altogether coming between.)

Jan. 30, 1881.

My Dear Nelly.

I suppose you are by this time once more facing the daily journey to Wakefield, and the tasks at school. I much hope that the latter do not entirely rob you of your time for private reading. I would always have some good book on hand, even if I only read it for a quarter of an hour a day.

I have now got for pupils four young ladies. The eldest is only fourteen, but they might each be taken for at least three years older than they are. I find them rather clever; we do English History and Geography together. One of them is always reading Homer, and she tells me that she would give anything to learn to read it in the original Greek. That is what you must do some day, mind that!

Your letters are frightfully scanty of information. Couldn't you tell me more about your neighbours, and all the people with whom you come in contact ? There must be something interesting now and then. Have you had any parties through the winter ? I suppose you couldn't ask many people to come in muslin dresses and silk slippers all the way out to Agbrigg. Yet I hope you won't be quite shut out from all your old friends.

It is terrible just now, walking about London streets, everything is covered with slush and mud. I spoil a suit of clothes every day: my very hat is sprinkled with dirt, it is hardly decent to appear in it. It is to be hoped you have a good pavement to walk on to Sandal station.

With much love, dear Nelly,

Affectionately yours,

GEORGE.

For a short time now, in addition to the ordinary dating of his letters to his brother, he made use of the Positivist calendar.

Tyrtaeus 93.

Jan. 30, 1881.

I hope you can see the *Pall Mall.* It becomes better and better, and is the recognized organ of our most cultured Radicalism.

I attended the meeting of the Positivist Society on Friday night, and we had a discussion as to whether the Society should make a public utterance on the state of affairs in Ireland and the Transvaal. It was decided to do so. I send you a copy of the Positivist Calendar for this year, which I got at the meeting. It was the suggestion Comte made for replacing the old notation by one more worthy of the advocates of the Religion of Humanity. Doubtless you will understand it. The 93rd year of the Great Crisis means, of course, the 93rd after 1788, 1789 being the first of the French Revolution, and hence of the new epoch.   I shall use the calendar in future.   It would be admirable as a lesson for children.   Keep the Calendar; I have put one up in my study.

The " Ballads " I like well, on the whole, though I profoundly wish they had not adopted the insensate plan of alphabetical arrangement.   When I was in Boston, Prof. Child showed me once an immense drawerful of materials for a great work on ballads.

A notable instance of Philistinism is causing much laughter in town just now.   You have certainly heard of the " Fleet Street Griffin " ?   This Griffin, on the top of a very ugly monument, was set up to mark the place where Temple Bar stood, and, as it appears, at the trifling cost of some £10,000. So great has been the outcry since its establishment, both on the score of public convenience (it blocks the road) and aesthetic requirements, that it is now all but resolved to put the whole thing down again, and, perhaps, remove it to another quarter! When I first looked upon the Griffin, I was constrained to burst into Homeric laughter—the thing is a disgrace to 19th century civilization.   But how about the £10,000 ?

It is such a thing as this that makes one rave against the blockheadism of so-called local governors. . . .   I look forward to a day when something of the civic spirit of old Greece shall animate one and all of our towns, when men will recognize their town as an individual member of the alliance of towns which makes up a nation—not merely as a collection of cotton-producing mills, or money-producing offices, but as one clearly-defined centre of intellectual life, which can only allow itself to neglect its noblest functions at the expense of all other surrounding towns.   From this point of view, I dislike the immense predominance of London.   Who ever sees a book worth having come from anywhere but London—I mean of course of English books ?   Yet of course this is altogether wrong. London is increasing in size past all reason, her evils growing simultaneously.

I am heartily glad of the thaw, but the slushy streets are unutterable.   I come home every day mud to the eyebrows.

Pheidias, 93.

Feb. 11, 1881.

I have just risen from the memoir of Carlyle in the *Times*.
I know well with what interest you will read it.   It is an
account of a life's work which gives one new supplies of energy,
fresh spirit to attack the day's work and make it a worthy link
between the efforts of yesterday and tomorrow.   Does it not
seem now as if all our really great men were leaving us, and,
what is worse, without much prospect as yet of any to take their
place.   Where are the novelists to succeed Thackeray, Dickens,
George Eliot ?   What poets will follow upon Tennyson and
Browning when they, as must shortly be the case, leave their
places empty ?   Nay, what *really great* men of any kind can
honestly be said to have given tokens of their coming ?   What
a frightful thing would be a living generation utterly made up
of mediocrities, even though the honest and well-meaning
exceeded the charlatans! . . .

Positivists say, let us devote ourselves to the study of man in
history, and, by the exercise of warm charity to all humankind,
work for the advancement of our species on the lines which
history teaches us to predict.   Indeed, having come to a settlement with myself on the subject of ordinary religion, I always
refer, in speaking of Positivism, to its *intellectual* side, its
inculcation, for instance, of a system of politics based upon a
study of the laws of human development, instead of mere
" politics " of expediency, and, in social matters, of ceaseless
efforts towards universal justice and light.   Of course, with
myself, its emotional side, the so-termed Religion of Humanity,
has also vast influence, and I can feel this enthusiasm for the
Race to be a force perfectly capable of satisfying the demands
usually supplied by creeds, confessions, etc.   But this, I am
sensible, is a matter of individual temperament, and far be it
from me to press the subject upon you.

I fear I have spoken much too positively about Easter, and
excited too many hopes.   It is by no means certain that the
Harrisons will take a holiday then, and so leave me free.   In

any case, I should dread the expense of the glorious plan you sketch out. If it could but be managed! Of course I am determined that, before long, every year shall see such an excursion for us both in company; I would not for anything put aside that hope. But it seems far too good to hope for just now. Yet I will not positively decide till the time draws nearer.

*   *   *   *   *

I am much taken up in the study of History just now, having to teach it so much. I should not be at all surprised if I found myself planning out a historical work one of these days. But where is the time to come from? In fact, I grieve to say that I spend at present no less than four hours every day in travelling backwards and forward—a quite impossible state of affairs. In fact, I seriously think of moving to the west end during the next few weeks. I think it would be to Notting Hill or thereabouts.

So Carlyle has been buried at Ecclefechan, I see, and not in the Abbey, as I confess I had hoped. Of course it was to be expected that he would express such a wish, but then the nation has a right to construct a Temple out of the graves of her greatest men. I see that no less than three lives are coming out. Carlyle left a fragment of autobiography, and Froude is editing it.

At the end of this month Gissing removed to rooms at 55 Wormington Road, Westbourne Park, in order to be nearer to his pupils, and, in view of this, writes to his brother on 26th Feb. 1881 :

I suppose it is vain to hope that I shall be settled in the new place for more than a few months: people who live from hand to mouth have to be content to do without the comforts of a fixed home. But at least I shall not walk myself to exhaustion every day, or wear out a pair of boots every three weeks, as of late. How I wish I could give you a real insight into my daily existence now and for the past years! But to do so would be to write a miserable letter, and why should I trouble you with such a one ?

To the same :

Xenophanes 93.

55 WORMINGTON ROAD,
March 6, 1881.

My new abode is far away the most comfortable I have ever had.   I much hope you will soon see my study; at night, when the blinds are down and the lamp lit, it is a wonderful room. I save an infinitude of time and fatigue.   How long shall I stay here, I wonder ?

I must be seriously thinking of my second Russian article. It has to go on the 17th April.   Now I have all my evenings free, I hope to get ahead tremendously with many kinds of work.   History is my special undertaking just now.

Love to all.   I really must try and write to the girls soon. Tell mother I am very grieved to hear she has not been well. Doubtless she will herself let me know how she gets on.

To the same :

Antithenes, 93.

March 13, 1881.

I have got thoroughly settled at length, and in every way benefit vastly by the change.   My study is a fine room, certainly more comfortable than any I have had.   To make things still better, Bertz is moving from Tottenham, and coming to live four doors away.   So here also I save time and expense, in addition to having someone quite near at hand to talk to.   I wish I could hear that you were coming up to London before long; we could gather quite a large party in my room, and be gloriously at ease after the lamp is lit.

I have at length heard from Remington, who sends me a cheque for *sixteen shillings*, author's share of proceeds up to last Xmas.   He makes out that 49 copies have been sold, and £24 odd spent in advertising.   Of course I have no check upon him;

and I must say I never expected to have a *cheque* either! So there is a pun. . . . .

I hope now to get some steady work at my book. My plan is to lock my door every evening from 5 to 9, and peg away. I bitterly bewail the loss of my mornings, when I am always in my best mood for writing. Still, I suppose I shall have some two months' freedom in the summer, and I should like to get so far ahead as to finish the novel in that time. Then comes the finding of a publisher. This time I will have a good one or none at all.

Every night from 11 to 1.30 I make a point of reading either a Greek or a Latin author. This I find quite necessary, to keep up classical knowledge. It is an ambition of mine to read Homer and the Greek tragedians as easily at least as I read Goethe, and I think I am at length on the road thither.

Glad to say, I feel up to the mark in health of late, and able to work long hours. With best love to mother and girls.

To the same :

Leonidas, 93.

April 24, 1881.

Many thanks for your glorious account of the Easter pilgrimage. To read of such things makes me unutterably wretched in my brick-and-mortar cage; such mentions of old country inns, of moor and mountain scenery, of sharp early-morning air—it is too much. You speak of our some day going over the ground together. I fear not; it is altogether too good ever to be realized. It is scarcely likely that I shall leave London again for years to come, if ever. And the worst of it is, I know how the quality of my work suffers from this pent-in mode of life. A few days of such bracing exercise would set me up with a completely new stock of ideas.

Thank goodness I have utilized this Easter as well as was possible; I have not yet lost a day for my novel. My plan is, as soon as the Harrisons begin work again, to get up at *six*, get breakfast over by *seven*, and write at novel till *ten*, when I have to go to the boys. I thus get three hours in the first freshness of morning strength. For I find that to sit down to fiction after a whole day of hard teaching requires an effort almost beyond my physical strength. With all this I fear me the book cannot be completed till August. It will be very long.

I have rather a fearsome business before me for May 5th, in the shape of an invitation to Harrison's, where there will be an assembly of Positivists to meet M. Laffitte, who is the head of all the Positivist associations. The man does not speak English, so of course French alone will be spoken in his honour. And I have not spoken French for five or six years. Well, I must read a French novel to brush up my phrases a little.

I have had letters from my pupils Bernard and Austin Harrison during their absence in the country. They are excellent little boys, and will make fine scholars, I am sure. It will be one of my greatest pleasures, I hope, to watch them developing year by year.

I have read a great deal of German these holidays, especially Eckermann's *Conversations with Goethe*, a most delightful book. Heavens, what a man that Goethe was; certainly no one comes between Shakespeare and him. I sincerely hope you will some day know him.

Among multifarious occupations, I am preparing a lecture on "Practical Aspects of Socialism," for a society with which I have connected myself. Its object (that of the Society) is an attempt to educate the working classes in some degree by means of lectures at their various clubs.

I see the German vice presidents of the Shakespeare Society have unanimously resigned in consequence of Furnivall's recent vagaries. By the bye, have you seen anything of the rather absurd representation of the 1st Quarto of *Hamlet*, in place of the completed play as usually given, which has just come off in London? Of course this 1st Quarto is a mere mutilated and pirated issue, as was common in those days, when successful plays were not printed. But Furnivall holds it represents Shakespeare's first sketch, and is better for acting than our form. Fudge! it appears to me.

Philopoemen, 93.   *To the same :*
                                        May 4, 1881.

First and foremost I have to give you astonishing intelligence. At length my packages have arrived from America, and I have spent two days in setting my new acquisitions in order. It is like a present to me, so completely had I forgotten what the boxes contained. Now at length I feel the satisfaction one has in completing a long and miserable phase of one's existence: with all my possessions once more around me I feel that in a certain sense a new period begins for me. My library finds itself wonderfully replenished, and I have been thus saved the necessity of some day purchasing many expensive but indispensable books.

What do you think ? They have sent me from Petersburg the four numbers for this year of the *Messager de l'Europe* for which I write my articles. It is a fine-looking periodical, about the size of the *Nineteenth Century*—rather thicker; but of course I can't read a word of it.

I have scarcely got into working trim after the Easter holidays. Did I tell you of my new plan of writing from *seven* till *ten* every morning ? I find it admirable, getting thus what I deem my *true* work done before the journeyman's work of the day begins. I rise at six, and have finished breakfast by seven. Of course I have to go to bed early, but I am so desperately set on getting on with my novel that I don't mind sacrificing the evening in part.

I am sorry to say I have not been in the best health lately. I am getting most frightfully nervous, indeed so completely nervous that I dread the slightest variation from my humdrum life. The door-bell ringing, even, or the postman's sudden knock puts me into palpitation and head-swimming, and I don't know what. This is very greatly the consequence, I know, of home circumstances, and I fear they will continue to work upon me. I only hope I shan't be rendered incapable of literary work; as it is, my writing has suffered the most grievous interruptions. I suppose a perfectly peaceful and intellectually-active life is one of those blessings I shall always only be looking forward to till there is no time left for it, and, according to my favourite quotation, " the night cometh when no man can work."

Best love to mother and the girls. I will write sometime—sometime—sometime.

To the same:

Vespasian, 93.

May 15, 1881.

I presume you saw in the *Athenaeum* the somewhat remarkable letter addressed by Furnivall to the seceders from the New Shakespeare Society? I should think the society is in a fair way to collapse.

I copy a notable telegram from Copenhagen which appeared in the *Standard* the other day. " A Royal proclamation has been suddenly issued dissolving the Lower House. It states that the King regrets to find the members wasting their time, being either incapable, or unwilling, to carry useful measures. During six months not a single useful Bill, not even a Bill of Ways and Means, has been passed."

Now how that would have rejoiced Carlyle! And indeed it is a refreshing utterance in these days of shams and make-believes. It is to be hoped the members will go home sadder and wiser men.

To the same:

St. Cyprian, 93.

May 22, 1881.

It is at all events good that you now know the exact date of your coming. I much wish it had been a little earlier that we might have had walks together round London before the winter comes on, but I dare say we shall be able to get two or three fine autumn Sundays as it is. There are several places within a radius of 20 miles which I much desire to visit, but fear I shall never do so without the help of your companionship —places like Barnet, Edmonton, St. Alban's, and many others.

I am at present going through English History in much more detail than ever before, a pleasure for which I have to thank the pupils I teach.

Did I tell you they now send me the St. Petersburg review
every month ?   Of course the only thing I can read is my own
signature, G.R.G., which looks remarkably pugnacious in its
English dress among the crooked little Russian letters.   Thank
goodness they are very punctual in forwarding their remittances.
But the work takes me very much time, and involves a terrible
lot of unprofitable reading.   You were right in saying that the
articles do not represent the full flavour of my opinions: still
I never say anything absolutely contradictory to my standpoint.
In future I am going to write with more freedom.   Despite
the preposterous press-censorship they seem to have been able
to print my last article intact, including the remarks on Most;
so that I shall be less guarded in future.   It is possible that the
review—being some 450 pp. long each month—may be among
privileged publications, and not classed with journalistic literature.   I know not.

These last days have been wonderful in their bright sunshine.   I suppose the leaves are out in the country—eheu,
eheu!   It seems a century since I saw a country lane, and
goodness knows when I ever shall.

Short letter this time, but I am sorely pressed with work.
Best love to mother and girls.

To the same :

June 19, 1881.

Your study-plan is very good, and, if you can stick to it,
will bring you through much work.   At present, it being quite
impossible for me to do any writing, I work something like this.
Before breakfast three Chapters of the *Germania* of Tacitus,
and some Roman History ; in the afternoon, History of the
Middle Ages (I contemplate a *Life and Times of Gregory VII.*,
some day); at night, political reading, whatever general literature I have on hand, and, last of all, 50 lines of Sophocles
—at present the *Antigone*.   At the end of this month I must
buckle to at my new Petersburg article.   Scarcely credible
that a quarter of a year has gone by since the last.

To his sister Margaret :

July 10, 1881.

Your last letter was a great improvement, both as to matter and length.

Martin Chuzzlewit is very fine, though I do not relish it quite as much as some others of Dickens; the story rushes backwards and forwards too much between England and America. Tom Pinch is, of course, good, though I fear there never was such a man, and Mark Tapley is, as you say, highly amusing.

I fear I cannot go much into detail regarding Arthur Hallam, as I have no biography of him in my library. But if you look in one of the glass-doored bookcases you will find a little volume called *A. H. Hallam's Literary Remains* which, I feel sure, has a memoir prefixed. He died in 1833 and was the eldest of the two sons of Henry Hallam, the great historian. Died on the continent and was brought home to be buried, I think in Somersetshire.

By all means ask every question that comes into your head. Green and the small histories of Smith would, I am sure, be a capital beginning. Read them with considerable care, seeking information in other sources regarding matters you are not quite sure of. It never does to use one book alone, always have others at hand, to check and amplify the information. For instance, I should advise you to use the large *Encyclopaedia* a good deal, in which you will find good information on many things in history. None the less I send you by this post Freeman's little book. For it is absolutely necessary that you should get a general idea of *all* European history before you can appreciate the parts, and here you have it capitally. Don't read it too quickly, but with thought, and, *above all*, with an atlas. *Never* read History without an atlas. Have you a classical atlas? If not, let me know at once and I will send you one. It will give me the utmost delight to know you are working gradually through these Histories: it will have a marvellous effect upon your mind. Let me know, at least once a month, what you do, *but don't hasten.* Don't trouble about the long German words. I'll tell you a secret. Always try to split them up into their component parts, and you will find you often needn't look for their meaning at all. Go on steadily and remember what I said about the effect of knowing one book in German thoroughly. Don't neglect the short Grammar at the end.

St. Bathilde, 93.
                    To his brother :
                                    July 10, 1881.

Now for your affairs, and first of lodgings. For my own part, I shall strongly advise the west end rather than the north. Really, I should be *désespéré* to have you come to London and then live utterly out of reach. I look forward to the month of September with vast delight. My holidays will be from beginning of August to end of September, so I shall be at leisure for a month with you.

With regard to Wakefield, how would it suit for me to run down for the week preceding the beginning of September, and then return to town with you ? Will you discuss this with mother ? More than a week, I fear, is out of the question, and even then I should have to beg for a room three hours every morning, as the progress of my book must be a serious object during those two months.

Your examinational plans require a good deal of thought. . .

I heartily agree with you that a very vigorous push should be made just this next year or so; it will leave you all the freer afterwards, to get the academical part of your life for ever done with—melancholy as the expression sounds.

Did you ever think of that grievously depressing aspect of life ? The essence of a great joy is the thought that it may one day be repeated; and yet the great and all-interesting epochs of life are done with once and forever—no second tasting of boyhood, youth, or the short period of mature powers. Eheu, eheu!—But what has this to do with passing examinations, prithee!

At all events, snatch a moment to write to me at greater length on the matter—especially about the suspect " coach."

You will be surprised to hear that my friend Bertz leaves on the 27th inst. for America. He is going to settle on a farm in Tennessee, in the Rugby colony founded just now by Thomas Hughes, of which you have doubtless heard. He has much liking for the country, so I think it probable he will be quite well off on his farm. He has given me some of his books, and will sell the rest (some 400 volumes) getting what he can for them.

By the bye, is it not Gosson who uses the phrase " Caterpillars of the Commonwealth " ? I find it also in *Richard II.* Act 2, scene 3 (the end).

You shall have my article week after next. It is the best hitherto, and I shall want opinion on it.

To the same :

July 29, 1881.

After next Monday my address will be 15 Gower Place, Euston Square, W.C. Yes, I am going back to the old locality, though not to the same house. I long for the neighbourhood of life and bustle and noise Here in this wretched workman's suburb it grows intolerable. I have found the most delightful lodgings I have yet been in; three rooms, one a proper kitchen, completely shut off by a door and staircase from the rest of the house The rooms are moderately spacious, and on the whole it is just like having a house to oneself.

Goodness knows when I shall again write at length to you; but do you do so, to keep me in spirits through the toil. I go on Monday.

To the same :

August 8, 1881.

I absolutely *must* complete my novel this year. If I do not it is as good as giving up all hope of ever finishing another book, for perpetual procrastination is like a disease, and bit by bit impairs every faculty. What I would give for a portion of the

spirit and energy with which I wrote the first book! I am
doomed to do everything under the most harassing difficulties,
in nothing is my path ever lightened, but rather forever more
and more encumbered.   I struggle with absolute anguish for a
couple of hours of freedom every day, and can only obtain the
semblance of whole-hearted application.   To say that I am like
a man toiling up a hill with a frightful burden upon his back is
absolutely no figure of speech with me; often, very often, I am
on the point of stumbling and going no further.

Do you think if I came on August 20th—that is Saturday—
and remained to the end of the month, I should be over-
burdening mother ?   I know well you will let me have a quiet
room and absolute peace for four hours or so every morning,
and that week and a half would be inestimably precious to me.
But it all depends on the date of your own coming up, for, as
you know, I wish to return with you.

Work on well, my dear Alg., as you are doing, and rejoice
that you are young [his own age being now 23] and have your
liberty to walk right onwards.   I, too, am young enough yet,
I suppose, but the months and the years go, go, with never a
better, but always a darker, outlook, and perhaps the best years
of all are already gone.   To look back on a wasted life must be
bad, but worse still, I think, to feel the waste actually going on,
to know what *might* be, and to be helpless.

Good-bye, dear Alg.

To his sister Margaret :

Sep. 18, 1881.

It is certainly your turn for a line at last.   It rejoiced me to
hear that you have got on so well with German.   " No day
without a line " was Luther's motto in translating the Bible
and that is the way to get through work.   Persevere, even if
you only do ever so little, and you will earn your Schiller.

Alg. and I get along together famously, and see a good deal
of each other.   On the other hand I fear you miss him very
much.   But do your very best to keep up good spirits.   Nothing

helps me so much in the effort as a determination that no day shall pass without a double duty discharged—first, the duty to oneself, in the acquisition of some positive knowledge; secondly one's duty to the world, in the doing of a kindly action, or, at least, the speaking of a kind word, to some other person. What more can one do, or indeed wish ?

The weather here is, on the whole, fine and warm, but I grieve to say, the morning mists have already begun to pay their visits, and will, of course, before long usurp the greater part of the day. Terrible enemies of mine, these same fogs and mists; they destroy my power of work and make my whole nature *limp*—soaked through, as it were. You remember the deplorable condition I was in, those wet mornings in Wakefield. How is young Muff [a favourite cat] ? Bless his old nose ! Grimmy Shaw begs me to send his compliments, and say that his health might be better than it is. He fears he is getting old; his fits still recur. He has strong thoughts, in the case of death, of making Muff his sole executor and legatee.

Good-bye, then, dear Madge, and let me know that you get on well, alike in health and spirits, and in the knowledge of the Germanic tongue. I am drenched in work; I don't know when I shall emerge dry.

Ever affectionately,

GEORGE.

To the same :

Nov. 9, 1881 (Lord Mayor's Day).

I am immensely ungrateful not to have acknowledged the knitted socks before this; but I am overwhelmed with unimaginable troubles, and must beg you to forgive me. Indeed I am very thankful for them. I know not whether you alone are responsible for the work, but I remember you spoke in a letter a short time ago of being engaged upon it.

Read away at Schiller, and, if you can possibly find time, read his life in Carlyle's works—a vastly interesting life it is. The man's was a noble nature, far above every meanness and vulgarity, and his poetry is the finest embodiment of idealism

which the world possesses.   Read all his ballads first; they are
the easiest in the language.   Then take up the *Lied von der
Glocke*, one of the most glorious poems ever written, but a
little difficult.   Make use of the translations in the bookcase,
whenever absolutely necessary, and, in any case, after reading a
poem read the translation for the sake of comparing it with your
own version.   Would it be too much to try a verse translation
yourself now and then ?

Glad to hear good accounts of Muff.   Grimmy Shaw (who
has just been knighted, and is now Sir Grimmy), rejoices in
much improved health.   He is an enormous cat, and a good old
animal.   It delights me that you have a good servant, at last;
also that you have made progress with house-keeping.   Think
over what we said as to the possibility of uniting intellectuality
with domestic efficiency.   Good that you have read *Hero-
Worship*, a book to be read many times and pondered over.
When you can read Schiller well, I will follow it up with a
Goethe—a still diviner man.

With much love, dear Madge,

GEORGE.

To the same :

Nov. 23, 1881.

I am always glad to have a good report of the German.
The only thing is, you ought of course to read some prose as
well as verse, for the difference of style.

Old Grimm waxes fat and sleeps much.   We get on wonderfully well together.   His old face seems to grow more intelligent
as he gets older, and he has very curious habits, some of them not
at all of a cattish nature.   For instance, he has taken to eating
out of one paw, sitting up and lifting bits of bread to his mouth
like a monkey.   He is rather ill-natured with my poor little
bird, and I have once or twice caught him on the very cage;
but for that he has been beaten, and now only ventures to look
up at the little chap with a very furtive glance.   At the present
moment he is fast a-snoozle on the hearth-rug, with his head
resting on one paw.

A society has just been formed in London called "The Browning Society" for the special study of Robert. Its meetings to the end of the year are open to the public, and Alg. and I think of going on Friday night to hear a paper read. Browning is a particular favourite of mine.

To his sister Ellen :

Nov. 23, 1881.

Many thanks for your kind letter, and the card you sent in it, which I think very tasteful. It is all the present I desire, to hear from you and know that you remember me sometimes, a cheering thought in the midst of this huge wilderness of a town, where no one has any friends and where one doesn't even know by sight—a fact—the people who live in the same house. Struggling for a living in London is very much like holding yourself up, after a shipwreck, first by one floating spar and then by another; you are too much taken up with the effort of saving yourself, to raise your head and look if anyone else is struggling in the waves, and if you do come into contact with anyone else, ten to one it is only to fight and struggle for a piece of floating wood. For people who are not anxious about to-morrow's dinner, life in London is very fine; otherwise it is a cruel sort of business.

I shall be glad to hear that you are well out of your examinational troubles and to have the promised letter when the time comes; till then, don't write; work on, doing your best, but not *over*doing it.

I often think of that glorious week I had with you all, of the song-singing and the tea-drinking, and the supper-eating. O, the comfort of it all!

The night draws on and I must walk out to post these missives, that you may have them in the course of tomorrow.

Grimmy Shaw is in excellent health, and sends respectful compliments to —— Muff Esq.

Ever affectionately, dear Nellie,

GEORGE.

To his sister Margaret :

Jan. 1, 1882.

Very best wishes for the New Year which opens here, at all events, with a fine sunny morning. I hope you begin it in better spirits than the last, seeing your way more clearly among all the difficulties and hindrances which are inevitable in the smoothest life-journey.

Thank you for the copy of Coleridge's poem, which, like all he wrote, is a model of sweetness and perfect expression.

Two of my pupils, when we ceased work for the holidays, gave me a very nice silver pocket pencil—a useful present.

I am on the point of beginning my serious quarterly labour, the article which I write for the Russian journal. It is always a tremendous toil. I sit down with much loathing, and rise from it—it takes me a fortnight—with infinite satisfaction. But it brings me in £32 a year, so I suppose I mustn't grumble about it.

I hope Muff grows in body and in mind. I suppose he has not given up his evil habit of sparrow-hunting.

To his sister Ellen :

Feb. 3, 1882.

Many thanks for your letter. You girls now-a-days have astonishing advantages over your mothers and grandmothers; it is only to be hoped you will make use of it for the only real end of education—improvement of character. If you only could know how much of the wretchedness of humanity is occasioned by the folly, pigheadedness, ignorance and incapacity of women you would rejoice to think of all these new opportunities for mental and moral training. For the cultivation of the mind goes a very long way towards the formation of a good character, say what they will. Who can *really* study Shakespeare and not be the gentler, wiser, nobler for it ? I have vast faith in imaginative literature of all kinds. If the choice had to be made, I would rather have a girl well acquainted with

Dickens, George Eliot, Shelley and Browning than with all the science in all the text books.   These writers show you what is meant by life and teach you to distinguish the good and the bad in it.   Never think you waste your leisure time in reading them.   And if you have not much leisure time now, you will have shortly.

Ever affectionately, dear Nellie,

GEORGE.

The faultless accommodation in Gower Place proved after all to be dangerously insanitary; after some illness, Gissing moved once more.

To his sister Margaret :

29 DORCHESTER PLACE,
BLANDFORD SQUARE, N.W.
March 8, 1882.

I believe it was you who wrote latest to me, so to you I will address a very hurried letter, which I hope you will communicate to all.   I am overwhelmed with many and dire occupations. I write, as usual, at midnight, wearied out.

My teaching work has extended fearfully of late.   I have now ten pupils—some in little groups; and am taken up with teaching from nine in the morning (having to set off at 8.15) till six at night.   Then comes private work of my own, so I have but little rest.   I have all meals here, save on Monday and Friday when I lunch with the Harrisons; they, in their inexhaustible kindness, insisted on this arrangement after my slight illness a while ago.   I have now two sons of Sir Henry Le Marchant to teach and, together with them, a nephew of the Duke of Sutherland.

Last Monday, Alg. and I, following in the track of the somewhat ridiculous excitement prevailing here now, went to the Zoological Gardens to see the famous elephant Jumbo—of whom you have doubtless heard.   There were 16,000 people in the gardens that day, and as, on the average, every person gave Jumbo three biscuits or buns, judge of the animal's size and appetite.   They have sold him to an American showman for £2000, and now find it absolutely impossible to fulfil their bargain: Jumbo refuses to stir.   A monstrous box has been made for him, but he can't be persuaded to enter it.   The papers swarm with letters, begging that he may be kept.   At the Gardens, thousands of letters are received, addressed to Jumbo, and containing—buns!   No one knows what will be the end of the affair; but most likely some twenty or thirty people will be killed.   Jumbo backed against his keeper the other morning, and if the man had not had the presence of mind to shout out the elephant's name, and so induce the beast to bend forward and look round, he would next minute have been crushed like a fly against the wall of the den.   Jumbo, by the bye, is eleven feet tall and weighs six tons.

Alg. is very hard at work, and now we are too far from each other to meet more than twice a week.   We manage to have Sunday evenings together, however.

I hope most sincerely that I shall be able to have an hour or two with you some time before next Christmas.   I am constantly thinking of those rare old German songs.   I much hope you keep them up; also that you get on with German in general. Alas, it is weeks since I read anything.   I have no time to look at a book.   All day I teach, and all night I scribble.   I am a weary mortal.   Tomorrow night I dine at the Harrisons. I will rush out and post this before I go to bed, as you will then get it mid-day tomorrow.   With much love to all and promises to write to all before long.

To his sister Ellen :

April 3, 1882.

Very many returns of your birthday, and may each one find you happier than the last.   How the years go by and how little have we to shew for our time, whilst our world has been travelling once right round the sun.   At your age you have not yet, happily, learnt to feel this lack of effectual labour. Every day you are making progress in your school studies, and the end of a year finds you appreciably advanced.   It is when we have long since passed away from school and all its tasks, when life is offering us lessons and problems so hard, so hard— then we are oppressed with this sense of standing still, and are saddened by the thought that, even whilst the end of our time is already drawing near, we have scarcely made a beginning of our work.   I often wish I were a carpenter, or a builder, or something of the kind; then at least one would sit down each night with the cheering consciousness of " something accomplished, something done," and the years would not seem a blank. The quotation reminds me that Longfellow is just dead— seventy-five years old.   Have you read of it in the papers ? I like his poetry and can often read a little poem and feel better for it.   He is not very deep; by the side of the great poets he sinks into insignificance; yet there is a quiet and sunny atmosphere in his work which often refreshes, when one is not in the humour for climbing the heights.

I was very glad to have the account of what you were doing at school.   You ask for advice as to the reading of poetry in your Easter holidays.   Did you ever read Cowper's *Task* ? I think you would find it very enjoyable.   I should like you to go carefully through it and let me have your opinion.   Then I want you to read all Goldsmith's poetry.   There is little of it, but what there is is perfect.   In learning by heart pieces out of *The Deserted Village*, one does not appreciate the real beauty of the verses; one must have them in their proper place in the whole poem.   You might, at the same time, read his two plays, *The Good Natured Man*, and *She Stoops to Conquer*.   Suppose now, you take these two men, Cowper and Goldsmith, and try, by degrees, to go through their *whole* works ?   It would do you infinite good to get, in this way, a complete and rounded study. Cowper's letters are wonderful, and all Goldsmith's essays delicious.   Think this over.

I hope all of you are quite well and enjoying the fine spring weather.   I much hope to come down to you some time during the summer or autumn, but it is just possible that I may be kept by pupils throughout the year.   I am aweary of it all.

Once more, best wishes, dear Nellie—love to ' Mother and Madge.

To his sister Margaret :

April 16, 1882.

I envy you most prodigiously your bit of open garden.   I know if I lived with you I should not use it much, since the sun in this sad clime of ours is seldom warm enough to allow of one reading in the open air.   But still the mere sight of it would be very enjoyable.   The idea of being in actual possession of a few roods of the earth's surface, and those free and open for the growth of green things, is very delightful.   One feels that, after years of living in two rooms of a London lodging-house, without even one inch of soil to oneself, seeing that one is suspended in the air, with others dwelling below, above, and all around one.   Yet, after all, there are summer evenings when it is possible to sit in the open air without shivering the flesh off one's bones.   I remember such here and there; strangely sunny spots in the landscape of bygone years.   I think of the various odours of the earth and plants and flowers, the buzzing of insects, the barking of a dog or the lowing of a cow in farm-yards far off, and the striking of the hour from mouldy old steeples.   At the seaside, too, I have known such evenings, sticking in the memory with the sound of the long, dying splash of small shore-waves, and perhaps the wheeling cry of a seabird.

Alg. and I often compare our notions as to the pleasantest way of spending a holiday.   I say how grand it would be to have a month in the Mediterranean; Alg. would not think of that in preference to the Scotch Border or the Hebrides.   I cannot get him to realize the gloriousness of seeing Italy, Sicily and Greece, Rome, Athens, the Ionian Islands—countries where every spot of ground gives off as it were an absolute perfume of reminiscences and associations.   Think of standing in the Forum, and saying to oneself—" Here on this very spot have Scipio and Sulla, Cicero and Caesar, Virgil and Horace, stood and talked; these very blocks of stone and marble have echoed to the noises of a Roman crowd, and beheld the grandest scenes of all history ! " Alg. says he would infinitely prefer the association of Flodden and Melrose. It is a strange difference of sentiment.

By the bye, what French are you reading now-a-days ? If you are free in that department, and could possibly make time, I wish you would go through Madame de Stäel's *Corinne*. It is a story of Italy, bright and warm with the sunshine of the glorious country, and written in a wonderfully eloquent style. Of course you always have some French book on hand, to be read, however slowly. Tell me if I shall send you *Corinne*. I will do so at once if you say yes.

Don't lose a moment in idle fretting over lack of time and opportunity. Better opportunities only come through the right use of such as we already have: be sure of that. When you cannot be reading, be thinking of what you last read, and make yourself master of all its meanings. Try and see into the truth of things, lower than the mere surface: that is what few people do. Good-bye for the present, dear Madge.

To his brother :

May 7, 1882.

I am like to have plenty of matter for my next Russian article. On opening the paper this morning I find the startling announcement that Lord Frederick Cavendish and the Under Secretary were shot dead last night in Dublin—some six or seven hours after Cavendish had been sworn in. This is brisk work, and it is hard to say what the result will be. Who will venture to take the position next ? It seems to mean certain death. Of course, some Irishman must take the place; why not Parnell himself ? One can't as yet understand this latest move.

Happily these matters don't greatly affect one, but from the kind of shock and excitement one experiences on suddenly reading such news it is easy to imagine how, in really stirring times, one's mere private troubles and annoyances would lose

their power of holding attention, and be merged in greater
interests.   In the time of the French Revolution, for instance,
it would not have been easy to brood over petty individual
difficulties.   Who knows but we shall yet make trial, in one
form or another, of this experience ?

I have been much delighted by coming across Cellini's
description of the moulding of his great statue of Perseus with
Medusa's head—you know the thing by sight ?   I have
perpetually wondered *how* this moulding of metal statues was
accomplished, *how* exactly the hollow mould was made. . . .

I shall to the end of my life look upon bookseller Allen
[referring to a small old bookshop at that time in Euston Road]
as a personal benefactor and bless his name.   You remember
our wondering what the price would be of a first edition of
Gibbon ?   Well, on going to fetch away the last volume of
Stephanus from your late abode the other night, I actually found
the very book outside Allen's shop, and—is it credible ?—marked
6s. 6d.!!!   Six quarto volumes, portrait and maps!   In
absolutely perfect condition, not a yellow stain, glorious print,
published by Strahan and Cadell.   This is 1s 1d. per volume!
And, what's more, the man told me he had had another copy
a few weeks before.   Of course it was impossible not to get this;
flesh and blood could not forego the possession of it, despite all
impecuniosity.

I suppose I shall hear in a day or two the result of examination.   I much hope it will be all right, as then you will not be
disappointed in your prospective Bamburgh sojourn.   By the bye,
I went to the Grosvenor and the Academy last week.   The
Academy was glorious, only so tremendously crowded that it
was difficult to get near the pictures.   I shall certainly have
another shilling's worth there before the 1st of August.   Some
of the landscapes were wonderfully fine; among them was a
large picture of Dunstanburgh, grandly done.   Sir F. Leighton
has several admirable classical pieces.   I regret hugely that you
should have left the Academy unvisited.   I felt every way better
for it.   It was the second best thing to an actual ramble on the
sea-shore to look at all those bright sea pictures, with their

L.G.G.   H

marvellous reproductions of sun, shade, foam and translucent water.   In fact, I can't really say whether I don't derive more positive pleasure from a fine picture of such things than from the reality.   In many ways there is grievous discomfort attending on a ramble among fine scenery—weariness of limb, heat of sun, showers, dust, wind.   Whereas, in looking at a picture your imagination enables you to realize at the full every most agreeable sensation, without any of the discomforts.   To be sure, it also makes you wish for the time to be in face of the reality, but it is a shallow philosophy which makes much of this.   Even that longing for unattainable conditions is the enveloping atmosphere of all life; one cannot escape from it.   And better it should take such a form, than any more violent, as it is apt to do.

Three fine lines I have just come across in *Catullus*, and which I must give you the trouble of making out, so rich are they in melody and meaning,—

" Soles occidere et redire possunt;
Nobis, cum semel occidit brevis lux,
Nox est perpetua una dormienda."

I must read more of the Veronian.

To the same :

May 18, 1882.

I had myself from the first but little anxiety as to the result of the examination.   I am heartily glad it is over, and that you have thus reached the happy term of life at which one may say: *Actum est de examinationibus !*   A most blessed deliverance. Though, for my own part, if I only knew of any examination which would by any possibility open up to me an active career in life, I would gladly sit down to prepare for it instanter. But this is too late, and the future holds forward no promise.

I hope you may enjoy Teesdale, etc.   The weather here is quite amazing; Italian skies from 5 a.m. to 8 p.m.   Regent's Park is wonderful.   For all that, I can't do without fires.   I tried it yesterday, and suffered enormously.

By the bye, I have been making out a form of Last Will and Testament. I think it is imprudent not to have something of the kind at hand, as, small as one's possessions may be, there is yet a preference in the mode of disposing of them. Now, I should be very glad if you would put this into legal shape any time during the next few weeks.

To the same :

May 26, 1882.

It is difficult to transport one's imagination away to the Farne Islands. I suppose they are the same as ever: the sea-birds calling about them, and the same wash of green breakers on those small stretches of sandy landing-spots. It is well to have such things in memory, for I fear there is not much chance of my ever realizing them again.

B. and I think of a walk out to Richmond next Sunday; that is if the weather changes. Last Sunday we had a pleasant ramble through the Chelsea Hospital grounds, interesting from being the Ranelagh of the past century. It preserves a strangely eighteenth century look still, which is heightened by the presence of red-coated pensioners.

This confounded landlady gets more and more disobliging. . . .

Shall be glad to have detailed account of the trip.

To his sister Margaret :

May 29, 1882.

I hope you are making use of this fine weather to get out on to the Heath and enjoy the glorious colours of earth and sky. Yesterday I had a long walk with a friend out to Richmond Park, and saw some of the most beautiful country scenery one could wish to revel amongst. In the midst of the splendid woods and fields which border the Thames in that part, one would think any large town was at least a hundred miles away.

It is Bank Holiday to-day, and the streets are overcrowded with swarms of people.   Never is so clearly to be seen the vulgarity of the people as at these holiday times.   Their notion of a holiday is to rush in crowds to some sweltering place, such as the Crystal Palace, and there sit and drink and quarrel themselves into stupidity.   Miserable children are lugged about, yelling at the top of their voices, and are beaten because they yell.   Troops of hideous creatures drive wildly about the town in gigs, donkey-carts, cabbage-carts, dirt-carts, and think it enjoyment.   The pleasure of peace and quietness, of rest for body and mind, is not understood.   Thousands are tempted by cheap trips to go off for the day to the seaside, and succeed in wearying themselves to death, for the sake of eating a greasy meal in a Margate Coffee-shop, and getting five minutes' glimpse of the sea through eyes blinded with dirt and perspiration. Places like Hampstead Heath and the various parks and commons are packed with screeching drunkards, one general mass of dust and heat and rage and exhaustion.   Yet this is the best kind of holiday the people are capable of.

It is utterly absurd, this idea of setting aside single days for great public holidays.   It will never do anything but harm. What we want is a general shortening of working hours all the year round, so that, for instance, all labour would be over at 4 o'clock in the afternoon.   Then the idea of hours of leisure would become familiar to the people and they would learn to make some sensible use of them.   Of course this is impossible so long as we work for working's sake.   All the world's work— all that is really necessary for the health and comfort and even luxury of mankind—could be performed in three or four hours of each day.   There is so much labour just because there is so much money-grubbing.   Every man has to fight for a living with his neighbour, and the grocer who keeps his shop open till half an hour after midnight has an advantage over him who closes at twelve.   Work in itself is *not an end ; only a means ;* but we nowadays make it an end, and three-fourths of the world cannot understand anything else.

Let me have your opinion on these points.

In a brief note to his brother at the beginning of June he writes :

Am getting on with a piece of work just now better than for the last two years. One volume as good as finished, and, on the whole, better than *Workers*. It is the last attempt. This failing, some other serious course will have to be taken.

And again on June 7 :

I must really write and tell of an astounding proposition which Mr. Harrison made to me the other day. I have not been able quite to grasp it till now. He proposes that I should go and spend September with them in Normandy! All expenses, he says, would be provided for, and he thinks the boys could have a couple of hours at lessons every day. Now at first this seemed *tout-à-fait impossible;* but, on thinking it over, it seems to me that it would be much folly not to overcome every difficulty in the way of it. I am not at all likely to have any pupils just then, and the gain in a hundred ways would be enormous. New scenes for novels, etc! Please communicate your serious advice.

First volume of novel finished this week.

B. asked me to go with him last night to the French Comedy Company, now at the Gaiety. We saw Sarah Bernhardt in " Frou-Frou." It was really most delightful, an entirely different thing from English acting. Last Sunday B. and I were taking our ease in a little public-house arbour out near Wimbledon Common, when we were startled by the sudden appearance of Ellen Terry. She came from her carriage with two children, and they drank cider, evidently much enjoying the rustic situation.

I expect you came back with some loathing to the " daily round, the common task." But it will have been a fine relaxation.

You will be amused to hear that certain carpet-rods are still *in situ* on my staircase—just as you saw them last.

To his sister Margaret :

July 12, 1882.

It is a pouring, dismal, indigestion-giving day. Yesterday, on the other hand, was in every way one of the most delightful days I have had for a very long time. I had an invitation from Mr. Frederic Harrison to go and see them in their country house. I got to Woking station about 9 o'clock, a trap was waiting for me and I was driven over to the house which is called Sutton Place, some 4½ miles from the station. It is most gloriously situated, amid such *real* country as I have not seen for years. There is not even a village within sight, at most two or three labourers' cottages to be seen over a great extent of landscape, and the nearest country residence about 4 miles away. All corn, grass and wood land, with the little river Wey winding through the heart of it to join the Thames far enough off.

The house itself is a marvellous place, dating from the wars of the Roses.

*   *   *   *   *

You can imagine what kind of a day I spent, and how little agreeable it is to wake up this morning to a hideous sky, a more hideous street, and most hideous work—for I am just now in all the agonies of my Russian political article, which I loathe.

To his sister Ellen :

August 19, 1882.

Many thanks for your letter. It does me good to think of you enjoying yourself so much. Don't trouble if you have no time to read. I am convinced that it is very necessary that you should give the brain a thorough rest for some weeks. When you get to be a hard-grained old creature like I am, then rest becomes of but little importance; but with you the process of physical growth is still going on, and it doesn't do to draw all the sap to the top of the tree.

I like to see your mention of the paintings in the Exhibition.

Endeavour to train yourself in the appreciation of art.   Whenever you look at a picture don't only ask yourself whether you
like it or not, if it pleases you, and so on, but try to find out
what the best points of it are, in which part of it the artist has
shown most skill, whether the drawing is good but the colouring
bad and vice versa, how otherwise the subject might have been
dealt with.   Some day we shall go over the National Gallery
together, and then can talk of these things.

Do you sketch at all ?   To do so, however imperfectly, is an
admirable training for the eye.   You accustom yourself really
to *see* in detail a landscape of which other people only get a
rough general idea.   There are artists who have so trained the
memory of their eye, that they can stand in front of a large
cathedral for a short time, and then go away and draw it in all
completeness.

To his brother :

Sept. 3, 1882.

On and after Wednesday next, my address will be :

17 Oakley Crescent, Chelsea, S.W.

Thanks for your last information.   Novel lies completed;
to-morrow I send it to Smith & Elder, though with the usual
doubts.   However, I have already begun a new one, and shall
so fare on, to do something ultimately, if human persistence
may prevail.

I have very bad news from Mr. Harrison.   Mrs. Harrison
still seriously ill.   Will put off my visit, perhaps finally; but
he will write again at end of month   [This refers to Nor-
mandy].

To the same on Sept. 20 :

Smith & Elder write me about my novel precisely what
I expected.   " It exhibits a great deal of dramatic power and
is certainly not wanting in vigour, but in our judgment it is
too painful to please the ordinary novel reader and treats of
scenes that can never attract the subscribers to Mr. Mudie's
Library."(!!)

Of course I could have told them all that.

To his brother who was staying in Bamburgh Castle,
on the Northumberland coast:

Oct. 6, 1882.

For the time, your lines have indeed fallen in pleasant places; I wish I also could get a whiff of Oceanus through the morning casement, and " hear old Triton blow his wreathed horn " in the breakers at the castle-foot.   Instead of that I am struggling bitterly with the old foe, the Russian article—less tangible this time than perhaps ever before.   My stray moments are devoted to theology and philosophy, especially the former, which always had much attraction for me.   I think I told you that the Harrisons had recommenced.

The pessimistic article is finished, but I shall not even try to get it published, seeing that it has developed into nothing more nor less than an attack on Positivism.   So far has my intellectual development brought me.   There is little hope that the *Nineteenth* or the *Fortnightly* would accept the thing, but, if they did, I should feel uncomfortable at the thought of Harrison reading it.   But I have other things going on, as soon as ever the bread-article clears the way.   I think there is little doubt that my work will ultimately follow the line which has been hinted at all along, I mean that of philosophico-social speculation.   I feel more inclination at present to write in this abstract way than to go on embodying theories in fiction.   But I suppose one cannot hope to strike the final course at all events before thirty.   Bread is the present desideratum, and the means of obtaining it grows doubtful.

Shall send you the *Hope of Pessimism* shortly, as I want you to understand this matter.

For all that, I have before my mind the plan of a very big novel, which will of course find embodiment some day.   Goethe's father used to insist on the boy's literary attempts, whatsoever they were, at least finding a complete form.   Incompleteness, eternal beginning and never ending, is the ruin of three-fourths of the intellectual men who at one time shew promise.

17 OAKLEY CRESCENT,
Day after Xmas Day.

MY DEAR ALG.,

One line to acquaint you with the fact that *Bentley* offers £50 (!!) for the novel.   Hurrah!

Always,

G. R. G.

To the same :

Feb. 3, 1883.

I send a good batch of proofs.   They are printing very quickly. . . .

Having visited the Rossetti collection at the Academy, and being delighted beyond all utterance, I determined to see the picture at the Burlington Art Club, so applied to Mr. Lushington.   He at once procured me a printed form of invitation. I go to-morrow.

I get on well with new book.   Hope to finish Volume I. by Easter, at all events.

If you possibly can, get hold of William Morris's *Earthly Paradise*.   This is poetry you will really like; all old stories told in Chaucerian style, and abounding in the quaintest archaisms.   Interesting articles on Rossetti in the new *Contemporary* and *Cornhill*.   That in *Cornhill* by Myers, very fine.

The title of the book which had been accepted by Messrs. Bentley, and was now being printed, was *Mrs. Grundy's Enemies*.   It was never published.

To the same :

Feb. 9, 1883.

I am sorry to say a little difficulty has arisen between the old man of the sea (*i.e.* the inhabitant of Tenby) and myself.   He has been reading the proofs, and comes to the conclusion that he must really beg me to soften certain features in some of the description and dialogue.   I send you his last letter, in reply to one of mine, in which I protested.   I sent him also some reviews of *Workers*, that he might see how such matters had previously been taken.   I have taken Harrison's advice, which is that, within reasonable limits, I should give way.   Accordingly I contemplate some little delay in publication.   Certainly I shall not quarrel with Bentley, on such unsavoury grounds.

Will send a few proofs to-morrow.   They are coming slowly.

You will have chuckled over my communication to Moy Thomas, in *Daily News*.   I was determined to strike a blow at "Mock Turtles."   Wonder whether outraged author will defend his piece next Monday.

Still in good spirits; hope you have reason to be the same. New novel progresses slowly, spite of distractions.

To the same :

Feb. 14, 1883.

No great progress to report.   The printers, however, have put on a spurt, and will, at this rate, finish Volume II. by end of week. . . . . I had much rather Bentley dictate desired changes, than run the chance of altering things which perhaps he would permit to stand.

I am somewhat low-spirited about the matter at present. Have been having a very *vive* discussion with Harrison to-day, in which he went very strongly against me.   I shall fight these prejudices to the end, cost what it may.   Have sketched following, to be put as preface to the book :

"This book is addressed to those to whom Art is dear for its own sake.   Also to those who, possessing their own Ideal of social and personal morality, find themselves able to allow the relativity of all Ideals whatsoever."

If this novel once gets forth, I shall write a magazine article on the points at issue.   I have much matter.   Pray send the critical letter you speak of.   I wish to goodness I had someone to take my part strenuously in the battle.   Can you suggest variant readings for the Preface ?

Never mind: I have that which never fails one—confidence in myself.   The day will come when I shall smile at the recollection of these initial difficulties.   Preserve this letter, and look back on it in the year 1890!

If this book creates some little fuss, as it probably will, I shall write a single volume to be entitled *A Highly Respectable Story*, in which I will give it the critics and the namby-pamby public in general to a somewhat amusing tune.   I could write the thing in a fortnight, and it would be *Satire* I can tell you.

Nothing yet from Bentley.   I do hope this annoying delay won't last much longer.   Doubtless he is waiting to read proofs of second volume, as well as MS. of third.

I get on with new work.   What I am now writing is, I can assure you, somewhat out of the common, and infinitely beyond anything I have done as yet.   When I read *Mrs. Grundy* in proofs, it seems miserably weak and frivolous by the side of what I am now doing.   The name, as far as I can judge, will be—*The Burden of Life*.   I shall very soon have finished Volume I.   This is good progress, considering numberless distractions.   There will be no sort of difficulty in getting to the end by the end of June.

To his sister Ellen :

Feb. 27, 1883.

I have sat down to occupy the half hour between breakfast and going out with writing to you and Madge.   This interval is always a vile one; I always feel ready to do all sorts of work just at this time, and yet have to face a morning's drudgery with pupils instead.   A dark and dismal morning like the present of course makes everything worse.

It will be pleasant to have Alg. at home again.   The old melodies from " Patience," will be resumed.   I hope you will be able to procure " Iolanthe " shortly.   The airs in it are not so taking as in " Patience," but I am not sure that much of it is not of a higher character.   On the stage it is wonderfully beautiful.   You have heard of Wagner's death; I suppose you have had no opportunity ever of hearing any of his music. I have only heard an occasional selection at times on indifferent orchestras.   I believe the operas are extremely grand, and well worth a visit to Germany to hear.

Do you, or does Madge, do anything at drawing yet ?   I suppose you, at all events, are too overwhelmed with the ordinary school routine to indulge in such things, but I hope the opportunity will come.   My own drawing days are for ever gone by, but I have a strong interest in art, as ever.   I have been spending some hours of late at exhibitions in London of Dante Gabriel Rossetti's pictures, which are very glorious.

I spent an evening in the east end on Saturday.   It is a strange neighbourhood, totally different from the parts of London in which my walks generally lie.   The faces of the people are of an altogether different type, and even their accent is not quite the same as that of the poor in the west end.   I rambled till midnight about filthy little courts and backyards and alleys, and stumbled over strange specimens of humanity.   I had a long conversation with a curious Welshman.   He informed me that he was "something of a scholar," for he constantly read the newspapers.   He was rambling about the crowded streets in his slippers, looking for his wife, who was shopping.

Let me hear if possible, with whatsoever information your life supplies.   This is a dull letter, but, as I said, I write at a dull time, and in expectation of my abominable slavery.   I shall be glad when Easter arrives; there will be a short breathing space.

Will you please tell Alg. to be sure to read an article on "The Theatrical Revival" in the February *Nineteenth Century*. Also tell him that my attack on "Mock Turtles" has resulted in an announcement that the piece will be withdrawn, and another substituted.

To his sister Margaret :

Feb. 27, 1883.

You will begin to wonder whether I still walk the earth ; or would do so, were it not, I suppose, for tidings occasionally furnished by a respected solicitor recently established in the

historic town.   Happily I am still working on, and, am glad to
say, feel in somewhat better health and spirits than has been the
case for several years.   Probably the approach of spring has
something to do with it.   Already there is a fresh glad breeze
by the river on sunny mornings, and I begin to think of the
days when the steamer will run to Putney, Richmond, Kew and
Kingston.   During the summer every Sunday will see me
going on the river either in one direction or the other.   For a
few pence one has a delicious sail, and the cobwebs of the week
are satisfactorily blown away from one's brain.   I, you know,
am just upon the north side of the river.   I like to cross over
the bridge to the south, and, on a sunny day, walk up and down
the edge of Battersea Park.   Then, looking over northwards,
I see the fine row of old Queen Anne houses called Cheyne
Walk, where numbers of interesting people have lived.

I wonder if you are likely to be coming to London again in
any reasonable time ?   May would be the month; the height
of the season, and before the too great warmth came on.   I
have made up my mind to get to Wakefield this year, and,
I think, it will be in August.   Till the end of July I expect
I shall be at my teaching incessantly—a fearful prospect.
But there will come a time of freedom.   And, in truth, I don't
think the teaching will go on for so very much longer.   Better
prospects seem to be opening up.   If the day of liberty arrives,
I shall not infrequently run down to Wakefield ; at least once
every three months.

Let me know once more what you are reading and what
thinking about.   I have had my British Ballads bound and they
make two very beautiful volumes into which I often look.
But indeed I read very little now-a-days; work of other kinds
occupies me almost exclusively.

There will be premonitions of spring on Heath Common by
this, I should think.   I should like to walk over it, with a pipe
and old Muff for company.

To his sister Margaret :

May 12, 1883.

Of Ruskin I have been also reading somewhat of late; especially one book you would glory in—the *Unto This Last* —his contribution to—or rather onslaught upon—Political Economy. I much wish you could get this somehow. The man is so horribly hard to procure, owing to his absurd fads in publication. Yes, I go with him very far, and can always exult in the mere glory of his English, which is, in prose, what Swinburne is in verse, the most artistic work of the day. His worship of Beauty I look upon as essentially valuable. In that he differentiates himself from Carlyle, whom else he closely follows. It matters little that his immediate schemes are impracticable ; to keep before the eyes of men the *ideal* is the great thing ; it does its work in the course of time. I wish you could see a photograph I frequently pass in a window in the Strand. It is Coniston Lake " Mr. Ruskin's View "— and certainly the point chosen must be the perfect one.

Well, he is, and always has been, rich and comfortable. Had he been poor, and with the necessity of struggling through a wretched existence of toil, his socialistic fervour would have, ten to one, exhibited itself in furious revolutionism, instead of this calm, grave oratory. Which of the two is ultimately better, I know not. Only this, I am growing to feel, that the only thing known to us of absolute value is artistic perfection. The ravings of fanaticism—justifiable or not—pass away; but the works of the artist, work in what material he will, remain, sources of health to the world.

To his brother :

May 13, 1883.

I am coming to the conclusion that the men who are capable of really enjoying all kinds of humour are among the rarest of all species. You yourself are, in fact, the only person I at present know to whom I can communicate fine shades of humour

with the certainty of being felt.   Of course one cannot instruct
a man in the understanding of humour.

In June he refers to a few breaks in work, and

writes to his brother :

I had a magnificent day on Sunday.   B. and I rowed up the
river to Richmond, and back; leaving at 10 a.m. and getting
home at 8.30 p.m.   The weather was perfect and the river
banks glorious.

To the same :

June 22, 1883.

Last Thursday I had a glorious time.   After doing the usual
work with the boys at Sutton Place in the morning, a whole
party of us drove from the house in the afternoon, and had a
picnic tea in the woods.

We reached a most superb point of view, called Newland's
Corner—certainly the finest prospect I ever beheld.   Thence
you see away over the Sussex woods, and also into Hampshire,
almost as far as Blackdown, where Tennyson lives.   The three
men and two maids laid our cloth under trees, whilst we ourselves lit a bonfire of dry boughs, and suspended kettle over it,
gypsy fashion.   Then a pleasant tea.

After that, a walk of a mile to a curious spot called " The
Silent Pool."   The pool is in the depths of a wood; it may be a
couple of hundred yards long, and comes from a spring which
bubbles up at one end, but it is impossible to describe the appearance of the water.   Though it averages ten feet of depth,
there is no spot where you cannot see every pebble at the
bottom, and, as the ground is chalk, the bottom looks quite blue.
Moreover you see very large trout swimming everywhere.
Lilies grow here and there on the surface, and fine trees come
down to the edge all round.

Then I left the party and walked some seven miles to Guildford, a very delightful old country town with ruins of a castle.

Nearly all the houses are genuine gable-ends. Then I had refreshment at a fine old hostelry and took train back to " Babylon."

In spite of taking this enjoyment he had written a few days before:

" Breaks in routine are always an unpleasant thing to me. It is so essential to keep the wheels oiled and going, and the habit of doing nothing is so fatally strong when allowed to exist even for a day or two. I shall not be able to write a satisfactory letter till I have once more some achieved ground behind me."

To his brother:

July 18, 1883.

My holidays [a break from his pupils only] have begun rather unpromisingly, with headache and inability to work, due to various strange complications and bedevilments in which no one has any interest but myself. But in a few days the mill will go again and grind on to the end of the task. I suppose I must very soon be hearing from Bentley, relative to " Mrs. Grundy." After all, how quickly the time has gone. The fretting and impatience of to-day becomes so speedily the half forgotten and inappreciable trouble of yesterday.

I am by degrees getting my right place in the world. Philosophy has done all it can for me, and now scarcely interests me any more. My attitude henceforth is that of the artist pure and simple. The world is for me a collection of phenomena, which are to be studied and reproduced artistically. In the midst of the most serious complications of life, I find myself suddenly possessed with a great calm, withdrawn as it were from the immediate interests of the moment, and able to regard everything as a picture. I watch and observe myself just as much as others. The impulse to regard every juncture as a " situation " becomes stronger and stronger. In the midst of desperate misfortune I can pause to make a note for future use, and the afflictions of others are to me materials for observation. This, I rather think, is at last the final stage of my development, coming after so many and various phases. Brutal and egotistic it would be called by most people. What has that to do with me, if it is a fact ?

For the present, then, *sufficit*. So often it happens that holidays are my worst working time. But I must struggle to the end of Volume III.

To the same :

August 3, 1883.

Curious that you speak of Boswell. I have been amusing myself with him these last few days. But—oh Heavens—have you read Mrs. Piozzi ? I had never looked into her anecdotes till last night, when on going to bed very early, I began to read them (printed in the last volume of my Boswell). Despite my situation I laughed so consumedly that I am sure I made myself worse. Do try to get the book. One or two stories are there told which surpass all conception of grotesque humorousness.

I hope you will enjoy your tramp. It seems a life-time since I was able to walk; and this just the finest time of the year. Eheu ! Eheu!

To the same :

August 23, 1883.

I have just read again *Redgauntlet*. The old fellow is very strong indeed in romantic situations. I must take a hint from him, and try to find parallel kinds in modern city life. I remember being impressed by this book when I read it before, and re-reading adds to my liking of it.

Real work is even yet at a standstill and will remain so.

No news in my miserable world. Day after day the same. I could say with Job " my days are as swift as a weaver's shuttle, and are spent without hope."

To his sister Ellen :

August 9, 1883.

I am grateful for your letter, which comes when I am in need of news from friends. I hope you are having for your holiday the bright sunshine that prevails here. My pupils write to me from Lucerne to say that they have had incessant rain for a fortnight, which must be nice. We shall scarcely get that here, I think. To me, however, it matters little, as I am hardly likely to walk out again till the summer is quite dead.

I rejoice to hear of your continued success at school. What you say of examinations I am sure is true enough. They certainly do not answer any end sufficiently important to justify their other harrassing attendants. It is unfortunately true that the real education of most people has to begin when they leave school, or, if it does not, they never become educated at all. I rather think that I owe very little of my culture—in the true sense of the word—to my formal teachers; though it is doubtless true they turn up and fertilize the soil for future use.

By all means give much time to your music, and the quiet readings on the Heath are also very good. I must hope you will some day be able to give me help towards something of a musical education. I want to get more insight into classical music than I have, to understand the various movements of a piece, and so on. At a really good concert I feel too much at sea; it must be remedied somehow.

That was delightful to get off to Fountain's Abbey. I was there years and years ago, but remember little beyond a point in the grounds where the guide stopped us, and then suddenly threw open a door, which gave a most magnificent view of the ruins down below. I wonder whether you saw the same. I was there, I believe with a lot of people, but who they were, I have no manner of recollection.

Now there comes a barrel-organ to play just outside. It will inevitably make my head worse, and yet, for all that I enjoy it. An organ is always an assistance to me in doing any kind of mental work.   So many people it simply drives distracted, they rush furious to the door, shake a frantic fist, and so on.

To his sister Margaret :

17 OAKLEY CRESCENT,
CHELSEA,
August 9, 1883.

Doesn't it seem to you that the above address is getting quite ancient, and a part of the established order of things ?   It rejoices me whenever I think of " fixity of tenure " here. Sometimes in walking about London I find myself in front of a house which I seem to know, and, on reflection say " Oh yes, of course I lived here once."   The names and numbers of most of my abodes have totally left me.   The present one however will not so easily be forgotten.   Unfortunately the people only propose living here for a little more than another year, so that it is vain to look forward to a longer tenure in my own case.   And indeed what my position may be twelve months hence is the most insoluble of questions, always has been and probably always will be.

To the same :

September 15, 1883.

No, no, you misconceive my position.   If I believed nothing but what I could prove, I should believe nothing at all; for nothing is capable of proof *absolutely*.   I mean this.   Taking for granted my powers of sense, I am quite justified in pursuing scientific discoveries, and saying that I can *prove* their truth; but I mean no more than that I can prove this *in relation to my own attributes*.   You remember I once spoke to you of Time and Space.   Granting Time and Space I will prove to you that a certain cave must be of a certain age, owing to the existence in it of stalactites which grow at a known rate; and I will also prove that the moon is so far from the earth.   But how about my own senses ?   They are powers given to me in some strange way, and they compel me to regard things after a certain fashion; but may not that fashion be something widely diverse from *Absolute Truth* ?   The colour-blind man will tell you that red is green, and so on, showing that the senses only guarantee certain conditional truths.

In very deed, I can prove absolutely, nothing whatever. Am surrounded by infinite darkness, and live my little life by the light of such poor tapers as the sun, moon and stars.   But I earnestly beg of you to understand that this position is compatible with the extremest reverence.   If you tell me you believe that the light has been brought to you, by means of a certain revelation, I cannot possibly say you are wrong.   I could only do so if my own senses were final arbiters of truth.   All I can say is that I am so constituted that I *cannot* put faith in the light you hold to me; it appears to me an artificial reflection of man's hopes.   My position with regard to the universe is that of Carlyle in the wonderful chapter of " Sartor " called " Natural Supernaturalism."   I pray you read that magnificent chapter again.

What splendid autumn weather—" Season of mists and mellow fruitfulness."   Oh, for the riverside on these glorious afternoons!   There is only one place in the world wherein to live, and that is *Chelsea*.

I am vastly better.

To his brother :

September 15, 1883.

Of course you see the advertisement of Macmillan's new magazine, and the astounding fact that they have printed 150,000 copies!   By the bye it is edited, I am told, by John Morley. Do get the first number, if only for the illustrated article on Rossetti.   Imagine such contents for $4\frac{1}{2}$d.

The sonnets of Shakespeare which I myself regard as the best—and some of them as perhaps the finest lyrical poetry ever written—are the following, Nos. 27-29, 30, 33, 44, 54, 55, 59, 64, 66, 71, 73, 86 (note the marvellous phrase " affable familiar ghost "), 90, 98, 102 (perhaps surpassing all), 106, 107

(yet what can surpass these ?)—no, no, 107 is unapproachable—
110, 111, 116, 119, 144.   Read these very often and with
extreme attention.   Every word is full-burdened with meaning,
every line is a cadence of music.   If you can anywhere point
me to richer volume of sound than swells in Sonnet 107, I
shall greatly thank you.

The interpretation of the whole string of Sonnets is difficult.
Of course much has been written on them, yet I myself have
come to a fairly satisfactory understanding.   Subdivide them,
by beginning a new canto with 40, another with 43 and the
last with 127.

To the same :

September 23, 1883.

I am busy with Landor.   I have got through the first
volume (*Forster's Life*) and am now in the *Imaginary Conversations*.   There are marvellous passages.   What do you think
of this for instance: " It is better to repose in the earth betimes
than to sit up late; better than to cling pertinaciously to what
we feel crumbling under us, and to protract an inevitable fall.
We may enjoy the present while we are insensible of infirmity
and decay: but the present like a note in music is nothing but
as it appertains to what is past and what is to come.   There are
no fields of amaranth on this side of the grave; there are no
voices that are not soon mute however tuneful; there is no name,
with whatever emphasis of passionate love repeated, of which
the echo is not faint at last."

This is perfect prose.

In turning over Tennyson I have been struck with his
felicity in putting vague notions into beautiful words.   *Vague-
ness* of form or of process is, of course, the most difficult of all
things to describe.   Read carefully Section LXX. of *In
Memoriam* noting especially the last two lines of the third
stanza.   Everyone must have experienced this, but very few
could put it into words at all.   Then again that verse in the
Dream of Fair Women describing the coming on of sleep,
beginning " All those sharp fancies by downlapsing thought."

Points like this interest me, like all matters of style.

By the bye, do make time for De Quincey's autobiographical writings, and the *Suspiria de Profundis.* Unsurpassed writing there. I learn a good deal by heart just now, both prose and verse. I believe it is good.

To his sister Ellen :

Sunday, October 14, 1883.

Sunday evening is generally a free time with me, and it is none too soon to think of writing you a line. I sent some scribbling to Madge the other day, which I hope would be agreeable to her in her early days amongst the strangers. You, I doubt not, are hard at work as usual. Let me know, if possible, that you keep well through it all, and that you grapple with examinations and the rest, without too much harrassment of spirit.

Here is a queer tale of Dean Stanley. Perhaps you know that he wrote a vile hand. On one occasion he wrote asking a friend to come to see him, and put in a P.S. " My station is Wokingham." The recipient showed this letter to an old lady who read it, and, on coming to the P.S. shook her head, sighed, and said " Ah, I can't agree with him ! "

" Agree with what ? " cried the other in surprise, marvelling that anyone should quarrel with so plain a statement of fact.

" Why," said the old lady " he says here—*my trust is in the working man.*"

No doubt you read of the interesting voyage that Gladstone and Tennyson took together in their holidays. Singular thing, the first poet and the first statesman of the day, two old fellows, going about in that way; and it probably never happened before. Gladstone said rather a fine thing of Tennyson in a speech on their return. " His work has been on a higher plane than my own, and his name will live when mine has been long forgotten," and I doubt not it is true, for, after all, art is the highest product of human life. Of course it pre-supposes civilization and all the triumphs that makes that possible. But so does the flower presuppose the stalk and leaves.

Did you read of the death of Tourguéneff, the Russian
novelist ?   He was, without doubt the greatest living writer of
fiction, and you must read him some day—of course in translations.   I possess two letters, on matters of business, which
he wrote to me from Paris.   They are of course valuable and
will become more so in course of time.

Oh dear, Oh dear; the wall between our house and the next
is fearfully thin, and there is some individual next door who
practices hymns on the piano all Sunday, *with one finger*.   I am
fond of music, but   ——.

Is Miss Milner [sister of Dr. Milner of Wakefield, the mistress of his first school] still in the land of the living ?   After
all, I owe her much; as all do to their first teachers.   Most
probably she has forgotten my name.

To his brother :

December, 8, 1883.

New novel will be finished on Tuesday.   I send it to
Chapman & Hall.   The name is *The Unclassed.*

To the same :

January 21, 1884.

Have got into the second chapter of new novel, and shall go
on at the rate of half a chapter daily.   I shall thus get it
finished early in the year, and have time by summer to look
about me in other directions if even this proves useless.

By the bye, if ever you have an opportunity, read Blackmore's
Lorna Doone.   It is a quite admirable book, approaching Scott
as closely as anything since the latter.   Scene in Devon, a
glorious locality.

To the same :

February 14, 1884.

I would make a chief point of the necessary union between
beauty in life and social reform.   Ruskin despairs of the latter,

and so can only look on by-gone times.   Younger men (like W. Morris) are turning from artistic work to social agitation just because they fear that Art will be crushed out of the world as things are.

In his lecture the other night on a new kind of storm-cloud he believes only to have appeared of late years, Ruskin more than hints that the degradation of the heavens is due to men's iniquity.   Strange sight, the old fellow standing up in the London Institution and rebuking his hearers like a Hebrew prophet!   Give this as an illustration of his extremes.

To the same :

February 27, 1884.

You remember that over the proscenium of the "Haymarket" is written:—"Summa ars est celare artem."   A fellow behind me there, the other night explained very loudly to a companion that this rune meant : "The summit of art is to excel nature" and went on to explain the derivation of *excel* from *celare*.

"Peril" at that house is inimitably played, such perfect acting I never saw.   Mary Anderson in "Tragedy and Comedy" is also very interesting.   I am going to see "Claudian" to-morrow night.   It is impossible for me to say whether I can be with you at Easter; I heartily wish I could, as I should enjoy the tramp enormously.   I fear it must all be left to chance.

To the same :

March 6, 1884.

If you want to get for the Library one of the most charming and delicate of modern novels, you should send for Besant's *All in a Garden Fair*.   I have just read it with really extreme delight.   Great part deals with a young man's struggles into literature, and is truthful enough.   But the summer atmosphere of the whole is delicious.

I have just got from Germany translations of five or six of Tourguéneff's novels.   They are published in the *Universal Bibliothek* at 3d. a volume!

To the same :

On March 16th :

The weather is simply astounding. An ordinary June is
nothing to it. Yesterday I was at Richmond and had a pull on
the river. Magnificent, I need not say, though the chief beauty
of Richmond is the foliage, and that, of course, is lacking as yet.

In addition to my new novel, I am at work on a play, which
I, at present, think of calling " Madcaps." I have the four Acts
sketched out, and think I can make something really good of it.
What odds will you take against me having a play out before
I am thirty ? I *mean* to, and resolutions have as yet borne
tolerable fruit with me.

To the same :

On April 28th :

I am sorry to say I am about to leave Chelsea. You will
be surprised to hear this. It is difficult to do, but self-preserva-
tion renders it unavoidable. This house has become very full
of people, and the position of my room leaves me scarcely ever
in quiet during the evening; my work has for some time been
at a stand-still owing to this, and that really won't do. I shall
go back into the old N.W. district, probably somewhere in
St. John's Wood; that is the true Bohemian locality.

Alas, the north side of Holywell Street is disappearing;
the glorious old Wych Street houses are no more. I wonder
if it were possible to photograph them. I fear not, on account
of the narrowness of the way. We shall live to see London an
irrecognizable city.

To the same :

62 MILTON STREET, N.W.
May 29, 1884.

I have begun a new novel—after several futile attempts—it
is always thus between one book and another. I should not
like to have to carry from here to Temple Bar all the paper
I have thus wasted during the last five years. Not waste,
however; it is indispensable.

I am very busy with Tourguéneff, at present: of course in German translation, and the man is glorious but, after all, there are two or three of his books obtainable now in English. You must get these whenever you can.

I am better off here than in Chelsea.

I have visited the Academy and Grosvenor. Some excellent pictures this year. Of course the usual glorious landscapes, which set one dreaming of flood and fell.

Did you see Ruskin's opinion of " Claudian " ? He went to see it *three* times. I have myself been twice; it is a magnificent piece of acting, and a more than tolerable play.

To the same :

Thursday, June 12, 1884.

Your account of the tramp is glorious; I would have given something to share it. I have forgotten the taste of the air in those outlandish regions. The Roman camp alone I should delight in seeing. You are fortunate in being able to store up such reminiscences. Heartily wish we could have a few days together at the sea-side somewhere in the autumn, but, from Wakefield, the distances are so great. I shall certainly come to Wakefield in August. I wish it were possible for you to come back with me, and walk, say from Chislehurst to Hastings, or something of the kind.

Throughout July I shall be going to Sutton again, two or three days a week ; I look forward with joy to the Surrey lanes.

I have found, by the bye, that Chapman's reader, who talked with me so sympathetically about the book, was no other than George Meredith. It is an excellent thing to have got his good word. His own novels are of the superlatively tough species (almost matching Harbottle chops). See, for instance, the beginning of " Diana " in the current *Fortnightly*.

My own life is too sterile and miserable to allow of my thinking much about the Race. When I am able to summon any enthusiasm at all, it is only for ART—how I laughed the other day on recalling your amazement at my theories of Art

for Art's sake! Well, I cannot get beyond it. Human life
has little interest to me, on the whole—save as material for
artistic presentation. I can get savage over social iniquities,
but even then my rage at once takes the direction of planning
revenge in artistic work.

Let me hear again as soon as you can. I suppose my present
very low spirits are attributable to the fever. In truth I am in
sore need of a holiday. It is just about seven years since I had
one.

To the same :

June 15, 1884.

To get rid of the vapours I went this afternoon by train to
Richmond, walked thence along the river to Kingston, had tea
there, and pulled to Hampton and back to Kingston, in a very
little boat, only just large enough to sit in and with outriggers.
The river glorious, but very full of boats, which made it very
nervous work without anyone to take the rudder. However I
progress in the art of keeping a look-out over my shoulder,
and sculling is becoming very easy to me. You must come here
some time just for the sake of a day or two on the river.

At Kingston I picked up a *St. James's Gazette*, which,
apropos of Tennyson's announcement that he can no longer
attend to strangers' letters and MSS. contained some marvellous
stories of Macaulay. A man wrote to him, an artist, begging
him, as he honoured art, either to hire or buy for him a cow,
to paint from. Another wrote asking an explanation of an
allusion in one of the essays, and, this being furnished, speedily
wrote again to say that he had forgotten the latter half of a
certain verse in Macaulay's *Horatius*, which he begged the
author to supply!

Another wrote from Scotland saying he wished to come up
to town and show Macaulay an MS. Would the latter send
him £50 for expenses ? And yet one more, a schoolmaster
submitted a pamphlet on British India. Macaulay pointed
out some errors, and in a week or two a new edition appeared
" Revised and corrected by Lord Macaulay."

The book [*The Unclassed*] was well advertised at the end of the week.   *Athenaeum, Pall Mall Gazette, St. James's Gazette, Spectator, Saturday Review* (specially good advertisement here), and doubtless some other.   I have no copies yet, of course ; you shall have one as soon as I get it—I am to have half a dozen.

To the same :

Monday, June 23, 1884.

You frighten me, or rather would do, did I not see that your strictures are the result of a misconception.   You evidently take Waymark's declaration of faith as my own.   Now this is by no means the case.   Waymark is a *study of character*, and he alone is responsible for his sentiments.   Do you not perceive this in the very fact of that *contradiction* in the book of which you speak ?   If my own ideas are to be found anywhere, it is in the practical course of events in the story; my characters must speak as they would actually, and I cannot be responsible for what they say.   You may tell me I need not have chosen such people; ah, but that is a question of an artist's selection.   You see, I have not for a moment advocated *any* theory in the book. Perhaps you have overlooked the few lines at the end of that very first chapter of Volume III. ?   There I speak in my own person, and what I say in reality contraverts all that Casti has just thought, if rightly understood.

And indeed your wrath re-assures me.   If indeed these characters can excite such repulsion in those who hold the accepted view of morals, then there is very little danger of their exercising an influence of a harmful kind.   They will only be enjoyed by those who are, like myself, purely neutral.

I shall amaze you yet more, but I must say that I myself hold the tendency of the book to be solely for good, though of course I had no such purpose in writing.   Look at the " garden party " chapter!

That alone demonstrates the possibility—nay, the essentiality of strongly human goodness connecting itself with the intellectual standpoint you so contemn.

But let me beg that you will not be so savage. After all, one must write what is in one to write; and I—I assure you very earnestly—I am in anything but a parlous state. And do not lose out of sight the fact that a man like Meredith can wholly praise this book, a man whose own writing has nothing whatever " offensive " in it, but yet is deeply intellectual. And remember, too, how much I have in my methods akin to Browning. I do wish the reviews would begin to appear.

But we must not forget that our grounds of actual and literary experience are so different that it is very difficult for you to understand me. Your opportunities have not yet led you to write like Balzac, Tourguéneff, Dumas, etc. Knowing all these men so intimately, I see that my own work is really anything but startling. Nor will you yourself speak so strongly in a few years. Now, for instance, your comments on Wood-stock. I assure you the man is very life-like; the only thing is that I have ventured to draw him more *faithfully* than any other English novelist would. Human nature is compact of strangely conflicting elements, and I have met men extremely brutal in one way who yet were capable of a good deal of genial feeling in other directions.

Now, I will make you a wager that, say in five years, you will re-read *The Unclassed* with far other feelings. I am so miser-ably alone in my position that I am driven into a certain self-conceit. The book is strong in its truthfulness, I maintain; its characters are types. Here and there will be found a critic to speak loudly in my favour, I doubt not. As regards the *tone* of the book, I myself, after reading anything, always say: " Now does this convey the impression that the author is human in his emotions, or the opposite ? " and I am very conscious that the tone of the present work is intensely human, strong with genial emotion.

And, I repeat, it is not a social essay, but a study of a certain group of human beings. Of course I am responsible for the selection, but for nothing more.

Well, well. It would be far pleasanter if I could write something which people would simply enjoy, and upon which you could feel disposed to congratulate me. I am glad you purpose writing again, and hope you will get this letter before you do so.

To the same :

Wednesday, June 25, 1884.

You say you are unwell. I hope it is nothing serious. Pray do not bother your head about the *Unclassed* any more, but let me know at once whether Mother could have me if I come down the end of this week, or on Monday. The Harrisons are going to the Lakes at once, instead of to Sutton, and I shall probably have them later.

I now want to get a week or two of thorough rest, in order to come back and settle to literary work in grim earnest. For it is sufficiently clear that upon that henceforth I shall have to depend.

Harrison takes precisely your view of the book. Yesterday we had rather a disagreeable talk about it, but to-night I have a very kind letter from him, and I will quote it to you—

" You can see that everything I said was based on admiration for your powers, and desire for your true success. Men such as you and I cannot speak too plainly and unreservedly when a very deep interest to both is at stake. I too have my ideals of art and social reform, to which I am no less devoted than you are, and for which I willingly give up a professional, a literary and a political career, all of which are in my hands. And it so happens that my ideals involve war to the knife with those which are professed by the hero of the *Unclassed*. I have known something of social revolt in many forms, and have had not a little sympathy with very many of its champions. I can feel it for almost anyone of the positive forms of social good. That of Waymark is to me mere moral dynamite. I make, as I told you, the clearest distinction between *The Unclassed* and George Gissing. I wish you every success, and think you worthy of success. Perhaps you are about to enjoy it. Far better judges than I think so ; and it would be difficult to be a worse judge than I am. I am, too, intensely prejudiced against the *motif*, and that may blind me to the art of the book, and its power of impressing the public. Be it so ; still I feel confident that the judgment of the social, or rather anti-social spirit of the book will prove to be that of the wisest—at least of the strongest party. Forgive harsh words that cover real good-will, and believe me, etc."

Well, one can't expect more than this from one pronouncedly hostile. He is wrong, I believe, for I shall make way in spite of opposition.

But now I need rest and a change most desperately; I do hope you will be able to put me up for a few days.

To the same :

Thursday, July 24, 1884.

Possibly your plan will best answer the purpose in view. Port Erin is a delightful spot. Only one thing, pray be very careful in the matter of bathing. I believe the Isle of Man has a bad reputation in that matter, there are currents and so on.

I am going daily to Sutton. This involves just three hours of train daily, and I am beginning already to pay the penalty in the form of headache.

It is quite settled that I go with the boys northwards on the 1st of August and leave there on the 15th. So that I shall hope to pass a night at Agbrigg [Wakefield] on the way home, if this be entirely convenient.

The house we go to is at the foot of Helvellyn, and we have a private boat on the lake. Doubtless the fortnight will be enjoyable.

Surrey is in its most delightful array.

Every inch of ground is green with astonishing richness of vegetation. The meadows and hills show a marvellous variety of colour—the latter exhibiting that intense blueness we oftener see in pictures than in reality. My daily drive from Woking, some three miles to Sutton is through one magnificent garden—

no other word describes the country.   No villas, no straight high road—only old farmhouses, and lane winding between thick hedges or open common land.   A population entirely rustic.   I have seen no part of England that matches it.

To the same :

BONSCALE, ULLSWATER,
Tuesday, August 12, 1884.

I shall be glad to hear of your Isle of Man experiences. I find I shall stay here till Saturday morning, and get home that night.   From Wakefield to Bonscale is only one ordinary post.

The weather has been amazing.   Not a drop of rain in the daytime since we came, but often refreshing showers at night. Only one drawback ; the great heat makes it misty and good views are not to be had.

Yesterday I mounted Helvellyn.   Bernard and Austin were with me.   I will give you a detailed account, which perhaps you will care to follow on the map.   A steamer runs from Pooley Bridge, at one end of Ullswater, to Patterdale at the other, and it calls at Howtown, a little bay close by us.   This steamer we took to Patterdale, getting there at 9.30.   From Patterdale the ascent begins immediately, though the summits are not to be seen till we are far up.   We took the track by Glenridding. *Horribile dictu*, this beautiful pass has been utterly ruined by the establishment of lead mines and smelting mills: the mountain sides, to a height of hard upon a thousand feet, are converted into mere quarries, and a great stream which rushes down with splendid leaps into the lake is made the colour of dirty milk by the mill-refuse.   Ruskin should lift up his voice, me-thinks.

Having passed these horrors we took a bridle-path steep and stony, which brought us by 12 o'clock to the summit of White Side whence we got our first real view of the heads of Helvellyn —indeed we had at first been misled into thinking that White Side was Helvellyn itself.   The sun at this time was terrific. Reaching this crest, there burst upon us a marvellous view.

To the same :

ULLSWATER,
Thursday, August 14, 1884.

You probably got a post-card this morning, written from
Grasmere.   I must give an account of the walk.

I took the 9.30 steamer from How Town to Patterdale,
and by 10 was well on the Ambleside road.   I passed Brother's
Water, and there began the ascent of Kirkstone Pass.   This is
a fine solitary road ; the clouds were low and rested on the dark
hills on either hand.   At the top of the Pass is an Inn, the
highest house in England.   Just as I reached it, the sky began
to clear, and coming over the crest, I all at once got the whole
12 miles of Windermere.   There is nothing grand about the
lake; the beauty of it consists in its size, and the fact that it lies
in an extraordinary broad valley, the hills on all sides sloping
very gradually for a great distance—green and splendidly
wooded.

On through Ambleside to Rydal, passing Wordsworth's
house, and the cottage which he at first inhabited.   One
painful feature of the district is the perpetual advertisement of
lodgings,—otherwise I should say the walk from Ambleside to
Grasmere is unsurpassed for delicate beauty.   And Rydal
Water is, beyond doubt, the loveliest thing I ever beheld.
Small, yet with several wooded islands; lying amid grand and
beautiful slopes, exquisite effects of light and shade; the little
river Rothay winding about, with footpaths and shadowed roads
here and there—the view from the ascending Grasmere
road is something never to be forgotten; I could scarcely leave
it.   The day, too, was perfect; sunny but not hot.   I noticed,
on the banks of the Water, grasses at least 10 feet high.

Then to Grasmere, where I saw Wordsworth's grave and
examined the village.   I was made angry by a huge red flag
which some disgusting inn-keeper kept flying in the middle of
the street.   A good many people in the churchyard and elsewhere, but nothing like an atmosphere of touristry.   I bought

a couple of Grasmere photographs, one of which I shall send to Mother.

So far I had walked some 17 miles from Patterdale. I purposed returning by another road. From Grasmere a mountain path leads between Seat Sandal and Fairfield up to Grisedale Tarn, and thence down to Patterdale, some 9 miles. This I undertook. Long before I got to the top of the Pass I feared I must give way, the climbing was so stiff, but I managed it, and the view from the height was superb. Below, Grasmere and the length of Windermere; then turning round the splendid descent of Grisedale from the Tarn to Ullswater. Going down was easy. I passed very near the top of Fairfield, and then under the crest of Helvellyn, looking up at Striding Edge, which was black as night. Of course I met no one on the road; the perfect loneliness —save for a few sheep —was half the beauty of the place.

So I caught the 6 o'clock steamer at Patterdale, and back to dinner at 7.

I shall leave here some time on Saturday, and be home again that night. Then begins hard work. But I am ready for it. I have benefited prodigiously by this fortnight.

To the same :

62 MILTON STREET, N.W.,
Sunday, August 17, 1884.

As always, it is the platform of the terminus which seems alone real, and all behind it a mere dream. Ullswater and Helvellyn are already fancies—irrevocably gone. But they were glorious at the time. The uproar of this street seemed so terrific after Bonscale, that last night I had the utmost difficulty in sleeping, tired as I was; and even when it came, it was very different from "the sleep that is among the lonely hills." Apropos, I took Wordsworth with me, and have enjoyed him more than before. He requires to be read amid his own scenes. Since seeing Grasmere, I

have constantly had ringing through my head more lines from
The Waggoner—

> " Dread pair, that spite of wind and weather,
>   Still sit upon Helm Crag together "

and many others of the kind.   And Rydal Water—ye gods,
there are few spots on earth like Rydal, be assured of that.

Your letter came to give me an accession of good spirits.

By the bye, did you get my post-card from Grasmere ?

I send herewith a view of Grasmere which please ask Mother
to keep, and some flowers I gathered on the fells above Ullswater.   I wonder what they are.

I had an hour in Penrith on Saturday—after reaching it by
steamer and coach, the latter the veritable old stage, delightfully
suggestive.

I am in amazing health.   More shortly.

At the end of August Gissing went down to Broughton Hall,
Lechlade, to examine the three boys of Mr. and Mrs. Gaussen.
This led to further extension of his social intercourse, and
in Mrs. Gaussen he found a kind friend, whose company was
always cheering to him.

He writes to his brother on September 1 :

I got down to Lechlade about 7 on Thursday evening.
Broughton Hall I found to be an old and interesting house.
It was one of the dower houses of Anne Boleyn, but the finest
portions of it have, unfortunately, been pulled down.

I was to have gone home on Saturday night, but they begged
me to stay till this morning.   There were two young Armenian
ladies of English birth staying also, and we had lively times.
In the afternoon we drove about the country, at night we had
music and reading aloud.

The country is rural to a degree that I had never imagined.
The sleepy old villages and hamlets were unspeakably interesting

to me.   The real name of the place is Broughton Poggs (what does it mean ?).   After service on Sunday morning, the village children come to the Hall kitchen, to take away jugs of soup for their dinner.

The most interesting visit we made was to Fairford, where there is a magnificent old church.   All the windows are painted glass, by Albert Dürer.   They are said to have been captured by an English ship as they were going from Holland to Spain. In the Commonwealth they were taken out of the frames, and remained long buried in a field hard by.   They must be among the finest examples extant.   Composition and figures glorious.

Another day to Burford Church—much of it 800 years old.

Not a new house in all the country side.   Of all lovely villages I ever saw, commend me to a certain East Leach, built on the two sides of an irregular little valley, with the river Leach, or rather the weedy stream so called, flowing under an old bridge.   Here, too, there is the curious sight of two parish churches within twenty yards of each other.   They told me it was common to build the churches thus, just where two parishes meet.

I asked a man on the road how far such a place might be. " Oh," he said, " it'll be three or four furlongs."

Other curiosities.   An inn sign called " The Five Alls." The explanation is this.   The old sign had five pictures : A king, with the subscription " I rule all " ; A priest " I pray for all "; a Doctor " I cure all "; a lawyer " I plead for all "; and a farmer " I pay for all."   Hence the " Five Alls."

On September 18 *to his brother :*

It has been, as always, terrible work to begin writing again. The task of getting into the fictitious world one has created always costs agony.   I sit down before the blank paper and feel I am in face of the impossible.   But a day makes all the difference.

To his sister Ellen :

18 RUTLAND STREET,
September 26, 1884.

This is a delightful letter you send me.

I am fearfully busy.   All the morning I am writing for dear life at a book I am bound to finish in a fortnight or so.   Then at 2.30 comes young Gaussen, and we work till 5.   Then tea together, and after it he works in my room till 8, whilst I again drive the pen.   My eyes are failing and my hand is positively cramped.

I envy you your *Villette.*   It is a noble book, full of wonderful character study, and with pages of English prose which will stand comparison with anything in the language.   Note for re-reading the chapter which describes her lonely life during the holidays at the school.

Also that grand passage which closes the book; you ought to learn it by heart.   By the bye the story was to have ended unhappily, but old Brontë in a rage commanded Charlotte to alter this.   She would only do so to the extent of leaving the fate dimly understood.

I must stop, my brain reels.

To his sister Margaret :

18 RUTLAND STREET,
HAMPSTEAD ROAD, N.W.
October 26, 1884.

I will now send you my best wishes, I cannot for the life of me remember your age, but that is nothing—seeing that I am at this moment in serious difficulties because I cannot tell whether I shall be 27 or 28 next birthday.   I do wish you would tell me, if you happen to know.

Doubtless you will enjoy Edinburgh.   I myself have been travelling of late, viz. to sundry drawing rooms, and mixing with the ordinary polite society of everyday London.   My life is strangely different from what it was three months ago.   I used to suffer from loneliness; now the difficulty is to get any time at all to myself. I am beginning pugnaciously to refuse invitations. Here is one for a *tennis party* next Monday, which I shall certainly not accept ! There is a line to be drawn somewhere and tennis really cannot be submitted to. Probably you are already an adept at this game, as it rages in country places.

I think there is no doubt I shall be in Yorkshire at Christmas, possibly for a week. The time goes fearfully: only about 6 weeks to the end of the year.

November 9 to his brother :

Eheu! Visits to tailor of late for dress suits, etc. A party the other night in Devonshire Street, Portland Place, and now again a private concert in Kensington Gardens Square to-morrow night.

Astonishing accession of acquaintances of late. Colonel Halpin among them, promise to call on the family of Dr. Macrae. Work goes on in spite of it.

New story of totally different kind, to be called, I think, *The Lady of Knightswell*, and to be in two volumes. In fact you will be surprised at the difference.

I am just engaged upon *Modern Painters* a marvellous book, very technical in parts, but abounding in true Ruskinisms of thought and diction.   It is rather spoilt for me by its theological mode of regarding æsthetic questions, but one must concede the man his standpoint. Certainly I shall go to the National Gallery and look at the Turners in a wholly new light; so much, at all events, one gets of direct instruction.

I picked up a beautiful folio of Jeremy Taylor's sermons at Allen's the other day for 1s. 6d.

On November 24 to his brother :

You will be amazed to hear that I have just taken a three years' lease of a good set of chambers in Marylebone Road and I have found a decent woman who will come in daily to do work. I fear I shall not be able to take possession till Christmas.

The rooms are in a huge block called Cornwall Residences. I shall be free from the thraldom of landladies and what is more be settled for a good long time. You must come up before long and see the place.

To the same :

7K CORNWALL RESIDENCES,
REGENTS PARK, N.W.
December 23, 1884.

Why do I not hear from you ? I now find a moment to write, after two days of horror. But I am right gloriously established, if you could but see this study. How grand it was to hear the postman's knock this morning at my own front door! Really there is here every convenience of a house, with none of the inconveniences. And I am settled for three years, at the least. The independence and seclusion of the place is amazing.

I am rather uneasy about your silence. Pray write as soon as possible. I fear I shall not get any Xmas letters sent to Mother and girls. Pray give them all my love, and describe state of affairs.

On January 2, 1885 he writes to his brother :

My sole feeling was one of surprise; it did not interrupt my work for an hour. I am getting very used to abuse in the place of criticism. Of course this thing is in execrable taste, and worthy of the author of *Gaiety Burlesques.* I have addressed a letter to the *Pall Mall Gazette* which they will print if etiquette allows; I am not quite sure of it. I had hoped you wouldn't see *Punch* this week.

Poor Bertz writes a letter of eight pages of lamentation, because the *Daily News* has spoken rather harshly of his book— yet every other review praises him highly. How would he take a real scarifying ?

I am hard at work again, doing my six pages every night; I shall soon have finished the first volume of new book.

To the same :

January 23, 1885.

I fear your silence means that you are still in an uneasy state of mind, and with nothing to communicate. I wish you were half as occupied as myself. I have pupils from 9.30 to 5, then six pages to write before midnight. This pupil business must somehow end before long. It is extremely loathsome. At present, however, they bring in £5 10s. a week.

We live in perpetual fog; the sky has not been visible for more than a week. I believe it is easier to breathe up aloft here than it would be in an ordinary tenement, still, headaches are induced to the detriment of work.

I hope you at all events keep in bodily health. Probably you will be sending a line on Sunday, though I know well how all but impossible it is to write when one's spirits are at low ebb. I myself am anything but cheerful. I have not entered a theatre for months, and the Strand is utterly strange to me.

Very hateful the account of all this throat-cutting in Africa. The way in which it is written about, shows the completest barbarism still existing under the surface; in fact the whole affair is amazing if one dwells upon it. Any day we may be brought into contact with the same slaughtering, evidently. The masses of men are still in a state of partially varnished savagery; the more wonder that anyone is able to rise above it.

Will you please thank Nelly for the pipe bag. It is admirable, exactly what I wanted.

To his sister Ellen :

Saturday, January 31, 1885.

A twelfth of the New Year gone, you see, and spring already coming upon us. The last few days it has been very warm. For that I am grateful; to me it makes all the difference between getting up in wretchedness and in tolerable spirits. I am mortally hard worked at present, teaching from 9.30 to 5, with only one hour's interval, and writing from 6 to 12.

Doubtless you are glad to have school toil over; I never yet met anyone who could honestly say the contrary. With this, life begins; henceforth there is time for education in the better sense of the word. I am so sorry that I cannot send the volume of George Sand which I promised; I am using it with a pupil and shall be doing so for a little while longer. Haven't you any readable French literature at home ? Of course our library is wholly wanting in foreign books; it is a pity. I dare not promise to get you a book as I positively have not a moment to go anywhere. I no longer feel like a citizen of London. Libraries, bookshops, museums, theatres, all are strange to me, even the very streets ; I wish it were otherwise.

Certainly follow up the 1687 to 1760 period, having got a grounding in it. Go over it for one thing in Morley's literature. Boswell you must absolutely fall to at once. The book makes an epoch in one's life.

I hope you will enjoy " Princess Ida," I wish I could see it with you.

You are certainly right; an animal cannot think of nothing. Victor Hugo suggests somewhere that their life is a species of somnambulism. But I should be disposed to fancy that they think very much as we do, only in a much more rudimentary way, being wholly without *general* ideas, or judging of each phenomenon separately.

I wish I were eighteen—and yet, I don't know, I dread the thought of learning life over again.

Yes, my rooms are as comfortable as ever; more so. You must some day see them.

Please give my love to Mother. I hope to see you all in the summer.

I have just reached the middle of a novel, to be called *The Lady of Knightswell* [this was published as *Isabel Clarendon*] which I hope you will be in a position to read before the end of the year. I think it may be finished before Easter. Tell me what you think of the name.

On January 31, 1885, *he writes to his brother :*

I am nearly in the middle of my new book, and hope to finish before Easter. I suppose it will fetch a price in the market, for it is void of offence, and not the worst thing I have done yet.

I live a hermit's life just now. Only on Wednesday I have to dine with the Grahame's. They are Scotch and musical. I dined the other night with a solicitor, member of the Savile Club, really a good fellow, and congenial in his talk.

On February 14 *to the same :*

I think I have not told you about the dinner party, at the Grahame's—there were twelve guests and most of them musical. We had excellent music; one girl played the violin really well. But you would have enjoyed the Scotch songs, admirably sung. They are capital people, and I enjoyed myself greatly.

Early in March I shall have young Gaussen to live with me for a month just previous to his examination. I expect it will bring upon me a good deal of visiting.

To-morrow I have to look in, during the afternoon, at the house of some Jewish people who have Musical Sundays. Really good singing to be heard. On the Saturday following I have a complimentary card for a private concert.

So I get music, without which it is difficult to manage. Fortunately there is always Bucalossi underneath, I am grateful to him, though he only plays Valses.

I wish I had the time to see *As You Like It* at the St. James's but the theatre is non-existent for me. If I can finish my novel by the middle of March, I shall take a week for sight-seeing. I shall be like a stranger coming up from the country.

On February 29 *to the same :*

We had an exciting incident here last Sunday night. I had just got into bed shortly after twelve, when I was shaken out

again by a terrific explosion, evidently in the buildings themselves. In two minutes I was downstairs. Everybody else
was rushing down, and, of course, everyone supposed dynamite
was at work. It proved to be a gas explosion in the flat on the
ground floor. The people had come home late, and, on
entering their front room with a candle, were blown up. The
window sash I found burning like a bonfire in the middle of
the street. In a very short time we had five or six fire engines,
and the burning was got under before any serious damage was
done. The inhabitants of the flat were brought to a place
close by and lie in a parlous state.

It was a very curious sensation in the first few moments.
One so often imagines dangers in the night, yet they never come:
here at length was palpably something of moment. The crash
was stupendous.

On March 14 to the same :

I am toiling incessantly ; by the end of next week I think
The Lady of Knightswell will be finished.

I have been in a sadly dyspeptic state, of late, it threatens to
become chronic ; yesterday I went to see a doctor about it.

You have seen the review of Meredith's new novel in the
Athenaeum. Is it not amazing that the man is so little known
or read ? He is great, there is no doubt of it, but too difficult
for the British public. What good thing is not ?

To his sister Margaret :

April 10, 1885.

I daresay it will be very good on the whole to have a rest.
Doubtless you will use your leisure to read a good deal. Doubtless Alg. has given you a good account of my abode, which I
think he seems to like. I hope you and Nelly will see it some
day, though goodness knows what state we may all be in this
time next year if the war with Russia begins. Of course it
will be the ruin of most people. It makes one sick of the
world and all it contains.

If you are reading French just now you will find the book of George Sand which I send very pleasant. *Le Chêne Parlant* and *La Fleur Sacrée*, are beautifully written.

It is nothing like spring here at present, very cold and cheerless, suiting well with the things that are going on.

I have got a book in the publisher's hands at present, but hear nothing about it. I want to begin another but it is really useless until we know whether there is going to be war or peace. If the former, then my occupation is as good as gone, and I shall write no more, at all events, till better days come, which, in such an event, will be very far off.

Why do not the bishops, priests, and deacons make their voices heard at such a juncture as this ? No, they are silent, and to me, such silence is incomprehensible. If it is not part of their duty to interfere against barbarism, then what *are* they expected to do ? Can you not understand the bitterness with which one regards their inactivity ? I fail to see in what we are better than the Greeks and Romans.

Please give my love to Mother and Nelly, thanking the latter for writing. I will write to both before long, if I can summon up spirits. At present I have little mind to speak to anyone.

On April 29 to his brother :

By hook or crook get hold of *Diana of the Crossways*. The book is right glorious. Shakespeare in modern English ; but, mind you, to be read twice, if need be, thrice. There is a preface, which is a plea for philosophic fiction, an admirable piece of writing, the English alone rendering it worthy of the carefullest pondering. More " brain stuff " in the book, than many I have read for long.

And on May 5 :

You would sympathize with the critic who said somewhere the other day about something " We have read this book with much mental discomfort." It amused me. *Wuthering Heights* is very grand. *There* is melodrama treated poetically: it is good to study and see the points of difference between it and the vulgar melodrama of every-day fiction. Am reading Italian now-a-days.

To his sister Ellen :

May, 1885.

It is twelve o'clock, I am just back from a delightful dinner party at Craven Hill, but I had better reply to yours to-night. I hope to come on the Friday before Whitsuntide and bring you back on the Monday morning ; I cannot afford longer time than that. You will be up for the Academy, Grosvenor, etc., and be able to see Irving in " Hamlet " I believe. I hope it will do you good.

June, 1885.

In early June his sister Ellen was with him for a fortnight.

Writing to his brother afterwards he says :

I feel considerable loneliness now Nelly has gone, it will require an effort to get back into the old order. I am re-casting *The Lady of Knightswell* into two volumes, it being Meredith's opinion that it would be better so. I work at it from two in the afternoon till tea, but it will take me a long time. Ready for October, I hope.

To his sister Ellen :

June 6, 1885.

I thank you very much for your letter ; I expected it this morning and it was very welcome. I have put myself to work in earnest. Yesterday I wrote from 2 till 10, and to-day I have continued from 2 till 8 finishing the first chapter. Unfortunately I could not sleep last night. When I am intensely occupied with fiction, the problems in hand fatigue my brain through the hours of sleep. I cannot get rid of them.

The attempt to work in the afternoon is something new.

I have never done it before, but I think I shall be able to continue.

It will involve going to bed early every night, but I am always the better for that. The difference between my present conditions and those under which I wrote the book before is so great that the results may well show a corresponding difference. I believe the recasting of the story will be much better than the old. But I shall say nothing to anyone till it is done.

To the same :

Thursday.

I have not seen Mrs. Gaussen since you left. No one person of course is like another, but her personality is remarkable in a degree you cannot perhaps sufficiently appreciate as yet. When you have been fatigued and disgusted through a few more years of life by commonplace, dreary people, shallow in heart and mind, you will get into the habit of resting in the thought of her.

I must tell you I have all but made up my mind to give up this fruitless struggle and misery at the end of July, when Grahame goes away. I shall, if possible, let the flat and go again to America, where it is possible I might get literary work, though I had rather end all that and work in a healthy way on a farm. The fact is that this kind of life is too hard, I can't endure it. I grow more and more low spirited and incapable of continued work. Suddenly in the middle of writing I am attacked by a fearful fit of melancholy, and the pen drops, I get nothing done. For hours I walk round and round the room and sicken with need of some variety in life.

Don't fret about this. You will understand it in a measure, and there is nothing so dreadful in going again to America. Don't alarm the people at home. I wouldn't say anything to them as yet. You see I am at the right (or the wrong) side of thirty, and even at forty plenty of men have begun their life's work. But there must be an end of the present conditions.

To the same :

July 3, 1885.

I thank you much for your letter, you cannot write too often, for I have perpetual need for the support of kind words.   I will just tell you briefly what I am doing.

Chiefly, being ill.   We are having our staircase painted, I have simply been poisoned.   I have had to abandon the study and work in the dining room, keeping door closed and window opened; yesterday and to-day I have been incapable of anything. But I think the worst is over.

My pupil has gone away to-day, a month earlier than was expected, so I am free all day long.   It is rather a serious state of things, but I must use it to get my book finished.   With effort, I think I can finish Volume I. by the end of next week, that is, if I can get bodily health.   The slightest disorder puts work out of the question: it is hard enough when I am well.

Last Sunday I lunched with the Apcars.

The plants seem still to flourish very well in the vases. But it is strange how little I regard the objects around me. When I lived in garrets with uncarpeted floors and unpictured walls, I was no less comfortable, in reality, than now.   These external things do not seem to influence my life, which is one of intense and unmitigated self-occupation.

I have to go out to buy sugar, and dread it; the grocers here object to sell sugar by itself, sometimes even refuse to do so, yet I cannot always order other things, and I cannot carry the sugar home myself.   These little things burden my life to utter misery.

I went to bed at 8 last night and shall not hold out much longer to-night, not having slept.   I have walked in the Strand to-day to escape the paint, but came back exhausted. I hope I can get to work to-morrow, it is the only way of passing the time.

Many thanks to you, dear sister, for your kindness and intelligent sympathy.

To the same :

July 27, 1885.

Please thank Mother very much for the good and kind letter I had from her on Saturday.   I was pleased to find her so well in health and spirits.   I suppose that you do not greatly suffer from tropical afflictions.   The heat to-day is simply terrific. I earnestly hope it will not endure.

Somehow I manage to do my daily quantum of work, though from 12 to 5 I find idleness indispensable.   I am well on in the second volume.

I hope to have finished the book by the middle of August. I shall, I think, alter the name and call it *Isabel Clarendon* simply.   I see no one and am not likely to till Grahame comes back in October.

Of Keats read everything.   To like Keats is a test of fitness for understanding poetry, just as to like Shakespeare is a test of general mental capacity.

I am just going to Mudie's, though goodness knows how I shall get there, through this heat.   Farewell.   With love always.

To the same :

August 2, 1885.

I am working hard at the first chapters of my new book *Demos.*   On Saturday I shall be interrupted to pay a visit to Reading.   I shall be back on Monday.

I have been several times of late to the National Gallery and am occupied with the earlier Italian schools.

I read a canto of Dante every day and derive vast satisfaction from it.   I am also reading Plato.   I am more and more determined to keep to the really great men, otherwise life is too short.

Let us think : Homer, Aeschylus, Sophocles, Euripides, among the Greeks: Virgil, Catullus, Horace, among the Latins: in Italian, Dante and Boccaccio: in Spanish, Don Quixote: in German, Goethe, Jean Paul, Heine : in French, Molière,

George Sand, Balzac, De Musset: in English, Chaucer, Spenser, Shakespeare, Milton, Keats, Browning and Scott. These are the indispensables.   I rejoice to say I can read them all in the original, except Cervantes, and I hope to take up Spanish next year, just for that purpose.   Now you will probably never go in for Greek and Latin, indeed I think you had better not, for the labour would be extreme.   But you must read the classics in the best obtainable translations.   Wait however till you have got a pretty thorough knowledge of the best in English literature.   German and French you must peruse day by day, if only for half an hour (that would amply suffice) and soon hope to pass to Italian.

Resolutely put aside useless reading; feed on the best quality of food.   There is nothing in the world to prevent you reaching a high standard of culture.   The use I can be to you is to urge you to begin in time on the right road.

Let it be understood that you are *studying*, that your life is arranged in a student's fashion and allow no one to pooh-pooh your course or lead you into trivialities.   I fail to see why you should not be a student as well as anyone else.   It is monstrous to go through the world blind amid such glorious things on every hand.

I read *King Lear* last Sunday.   I rejoice to find that with every added year of age Shakespeare becomes greater to one, and fuller of intelligible meaning.   No words can express the greatness of *Lear*; no other man ever lived who could have conceived it unless it were Michael Angelo who in some respects perhaps got beyond Shakespeare.

To his brother :

August 5, 1885.

I am reading Crabb Robinson's *Reminiscences*, a book you would enjoy.   It abounds in stories regarding Coleridge, Lamb, Wordsworth, etc.   Lamb he was specially intimate with. There is one entry " Looked over Lamb's library, in part. He has the finest collection of shabby books I ever saw; such a number of first-rate books in very bad condition is, I think, nowhere to be found."

A story of Blake has excited my laughter.   " He said he had been much pained by reading the Introduction to *The Excursion*. It brought on a fit of illness."   Subsequently in a letter to Miss Wordsworth, Robinson says the illness was " a stomach complaint which nearly killed him ! "

The Diary is in three big volumes, but they are wonderfully entertaining.   I remember the book coming out some ten years ago.   Robinson was a man of curious modesty.   There is a note closing his remarks in the year 1820, " A year which I have enjoyed as I have the former years of my life, but which has given me a deeper conviction than I ever had of the insignificance of my own character."   And I fear he was right. There is much Philistinism in his way of talking and viewing things.

I do not go out and have nothing to tell.   I thought I had better apprise you that everything goes as well as it can be expected to.   Regularity of work has a singular way of making time, at the same time long and short.   The days go by with amazing rapidity and yet it seems very long in looking back to last week.   I write about 8 hours a day.

To his sister Ellen :

August 6, 1885.

I believe the book will be finished this week.   The second Volume is a crescendo of wretchedness and I am in a fever with writing it.   But this time I know that it is good, say what anyone will.

The toil has been tremendous.

Let me have a detailed account of your progress in Keats and Coleridge.   We will see if we cannot go through English poetry in this way.

I am just reading Mark Pattison's *Memoirs*.   At the beginning he says:—" All my energy was directed upon one end—to improve myself, to form my own mind, to sound things thoroughly, to free myself from the bondage of unreason and the traditional prejudices, which when I began first to think, constituted the whole of my intellectual fabric." Now there is a statement of the objects of culture, admirably put. Everyone capable of self-culture should remember those words and act upon them.

Mark Pattison, by the bye, was the brother of "Sister Dora," whom I daresay you have heard of. A singular pair, to be brother and sister.

I have not time to write much and indeed I willingly rest my hand from the pen when I can.

To his brother :

August 9, 1885.

I have just finished Crabb Robinson. Really I know not a book in which there is such an amount of literary reminiscence. Crabb was born in 1775 and died in 1867. His intimacies ranged from Goethe to Stopford Brooke. The stories are endless, but especially rich in their information regarding Wordsworth, Coleridge, the Lambs, and Flaxman. With all these he was on terms of fullest intimacy.

By the bye, I must quote a couple of lines he mentions taken from Joseph Cottle's " poem " on the Malvern Hills :

" It needs the evidence of close deduction
    To know that I shall ever reach the top."

This must go together with *How Hard It Is* and *Loathsome Potter*.

How I envy you the experience of country life ! To me it seems as if everybody but myself has opportunities of studying various phases of life. I wish I had your intimate knowledge of the Wakefield life and people, and now your acquaintance with the life of a farm. Nothing of that useful kind comes in my way.

For three weeks I have not opened my lips, except in entering a shop or in speaking to my servant. I find it difficult to talk even to that amount, one gets unused to the sound of one's own voice.   But I have been very hard at work and my energy has not failed, as it is wont to do.   To-night I finish *Isabel Clarendon*.   I have done my best to make the story as realistic as possible.   The ending is as unromantic as could be, and several threads are left to hang loose; for even so it is in real life; you cannot gather up and round off each person's story.   But this time I believe the work to be good.   Yesterday I wrote for nine hours, and at last in that peculiar excitement in which one cannot see the paper and pen, but only the words.   I kept choking and had my eyes painfully moist.   I don't think the result of this can be worthless.

Mark Pattison's *Memoirs* I have just read with very great interest.   A book so wholly taken up with student-interests I do not know.

Well, I have not lost the last couple of months, at all events. But I must get on with the planning of a new book.   It does not do to pause so long between, one must be incessantly at the publishers.   I shall stick to the plan of two volumes, it is speedier work.   I believe it will come to one before long with most writers.

To his sister Margaret :

August 12, 1885.

I take it that you are home by this time.

This is a letter-writing day with me, for I am just free of my work for a few days, having finished my book and sent it off.   Now is the time for a breath of sea air, if I could get it. But I shall not be able to leave London this year, it seems. I begin a new book at the end of the present week.

I am resting my mind by reading Italian.   Dante I am engaged with at present and he is glorious.   I should advise you to take up Italian, when you have read a little more French and German.

London is deserted; only some three million and a half people remain to await the coming of next season.   All the houses round Regents Park are shut up, and the sight of the

darkened windows does not make one cheerful.   I myself live
in utter solitude, it is more than three weeks since I opened
my lips to speak to anyone but the servant.   This is a dolorous
state of things, and I fear is likely to last till October, when my
pupil will come back again.   Perhaps, on the whole, it is favourable to work.

You do not tell me what you have been reading of late.   In
your leisure you ought to get through a good deal.   Do not
lament that you are not able to procure new books.   I often
wish that I was strictly limited to a library of really good poets
and historians; it would be vastly better in the end.   One
ought to get as much as possible of the very greatest—Shakespeare, Milton, Spenser; yet how seldom one takes them down.

To his brother :

August 13, 1885.

Alas, it is impossible; I shall not be able to leave town this
autumn, for the work that lies upon me is heavy.   I have
made up my mind to finish the next two volumes (I don't think
I shall ever again write three), before winter.   It is high time
to put aside all paltering and face the publishers resolutely.

I have just finished the first three cantos of the *Inferno* in
the original.   Ye Gods, what glorious matter!   It is preposterous to read it in a translation though Cary is as good as
any translator could be.   But the metre, the music, all is gone,
and so much depends upon it.   I rejoice in this new faculty:
I shall go right through the *Commedia*, and can finish it, I
think, by Christmas.   I feel to have gained a new sense, a
new power.   Next year I shall take up Spanish and read Don
Quixote.   Italian is not difficult, to one who knows Latin,
but the easiness only becomes apparent when one has got over a
few initial difficulties, particles, etc.   I wish I had an Italian-
Latin dictionary.   The words are strangely and fearfully altered
very often, and, of course, a great number are Teutonic.

I have also in hand *Milman's History of Latin Christianity*,
six big volumes.   It is curious that I have such a decided taste

for ecclesiastical history.   I revel in the old heresies, Pelagian-
ism, Nestorianism, Monophytism, etc. etc.   The truth is partly
that it all stands in such close connection with the fall of the
Roman Empire.   Milman goes from 1 A.D. to the Reformation,
thus supplementing Gibbon.   My Dante studies will go well
therewith: and all together they lead up to the Renaissance,
which also interests me deeply.   The attainment of Italian
will make the way more practicable.

Later in August he writes to his brother :

I have just bought *The English School of Painting* by Chesneau,
with a preface and notes by Ruskin.   Some of the notes are
characteristic.   Where Chesneau says that there has been no
English painter of genius since Turner, Ruskin notes " This is
rather too hard upon us, my good French friend.   There has
not been, and will not be, another Turner, but we have had
some clever fellows among us since, who would have made a
good deal more of themselves if they had better minded what
I said to them."

I am waiting to see if the sun will come forth; if so, I mean
to go up the river as far as Hampton, to think out one or two
points I cannot get clear.   Really, Sunday is an intolerable day
in town; the silence instead of refreshing, as it would in the
country, merely weighs upon one, suggesting ennui and afternoon lassitude—that most hateful of conditions.

It is fine to see how the old three volume tradition is being
broken through.   One volume is becoming commonest of all.
It is the new school, due to continental influence.   Thackeray
and Dickens wrote at enormous length, and with profusion of
detail; their plan is to tell everything, and leave nothing to be
divined.   Far more artistic, I think, is the later method, of
merely suggesting; of dealing with episodes, instead of writing
biographies.   The old novelist is omniscient; I think it is
better to tell a story precisely as one does in real life, hinting,
surmising, telling in detail what *can* so be told and no more.
In fact, it approximates to the dramatic mode of presentment.

In comparing London life with life in the country, he writes
to the same :

Yes, there is very much to be said for civilization, if one is in a position to enjoy it.   What advantages of civilization have I for instance ?   I live a very hermit's life; weeks pass and I do not exchange three words with a soul.   I cannot afford theatres, for the gallery and pit have become loathsome to me. I have not time really to visit the museums; I pay an enormous rent for the privilege of living in barracks.   I would, at present, give a year of my life for six months of true country, with the rest of autumn soberness, with leisure to read Homer under a cottage roof.

You will see there is a very considerable change in my view of London on the whole.   Yes, it has been coming on for some time.   It is highly improbable that I shall ever have an income to render it possible, but, if I had, my first move would be to a village not more than 40 or 50 miles away.   Whence I could come up if I needed to, or it pleased me.   I should not feel the hateful pressure of London so much, if I had congenial friends to roof me at times; if London becomes a number of pleasant familiar houses, well and good, it is delightful.   But there is no chance of that.   The Gaussens are just going out of town; there is an invitation to Broughton, but I do not think that I can go.

To his sister Ellen :

August 24, 1885.

Enjoy your sea-side to the utmost, it will set you up for the rest of the year.   Yesterday I went into Surrey to spend the day with the Frederic Harrisons; it was a journey of about 40 miles.   I went to Godalming station and then walked 5 miles to their house at Elstead.   The more I see of Surrey the more convinced I am that it is the ideal of English rustic scenery.   One could not be more remote from London.   The Downs are glorious and there are limitless tracts of wood and heather.   From a height, we had a view right away over

Hampshire towards Portsmouth.   And the country people are utterly unsophisticated, no breath of town has touched them. The Harrisons have an exquisite one-storeyed house, with tiled roof, standing in a large garden and divided from the village street—a village of ten houses—by a wall.   The house is three hundred years old.   The day was magnificent, and I really enjoyed it immensely.   On coming back the train got fuller and fuller as London drew near.   Sunday night is always a terrible time for travelling.   But Elstead was far beyond the reach of ruffiandom.

I have written the first chapter of my new book [*A Life's Morning*], and am now re-writing it—a matter of ten pages. It always requires some labour to get the first chapter satisfactory, especially when, as in this case, it contains a rapid survey of many years.   But I think the re-writing will suffice.   I hope to finish the first volume by the middle of September.

Very many thanks for the dialect books, they are exactly what I needed.   I will send them back to Wakefield before long.

I have nothing in the world to write about.   I see no one and go nowhere.   So this must e'en suffice.

To his brother :

September 22, 1885.

Doubtless you are toiling on; I, too, thank Heaven, grow in the faculty for work.   I shall soon have done the first volume of my new novel, and my general studies progress.   I am busy with the Art of the Renaissance just now; it does me good in detachment from the vulgarities of the day.   Less and less I am dependent on newspapers and the external life of London; i' faith, I have no time for them.

How do you get on with Daudet ?   Is he not purely delightful ?   The style is admirable, and the characters intensely real.   Few French novelists have written more humanly.

Do you see the report of the row the Socialists have had with the police in the East End ?   Think of William Morris being hauled into the box for assaulting a policeman!   And the

The devil is such a man doing in that galley? It is painful to me beyond expression. Why cannot he write poetry in the shade? He will inevitably coarsen himself in the company of ruffians.

Keep apart, keep apart, & preserve one's soul alive, — that is the teaching for the day. It is ill to have been born in these times, but one can make a world within the world. A glimpse of the morning or evening sky will give the right note, & then we must make what music we can. I hope you are getting to enjoy Livy. His Latin is glorious, — history set to the organ. Do you not feel that your powers of intellectual & aesthetic appreciation grow with time? To me that is the only compensation for getting older. I read "Lear" the other day, & never before enjoyed or understood it so well.

I was looking this afternoon at a picture by Turner of "Richmond from the moors." It must indeed be glorious, if that represents it. Oyes, there is an enormous advantage in living amid such scenery. It educates both eye & mind.

Money or no money, I must try to get to battlefield for Christmas. I hope to finish my novel by the end of October; that is good advancement. I am to hear in a day or two from Chapman about "Isabel Clarendon." It is impossible for him to refuse the book; it is good. I suppose you will also spend Xmas at home?

On Sunday a man was sent to call on me by Mrs. Sansom, — just about to go in for his Law Final. No particular interest, but I have promised to look him up on library of Law Institution — I shall judge the time.

Thank Heaven, I have made use of this summer. In writing I feel unmistakable increase of power; the persistent study of English style is beginning to tell. I write more slowly than ever, but with infinitely more savour. By the bye, I have called my heroine "Emily Hood". You don't think the associations of that name are too strong, do you?

I must away to Dante, who grows upon me. Do not write to the detriment of your work, but let me have a note when possible.

Yours, dear Alg.,

George Gissing.

magistrate said to him: " What are you ? " Great Heavens!
Morris answered : " I am an artist and man of letters, I believe
tolerably well-known throughout Europe." Of course he
should not have said that, but it was enough to drive him to it.
But, alas, what the devil is such a man doing in that galley ?
It is painful to me beyond expression. Why cannot he write
poetry in the shade ? He will inevitably coarsen himself in
the company of ruffians.

Keep apart, keep apart, and preserve one's soul alive—that
is the teaching for the day. It is ill to have been born in these
times, but one can make a world within the world. A glimpse
of the morning or evening sky will give the right note, and
then we must make what music we can. I hope you are
getting to enjoy Livy. His Latin is glorious—history set to
the organ. Do you not feel that your powers of intellectual
and æsthetic appreciation grow with time ? To me that is
the only compensation for getting older. I read *Lear* the other
day, and never before enjoyed or understood it so well.

I was looking this afternoon at a picture by Turner of
" Richmond from the Moors " [in Yorkshire]. It must
indeed be glorious, if that represents it. O yes, there is an
enormous advantage in living amid such scenery. It educates
both eye and mind.

Money, or no money, I must try to get to Wakefield for
Christmas. I hope to finish my novel by the end of October;
that is good advancement. I am to hear in a day or two from
Chapman about *Isabel Clarendon*. It is impossible for him to
refuse the book; it is good. I suppose you will also spend
Xmas at home ?

On Sunday a man was sent to call on me by Mrs. Gaussen—
just about to go in for his Law Final. No particular interest,
but I have promised to look him up in library of Law Institution—I shall grudge the time.

Thank Heaven, I have made use of this summer. In
writing I feel unmistakeable increase of power; the persistent
study of English style is beginning to tell. I write more
slowly than ever, but with infinitely more savour. By the bye,

I have called my heroine " Emily Hood." You don't think the associations of that name are too strong, do you ?

I must away to Dante, who grows upon me. Do not write to the detriment of your work, but let me have a note when possible.

In October, writing to his brother :

I am very seriously thinking of beginning exclusive vegetarianism. Toil is the order of the day. No use blinking the fact. I am relentlessly cutting down odds and ends of leisure. My great enemy is the temptation to *eat* too much, heaviness ensuing. I think vegetarianism will help here.

I have finished, thank Heaven, the first volume of my new novel, so you see that I am not idle. The blessed certainty of progress in the achievement of a fixed daily task! The end comes before one knows of it.

The publishers' lists terrify one. Such mountains of literature. Yet how little of it is of substantive value. Familiarity with the market rather encourages me than otherwise, in the department of fiction, for, in truth, there is no one now writing, save and except Meredith whose novels are to be taken seriously.

Read the advertisement Chapman has in the *Athenaeum* this week after " Evan Harrington." I am just re-reading the book in the beautiful new edition. It is incomprehensible that Meredith is so neglected. George Eliot never did such work, and Thackeray is shallow in comparison.

Heigh ho, the wind and the rain! A fearful morning. Am despatching correspondence to have the latter part of day for my unpostponable chapter. What say you ? Two complete novels between June and November, not bad ?

I had a magnificent day in Surrey last Sunday. I am convinced that there is no such rustic scenery in England as untouched by town influences as if it were a couple of hundred miles from London.

There are yet four months of the year left, and a vast amount can be done in that time. I myself hope to have written some four volumes before the beginning of 1886. It is only

incessant work which brings results, and one's consolation lies
in the fact that the vast majority of men do not work at all.

Again in October he writes to the same :

I work on desperately; 20 MS pages (40 print) of the new
book done.   Surely I shall get a footing now before very long.
Confound it, I only want a couple of hundred a year.   I am
certain of it if I can live another two years or so ; just now is
the climax of struggle, I believe.   Thank goodness my powers
obviously grow; but I fear I have been led from my right track
in *Isabel Clarendon* and *Emily* [*A Life's Morning*].   We shall
see what people say to the former.

To his sister Ellen :

October 9, 1885.

Assuredly I ought to have answered your letter before this.

Last night I finished Volume I. of my new novel.   The end
of it has cost me a great deal of labour and I shall probably have
to re-write some pages.   But I must on with Volume II. and
try to finish it by the end of this month or so.

I miss music grievously.   No doubt, as you say, Beethoven
leads; in my brutal ignorance I can only gather opinions second
hand, but it is clear that Beethoven ranks with Michael Angelo
and Shakespeare.   And, like them, I expect he requires vast
study to be thoroughly enjoyed.   One ignorant of music can
never hope even to get pleasure from his greatest work, or at all
events, not the pleasure designed.

I approach the end of the *Inferno*.   Dante is far from easy,
and dictionary work continues considerable; but it is speedily
re-paid.   I hope to get on with the *Purgatorio*, but can scarcely
hope to finish the whole work for many months.

I have on hand George Meredith's *Evan Harrington*.
Chapman is publishing a new one volume edition of Meredith's
works.   I have read most of them and shall now go through
them again.   It is amazing that such a man is so neglected.

For the last thirty years he has been producing work unspeakably above the best of any living writer and yet no one reads him outside a small circle of highly cultured people. Perhaps that is better than being popular, a hateful word. You must read him someday, but not till you have prepared yourself by much other study.

On October 22 to his brother :

I am just finishing a second very thorough reading of the *Inferno*. I feel that I get to know it. Many passages I have been learning by heart. There is one about the necessity of toil which has helped me immensely.

I grow to be a machine of regular exertion. My hours are arranged with extreme precision, and, whatever the mood, I force myself into the requirements of the time. Alas, I sat the other night for three mortal hours over *twelve lines*, and they were poor lines too. Of course that meant over-fatigue, but there is no help.

On October 31 to the same :

Meredith tells me I am making a great mistake in leaving the low-life scenes; says I might take a foremost place in fiction if I pursued that. Well, the next will in some degrees revert to that, though it will altogether keep clear of matter which people find distasteful. I shall call it *Demos* and it will be rather a savage satire on working-class aims and capacities.

To his sister Ellen :

November 4, 1885.

Yes, Byron is very different from Keats, but there is rare force and fire in him. All that relates to Italy in *Childe Harold* is magnificent—though perhaps rhetoric rather than poetry. You ought to know by heart all the lines on Rome. I wonder whether you have the right feeling about Rome ? Alas, you read not Latin: alas, alas. For me Rome is the centre of the Universe. I must go thither and that shortly, if I beg my way.

I dare not read a book about Rome, it gives me a sort of *angina pectoris*, a physical pain, so extreme is my desire to go there. And I shall not wait much longer. I can get very cheaply to Naples by the Oriental steam-ship.

Now I will take you into my confidence. My new book called *Emily* is dispatched to Smith & Elder; but *under a pseudonym*. The reason is that Chapman has, at last, as good as promised to take *Isabel Clarendon* and I fear I cannot publish two books with different publishers, at the same time and in my own name. So I call myself " Osmond Waymark "—the name of the hero of my last novel, himself a man of letters. I fear *Emily* is rather poor, and ten to one I shall not sell it. But I shall try hard. Chapman will make me the offer to-morrow.

To-morrow I begin my new book, which is to be called *Demos*. Alas, it must be in *three* volumes. It will deal with Socialism and the working classes, and from a very conservative point of view. I mean to give three months to it, and to make it worth reading and worth having written.

I am buried in Dante—have reached the middle of the *Purgatorio*.

I am glad you have read *Childe Harold*. I think you might now journey back to Milton, and go through his *Paradise Lost*. Milton is to me constantly becoming of more importance. I advise this now because he was everything to Keats—he and Spenser. You will be able to detect his influence in *Hyperion* especially. I take it for granted that you know all Milton's shorter poems by heart. But I fear you do not know the Sonnets and they are grand.

By the bye, for relaxation read Leigh Hunt's *Stories from the Italian Poets*. To this day I remember them well. They will give you a foretaste for Dante whom you will, of course, some day read in the original.

On November 5 to his brother :

To-day I have sent my second book *Emily* to Smith & Elder, but under the pseudonym of " Osmond Waymark." It is impossible to have two books in one's own name out at the same time; so I have no way but this.

I can finish my next book—to be called *Demos*—by the end of January, I think, so that perhaps even that may come out in the spring season. I fear I have erred greatly in leaving my special line of work.

I am at the middle of the *Purgatorio* and get health from it. The *Paradiso* will be stiff, as it is almost all theological argument

To his sister Ellen :

Sunday, November 22, 1885.

Your letter is good and kind.

The coming of proofs has rejoiced me. *Isabel* will be out before Christmas.

I have finished a third of the first volume of *Demos*, with much toil and endless re-writing. It is more elaborate than anything I have done yet, and the plot has cost me hours of construction, so that I have scarcely done any reading of late. And now I am obliged to go about attending Socialist meetings. To-night I go to one at the house of the poet Morris in Hammersmith. You know Morris, though I fear, only by name. His taking to Socialism is extraordinary, seeing that the man's life has hitherto been devoted to Art, and his poetry is of the same school as Rossetti. I hope to see him to-night.

But, in truth, *Demos* will be *something*, I assure you. I cannot hope to finish it before the end of January, if then. But I hope to have it ready for the Spring season. Mark my words—it will be something at last.

On November 26 *to his brother :*

Last night I got a note from James Payn, who reads for Smith & Elder, asking me to come and see him. He was enthusiastic. In any case they will publish and give me £50, and it is *just possible* that he can run it [*Emily* changed to *A Life's Morning*] through *Cornhill* in which case I shall get much more. But that is uncertain, and the decision must wait a little.

To his sister Ellen :

January 17, 1886.

Why so long a silence ?   Is there rage at anything ?

Isabel is to appear in February.   The proofs are all long since got rid of.   I send you proof of the title page, which please return.

Demos progresses.   I am near the end of the first quarter of the second volume and am getting ahead more quickly than for a long time.   Yesterday I wrote what was equivalent to 24 pp. of print.

I must not write much for my head aches.   But pray let me have a line.

Bright spring weather the last few days, it can't last.

I have good hopes of finishing *Demos* by the end of March. I hoped to have done long before, but progress has been slow. However the way is clear before me now.   I read scarcely anything, only a little Greek and Italian.   We [his brother was with him at this time], have a subscription at the Grosvenor, but there is small time to give to it.

Did I tell you I was teaching the Bishop of Hereford's boys ?

To the same :

January 31, 1886.

In three days I shall have finished Volume II of *Demos*, and I don't think the last volume will take me long.   It is good, that I know perfectly well, and if I am not mistaken it will bring me a little more bread and cheese.

I have been thinking over our London doings.   Everything delightful is made doubly so by the thought of its value in the future.   To look back upon enjoyments is half the satisfaction of life.   I don't think you will ever forget that first peep of London, shall you ?   That walk about the City, the first glimpse of St. Paul's with the sun on it, the view from Hungerford Bridge, the view from the dome of St. Paul's!   You remember too, that glorious concert at the Albert Hall—perhaps that has slipped your memory? You will never hear "I dreamt I dwelt" sung more splendidly than it was that night, nor perhaps, "Come into the garden, Maud" by old Sims [Sims Reeves].

Then there was the evening at Mrs. Gaussen's. Ella had a poem in a local paper a few weeks ago—the poem she read to you.

An unknown man wrote me a letter the other day about my last book, very complimentary, and ended up by saying he felt sure my name was "John Robertson"! Who John Robertson may be I know not. The incident was amusing.

I have been so fearfully busy that my Dante has fallen into arrears, but to-day I have read two cantos, and hope to go on now to the end of the *Paradiso*. I do scarcely any reading—French by preference.

Try to read this scrawl, dear sister, and think of the old days.

To the same :

March 14, 1886.

I have just sent off the last proofs of *Demos*. You will see by a huge advertisement in the *Spectator* that the book is to be out in a few days.

I have got the cheque for £100.

It delights me to have your praise of *Isabel*. Yes, I think the end was inevitable—at all events in real life, and between people of such character.

Ah, but you will forget all about that book when you read *Demos*. The heroine, by name Adela—you will think delightful—so she seems to me at all events. The book is going to be a huge success, I don't doubt it. The turn has come at last.

Don't know when I get off to Paris, but not for a week yet. Must see *Demos* out.

IV

DEMOS TO FIRST VISIT TO ITALY
(1886-1888)

His brother Algernon was with him at Cornwall Residences throughout this year of 1886, to whom he writes from Paris on March 22 :

I am vastly at home and the sights of this unspeakably beautiful town are rejoicing me.

I imagine what it would be if one found oneself suddenly in the middle of the Athens of Pericles. No whit less interesting is this—incredible, unimaginable. I have been on the " Place de la Bastille." No trace of the Bastille remains. I have mused strangely over the things that quiet place has seen. This morning I went to the " Morgue," which was at once very horrible and very simple.

This Latin civilization is astonishingly different from our own. I could tell you curious things.

Wonderful scene in the great markets. Astonishing good humour of all and sundry. Women of the lower classes seldom wear anything on their heads, but have the most elaborate method of hair dressing.

It is the beginning of a new life. Ah, if you saw the bookstalls, illimitable, not to be counted.

But the Opéra crowns everything in modern architecture. I never knew what a public building could be.

I am in the shadow of the Sorbonne and close to Notre Dame.

Later in March he writes to the same :

I have a letter from Frederic Harrison this morning, acknowledging *Demos* with much compliment, though a protest against my aristocratic temperament. He says " Your book looks like going to be a striking success. The advertisements are phenomenal, and paragraphs ran round the press with suggestions of mysterious authorship." [*Demos* was published anonymously.]

I think I shall return on Thursday evening, so as to be in London on Friday.

To his sister Ellen :

Paris, March 29, 1886.

I hope Mother got the letter I wrote the other day, and that you all read it. I am writing in a café on the Place de la République.

To-night I go to see Sarah Bernhardt in one of her best parts.

After London the restfulness of Paris is indescribable. All the people here seem to be taking repose or enjoying themselves.

Yesterday I was in the Louvre again. I have sat for a long time before the Venus of Milo, which stands in a little court of its own.

To-morrow morning I think of going to Versailles.

Liszt is just now the centre of excitement here. He and Pasteur divide attention.

To the same :

7K Cornwall Residences,
April 15, 1886.

I am waiting to hear from you your opinion of *Demos*. What you wrote me about *Isabel* was intelligent and just, and I should like your real thoughts about the new book. It seems to be doing well. I asked for it at the Grosvenor the other day, and they told me it was impossible to let me have a copy just yet, as it was " in very great demand." Smith & Elder send me all the reviews, and I have now a good batch of them— some serious, some imbecile.

The *Spectator* review is admirably written. The next best is one in the *Guardian* which has come to-day. It is rather amusing to find myself praised in a church organ. I suppose the book may already be counted a success.

I am toiling at the commencement of another story, but as yet only in my head. I sit for some hours daily in meditation, and little by little the thing grows. I hope, by the end of this week to be far enough advanced to give names to my people.

It is long since I heard about your reading. I am going to send you Browning's *Balaustion*—you can of course return it before long.

The season is beginning ; the streets are bright and crowded. If it only were possible for you to come like last year ! Well, never mind, there is plenty of time yet, and, on the whole, remember that everything is going well. In another couple of years it is not impossible that I shall have a very tolerable income.

Grahame returns the end of this month. I rather grudge my mornings, but cannot yet surrender £2 10s. a week.

To his sister Margaret :

April 28, 1886.

Thank you for news. I am glad you liked *Balaustion*. Yes, all Browning is difficult and can only be appreciated after many readings.

I am toiling fearfully over the construction of a new book [*Thyrza*], and fear I shall not begin the actual writing for a week or so yet. I have to go over a hat factory, a lunatic asylum, and other strange places ; also to wander much in the slums.

We heard Mme. Albani sing in " The Messiah " at the Albert Hall on Good Friday. It was grand!

I must not write more as the time goes by.

To his sister Ellen :

April 29, 1886.

I do hope your throat is better. This is a vile time of the year, hot one day and cold the next.

You will be glad to see the advertisements of *Demos* in the *Cornhill* I am going to send.

I am delighted that you have read *Paradise Lost*. I now want you to read Homer—Virgil—Dante.

You are now quite ready for the greatest poets and ought to get a pretty good knowledge of them. And Homer must come first.

Toiling on at my new book. Every book is harder than the one before, I find, but the next shall also be better than anything preceding. At last I shall have a public to attend to me at all events. But I can scarcely get done before October or so.

What about your portraits ? I want one.

To the same :

May 8, 1886.

I am glad to have your portrait. I shall open the pages often, and look at it.

I called on Payn yesterday. He is tolerably satisfied with the results hitherto of *Demos*. They have sold 500 copies and others are beginning to go off more quickly.

Chapman had an announcement of *Isabel* in the " Literary Notes " in an evening paper the other day. Goodness knows when it will see the light. I am glad you feel a special liking for the book. *Demos* is, of course, vastly better from a literary point of view, but I shall always like *Isabel*. Doubtless when it is published it will be a flat failure.

I have not fairly begun the new book yet.

Grahame will be back next Thursday, then begins double toil. No chance of it ending yet. But Payn tells me he will be glad to see my new book. If only it was ready!

Alas, I have not opened a book for six weeks, and am not likely to. Never in my life was I so long without reading. But now I must write for sheer bread and cheese.

To the same :

May 21, 1886.

The more I think of it, the more I am surprised that you find the first two volumes of *Demos* dull. Other people with not half your imagination, say just the opposite. I wonder what the truth is.

I have finished about 70 printed pages of the new novel. Not an idea what I shall call it.   In parts it will be rather grim, and the ending tragical enough.

I send an autograph; who in the name of wonder can desire it from such a wretched beast ?

Try hard after the art of living in the Present.   We waste our lives by neglecting this—always living in mere expectation. You can effect nothing by worrying yourself.   Take every reasonable step, and then let matters rest—you yourself making progress the while.

I am glad to think of your reading Homer.   He is the fountain head of most modern poetry.   He has the world all fresh before him, and no fear of not being original.   To read him is like standing in the light of sunrise and seeing the world renewed.   Of the Greeks he was the Bible—the philosophers quote from him as moderns do from the Jewish Scriptures. When you have read Homer, your thought will be enriched with knowledge of an era of human history.

I regret that few people seem to understand and appreciate Adela Waltham.   I fancy she will always be a great favourite of mine.

They tell me it is a poor season; nobody has any money, no parties, etc.   No matter; one can work.

Alg. and I went to a concert at the Albert Hall on Wednesday night.   Sims Reeves, Christine Neilson, Mme. Trebelli. Pachmann played some Chopin.   Sims (very weak in the knees), and Neilson sang the duet from " Lucia di Lammermuir " not a little glorious, you can imagine.

The Colonel called the other day and talked excitedly of *Demos*.

> *To his sister Margaret :*
>
> *June* 13, 1886.

You are long silent, but then so am I.   I trust you are better in health, and that something of comfort comes into your life from the world's thought and action.

I am past the middle of Volume I of my new book, which

at present I think of calling *Thyrza*.   My progress is slow, for I
have to slave still during my mornings; but I believe the day of
emancipation is within sight: Two signs of its coming (1) *Demos*
is just published in Germany, in the Tauchnitz Collection.
(2) My publisher called here yesterday to invite me to dinner!

My days of reading seem to be over.   I have scarcely opened
a book for weeks.   If only this thrice-hateful teaching would
come to an end!

I suppose Nelly will enjoy herself at Southampton.   Strange
this friendly association with people ;   I suppose the day will
never come for me when I shall have intimate acquaintances
among people of ordinary family life.   Yet it would be pleasant
in its way.   I readily get impatient with such people, and, I
fear, am rather apt to display my contempt for them, but still
they might put up with me.   I even venture to think they might
profit by me, in a sensible way.   Yet it would be awkward if
they came to recognize their portraits in my books!

Prithee write a line before long and say, if possible, that you
feel stronger.

To the same :

July 31, 1886.

I am grieved to hear that you are anything but well again.
I wish it were possible for you to get away for a while.   But
everything will be better as soon as you have abandoned that
horrible corner of England and are come to live in Surrey.
The climate will certainly suit you far better and life will be
far fuller of interests.   We want [his brother and himself] if
possible to get a house quite near the Downs, somewhere between
Dorking and Guildford ; glorious country.

I am living at present in Lambeth, doing my best to get at
the meaning of that strange world, so remote from our civilization.   My book is practically still to begin, but I believe it will
be my best yet.   I have the strangest people and scenes floating
in my mind.   To-morrow, a Bank Holiday, I must spend in
the street ; there is always much matter to be picked up on
such days.

It is a strange thing that I never do much work during the summer months.   My productive time is the autumn and winter.   Grahame goes away in a week, for two months.   I shall be free all day long; one can get over much ground in that time.

I am reading little.   Hour after hour I sit thinking over my book and the time goes only too quickly.   It is a grievous thing to have to sacrifice every morning, but I see no way out of it, just yet.

I still, now and then, receive a review of *Demos*.   There was one in the *Queen* on Saturday, favourable as usual.   I believe *Isabel* has been pretty well reviewed.   I have no opportunity of seeing what is written except by chance.

The writers who help me most are French and Russian; I have not much sympathy with English points of view.   And indeed that is why I scarcely think that my own writing can ever be popular.   The mob will go to other people who better suit their taste.   Day by day that same mob grows in extent and influence.   I fear we are coming to a time when good literature will have a hard struggle to hold its footing at all.

To his sister Ellen :

July 31, 1886.

Long before this I ought to have replied to your kind letter from Scarboro'.   Don't think I put it aside without further thought.   I always value much any proof that you think of me and my work with sympathy.   How impossible for me ever to live the ordinary kind of domestic life!   Solitude has long since been an essential to me.

My book is in sad case.   It comes to this, that everything hitherto done has to be cancelled, and a new commencement must be made at the end of next week—that is when Grahame leaves town.   This is not what I had hoped, but I can't say that I am much depressed about it, for my work is not lost ; the book eventually will be all the better for so much preparation. I am again day after day in Lambeth ; this morning I got home only at 2 o'clock. Ah, but you will see the result, I have a book in my head which no one else can write, a book which will contain the very spirit of London working-class life. Little by little it has been growing ; it will be a stronger and pro-founder book than *Demos*. But alas, it cannot be finished till the end of October, I fear. No matter : there is nothing to be done by hurry.

It will be very delightful when you come to your home in Surrey—then there will be a possibility of meetings oftener than once in two years. I know well how you will all like the beautiful country south of the Thames. Alg. and I are looking about for houses.

I am so glad you have had good holidays this year, may they have put you in good health and spirits. Get on again now with your reading—old Homer and the rest.

With me it is a constant aim to bring the present and the past near to each other, to remove the distance which seems to separate Hellas from Lambeth. It can be done, by grasping firmly enough the meanings of human nature.

To the same :

August 20, 1886.

A large box of flowers which has just come from Broughton is a reminder that I have not written to you for over long.

I am delighted beyond measure at your progress in French. Is not *Consuelo* purely delightful ? It is a study of the artistic nature. How glorious is all that free, joyous, southern life! What poetry is in the book! What a sweet musical style! George Sand is a right splendid woman—I have just been reading some volumes of her letters, and those of the later years made me think of Goethe, so calm and wise they are—indeed she resembles Goethe in many ways.

Tell me when I shall send the other volumes. Ah, I read it first—and indeed George Sand at all first—in the free library of Boston (U.S.A.). There I read ten or a dozen of the novels straight away. What a joy to look back on that first revelling in pure artistic work ! Hold on to the spirits of the great artists, and scorn the contemptible littleness of the mob.

An extremely laudatory notice of *Demos* in the current *Saturday Review.*

Only half my first volume done yet, but at length the initial difficulties in very truth subdued. I shall now get ahead.

See what John Morley wrote in a private letter to Frederic Harrison the other day :

" I have been reading *Demos.* Is it Gissing's ? I suppose so. There is some masterly work in it. One page, that describing the East End graveyard—contains a passage which is one of the most beautiful in modern literature And there is genius throughout."

That is worth having !

It will be delightful when you are down here in the South. We shall talk often. Don't get to despise or dislike me before you thoroughly understand what I aim at. That will come with reading and thinking. But most of all, of course, from thinking over my books.

To his sister Margaret :

September 27, 1886.

I am just back from the Sussex coast, whither I was driven last Thursday by sheer breakdown. I went to Brighton, but found the place impossible ; a more hideous and vulgar seaside town the mind of man has not conceived. So on Friday morning I walked along eastward through Rottingdean, Newhaven, Seaford to Eastbourne. And here at length was rest.

Surely there is no more beautiful watering-place ; it is handsomely built with broad, clean streets, almost all of them avenued with fine thick chestnuts. To the east is Pevensey Bay, a splendid sweep to Hastings: immediately west is Beachy Head, a grand chalk cliff about 600 feet high. Behind the magnificent stretch of the South Downs.

The calm was wonderful.   On the top of the Head I could light my pipe without sheltering the match.   I could sit each night on the shore till 10 o'clock feeling perfectly warm and comfortable.   It is clear that Eastbourne will in future be my health resort.

I see that Saturday's *Athenaeum* mentions that a new edition of *Demos* will be published this autumn season.

I think the new book will be called *The Idealist* though I am not yet sure.   Alas, it cannot be finished till Christmas, but I have come back with renewed health and vigour.

Frightful weather on my arrival here—violent storming of wind and rain.   Winter has begun.   Well, it is always my best time for work.   I draw my writing table up to the fire, and forget the outside misery.

Please tell Mother of my goings on.   I will write to her shortly.

To his sister Ellen :

November 22, 1886.

Many thanks for your kind letter.   May your good wishes have fulfilment, that the future may be bright for all of us.

I fear I cannot possibly be at Wakefield at Christmas.   I shall not have finished my book till the end of the year, and then I must at once get it disposed of.   There is small probability of my leaving England till February, for I must get the proofs off hand first.

But I tell you the book will be worth something this time. I feel it is far better than anything I have yet done.   Yes, you will like it I know.   It will be called *Thyrza* from the name of the heroine " Thyrza Trent."   She and her sister Lydia are work girls in Lambeth, and I firmly believe they will be two of the most delightful characters in fiction.   I write with fever and delight.   Am nearing end of third volume.

Demos appears on the 26th as you know.   I hope they will send me a copy or two.

So all goes fairly well.   Read on, read on!   I am studying Florentine history.   If I get to Italy, I shall not be able to go further than Florence. Rome for next time. But Florence will be enough.

Much love to you. You will have a happy Christmas and think of me finishing my book. Poor Thyrza will die, alas !

To the same :

December 16, 1886.

A word in reply to you. I shall think of you much next Tuesday and Wednesday. I daresay you are quite old enough to travel by yourself. Of course it would be better if you had someone with you, but after all the self-reliant woman is the best, one that would go from here to San Francisco with perfect ease and simplicity. It becomes a woman to have knowledge of the world, and not to be a helpless puppet.

No, I have not been getting on at all well but I think in the three weeks to come I shall finish *Thyrza*. But Italy is not for me as yet, I can see that ; there are far too many obstacles. A holiday I must have before beginning the next book, but how and where I know not. Perhaps at Lands End for a week or so. Perhaps only Beachy Head. I don't feel well, and certainly want a rest, but the difficulties are very great.

I have decided to give up Grahame next Midsummer ; so that after that it will be sheer writing for bread, possibly for starvation. There is small hope to look forward to.

I went to the Ballad Concert at St. James's Hall the other night and heard " When Other Lips " among many delightful songs. But I couldn't quite enjoy things, the weight is too heavy. In waiting an hour for the beginning of the Concert I read three or four cantos of Dante. Have read much Italian of late.

I send *Consuelo*, Heine and the *Buch der Lieder* which to me was the beginning of an epoch of intellectual life. You are on the right way ; go on strenuously to read and think.

To the same :

December 28, 1886.

Your letter, always a pleasure, comes pleasantly on Christmas morning, which was bright and crisp.

Have you finished the first two volumes of *Consuelo*? Before I sent the third to you, I was glancing into the pages for half an hour and I was drawn on to read all about the Canon's garden and the flowers that grew there. Heavens, what writing ! Ah, if one had the pen of George Sand.

There is a glorious statue of her in the *foyer* of the Théatre Français a seated figure, beautiful, dignified, wise. In her old age she had something of the calm wisdom of Goethe, and her letters are wonderful. You must let me send you half a dozen more of her books after *Consuelo*.

I sent you Heine's *Buch der Lieder*, one of my most precious possessions. Poor Heine ! I made a pilgrimage to his grave in Paris. In all literature he is one of the men most akin to me. But you will not understand him till you have read his prose as well as verse.

I am a quarter through the last volume of *Thyrza*. It is good, better in many respects than *Demos*. Last night I cried myself into illness over a chapter as I wrote it, and this cannot be balderdash. I value the book more than anything I have yet done. I hope to have finished it in little more than a fortnight, if I have perfect peace.

My best love to you, dear sister, and may you do good work in the New Year.

To the same :

January 16, 1887.

I have received the books you return. Good that you have read *Ekkehard*, it will have given you an interest in Virgil. It will be glorious when you can read Dante, but in that I shall have to give you a start. In an hour or two I can save you three weeks' toil.

I read mostly Greek at present.

Thyrza was finished yesterday morning. Thyrza herself is one of the most beautiful dreams I ever had or shall have. I value the book really more than anything I have yet done. The last chapters drew many tears. I shall be glad when you know *Thyrza* and her sister. The vulgar will not care for them, I expect.

I hope very soon to begin another book. Am very well and able to work steadily. For a week or so shall prowl about London getting hints, etc.

In January 1887 Gissing went for a short rest to Eastbourne. He writes to his sister Ellen :

I have been to Pevensey this morning. The castle is one of the finest ruins I ever saw.

I came across a wonderful man yesterday, one Stephen Blackmore, a shepherd away on the Downs. He has been all his life collecting relics of the stone age, arrowheads, etc., and has a great collection in his house. I went home with him and saw it. He knows Sir John Lubbock and sundry other people of the kind; I found him studying *Man before Metals* one of the International Scientific series. Shall go to see him again before I come away.

I walk twenty miles daily and feel vastly the better for it; I walked for five miles at least holding my hat with both hands, there is a gale blowing to-day. But the town itself is wonderfully sheltered by the hills.

Everybody is out of work here. Processions of a couple of hundred men daily tramping silently and in miserable order. Wherever I go, I am stopped by decent men on the road who beg. And now the fishermen tell me there is absolutely no fish on the coast! I should think the Corn-law years cannot have been much worse.

To his sister Margaret :

Tuesday night, March, 1887.

The snow has just disappeared ; to-day a rioting north-west wind and grand sunshine.

I see that Hardy has a new book out, *The Woodlanders*. He talked to me about it when I saw him last year. Reviews seem to think it good, but reviews are never worth anything, on one side or the other. By the bye, I am not going to see any of *Thyrza*. I shall instruct Smith & Elder particularly not to send me any. They irritate me and interrupt my work.

I am half through the first volume of *Clement Dorricott*, which is good progress. I work all day long at it and I think half through the night. It must be done by the end of June, and will be before that at this rate.

Well, we may expect to see the sun once a week henceforth. Ah, if one lived in Italy! Well, well, there is no hope of it.

To his sister Ellen :

April, 1887.

I have just finished Volume I of *Clement*. What say you to that for work ? Considerably less than a month—and good I tell you, good, good! It looks as if the whole will be done by the end of May.

Good Heavens, what I would give to look in and talk for five minutes with you all! I should come if the expense were only half what it is—though I am in dire money straits.

Am in splendid health, as always when I write my eight or nine hours a day. Rush at Volume II to-morrow morning, all is ready in my head. A strong story, and some tremendous situations toward the end. My hand shakes still with the excitement of the last chapter, which foreshadows dire things.

I read scarcely anything except a play of Shakespeare every week ; no time for more.

April 3, 1887, to his brother (in Northumberland).

I expect you make rare progress these light mornings. Even I am generally at my desk by 8 o'clock, breakfast over already. No sign of publication of *Thyrza.* Surely no book ever had such pre-advertisement, seven or eight weeks.

I am in the second volume of my new book. I propose to call it

CLEMENT DORRICOTT
(A Life's Prelude).

I wonder what you think of this title ? I am in strong hope to have finished the book before the end of May.

There was snow here the day before yesterday, but on the whole the weather is very spring like. A fair amount of sunshine. I have dinner at 12, and then walk exactly round the Park, returning by Marylebone Road. I have tea at 3.30 and am at work by 4.

I have been trying to read Kingsley's *Westward Ho,* but cannot get on with it. It is really a boy's book, terribly out of my line.

To his sister Margaret :

April 12, 1887.

The weather is very glorious just now. To my astonishment on Friday morning I learned that it was Easter time. My life is that of a hermit, and I do not even take a newspaper.

I am reading again *Villette.* Charlotte Brontë I find more and more valuable. She is the greatest English woman after Mrs. Browning. George Eliot is poor in comparison with her. No page of her is without genius, and she wrote a style such as you find in no other writer. She strengthens me enormously.

Homer and Shakespeare are my other authors just now. In the latter I am attending to the obscure plays. Old William always rejoices one's soul. Homer—well one cannot speak of him, only think.

To his sister Ellen :

7 K.   *Sunday.*

Proofs that *Thyrza* is making its way begin to reach me. I have had an enthusiastic letter from an East End vicar, a man of sixty-two.   He is coming here to see me on Tuesday. Tells me that he was a school-fellow of Rossetti; I think him an interesting man.

Then I had an invitation to be an honorary steward at the annual dinner of the Newsvendors' Provident Institution.   This I have respectfully declined.

I have been at the British Museum this last week reading mostly French—and a big book about Rachel the great actress. You know *Villette* ? and you know that chapter in which Lucy Snowe goes to see the actress whom she calls " Vashti." That was Rachel.   If you have it not by heart, prithee turn to *Villette* and read that description of her acting.   One of the most glorious pages in English literature.

I am thinking over a mixed volume of critical essays and social musings which I hope to write some day.   It has long been in my mind.   Have a bad sore throat—deep winter again.

To his sister Margaret :

May 6, 1887.

You are thinking that I have wholly forgotten you.

Nay, but I have been direly busy.   I am past the middle of Volume III of *Clement* and I must get it finished.

You saw a goodly advertisement of *Thyrza* in the last *Athenaeum.*

I have just had an invitation to dine with S. again.   But I have declined.   It is my rule henceforth to dine with no one. My solitude makes me more and more unfit to meet with people who are lighthearted, and it is better not to make pretence. So henceforth I shut myself from all acquaintances and simply work on.   I cannot get to know the kind of people who would suit me, so I must be content to be alone.

To his sister Ellen :

May 14, 1887.

I have just seen a quotation from this notice in the *Athenaeum*.
Thank you.   Now is it not extraordinary that—as is very
clear—*Thyrza* will be thought far more of than *Demos*, yet
I assure you there is nothing like the same power in the book.
It will be a long time before I do anything better than *Demos*
artistically.

Bertz writes that *Thyrza* cannot possibly be popular, because
it has no plot.   I myself thought and said the same, yet look at
the amazing first sentence of the *Athenaeum* review.   Nay, there
is no understanding it.   The quotation on the title page is from
the glorious idyllist Theocritus.   It means " But we heroes
are mortals, and being mortals, of mortals let us sing."   Alas,
how little these reviewers comprehend (apprehend, I should
say), of my real meaning.   In truth I think of very little but
Art, pure and simple, and all my work is profoundly pessimistic
as far as mood goes.   Never mind, if I live another ten years,
there shall not be many contemporary novelists ahead of me,
for I am only beginning my work.   Thirty years of age this
coming November.   Well, Scott and Thackeray did not begin
till they were forty, and did a vast deal after that.   I don't
know where you will find room for my books by that time.

To his sister Margaret :

May 26, 1887.

I am taking a brief holiday, a cold has robbed me of half a
week, but yesterday and to-day I have enjoyed myself.

Last night I went to Drury Lane, and heard *Lohengrin*,
the first opera of Wagner that I have heard performed.   Unfortunately it did not impress me so much as it ought to have
done.   I don't believe anybody can enjoy the music at first
hearing; at a second it becomes quite a different thing.   Now,
for instance this afternoon I have heard at the Albert Hall the

overture to *Tannhäuser*, and having heard it previously, I enjoyed it beyond measure.

Then again at Drury Lane last night the singers, though thought a good deal of, were not really fine, and in singing my ear makes rather exorbitant demands. There was a tremendous house and most strict suppression of all applause in the course of the acts.

I always enter that theatre with a heavy heart. To think that those walls heard the voice of Edmund Kean, of Macready and other fine actors, and that now it has become the home of the vulgarest kind of popular spectacle (the opera season is an exceptional affair).

I must write Nelly a line, so I will tell her about a concert I have been to to-day and she will tell you.

To his brother :

May 26, 1887.

Your favourable remarks on *Thyrza* rejoice me. Of course, I wanted to know what you thought of the book. Well, I am only beginning. I have asked Smith & Elder not to send me the reviews, so cannot send you any. But I see the *Athenaeum*, and there are highly favourable quotations in the advertisements —said advertisements being huge, and taking up just one third of the column. It is sufficiently obvious that people like it better than *Demos*.

Ah, but this afternoon. I have been to a concert at the Albert Hall where Patti has sung ; first appearance since her return from America.

Great heavens, I would have stood at the gallery door two days and nights to hear those six songs she sang. It is a glorious memory for a life time.

Well, it is the acme of singing in our day; the sopranos now living cannot go beyond it. Albert Hall was packed—at 3 in afternoon—and the enthusiasm and reception of Patti! When she sang, the other singers came together at the entrance to the platform to listen. It was delightful to see them crowd

about her as she went away.   " Why haven't I got four ears ? "
cried somebody sitting near me.   This kind of thing is an enormous assistance to me; it makes me well in body and mind for
a month to come.

Your descriptions of local life continue full of interest, and
there cannot be a doubt that if you write a book of such matter
it is bound to be accepted.

Well, it is time to get to work again.   I suppose Grahame
will really go his way at end of July, and then comes the battle
with a vengeance.

Hideous burning down of the Paris Opéra-Comique last
night.   Am busy just now with the subordinate Elizabethan
dramatists.   Rare matter for a May morning!

On June 13 to the same :

Have not begun a new book yet, as I am anxiously waiting
to hear from Bentley.   Do little but read Greek.   I thank
heaven that I shall very soon have as tolerable a command of
Greek as anyone who is not a professed scholar.

That has been my ambition for many years, but Greek takes
a long, long learning.   I have not once been away from London
streets since sunny weather began, and I suppose I shall now
have to resign the hope of a holiday for this year.   I absolutely
have not the energy to go anywhere alone.   I should like to be
at Richmond, but cannot face the trouble of getting a ticket and
going by train.

On June 28 to the same :

Some foreign booksellers have written to me about a German
translation of *Thyrza*.

I am beginning a new book.

Anderson has inveigled me into dining with some interesting
people at Blandford Square next Friday.

The " Jubilee " was amazing.   At night all the great streets
were packed from side to side with a clearly divided double
current of people, all vehicles being forbidden.   You walked

at the rate of a funeral horse from top of Bond Street to the Bank, by way of Pall Mall, Strand, etc. Such a concourse of people I never saw. The effect of illuminated London from the top of our house here was strange. Of course I didn't try to see the daylight proceedings.

I am more anxious than I can tell you to hear what success you will have with the present book. The future—the future!

To his sister Ellen :

July 8, 1887.

Better again somewhat, as was to be expected. I wish your pupil had ceased sooner—it would have been pleasant if you could have spent a few days here.

I am going into Surrey to-morrow, to study one or two localities which I need for *Dust and Dew*. Excellent name that !

My next book must be a strong and important one, even though I starve a little in the writing. Every day I have proofs that people of some weight take an interest in my books.

I cannot and will not be reckoned among the petty scribblers of the day, and to avoid it, I must for a time issue only one novel a year, and each book must have a distinct character, a book which no one else would be likely to have written. I have got a solid basis, and something shall be reared upon it.

Don't desert me in the struggle, and try and have some faith in the result. I want money and all it will bring very badly, but I want a respectable position in literature yet more. When I write, I think of my *best* readers, not of the mob. The demand for my books is steadily increasing, and will do. Mudie, I hear, took sixty copies of *Thyrza* to begin with, and has sent for another twenty-five since. Over against this put the fact that he has just taken 2,000 of Rider Haggard's new book.

Two things I aim at in my work: the love of everything that is beautiful, and the contempt of vulgar conventionality. Only a few people understand, but more will do so in time. Only help me by some degree of hopefulness, and some day we will laugh at starvation at the top of Beachy Head.

On July 10, 1887 *to his brother :*

I dined with the Smith's last Sunday, and had much talk with Smith about the Brontës. Strange to think that he positively knew them. Described his astonishment when Charlotte and Anne came into his office one day, to declare their identity. Charlotte silently holding out a letter of his own addressed to Currer Bell.

The *Pall Mall Gazette* had an article the other day headed " George Gissing as a Novelist." Reviewed all my books. Poor stuff said to be written by Stead.

On July 24, 1887 *to the same :*

I think I told you I go to Wakefield next Friday. My stay may perhaps reach a fortnight, but not longer. I suppose you are still in Worcestershire.

I dined with the Grahame's last night, and had an interesting talk about the British Museum Reading-room with the daughter of Dean Bradley. She is working for the *National Biography* and goes to the museum daily.

On Wednesday I go to Putney to visit Mrs. Richmond-Ritchie. She began by sending me a circular of recent meeting in Lambeth and, in reply to my reply, said she hoped I would go and make the family's acquaintance. It will be interesting.

Dined at George Smith's a fortnight ago, and had a very pleasant evening. Well, I have consented to go on with the boy Grahame still, and perhaps it is very well that the thing so arranges itself. It is valuable to me in keeping up the classics. By the bye, I have just finished a complete reading of Theocritus, of which I am rather proud. His vocabulary is very stiff. Am going on now at Aristophanes, who is considerably more difficult as he abounds in slang.

Many thanks for naming the flowers. I had no idea wild thyme was so abundant; it covered the Downs. Of course it is purple.

To his sister Ellen :

August 25, 1887.

It is good of you to send your thoughts, and thus help me to get over this time of somewhat impatient waiting.   Indeed I wish I could sit with you in that same orchard and get a glimpse of Cotswold.   I can understand that you found it enough to ponder.   People at large are ready enough, all of them, to sit unoccupied, but the thoughts of most at such times are concerned only with the petty affairs of their daily life; one in five hundred know really how to *muse*.

There is a great difference between turning over in one's thoughts the colour of Mrs. Scrubb's dress or the shape of Mr. Grubb's whiskers, and really dwelling at peace upon the suggestions which make themselves heard in the whispering leaves, and creep near to one in swaying shadows.   Old Carlyle's gospel of the miraculousness of everything about one is, in truth, obvious enough, but one needs perpetually to be reminded of it.   I, for my part, can well spend an hour in marvelling over the growth of any green spray, and I am sure that every hour really so spent quickens all one's perceptions henceforth.

I am spending this week over a dialogue of Plato.   Next time I have a holiday, I shall read some Plato to you— especially the speech of Socrates at his trial.   It is one of the most inspiring things I have discovered in the world's literature.

I often think of that story of Lady Jane Grey sitting on a summer's morning reading Plato.   A strange thing that it has taken these centuries to get back—to begin to get back to the ideal of woman's education which the Elizabethans had.   And who has time nowadays to read Plato ?   Perhaps fifty people in the United Kingdom—if so many.   Well, there is no reason why *you* should not, before many years have passed.

I am just going into town to look up some things in the British Museum—I hope to finish my book by the end of the year.   I daresay it will be all the better for having grown thus long in my mind.

Thank you, dearest, for all your care to help me along with your sympathy. I think I am beginning to share some of the advantages of old age, for, as long as I can stick undisturbed at my books, I trouble very little about the things that are beyond my reach; it's only change and unsettlement that remind me of loneliness. But the majority of mankind have to seek their comfort in forgetfulness rather than in any positive good.

To his sister Margaret :

August 27, 1887.

I am delighted that you took so much interest in my rough and ready translation of old Homer. If possible we will have many more such readings. You might, at all events, glance through Cowper's version; it will be some help.

Last Sunday evening I spent on Clerkenwell Green—a great assembly-place for radical meetings and the like. A more disheartening scene is difficult to imagine—the vulgar blatant scoundrels! Rather than with such, I can sympathise with the most bigoted frequenter of the littlest of little Bethels. May we not live long enough to see democracy get all the power it expects!

Very warm and bright weather again. The trees here have scarcely begun to shed their leaves as yet.

To the same :

September 11, 1887.

About a quarter of my fresh volume is finished, a satisfaction seeing that that portion costs more labour than all the rest of the book. But I shall not have finished much before Christmas under the most favourable conditions. Bodily ailments as usual have oppressed me.

On the back of the *Athenaeum* I am about to send, you will see Cassell's advertisement of a new Shakespeare at a portentous price. And after all I will warrant the illustrations are worth little or nothing. Illustrations to Shakespeare I cannot away with; they destroy my pleasure in the reading. Now and then I have something of the same experience after seeing a performance of some play; in reading that play one begins to think of the *acted* scene rather than of the poetical picture. Even to this day I cannot read Touchstone without hearing Compton's voice, whom I saw play the part twelve years ago. That, of course, is a testimony to the power of the actor, but I decidedly prefer to hear that inner voice which is solely the creation of the poet.

Smith & Elder announce the collected volume of Thackeray's letters. Well, I cannot say that I care for them, and I think the unlimited praise showered upon them by reviewers is merely a sign of weak-mindedness. The letters are not such as stamp a great man. Thackeray *was* great, undoubtedly, but here he does not show it. In his moods of reflection I never saw anything (I speak still of his letters), at all apart from the commonplace. Of course a man has to adapt his writing to his correspondent. Compare with them a letter of Charlotte Brontë's. Great heavens!

I shall go to see Mrs. Ritchie in about a week. I suppose she won't have forgotten who I am by that time.

On September 19 to his brother :

This terrible attack of winter will not have been very cheerful for you, I am afraid. Long ago I have begun fires.

The title you mention I have never heard; I cannot think it has ever been used. I myself like shorter ones, if only thinking of the mechanical difficulties which arise from many worded headlines and letterings.

It is just possible that I might come to you [in Worcestershire] for Christmas and then go on to Wakefield, but all depends on progress. I miserably want an opportunity of seriously studying some country scenes. I don't see how it is ever to be got.

On October 6 *to the same :*

I am glad to see your writing again.   Doubtless all your time is taken up.   I am labouring on the first volume of *Dust and Dew*.   Now writing it for the third time.   I mean this next to help me.

I had to spend two days in Essex last week, getting material. I walked to Chelmsford, slept there, and thence to Maldon, at the mouth of the Blackwater.

To his sister Ellen :

October 16, 1887.

In a few days I finish the first volume of *Dust and Dew*, now I warn you in advance that you will not find this book as *entertaining* as *Thyrza*.   It is very serious indeed and deals with some of the wretchedest problems of this huge London. One cannot always be showing the pleasant sides, there will be very little indeed that is pleasant in the story.   But I believe it to be artistically stronger than anything I have done yet, and I fancy it will excite a good deal of attention.

I go to Grahame every morning, and work steadily each evening from 4 to 11, with a mouthful of bread and butter and a cold cup of tea at 8.   I am in singularly good health, better than for a long time, indeed I can work those seven hours without the least feeling of weariness, and since my daily walk round the park, I believe, I even suffer less from indigestion.

You will think I am entering on an ideal state of existence.

I can understand that you enjoy your return home and get to work with gusto.   Pursue your Latin with quiet steadiness, and you will find the difficulties vanish before long.

My best love to you, dear sister, try and keep in good spirits. I rather think my own gloomiest days are over.   I begin to be content with my lot and find it enough to work all through the day.   Soon enough the night cometh.

To the same :

November 4, 1887.

I have a lot of indifferent news for you.   A week ago I got a letter from H. asking me to give B. a lesson every evening from 6 to 7.   Of course, I could not refuse, and of course, all my work is at an end.   It is a miserable thing; goodness knows when I shall get my book done.

Then comes a letter from James Payn saying he is going to use my old old story *Emily* [*A Life's Morning*], which you have forgotten all about I suppose—for the *Cornhill.*   He wrote in hot haste and demanded a better title by return of post.   I suppose it will run for about six months, beginning probably with the New Year, or perhaps next month.

Alas, alas, I hoped to have my new book ready by Christmas. I have been all but laid up for a week with severest lumbago, only just able to walk to Baker Street station.   Of course I have done nothing for it but it is somewhat better now.

Don't work too hard, but try to keep a quiet mind.   Surely we shall have a holiday next year—but there is no knowing.

To the same :

November 13, 1887.

You have done wonderfully in Latin.   If I had one single five minutes free in the week I would try and give you some help at beginning Virgil, but I am driven too hard, and it must wait for a little while.

The name *Emily* was deemed too unattractive to the mob. And now we find that *Her Will and Her Way* has been used. Accordingly I have suggested *A Life's Morning* which I think better than the other.   This will probably be final.   I shall have the magazine and will send it you.   But I warn you the whole is feeble.

I am not yet at middle of second volume of the other book. At most I get four MS. pages done daily.   It is a grievous thing just when it is necessary that I should do my best work to have to work at weary intervals.

Grahame goes at end of year to Cannes. But there is no relief to me if I still have B. in evenings. I can do little or nothing before 4 p.m.

Tremendous row in London between police and mobs. Meeting to be held to-day in Trafalgar Square, in defiance of police prohibition.

You have read about the critical state of the German Crown Prince. What a noteworthy fact that, just because he happens to be a man of common sense who would govern reasonably, all Europe is in tremors lest he should die! It shows how rare such a man is among governors; shows too what unspeakable fools are the masses of mankind, who confess that they cannot do other than be led into quagmires by any ruler who happens to find a pleasure in seeing them there.

Civilisation! With all the European peoples desiring to live in peace and comfort, the mere fact of one man's death and his son coming to the throne, might, in all probability, lead to wars of incalculable duration.

To his sister Margaret :

November 13, 1887.

I rejoice exceedingly that the doctor has put your mind at ease. Take care in going about your charitable excursions.

I am glad you go on with Homer. It seems many ages since I used to sit and read him to you. I have just been reading with Grahame several of my favourite passages: the weeping of the horses, the death of Argos, etc. Grahame is a wonderful boy not quite sixteen yet and he will soon know almost as much Greek as I can teach him. Practically his mind is already mature. If he continues at this rate, he will be a most exceptional scholar.

My work goes very very slowly. I am so wretchedly tired every night. But I *must* have it done early in the New Year.

A daughter of the Dean of Westminster, by name Mrs. Woods, has recently published a novel which I think more remarkable in its way than anything since the Brontës. It is called *A Village Tragedy*. You remember I met a sister of hers not long ago. I have written excitedly about the book to Bentley, the publisher, and he tells me he has sent my letter on to the author. As a matter of course, the book has been passed over by the critics in as good as absolute silence!

Oh, unutterable, long-eared asses!

To his sister Ellen :

December 6, 1887.

I am sending you one of the best of Tourguéneff's novels and I shall be disappointed if you do not enjoy it vastly.

Read in this week's *Spectator* what Arnold says about Russian novelists. Tourguéneff is a man I glory in. The proper names may give you a little difficulty but only for a day or two.

I am in the third volume of my new novel, spite of diffi-culties. On the 19th I have an invitation to the Deanery, Westminster.

Went last Wednesday night and saw the French Company play Molière's *Tartuffe*.

I rejoice to hear of your musical studies.

By the bye, don't abandon " Faust "—you will get most good from it when you are quite familiar with the text. I think there is little doubt I shall be with you early in the year.

From about this date onwards Gissing has preserved his diary. On December 27th he notes :

After a fortnight's break in writing, resume *The Insurgents*. Have reached middle of third volume but I see that much must be re-written. Began it last July, and have toiled ever since. To-day returned to Chapter I, which I must have written six times, and again re-wrote it. But to-morrow it will once more be cancelled, I see. Cannot hit the right tone. Wrote 4-10.

To his sister Ellen :

December 28, 1887.

I had a delightful evening yesterday at the Deanery, Westminster. It was an "at home", hour 9.30. By 11 o'clock some fifty people were present. My chief object in going was to meet Mrs. Woods, the author of *A Village Tragedy*. Her face is that of the Tragic Muse, a wonderful face! She only occasionally comes to London. Our meeting was very cordial, for I had written an enthusiastic letter about her book to Bentley, who published it, and Bentley forwarded it to her. She also had talked of me with the Frederic Harrisons.

I got home at 12 o'clock feeling better than I have done for a long time.

Perhaps you don't know that when I am in good spirits I can talk consumedly. One young lady, I don't in the least know who she was, though Miss Bradley introduced me to her, evidently found much amusement in the hodge-podge of literature I turned out for her benefit. She was one of the cold and dumb species of English young ladyhood, though not brainless, for she knew something of literature; I determined to break down the barrier of formality, and in a quarter of an hour did so most effectually.

Last Saturday I attended a lecture on Art at Willis's Rooms, and there, lo and behold, was the great Oscar Wilde. I looked at him with no little curiosity. He is growing enormously fat and is conforming in attire to conventional standards. Alas, he has even shortened his hair.

I feel well at present, and vigorous. Something will be done yet.

Diary :

December 29. Wrote from 2-10, a good spell. Finished Chapter I, revised II, and did something at III. Curious similarity between Chapter II and the opening of Mrs. Wood's *Village Tragedy* ; but mine was written long before I read her book.

January 6, 1888.   Wrote from 3 to 9 but with no results :
it must all be cancelled.   Never mind, have recast the chapter
in my thought and will go at it again to-morrow.   My patience
is inexhaustible.

On *January* 8 *to his brother* :

I have got into a very shaky state of health, and need a
change much but I cannot see how I am to get it ; I want to
go to Wakefield, yet for my health that is no use at all; indeed
nothing is, but the sea; yet I know not how to afford time or
money for both things.   It is very certain that before the long
summer's work with Grahame begins, I must have a very
decided holiday.

My book cannot be finished before the end of February
now.   Those lessons have been the ruin of me.

On *January* 11 *to the same* :

My present intention is to go to Paris as soon as ever my
work is finished, that I feel to be a necessity again.   Thence I
think I should run to Wakefield, for at all events a few days,
and thence to you.

I think I shall have something strong in hand, if ever I can
get done.   The first volume I am re-writing for at least the
fifth time, and, for a wonder, I feel tolerably satisfied.   I
manage to get my walk round the Park each day again, and
that is a great help.

On *January* 23 *to the same* :

What are your hours of work ?   It is a fearful question
with me, complicated by dyspeptic sufferings.   On Wednesday
I am free from all teaching for a couple of months, and I am
going to do as follows: Breakfast 8.30 to 9, write from 9.30
to 1.   Then take a cup of cocoa and bit of bread and butter,
but make no serious break.   Write again till 4.   Then have a

solid dinner and use the evening for reflection, reading, walking, etc. I believe this will do. I am going to leave off tea again; I am convinced it explains many of my ills. To-night am feeling ill and can't work.

Diary :

January 25. A terrible day, got up with a headache, from 9.30 to 2 wrote—or rather struggled to write—achieving not quite two pages. Suffered anguish worse than any I remember in the effort to compose. Ate nothing at 2, but started and walked to Hampstead and back. Head a little better. Dined at a café extravagantly spending 1s. 9d. At 7 tried to write again, and by 9.30 finished one page. However this completes Chapter V.

January 27. After a hopeless struggle with illness went off to Broadway [Worcestershire, where his brother lived], departing as usual, half an hour after getting the idea. Could not let Alg. know in time, so passed the night at Evesham, staying at " Rose & Crown." Was awakened by the chimes at midnight, the first time I ever heard them ; made me feel I was in Shakespeare's country.

Saturday, January 28. Walked on to Broadway, 6 miles. Alg. met me half way on the road, with his little dog. Delighted with their cottage.

February 4. Returned to London, after enjoying myself much. An invitation to dine with the Cookson Crackanthorpes forwarded to me, of course had to decline.

Much improved in health. Thought carefully over the remaining portion of my book, and got it clearly arranged. Take the new evening paper the *Star*—furious radicalism and useful to me.

February 5. Bad headache. Evening spent in Clerkenwell,

wandering. Took up *Tatler* again, the latter is refreshing. To bed at 11, in hope of work to-morrow.

Tuesday, February 7. Two days of blank misery, incapable of work; feeling almost ready for suicide. This evening a little light comes to me. Will it be credited that I must begin a new novel ? I am wholly dissatisfied with the plan of what I have been writing. This terrible waste of time. I dare not tell anyone the truth; shall merely say that I am getting on very slowly.

Wednesday, February 8. Did actually begin a new story, to be called, I think, *Marian Dane*. What is more, wrote the whole of Chapter I, 8 pages. Sat from 9-12 and from 3-9. Had a good walk round by Kilburn.

February 9. Wrote four more pages, but decided that I must begin once again. The work has only been preliminary.

February 13. After days more of misery, gave it up and came to Eastbourne. Took two rooms at 27 Brightland Road. No one in the house but the landlady, a poor old single woman. Bad cold weather.

February 14. Got to work in the evening and wrote five pages of the first chapter again. In low spirits and sleeping poorly.

On February 16 *to his brother :*

Already I feel vastly better. Yesterday Roberts came down and will stay till Monday. This afternoon we walked over the Downs to East Dean, and it was one of the most wonderful walks I have ever had. An east wind was blowing so terrifically that in places one could scarcely stand, and the new fallen snow was drifting into heaps of four and five feet deep upon the sunk road, the wind now and then blowing it in showers across the country. There were superb effects of distance.

To his sister Ellen :

EASTBOURNE,
February 18, 1888.

Your letters are very cheering to me, and have helped to improve my state in general. Beyond doubt I am improving vastly. Roberts has been here for some days and we have walked some 12 miles daily, plunging defiantly through snow, and in the teeth of a deadly east wind; strangely, it has given me no cold.

Yesterday we went to Pevensey. The old castle looks rather grim in such weather.

I have done no work yet but Roberts goes to-morrow morning, and I daresay I shall settle down very soon. My head is much clearer and I can face things in something like a hopeful spirit once more. But the *Cornhill's* story [*A Life's Morning*] is disgusting me, and I feel it gets poorer and poorer; I can only hope that it will very soon be forgotten.

Diary :
February 29.

Think a good deal of my novel, the *old* novel once more, upon which, I have no doubt, I shall re-settle when I get back to 7K. Have got tolerably full notes for Volume I. Story substantially the same as before, but details a good deal altered.

I broke off this writing to go to Lewes, where I spent a snowy afternoon. At 5.30 I was home again. A telegram waited for me. I caught the 7.45 train and was at 7K by a quarter to 11.

To his sister Ellen :

7 K *Saturday, March* 3.

I have been wishing more than anything that you could come for a few days, but I feared your work would make it impossible. If it be anyway possible, I beg you to come on Monday or Tuesday. If you could catch the 9.20 you would be here by 1 o'clock and I could meet you at King's Cross.

Yes, I am indeed wretched and cannot do anything till I have relief of some kind, and this would be the very best. Thank you a thousand times for suggesting it. Send a post-card to-morrow—and yet, I don't know whether it would reach me in time.

Diary :

March 10. Have had a violent cold since Wednesday night. Better to-day. On Monday, please the Fates, I begin work.

March 14. Still wasting time. Ill and in wretched spirits. To-night a letter from a certain Fanny Le Breton, who writes wishing to translate *Demos*. She is also reading *A Life's Morning*. I have always imagined it the most un-likely thing for a new English writer to find readers in Paris.

To his sister Ellen :

March 14, 1888.

Your letter cheered me as your letters always do. I am still far from beginning to work. I never remember the time when I felt such great and persistent bodily weakness, with corresponding inability to exert my mind. I took up a pen on Monday, but could not frame a sentence; in blank misery I sat for half an hour staring at the sheet of paper, then turned to stare for hours at the fire.

I begin to think that the air in this part of London is proving fatal to me. Everybody draws attention to the fact that the fumes of Baker Street Station must be poisonous, and I daresay there is something in that.

I speak very seriously when I say that I feel to be growing weaker and weaker. I cannot reconcile myself to the thought that my life's work is over, there is still so much I want to do. I have so much to say. It is useless to ask advice. I must act on my own responsibility, of course.

I suppose I must inevitably remain here till I have a book to sell. But when I shall be equal to work I know not. My cold is very bad and a cough has added itself.

Will it be better when days of sunshine come ? Perhaps so. I must just wait and see. But another winter I cannot face here; seriously I do not think I should live through it.

All day long I do absolutely *nothing*, I do not even read. Goodness knows how I get through the hours.

It did me good mentally to talk with you for those few days, but they were so few.

I think we should soon understand each other, if we only had opportunities. But the opportunity will never come, never. This life—short as it is—is thrown away. We act and think as though we had a literal eternity before us. I am delighted with the living interest you take in such things as Browning's poetry. It is such a sign of health. At present I *cannot* interest myself in anything ; I do not live, but merely support existence. You will get so used to this kind of querulousness that you will pay no attention to it—which perhaps would be the best thing that could happen. What *is* the use of complaining when there is no remedy ? Yet it seems so miserable that a man at my age should be so utterly companionless. What I want is domestic society. I want to know a family of people with whom I could have restful intercourse. If that were gained, it would matter little where I lived. It will never benefit me to take change of air or anything of the kind, so long as I am a hermit wherever I go. I merely carry a desert with me.

When I am writing, I can partly forget myself in the words. Write I must, it is the only refuge.

Well, here is a great abundance of dreariness—you will scarcely get to the end of it.

Diary :

March 19. Felt greatly better in body and mind. Began a novel to be called *The Nether World* and wrote six pages which satisfy me.

To his sister Ellen :

March 25, 1888.

Yes, I feel better than for a very long time. I am working well and see a long course clear before me. Once more I have the true joy in my imagination, which has failed me for some twelve months. By the bye, now that I have read the proofs of *A Life's Morning* to the end of the August number, I begin to see that the story is by no means contemptible. It is the method of publications which is at fault—vile method. Wait till you can judge the work as a whole.

Many thanks for your letter, it helped me a great deal. All will go well so long as I can work.

On March 20 *to his brother :*

Pray send your book at the earliest possible moment. By dint of cod liver oil, fat bacon for breakfast, dumb-bell exercise, etc. I am feeling much better and am doing good work at last. At the same time I am reading much general literature (having taken a Grosvenor subscription), and your work will be the opposite of a disturbance.

To the same :

March 26, 1888.

I have given the day to your novel. On finishing it, I find that two remarks first of all occur to me. I am astonished at the sudden advance it shows on *Crakehall*, I am delighted with the progress shown in the book itself. For, though the first chapter is capital, I have no doubt that the second volume as a whole is much better than the first. That is a very hopeful thing.

I believe the story will generally be found interesting, distinctly interesting. The treatment, the style, are not to be compared with those of the average work of fiction. Here and there I find admirable bits of writing, especially those passages in the first volume descriptive of scenery in foreground. These are very strong. About the whole book there is an unmistakeable tone of intellect. The quotations are very judicious; the reflections are often original, never commonplace.

The book is a good book, a greatly promising book. Your next will be, I know, very good indeed. I think it likely that you will have harder, rougher characters—less given to the melting mood. There is much hope in the future for you.

Diary :

March 29. Morning spent in Clerkenwell.

April 2 (Easter). Spent day at Crystal Palace and brought back a lot of good notes.

To his sister Margaret :

April 15, 1888.

I suspect you would have some sympathy with the view taken of me by the writer in *Murray's ;* you would chuckle to yourself and say : " I wonder how the ruffian will like this ! " But on the whole it wasn't bad. I have no ambitions to dance jigs before the public. You would wish for a more sanguine tone of writing, but that kind of thing cannot be affected. I am not sanguine with regard to any of the affairs of men.

The beginning of warm weather reminds me that to you it is anything but agreeable. I do hope you will be able to get through these few months without much weariness.

They have just sent me from Broadway a great quantity of rock-cakes, beautifully made and very delicious. But I have the utmost difficulty in knowing when to eat them, so as not to interfere with the clearness of my brain. At last I have hit upon the plan of having them for breakfast, as I go out at once and walk off the indigestible results before it is necessary to sit down to work. A few friends keeping me constantly supplied with rich cakes, would put a most effectual end to all my progress.

To his brother :

May 4, 1888.

Various people have brought under my notice several very good reviews of your book. I hope they may be of use to you. There is clearly a field open for your activity. By the bye, the *Saturday* was facetious at my expense; Grahame showed it me with much chuckling. Socialistic! quotha. Well, perhaps so after all. It was an excellent review for you.

I am working under many ills.

Practically it is decided that I *let* 7K early in the autumn, and leave London for at least a year. Don't quite know whither I shall go, but all sorts of things are in the balance at present.

Diary :

May 8. A day of blankest idleness and misery. Afternoon to Grosvenor where I got Volume I of Hardy's *Wessex Tales*, and Volume II of Vernon Lee's *Journalia*. Read them both in an hour and a half then paced my rooms in agony of loneliness, this becomes intolerable; in absolute truth I am now and then on the verge of madness. This life I *cannot* live much longer, it is hideous.

May 10. A day of wretchedness of course—trying to read *The Virginians*. Went to the Temple Bar news-room and saw that in Gladstone's article on " Robert Elsmere " (*Nineteenth Century*), there is a reference to *The Unclassed*, the only modern novel he mentions. The oddest thing that Gladstone should be the man to revive mention of that book. He calls it " A novel of the speculative and didactic class." There is justice at all events.

May 20. This morning beheld an idiotic experiment. I rose at 5.30 (glorious sunshine), made a cup of cocoa at 6 o'clock, and sat down—to write ! The result was that by 7 o'clock I had written five words, and had fretted myself into a headache. This has solved decisively the question of Walter Scottian work in my case. It is wholly out of the question.

June 3. Strange how sternly I am possessed of the idea that I shall not live much longer. Not a personal thought but is coloured with this conviction. I never look forward more than a year at the utmost; it is the habit of my mind, in utter sincerity to expect no longer tenure of life than that. I don't know how this has come about; perhaps my absolute loneliness has something to do with it. Then I am haunted with the idea that I am consumptive. I never cough without putting a finger to my tongue to see if there be a sign of blood. Morbidness—is it ? I only know that these forecasts are the most essential feature of my mental and moral life at present. Death, if it came now, would rob me of not one hope, for hopes I simply have nor e.

June 8. Have taken up *Elle et Lui* for odd moments. Do other people re-read books to the same extent as I do ?

To his sister Ellen :

June 3, 1888.

Your jottings are always welcome; they remind me that your thoughts turn hitherwards constantly, and give me assurance that you are well. That daily walk must be getting serious, now that the weather has decidedly taken a turn for warmth. You must not expect to do as much work now-a-days as in the cool months; a couple of hours of rest after you return home is absolutely essential.

My book makes decent progress, and I think there is no doubt I shall have finished by the end of July. I still see occasionally a review of *Joy Cometh* [by Algernon Gissing], and always in a favourable vein. The book is still advertised too. I am anxious to see what the *Spectator* will say, but that may be months ahead.

A dark story, this I am now working at, but it will be one

of my strongest, I think.   I am getting in to the end of the second volume.   By the bye, the title I have finally decided upon is *The Nether World*.

Fortunately no one troubles me with invitations this season.   In all probability, I have secured this freedom by my constant refusals.   In fact, I have never had so little correspondence as during the last fortnight; I think not more than two letters have come each week.

On June 6, 1888 he writes to his brother's wife :

Great heavens!   That little study!   I remember above all the extreme quietude one enjoys there [referring to his brother's cottage in the country].

Here there is an incessant hissing of steam from the Baker Street Station; it seems to annoy me somewhat more than formerly.   But that is, of course, a necessary consequence of my resolve to get away from it—a singular psychological fact. Nothing helps one to endure evils so well as a conviction that they are inevitable ; once let a glimpse of rescue occur, and henceforth one frets as though every pain were doubled.

To pursue the argument to its largest issue, only the impossibility of escaping the miseries and risks of life makes mankind at large so placid in the midst of them.   Let there come some prospect of a vastly better existence, and how the earth would ring with impatient outcries.

To his sister Ellen :

Sunday, June 17, 1888.

Cloud and rain, temperature like that of January.   I cannot sit at night without a fire.   Last night I was so cold and miserable and incapable of work that I went off to the theatre and, as usual, did *not* enjoy myself.   In fact, not for years have I enjoyed myself at any play.   The stuff is so amazingly poor, and the actors so far beneath contempt, and I myself so unable to get out of the every-day mood.   But for this I should have

exactly finished Volume II.   It frequently happens in that way.
However the end of the book is in sight.

Väter und Söhne is a stronger book than *Die Neue Generation.*
Bazeroff a wonderfully drawn character; I have some doubt
whether you will understand this typical nihilist.   It is the
purely negative mind, common enough now-a-days in men of
thought.   And how clearly I see Mme. Odinzoff!—Well,
well, it is a great advance for you to have made the acquaintance
of Tourguéneff.

I have been sensibly heavy-hearted about that poor Emperor.
The pity of it!   Of course his death is a blessing, but the end
of his life was very dolorous.   And it is now all but certain
that there will now be wars and upsets and general barbarism.
Friedrich was at all events a civilised man; this son of his
seems to be a mere military blockhead.

I have just been reading some German translations of plays
by a Norwegian called Ibsen; extraordinary productions.
There seems to be a very active literary life in Norway.

Diary :

June 19.   No sunlight.   Wrote 3.30 to 9.45 and did a
little more than four pages, hard, close writing.   Embodying
many notes.   How easily I used to write when I never used
notes at all, but improvised straight on!   I think I may congratulate myself on advance in artistic method.

To his sister Ellen :

July 3, 1888.

I went to the Smith's last night and enjoyed myself vastly.
They are particularly kind.

That wonderful old woman Mrs. Procter was there (Barry
Cornwall's widow).   Goodness knows what her age is ;   her
energy is amazing.   She knows all the living great writers intimately, and has been the friend of all back to the Byron and
Shelley time.   She told me a story about Browning.   He had

dined with her the other day, and, after going away, found he
had taken the wrong hat, and returned.   In the meantime, a man
who had also been dining (a guardsman), was just saying to Mrs.
Procter " By the bye, who *is* this Mr. Browning ? "   And at
the moment Robert put his head in at the door!—the guardsman
had never heard of the poet.

That reminds me.   My neighbour looked in the other
evening and picked up *Villette*.   " Is this a good book ? " he
asked.   " Why," I said, " you know it's Charlotte Brontë."
" Charlotte Brontë ?   Is she well-known—I've never heard of
her."   And this man is the Queen's printer.   It is scarcely
credible, but a fact.

It was a wonderful evening.   The Smith's house has a large
balcony, and a lot of us (we were some twenty altogether), sat
out there, smoking, drinking coffee, hatless, shawl-less; a glorious
moon in the sky, right before us.   I felt thoroughly well and
content and hopeful for the future, and answered people's
questions merrily about *Thyrza*.   Then Mr. Smith came and
sat down by me, and I said: " Come now and tell me all you
can about the Brontës."

So he began his stories.   It was a wonderful thing to think
that this man had entertained Charlotte in his house some forty
years ago, just as he was now entertaining me.   (He is about
sixty-four, hale to look upon—a great traveller.)   Of course
he was a young man in those days, and he hints that he is the
original of " Dr. John " in *Villette*.   It is not unlikely.   He
says that he did actually accompany Charlotte to see Rachel act,
as in the story.   Charlotte had a strange weakness; she was very
vain of her narrow waist and small foot, and she laced herself
so tight as to injure herself.   One day she attended a lecture
of Thackeray's, and, when she went up to Thackeray to
speak to him after it was over, he suddenly exclaimed to someone
standing near: " Oh, let me introduce you to Jane Eyre!"
A day or two later, Charlotte was in the Smith's drawing-room,
and Thackeray came in.   She rose and gave him a prime scolding
" Suppose you came down into Yorkshire, do you think I
should present you to people as Mr. Pendennis ? "

Well, all this is glorious. A happy thing that I have not
come too late to talk with these people; if I live thirty years
more, the memory will be interesting.

Another story I must add. Browning was dining some-
where quite recently, and a lady at the table was talking to Mr.
Smith about him. Indicating another lady opposite, she asked
Smith in a low voice: " Is that Mrs. Browning ? "

Heavens! The ignorance of people.

Diary :

July 8.   In morning to Mile End Waste, for a strike meeting
of Bryant & May's match girls. Very few of the girls themselves present. Speeches from Mrs. Besant, Burrows, John
Burns, Cunninghame Graham, Clementina Black, Stewart
Headlam, etc.

On the way home had an experience familiar enough and
horribly distressing; of a sudden, like the snapping of a cord,
I became aware that the plot of my story, as arranged for the
next few days, would not do. Sat late brooding, and had a
troubled night.

July 9.   Woke to the most miserable distress, striving vainly
to see my way in the story. Seldom have I suffered keener
mental pain. Thought, thought at the rate of a hundred
thousand miles an hour. Dressed in a suicidal mood. Fortunately a bright morning or it would have been worse with
me. In afternoon, still thinking, and at length reconciled
myself to a scheme. But could not write; brain too much
fagged; weather almost cold and since noon very cloudy.

July 10.   To get story in order, had to go back and re-write
two pages at end of Volume II, and four early in Volume III.
Finished both places, so that to-morrow my work is clear
before me again. I think I can go on to the end now.

To his brother :

July 8, 1888.

I quite understand your occasional want of some modern fiction.   I have just the same need myself, at times.   Comparison between that and one's own work is necessary.   I, too, find that it is not advisable to strain the mind over any incongrous subject when at work on a story.   The fact is that a few hours' imaginative work take more out of one than is commonly suspected, and much recreation is required in order to keep it up.

Diary :

July 13.   Fine, warm day, thank heaven.   Wrote only from 3.30 to 6.   Did two pages.   The capture of Bob Hewett and the excitement of them made me so ill that I could do no more.   A disappointment this.   Walked about the streets till 9.30.

July 15.   Ceaseless rain from morning till night.   Thought I might work, but, as usual, the Sunday effect was too strong, so contented myself with planning the three chapters that remain to end of book.   In these wish to emphasize that the idealistic social reformer is of far less use than the humble discharger of human duty.   In the afternoon lit the fire and passed quite a pleasant winter evening—absolutely indistinguishable from an evening in December.

July 21.   Wrote 3 to 10, doing nearly five pages.   This leaves two and a half to finish to-morrow.   To think that I should write these words at last.

July 22.   Wrote from 8.30 to 11 in the morning and from 6 to 8 at night so long did it take me to finish the last two and a half pages.   However, I can write here: Finished *The Nether World.*

To his brother :

July 19, 1888.

I think I go to Wakefield next Wednesday: at all events you had better direct thither after that day.   Where I shall be in the winter, goodness knows.   I *rather think* Paris, but it depends on what I do with my book.

Nothing for it but working steadily on with the daily task. I find Scott's diary in his decadent days occasionally a good impulse to persistent toil.   But more than any other book, for that purpose, does Forster's *Dickens* assist me.   At least every other day I am reading a scrap here and there.   The vigorous artistic energy of the man, the seriousness with which he takes his work—the accounts of his progress—I find extraordinarily helpful.   As example of what I mean see page 140 (second column) and first column of 141.

It seems to me that *A Lion of Cotswold* is an admirable title—especially in that it strikes the note of your chosen subjects.

Diary :

August 22.   [Agbrigg, Wakefield.]   Days spent of late worse than idly.   Reading a little, however.   *Hermann und Dorothea* and Odyssey.

September 2.   Time has been wearing on.   Frame of mind nervous and discontented.   On the whole have determined to go to Paris.   Have been reading six books of Odyssey translated aloud to Madge.   The atmosphere of Wakefield would soon make the completest dullard of me.

To his sister Ellen, then at Scarborough :

AGBRIGG, WAKEFIELD,
August 30, 1888.

A fine day here at last: may you be having the same.

I suppose you are well and cheerful.   For my own part, I feel much better than during the first few days after my return from Seascale. A certain cheerfulness has taken possession of me: I cannot think whence it comes.

I have read six books of the Odyssey to Madge, and I hope we shall be able to go on, though we shall scarcely reach the end before your return.

I was very glad indeed to hear that you had found Anne Brontë's grave. The man's readiness to indicate it would seem to prove that it is occasionally asked for.

Strange to think of Charlotte Brontë having stood on the spot, at the time, of course, regarded by those with whom she had dealings as an insignificant stranger. These revenges of time are very palatable to me. I think of such cases with a sort of exultation over oblivion, a rebellious triumph over the world's brute forces.

I have been reading Crabbe of late. I knew little of him and find him particularly interesting. His verse stories anticipate in a remarkable way our so-called " realistic " fiction ; they deal with very low life frequently, and in a way wholly original at that time. The description of locality, too, is minute, in a way which only modern prose writers have made common; he delights in the dreary and depressing scenery of the Suffolk coast, in squalid streets, in poverty-stricken chambers. Curiously enough, I find he actually wrote several prose novels, but they were destroyed, because his wife was of opinion that he had not succeeded so well as in verse. I should like to have read those productions. Evidently he anticipated at a long interval the now prevalent school of art.

I am always glad to have *assimilated* a new man. The mind feels richer for it. Something of Hawthorne I have also been reading. Besides his exquisite style, there is in Hawthorne an independence of conventional view which makes his work very valuable to all who are reading for the maturing of their thought. One does not easily get weary of him.

To the same :

SMALLBROOK COTTAGE, BROADWAY,
WORCESTERSHIRE. *September* 13, 1888.

The weather has been perfect—absolutely perfect.

What a day had I yesterday at Stratford! From dawn to sunset an unclouded sky, warmth of the most genial kind, just tempered by a breeze you only felt in walking on. For two hours I lay on the edge of the churchyard, looking over the town; innumerable were the pipes I smoked. Deep were my meditations. Without any effort or recollection, scraps of William kept coming into my mind; and the one which recurred most frequently and which was of most soothing efficacy was :

> " We are such stuff
> As dreams are made on, and our little life
> Is rounded with a sleep."

The house I did not enjoy. If I could have wandered from room to room alone! But to be pestered by garrulous old women, bent on explaining to you the meaning of " quarto " and " folio " and gravely reminding you that Sir Walter Scott was " the celebrated novelist "—no, this disabled me from really looking at a single thing. For one sees not with the bodily eye alone; the spirit must be unruffled and able to reflect external things like a still lake; otherwise, profit of gazing there is none.

Shottery was another matter. Save that children ran forth from the garden of Anne's cottage, holding flowers which you were expected to pay for, there was nothing to offend. And the village is very beautiful, old, quiet, intersected with lanes and pathways, surrounded with undulating meadow and corn-land. Here without all doubt William has often and often rambled in days when he had little foresight of *Hamlet*. ("Who's that gone by ? " some cottager would ask in the evening; and the answer would be, " Why, I believe it was young Will Shakespeare, but I didn't quite catch his face.")

Diary :

September 24. A letter from a stranger, Rev. George Bainton of Coventry, who says he is going to deliver a lecture on art of composition, and is writing to one or two well-known authors " requesting them to give him hints as to their own methods of study in such matters." Wrote a rather long reply.

V

FIRST VISIT TO ITALY (1888-1889)

In September of this year Gissing went with a friend to Paris and from thence to Italy.

In his Diary he makes the following entries :

October 2, 1888.   Went to the Salle des Conférences, 39 Boulevard des Capucines, at 8 o'clock and heard Louise Michel on " Le Rôle des femmes dans l'Humanité."   I had expected to see a face with more refinement in it ; she looks painfully like a fishwife.   Dressed with excessive plainness in black and wearing an ugly bonnet.   Much fluency, of course, and signs of intellect.   Demanded absolute equality of women with men in education and rights.   At one place she raised indignant protests by describing, to illustrate her own courage, the artistic beauties of *les incendies*, " comme une aurore," during the Commune outbreak—cries and hisses interrupted her.   I had to reflect a moment to enter into the feeling of these people.   We English have no fresh memories to stir us in this way.

October 3.   Nelly sends letter from Smith & Elder.   They begin by saying that my books as yet do not sell at all (*Thyrza* only 400 copies), and offer £150 for *The Nether World*.   I accept.   This will enable me to go to Italy.

October 4.   In evening to hear Sarcey on Daudet's *L'Immortel* at the Salle des Conférences.   A great treat.   He objected strongly to Daudet's *personal* pictures, but soon put aside that subject and went through the novel, reading passages and bestowing rapturous praise on the style, the peculiarities of which he discussed. Inspiriting to hear work thus dealt with. Delightfully dramatic manner of reading.

October 6. Cloudy but some sunshine. Two hours in morning among the antiques of the Louvre. Evening to see adaptation of Dostoïevsky's *Crime et Châtiment* at the Odéon. Effective here and there, but on the whole poor play—inevitably so and poorly acted. Paul Mounet played Rodion; made him too much a melodramatic Hamlet. One of the two murders is cut out; alas! how much else also, from D's marvellous book! Sonia very poor.

October 7. Bright day, but bitterly cold wind. Rose in astonishing health and spirits. The knowledge that I am safe from penury for a year has helped me wonderfully. Working hard at Italian. Afternoon two hours among Italian pictures, and Renaissance sculpture at Louvre. Saw the new monument to Gambetta in the Place du Carousel; a winged lion at top; rather pretentious and noisy affair.

To his sister Margaret :

33 RUE LINNÉ, PARIS.
October 10, 1888.

I am glad to hear that the cartoons [Raphael's] arrived safely and that you have already hung them; may they be a constant source of interest. Of pictures I am just now having as much as one could desire. Each day I spend several hours either at the Louvre or the Luxembourg and delight myself amid wonderful things.

As well as my picture studies, I am working hard at Italian. What for? say you. Ha, ha! Believe it or not; if all goes well, in a month's time I shall be in Italy! We have decided to go to Naples. I shall look out from my window every morning at Vesuvius; I shall walk about in Herculaneum and Pompeii; I shall look all day long at the blue bay of the Mediterranean! This is news if you like. More of it before

long.   For the present, good-bye.   I do hope the hard weather
is not trying you too much.

Diary :

October 13.   In evening to the Odéon.   "Athalie" with
Mendelssohn's music.   Athalie by Mme. Aimée Tessandier.
Well, I didn't greatly care for her.   It is the first time I have
seen one of these great classical pieces, and I have read so much
about Rachel that I am easily disappointed.

October 14.   Strange that I, all whose joys and sorrows come
from excess of individuality, should be remarkable among men
for my yieldingness to everyone and anyone in daily affairs.
No man I ever met *habitually* sacrifices his own pleasure, habits,
intentions to those of a companion, purely out of fear to annoy
the latter.   It must be a sign of extreme weakness and it makes
me the slave of men unspeakably my inferiors.   Now here is P.
It would take an hour to write down all the things I do and say
in one day just to suit his variable moods and temper.   Why do I
catch a bad cold waiting for him outside a shop where he is
purchasing follies ?   Why do I stint myself of butter that there
may seem more for him ?   Not out of affection, most surely,
but mere cowardice.   I never dare say what I think, for fear of
offending him, or causing a misunderstanding.   And this has so
often been the case in the course of my life.   Therefore it is
that I am never at peace save when alone.

This morning went to High Mass at St. Eustache.

Went to the Louvre.   Salle des Dessins 5—an exquisite
study of drapery by A. Dürer.   Approaching Da Vinci, and
especially reminding one of him after the rough work of
Annibale Carracci in Salle 4.   Splendid copy by Rubens of
horsemen fighting, by Da Vinci.   (Why is not this scene
horrible to me, like, *e.g.* the war scenes of De Neuville ?   Is it
because the costumes are antique, and war can be accepted as
an accompaniment of earlier civilization, but is revolting in
connection with the present ?)   Salle 11.   Splendid horses by
Géricault—just walked through the most modern French

Gallery. Thomas Conture's large picture "Les Romains de la Décadence" gives me pleasure. The central woman's face— noble, satiated, self-dissatisfied—pleases me much. Looked at Greuze's "La Cruche Cassée," one of those pictures of which I cannot say anything definite at once. Coming down turned into the Sculptures. The Venus of Melos gleams very pale at the end of a long gallery, against a dark background, and contrasting with the yellow marble of the Borghese Mars in the foreground.

October 17. All to-day (weather glorious) suffering from influenza and throat. Went out in morning, rest of the day sitting by fire reading *Italienische Reise.* I remark that Goethe had got exactly into my own state with regard to Italy before his visit there ; he says he could not bear to read a Latin book, or to look at a picture of Italian scenery ; again and again I have felt and expressed that, these last three years.

October 18. Wonderful weather, but unable to go out all day; severe cold. Of course it happens that Mlle. Le Breton sent a ticket for the Chambre des Députés, for to-day. Read at Goethe and Baedeker's introduction to Italy, the articles on art.

October 19. Out in the morning. I experience at present a profound dislike for everything that concerns the life of the people.

Paris has even become distasteful to me because I am living in this quarter. All my interest in such things I have left behind in London. On crossing the Channel I have become a poet, pure and simple, or perhaps it would be better to say an idealist student of art.

To his sister Ellen :

OFF TOULON.
October 28, 1888.

It is no use ; never, never, never, shall I be able to tell you what I have seen since yesterday morning, and what I behold

at this moment.   The valley of the Rhone is indescribable.
I have never yet known what sunlight is ; I have never seen
autumn colours on trees.   All along the Rhone there are
multitudes of poplars.   You know what we call "old gold";
well, imagine that with the brightest possible sun gleaming upon
it and you yet cannot conceive what these trees are like.   And
the vineyards, 200 miles of them.   The dead vine leaves are
sometimes patches of brilliant scarlet.   But how am I to
describe the sunlight—the atmosphere—the distances ?

I suppose it is because I have lately spent so much time
looking at pictures.   I cannot realise what I now see.   It
seems to me merely like a wonderful picture gallery.   I woke
in the night and in vain tried to believe it.   It makes me choke
in the throat and tears come to my eyes.   I am sitting on the
deck of the steamer, and every time I look up from the paper
I seem to be dreaming.   The sun is almost too hot ; there is a
delicious breeze ; the sky is purple-blue, with scarcely a little
yellow cloud here and there ; the sea is ultramarine.   We are
coasting.   The coast is mountainous all along; strange great
rocks of limestone, mostly very bare.   Against the sky the
mountains look a sort of hot grey and the shadows are of
wonderful depth and sharpness.   All along the shore are
villages, each house a dazzling speck of white.

I saw, of course, but little of Marseilles.   The principal
street is called Rue Cannabièri and it is famous for its gorgeous
cafés and restaurants.   I strolled along it at 10 last night ; and
certainly never, not even in Paris, saw so much brilliance in so
short a space.   This morning we embarked at 9.   My room
by the bye (at Marseilles) opened on a large garden of beautiful
cypresses and with a few aloes.

The peculiarity of the appearance of the landscape is, I believe,
that at a little distance everything seems translucent.   You
seem to see the light of the sky *through* the mountains.   I have
thought of sketching outlines, but the idea is absurd.   There
are no lines only gradation of colour on colour.

Let no one tell me I am in the 19th century, nothing of the
kind.   Nothing later, at all events, than the conquests of the

Saracens. But rather I am in times long before that. These are the mountains that the Greek colonists saw. The sea and the shore having nothing altered since the times when Carthage was the great Empire of the Mediterranean.

The end of October, and here I bask in delicious sunshine ! I write and read on the open deck. Ah, that you could be here ! 5 p.m. The sun is just setting over one of the little Ile d'Hières. Westward, all the mountains about Marseilles and Toulon are bathed, etherealized in a light half yellow, half purple. To the east, the sky is growing a darker purple and the land of the same colour. My first Mediterranean sunset ! The bell is ringing for dinner, but I shall stay a few minutes longer.

I have just made the acquaintance of an American from Mizzouri who is going to a Roman Catholic college at Rome, to study theology for five years. We have smoked a cigar together on deck, under the milky way, which is wonderfully bright. The lighthouse shining near us, so that we are not very far from Nice.

October 29, 6 *a.m.* Look through port-hole of cabin and see sun rising over Corsica, which is close by, very high mountains, some with snow in the top gorges. A wild beautiful island, valley after valley; rugged with dark vegetation, white villages down by the shore. Cloudless sky; sea perfectly smooth.

10.45 *a.m.* First sight of the shore of Italy. It is growing beyond Elba, stretching in both directions—the hills of Tuscany. Hurrah ! Behind is Corsica, the snowy heights glorious in sunshine.

I don't know how to give you an idea of the colour of the scene. The sea is certainly blue, but a sort of black blue. The sky . . . . ? Well, that is not *blue* in the ordinary sense. In the whole hemisphere there is not a speck of cloud. At the horizon the colour begins a pale blue grey, the line of the sea violently clear against it; it darkens upwards and at the zenith is a *misty violet* rather than blue of any kind. The island of Giglio is now ahead. Dolphins leaping about in the sea.

4.45. The sun setting behind Corsica. Giglio a glorious rose colour.

Corsica very faintly outlined, beyond the translucent shape of Monte Cristo. Elba still well in sight. The sun, though it is just on the horizon, too bright to be looked at.

5 *o'clock*. The sun gone. Corsica has become a very dark and well defined line of mountains, instead of the faint outline of before. Monte Cristo is like a flat silhouette in the distance. Giglio has lost its colour, and become a stern grey.

October 30. Up on deck just in time to see the sun rise. We are now among the islands which come before Naples. Again not a cloud visible. Though we are so far from land a little bird is flying about the vessel, something like a canary. Don't understand how it got there.

10.20. Off Gaeta. Very fine mountains, with a few yellow clouds on them. The colour a distinct pink grey.

12.45. Vesuvius at last! Misty but a great form looming out, with pillar of smoke rising; not black smoke but tinted *pink* like a cloud. A similar line of smoke lies above the top of the mountain.

Capri has come out behind Ischia.

The smoke of Vesuvius is blowing towards Ischia, a sign of fine weather.

The peninsula of Sorrento full in view. Just entering the strait between mainland and Procida.

Here I stop, address the letter down in the cabin, and post it as soon as I land.

Diary :

October 30. In the Port of Naples at 4 o'clock. There followed an indescribable scene. As soon as the ship approached, there came forth dozens of little boats, the boatmen roaring out the name of hotels which they represented. Of course in language quite unintelligible to me. The uproar was deafening. Fortunately P. had made acquaintance with two Italians on board, who were able to undertake the bargaining for a boat ;

at length eight or nine of us got into one, with a great quantity of luggage.   P.'s and my luggage amounted to nine articles—a terrible job to keep an eye on them.   As we pulled towards the custom house began a yet more terrific struggle.   First of all we had to fight with porters to keep our luggage; then when it was once on the table, we were crushed in a roaring, struggling crowd.   No attempt at order; I suppose this scene could only have taken place with an emigrant ship.   Providentially, we yielded ourselves to the directions of a shabby but lively little fellow who seemed to speak every language.   The wild and grotesque gesticulations all about us.   Baggage strictly examined, as we came from France, and the abolition of the commercial treaty is just now giving much trouble.   P.'s tobacco pouch and two packets of tea sent off to an inner office but eventually returned to us.   Then again a fight between the porters authorised by our little fellow, and all the others about.   At last, out we went in procession after our truck, and going we knew not whither were led to the Albergo New York, just opposite the lighthouse.   With much difficulty we got settled about a room for two nights and paid all charges.   The little fellow shook hands with us all effusively.

November 3.   At midnight, last, a tremendous storm.   I was awakened by the thunder, which did not rumble, but went off in great claps like artillery.   Wind roaring and furious rain, incessant lightning.   The sea was already very rough when I looked at it about 4 o'clock.   I find it was scirocco yesterday; I have speedily come to know what this means.   All day I could scarcely drag one limb after another.

This morning a splendid N.W. wind and very clear sky. Felt well again and ready for a long walk.   Went through the *grotta nuova* and Fuorigrotta.   From Fuorigrotta to Bagnoli, a walk of about a couple of miles, along straight road between vast vineyards, pines also growing on either hand.   The autumn tints are little noticeable, nothing like that wonderful Rhone Valley.   Saw great numbers of little lizards darting about the banks.   The vineyards are not hedged, or walled, but protected by great trenches. At Bagnoli found the sea breaking in great waves on the rocky shore. The sky is to S.W. black as night, but all the rest blue and laughing. Tempted onwards, and soon came to Pozzuoli, where I had to face a combat with swarms of guides and carriage-drivers who swarm before the gate by which you enter the town. A happy lie saved me. " Ho gia tutto veduto! " I cried, and my trouble was at an end. But a scrubby little naked-legged boy stuck to me through the street. I was looking for a wine shop (having already eaten two rolls and two pears which I had put in my pocket) and he, observing this, kept recommending a place.

In vain the attempt to throw him off; I yielded at last and let him guide me into a paltry little " osteria." There I had half a bottle of wine and the ragged boy, very good tempered, sat by me. When I had finished, I poured out half a glass, and, with a soldo, gave it him to drink, saying " Non seguite piu." He obeyed me.

Glorious little town, Pozzuoli, richly Italian, full of colour. Remember the little square, with fountain and two statues; the delightful little port (best of all) and the little public garden, with its streets, where I sat and smoked a pipe, and looked at the ships, and over to Baja. One of the soft Italian organs played the while. I felt happy, more than happy.

Went back to the shore and picked up a lot of pretty shells— some for mother. Day got brighter still as I went on. I stopped a little short of the Baths of Nero, reserving Baja itself for another day.

This morning a little girl came to take away a cup of coffee in one of the odd little tin vessels, with a cap, which are common here for that purpose ; her hair was a perfect black and very curly, whilst her face was exactly that of an angel in one of Botticelli's pictures which I remember but cannot indicate.

November 4. An excessive weariness always comes upon me in the evening. For one thing to walk about Naples is to be constantly climbing—a severe exercise.

We are not troubled here with bulletins to fill up at hotels and lodgings.   In every way I prefer the life and customs to those of France.   Singular that I even feel a sort of pleasure in being under a monarchy once more !

November 5.   The date reminds me of bonfire day; how far I am from such associations.   Started early for a walk about the east part of the town.   Turned from the port up the Strada del Duomo and explored several by-streets, the Strada Anticaglia especially, where traces of the theatre in which Nero performed are still to be seen.

Should have mentioned that in the morning I bought several books: Leopardi's *Poésie et Prose.   Le Mie Prigioni.   Canti Popolari Tuscani*, and lectures by Mariani on Italian literature in 18th and 19th century.

November 6.   Getting anxious to have a letter from England —in a day or two I suppose.   Do nothing much but read Italian.

To his sister Ellen :

VICO BRANCACCIO, NAPOLI.
November 9, 1888.

I find I have so much to say and, at present, so little time to give to letters (and indeed I am worn out generally when I sit down) that I shall be obliged to ask you to read this to the others.

On the 9th November how would you like to be sitting in a huge room with the windows wide open, a room in which there is no fireplace and of which the floor is tiled ?   Well, so it is with me since my arrival and all I have to complain of is the heat.   The weather has been wonderful since my arrival. One day indeed we had the scirocco ; the effect upon me was that I could scarcely walk a yard and passed the day on the sofa prostrate.

Let me try to put down a list of the impressions one first receives in walking about Naples.

Morning and evening the streets are thronged with large

herds of beautiful goats, the milk is much sold. They all have
bells and the result is a constant tinkling everywhere.

Everywhere you meet monks. It is like living in the
middle ages. Other clericals swarm and, like the rest of the
Neapolitans, saunter along at the rate of a mile an hour.
Never do you see a person hurrying.

The extraordinary structure of the town. It is built on the
side of a mountain and I have never had such severe exercise
as in walking about the streets. But I am glad I delayed no
longer in seeing Naples, for every year it is becoming modernized
and sanitarized. Enormous pullings down and rebuildings are
in progress. A pity, but inevitable. If you could see the
Strada di Chiaia at 5 o'clock in the evening! It is one of the
main thoroughfares and along it passes the stream of carriages
returning from afternoon driving along the esplanade. Well,
the Chiaia is nowhere as much as six yards broad, and in parts
like other streets has no pavement for pedestrians. Every
moment you think you must be run over but there is really
little or no danger, for everything goes on at such leisurely pace.
And the roaring, bellowing, shrieking! Every Neapolitan
shouts on every possible or impossible occasion.

The paving of the streets. It is all with lava, and in enormous
blocks placed diamondwise—a strange effect.

The colour of the houses. Those which prevail are white,
salmon colour and bright yellow. Everywhere flat roofs, often
converted into gardens. Round the door is often a border of
bright blue. All the larger houses are built round a courtyard.

The amount of fruit everywhere. I buy white grapes at one
penny a pound—figs at about the same rate—three new lemons
(green inside and out) for a penny—tomatoes for almost nothing.
Of course the figs are just off the tree. Everywhere oranges
are ripening.

The multitude of donkeys and mules, but especially of
donkeys. *Never* is the sound of the donkey's braying out of
your ears. They run up and down the "gradoni" heavily
laden with costermongers' baskets, which, by the bye, are always
decorated with fine branches. Donkeys and mules and horses

all have extraordinary harness, a pile of glittering and jingling metal, surrounded with a thing like a weathercock.

The constant presence before your eyes of the sign " Banco Lotto." This means a place where lottery tickets are sold. The lotteries are legal and drawings take place every week.

I could go on at any length. How much I must be content to tell you when I get back to England.

I am half way up the hill from the sea. My window looks over Posillipo, and by putting out my head I can see one end of Capri. Thus I get all the sunsets.

Living however can be called cheap enough. For breakfast I go out and have a cup of coffee, two rolls and a piece of butter. At mid-day I eat wherever I am, bread and fruit; all I can possibly eat I buy for 3d. and a bottle of excellent wine costs 4d. At night I go to a Restaurant and there have soup, meat, vegetables, fruit and wine.

I am in despair when I turn to speak of the aspect of the country. No words can give the faintest idea of it ; no painted picture is any use. You must come here or be content to know nothing about it. I have not yet been far; Capri, Pompeii, Vesuvius, are still in the background. But I have been to Pozzuoli (Puteoli) and Baja (Baiae). The Bay of Pozzuoli appeals to me even more than that of Naples. Vesuvius is too tremendous a spectacle for constant looking at—but the Bay of Pozzuoli with its green and blue sea (dashing up in great waves these last few days), its capes, its views of islands—no, I can say nothing about all this.

The first two nights I was here Vesuvius was enveloped in clouds, the third night I looked in that direction and there I saw a light like that of a great red bonfire up in the sky, very strange and impressive. The mountain has two summits, the lower called Somma; its slopes are one vast garden, the richest region of the world, wonderful to look at from a height, so infinite does the space seem, so indescribable are the colours.

To speak a little more of practical matters, a serious difficulty is the language. With educated Italians I can get on well, but the Neapolitan dialect is terrific. Imagine a foreigner beginning his experience of English at Sowerby Bridge—or even on the borders of Scotland! That would be a parallel. Even an Italian of northern origin with difficulty understands the people. I can manage now for all I want in the shops, but for real practice in Italian, I must wait for Rome and Florence.

Now here is a poor account of a walk I had the other day. I set out towards Posillipo. The hill of Posillipo, which, as you will see, separates our part of the Bay from Pozzuoli, is pierced by two enormous tunnels, one of them of Roman making. I passed through and came out at the village called Fuorigrotta, thence walked along a straight road to Bagnoli. The road runs between vineyards (that is a feature of the country you must always bear in mind, vineyards of miles in extent everywhere), and is bordered with beautiful pine trees. The walls and ditches swarmed, swarmed with lizards, which darted about in the sun. The vines are, of course, dead, but the old leaves show fine colours.

At Bagnoli I came to the sea. The sand is very dark brown. I picked up some beautiful strange shells, of which I keep a lot for mother. Of course there is no difference of tide, always at the same level.

On to Pozzuoli. Ah, the delightful little town—once the greatest port of Italy! Everything seems miniature now. A little harbour (glorious colour of sea and sky) and near it a little public garden planted with palm trees. There I sat for an hour and smoked a pipe, watching the sailors, and myself an object of much curiosity to the inhabitants. Of the intense picturesqueness of the houses nothing can give you an idea. By the upper windows hang great clusters of tomatoes and other fruits, gathered and put there for keeping, I suppose.

On by the sea until I came to a small lake separated from the sea by a dyke along which the road goes. This is the Lucrine Lake, made into a port by Augustus, and then very celebrated for its oysters. Here I turned inland a little distance until I came in sight of another little lake, deep in hills. An old boatman quite alone, stood by the bank and, as I came up, he pointed to the water and said solemnly " Il Lago Averno."

Yes, it was the Lake Avernus. I had a talk with the old fellow in a queer fashion and bought some shells of him.

Back to the shore and then on till I came nearly to Baja. I brought my walk to an end just in view of it. Well, you know all about Baiae. Here Virgil and Horace and Cicero have many a time walked, Horace often speaks of it in his poems, it was the fashionable resort of the Romans—now a poor little village. But behind it is a view of the fine mountains of Ischia; Capri is right south; the shore is wonderfully lovely. And these things Horace saw just as I see them. No, no ; one can't speak of it !

Yesterday I climbed up to Camildoli, where there is a monastery and where you have what is called the finest view in Italy. Again, no possibility of describing it. There was no speck of cloud on Vesuvius, and the smoke of the mountain was rose-colour. The monk who led me spoke very good Italian ; when I told him I was an Englishman he said smiling " Si dice che v'è molta nebbia " (" They say there is much fog there ! "). I assured him he was not mistaken. A very clean monk in a fine white gown.

Next Sunday I shall go to Pompeii, on that day admission to the town is free, on other days you are charged 2 lire.   And then in a few days I think of making a longer excursion to Paestum and Salerno and Amalfi. When I shall manage Vesuvius I can't think. Impossible to do the climbing on foot. There is a rope railway up to the Crater, but then they charge you 25 lire, I think ; and besides, it is an ignoble way of ascending.

Already I have been to the foot of the mountain. There is the town of Torre del Greco which has several times been destroyed. I went to the sea shore and the sight was extraordinary. All the rocks are volcanic scoriae, quite black. Wherever the soil is turned up you see that all is black, and burnt. Do you want any—what do you call that stuff—yes, I mean pumice stone ? No doubt whatever this town will again be burnt and crushed some day, at present it is busy and noisy and cheerful enough. It sends a fishing fleet every year for coral and I saw notices on the wall that the school for instruction in coral carving had just opened.

I broke off to go to the window to look at the sunset.   I think we are going to have a storm.   The sea is ominously calm and Capri is very clear, a sign of rain.   In the street below, a herd of goats is just tinkling by ; of course a donkey is braying.   At 5 o'clock I shall go to dinner, but I will first finish this letter.

You cannot tell how glad I shall be of a letter.   Last night I had one from R. and one from B., but both live at a shorter distance than you, so could write more quickly.

I made the oddest acquaintance yesterday in the village of Soccavo.   Very tired, I went into a little hotel place to get some wine.   The landlord was a young man of very intelligent appearance, from the north of Italy, so that we could talk. When he learnt that I was an Englishman, he exclaimed that he had three English books.   They proved to be *Verdant Green;* a translation of *Paul et Virginie* and an odd volume of Hannah More's works.   A friend had given him these.   He could not read a word, but vastly enjoyed the illustrations to *Verdant Green.*   We had quite a long talk and he introduced me to his wife and baby ; " Mia figlia," he said.   Certainly I shall go to see him again.

On the road there passed by a large open cart, piled with some hundred weights of a purple mass of stuff which I couldn't make out.   As soon as it had gone by, a scent came on the wind, which at once told me what the stuff was.   Simply the crushed remnants of grapes, out of the wine presses.   The plane trees are in fine autumn colour just now.   Yesterday I came across a great quantity of flowers, growing in a wood, that looked like large violets.   I wish I knew what they were.   Of course I am miserably ignorant of most of the flora.   But I know the pine, and the palm and the cactus.

On the shore of Lake Avernus I gathered some wild thyme, I think.   Here is a piece for you, and a piece to send to Alg. Think!   From the Lake Avernus!   But I shall bring back lots of mementoes.

Much love to all who read this scribbling.   Let me hear. I live in a sort of half craziness, and it will be long before I can write coherently.   Ask mother to send a line.

Diary :

November 11.   Left Naples by 10.25 train for Pompeii, choosing to-day because admission to the ruins is free.   Took with me a wallet of provisions.   Of the visit itself little can be said; like everything else here it exceeded my expectations.   I will jot down points that interested me.

The lizards running about the sunny old walls—the huge irregular blocks of lava of which the paving consists, with the deep ruts of wheels; how long wearing this must prove!   The high narrow pavements; that approaching the theatres is worn quite hollow.   The little barbers' shops in the Strada di Mercurio, with its block of stone in the middle for customers.   I gathered some ferns there.   The fine face and figure of the wounded Adonis in No. 18 of same street.   I understand now, of course, vastly better the arrangement of Roman houses.   The streets are certainly very narrow.   The theatres rejoiced me. Remember the deep cutting for the curtain, and the three doors on to the stage.

A superb view from the top of the Temple of Jupiter. A good deal of snow on the Apennines.   Surely few towns are more exquisitely situated.

The extraordinary and delicate care with which the place is preserved.   Whenever a piece of stucco has been loose, there is a little iron clamp to hold it.   Wooden beams often inserted above doors showing that a process of rebuilding has, at times, been carried out.   What a place of stucco, it was.   Delightful perfection of the divisions into *regiones* and *insulae* and streets and numbered houses.

As I had no train back until 6.14 and it was impossible to wait after sunset in the cold, I set out at 4.30 and walked to Torre Annunziata.   There waited a little and caught a train which took me without stopping to Naples.

Detestable spirit just now between France and Italy.   Constant talk of war.   But what I see of the Italian papers are nothing like as bad as the French, which become hateful on questions of international politics.

Tuesday, November 13. A day just like many a warm sun-less autumn day I have known in England. Not a ray of sun-light from morning to night. In afternoon walked to Campo Santo, in the Strada Nuova di Poggio Reale. From the Poeta Capuana the road leads to the most disagreeable part of Naples, made especially oppressive by the lowering sky. Great blocks of working class lodgings are being built here; if one or two points were lost sight of, one might be in the East End of London, for the buildings are exactly like the model lodging blocks. The smaller houses indescribably filthy, the ugliness of the district cannot be described.

The Campo Santo occupied me for an hour and a half. Most curious the custom of burying in niches. Here and there great walls stand constructed for this purpose—apart I mean from the tombs—with six or more niches one above the other, and any number lengthwise. At first I supposed that the oblong marbles were merely commemorative, and that the graves were in the ground below, but one or two open niches showed the fact. At each end of the marble covering is a keyhole, and other orifices just enable one to look into the interior; in one case I distinguished a skeleton so that it would seem coffins are not used. And I don't see how they can be, for the holes are very small, yet in many of them one reads an inscription like this : " Lorenza S. per se e suoi." The only name I recognised was that of Thalberg. On the front of a great building, large enough to be a church, was written " Sigismondo Thalberg."

Very noticeable is the common custom of putting a portrait bust on the tomb, however insignificant the man. These busts are well executed and obviously good likenesses; realism is perfect, even collar, tie, waistcoat, etc., being carefully carved.

But the most astonishing of such things was the grave of a certain " Giuseppe Manensi " near the main entrance below. An elaborate marble pedestal, with stairs, etc., is crowned by a bust of a military looking man, with imperial moustache and the kind of beard called " goatee." Below the bust stands a life-size group of four persons—the wife and three children. The lady rests on her right arm, against the pedestal of the bust;

she is most elegantly dressed with much lace about her garments. Two little girls are before her, one holding flowers, the other clinging to her hand; and near is a little boy holding his hat. All are patent likenesses, and the effect is most ludicrous, a hideously commonplace representation of modern grief. Who on earth suggested this thing? It is very recent; I suppose a speculative sculptor proposed it to the widow. Oh, the expression of that wretched boy, who is holding his hat!

November 15. See in the paper (I read the *Corrière di Napoli* every morning) that the public scriveners under the window of San Carlo have notice to move at the end of the present year. Indeed it was high time I saw Naples.

To-day is published in three volumes *A Life's Morning*. I rejoice unspeakably that I am out of the way.

November 18. After some doubt whether I was well enough to go I started by the 10.25 train for Salerno, purposing an excursion of some days. Glorious view of Salerno from the railway at Vietri and between the tunnels by which S. is approached. On arriving had a meal and without stopping to see the town, took a " carrozza " for Amalfi (5 lire and *mancia*). As soon as we got to Vietri on the road, up drove two other carriages, and the three rascals attempted to make me change, on pretext of a fresh horse being needed. Easy to imagine the fix in which I should have been had I yielded. " Questo è mio fratello," said my lying driver, pointing to one of the others, not the least like him. A brief " non voglio " put an end to the matter, and on we went.

Monday, November 19. [At Amalfi].
A day of hard incessant rain ; landlord tells me the weather changed at midnight. A very decent fellow, the landlord, who had the sense to speak Italian slowly and clearly to me. Made a few attempts to see the town and neighbourhood.

Made two sketches from my window; one of a round tower, that stands clear against the sky on a height; the other of the Campanile.

November 20.   Started early and drove back to Salerno; weather again calm and sunny.   Many butterflies flitting about. At Salerno just caught the train southwards, and at 12.45 was at Pesto.   Train full of peasants; most of them had good handsome faces, and by their talk seemed good fellows.   All along rare views of the Apennines.   As we neared Pesto passed a few herd of buffalo; but they are practically the same as cattle, and graze placidly and unalarmed by the train.   The land getting rapidly cultivated all along the route of railway.

At Paestum, for a delightful change, there is no pestering by guides.   I walked straight to the Temple of Ceres in peace. Only one party of three or four Germans had come down by same train.   Here discovered for first time a mistake in Baedeker; he says the guardian's house is by the Temple of Ceres, whilst it stands by that of Neptune.   Before entering latter bought four *soldi* of cheese at a vile little "osteria," the only one in the place, and was cheated shamelessly—a piece of one inch solid.   Paid a lira for admission to the space where the two main temples stand; guardian very decent fellow, speaking good French.   When I had entered two women came up, and asked me if I wished to buy refreshments—but did it respectfully and quietly, and accepted my request for a mere half bottle of wine, without the least pestering.   Perhaps wife of the guardian.   So I ate my bread and cheese in the Temple of Neptune and drank the wine, which was very sweet.   Calabrian, the woman told me.

Owing to the necessity of taking train back northwards, had only two hours altogether—grossly inadequate, of course.   The stone of the temples has become honeycombed wonderfully; here and there incrusted with what seems to be petrified fungi. In every crevice are pretty coloured snails; I brought away several.   Many lizards.   The ground all about thick with a rank vegetation   Everywhere quantities of what I had hitherto taken for wild thyme, but which a note from Alg. tells me is peppermint.   The Temple of Neptune is a golden brown; contrasts strongly with the white of the so-called Basilica, next to it.   I picked up a fragment of marble, and, at same time, a bit of the travertine; the one quite cold in the hand, the other warm.

Exquisite views all round. Blue line of sea, with Capri and the Sorrento peninsula. But the most striking is to stand in the middle of the Temple of Neptune, and then glance towards both ends. At the one, a very narrow strip of the bluest possible sea, only that; the other way, a splendid valley rising upwards on the mountains; both these seen between the grand Doric columns. Think that these columns have echoed to the Greek speech!

It was intensely still. A carter going by, uttered the peculiar wailing song, so commonly heard about here; his horses' bells tinkled. Between the two Temples, a donkey, laden with a sack, was grazing. Clouds began to thicken; the rays of the westering sun came through them, making the other clouds on the mountains a rich colour. The ordinary colour of the crags in sunshine I cannot express. I mean it is a peculiar tint for which I know no name.

A few farm houses stand in the neighbourhood. A field where farm oxen were turning up the black earth are marked with stones which once built Paestum—the ruins of a great city! The remains of the city wall very vast and impressive.

At Battipaglia (as in coming) had to change, and there decided to stop at Pompeii for Vesuvius to-morrow. At Nocera station, women crying, " Uova fresche ! (pronounced fresh-che) Mele ! Pere !" The porters when the train is ready to start, first cry "Partenza!" then a moment after "Pron-ti!" By the bye, I find the Italian officials everywhere polite and intelligent. My experiences with them are much pleasanter than with the French.

As I walked from Pompeii station to the Inn, the moon rising, right in front. On my left hand, the dead town in darkness, and behind it the bulk of Vesuvius, with an angry glow. On either side of the road, plane trees. Put up at the " Soli," a capital place. Found a lot of Germans there, good fellows. The amusing waiter, Giuseppe.

Painting on walls of the eating room. My bedroom is a

little outhouse built at the back of the garden, into which my door opens straight.

Here made an acquaintance J.W.S.; at dinner he was talking German—very fluently, but in a way that betrayed him as a foreigner. Something in his accent reminded me strangely of— I knew not what; of something very familiar. After dinner it came out he was a Yorkshireman, and with a strong Yorkshire accent: there was the secret. Related to Wakefield people. Was delighted to hear I knew them. He had been in Italy seventeen years.

November 21. Ascent of Vesuvius. Started at 8.30 on horseback, guide also on a horse. Fine day, on the whole, but rather too misty for a good view, a spot of rain once or twice. At Boscoreale stopped and had a bottle of white Vesuvian wine; tastes very like cider. I had fears about my horsemanship; however I stuck on without difficulty, even when we galloped, but the bruising and abrading was awful. The ascent at first through vineyards, some of "Lacrima Christi." At point where the climb begins we left our horses and also the food. Found it impossible to get rid of the two "ajuti," who, at expense of 3 lire apiece, insisted on lugging me up the steep parts, by means of a cord. The pleasure greatly spoilt by this needless nonsense; nowhere is the climb difficult; the only thing is, it means the ruin of a pair of boots. As you get to the top it is difficult to avoid taking the sea for sky, especially with a little mist on it; Capri I constantly took for a high cloud, until I corrected myself. At one point much suffering from sulphur fumes, but soon got through this. Did not venture on to the inner cone; it smoked furiously and looked red-hot; I should have had no boots left at all. Ground covered with bright yellow sulphur; collected a lot of pieces. Much activity of volcano; vast volumes of smoke, constant vomiting of small stones; the smoke of a dark rose colour at times. Inside the incessant noise as of a foundry—a throbbing, beating, with a huge burst now and then.

Down again to the horses. A lad, who had taken care of

them, I found was called Raffaello; and my guide's name I found afterwards to be Michelangelo.   We ate our lunch, I sharing mine with guide.

At Boscoreale, in the little inn, found an American lady, who with *strong* accent, instantly cried out to me, " *Can* you speak any Italian ? "   She said her husband and daughters had gone up the mountain and she was waiting their return; in a state of exhaustion, and couldn't speak a word of anything but English, to ask for food.   I ordered for her a beefsteak and raw tomatoes. Much gratitude, and she came to the door to see me off.

Heavens, the state in which I reached home !   Knees and backside and bottom of spine seriously abraded; also knuckles, with occasional clinging to pummel.   Not a bone that didn't ache.   It would have been nothing, but for the riding.

Going to my bedroom through the dark garden, I met a little lad belonging to the house.   " Buona sera, signore " he said, and I replied "Buona sera."   Then " Va bene, signore?" "Va benissimo! "   "E una buona parola ! "   Curious reply that.

November 22.   Little thought, last year, where I should be spending next birthday.   Decided to run over to Naples, and back again at night in order to go with S. to Massa Lubrense to-morrow.   Took 7.30 train back to Pompeii.

Friday, November 23.   Set out walking with S.   Little short of Castellammare overtaken by two of our Germans, in carriage, they persuaded us to mount.   Had wine, and took, all together, another carriage for Sorrento.   Through Vico Equense.   This side of the peninsular very different from the other; for most part a long slope upwards, richly covered with olives and *agrume* (the general name for oranges and lemons). The first glimpse of Piano di Sorrento, delightful.   Not really a plain but a gently rising wide and deep lap, surrounded by mountains, and with a sheer line of high cliffs all along the sea front—a singular effect.   Through Meta—then pulled up at Sorrento—the town of Tasso.

Here the Germans remained for the Capri boats, and S. and I walked to Massa.   Wonderful walk.   Half way, one of the

richest views I have yet seen. Vesuvius right opposite, perfectly cloudless; right, Piano di Sorrento, with its upward sloping
olive-hills. Far below my feet, the little Marina of Sorrento,
with its boats drawn up. All around, gleaming limestone hills,
and in far distance, Naples—the long salmon-coloured line of
houses, from Posillipo to Torre Annunziata, and Camaldoli
rising up behind. Capri and Ischia both in sight. The sea
foaming under the tramontana, which was strong. Over all,
sunlight from the west.

Reached S.'s house—Villa Cozzolino. He is building an
addition to it, and things all in disorder.

November 24. Walk with S. up to the Castle of Santa Maria.
Splendid view of Capri, close at hand. Brilliant sun. We
passed the house where Murat lived, and whence he viewed the
capture of Capri by French. His rooms still kept as he left
them, precisely.

November 25. A fine morning. The limestone crags
gleaming against intense blue of sky. Wonderfully rich vegetation. Baedeker says the flora has 800 species. Vesuvius
cloudless; wind from west. From Piccola Marina over to the
Grande, and thence in boat to Grotta Azzurra; a little difficulty
in entering, owing to the swell of the sea. The blue of the
water indescribable, but only near entrance. I expected to see
the rocks all round blue with reflection, but it was not so ;
perhaps insufficient sunlight. The silver gleam when the oar
was moved in the water. A splendid view of the sheer crags
as we rowed by, going and returning. Corals on the rock just
below water mark; boatman said they were too hard for use.

The pellucid green water near, and in the harbour, almost as
wonderful as the Grotta; the weed at the bottom at great
depth, green beyond expression.

In the afternoon found my way up to the Villa of Tiberius.
The Salto di Tiberio an awful height, a stone seemed to be a
whole minute or more in reaching the bottom. Baedeker says
the height is 738 feet, and that the highest cliffs at the east are
1,000 feet sheer! Drank a glass of white wine at the little

" osteria " by the Salto, and took a rose (blooming in a garden) from the corner there; also wrote my name in visitors' book. Then on a little higher to the ruins of the Villa. A talkative old woman presented herself as guide; she said the place was the property of herself and two or three brothers and sisters. A fine peaceful cow stabled and ruminating in part of the ruins. A very few traces of mosaic, all else gone—except indeed the beginning of a paved roadway which seemed to run downwards to the sea, and which had a double track for wheels, as if vehicles used to be hauled up. The lower part covered with earth; the ground of a peasant who refuses to excavate. Brought away a little bit of mosaic stone. Talk with the hermit who was here by his chapel. Lightning is constantly striking the place; he showed me the marks of the last bolt, which fell in September last. The hermit happened to be absent in Capri; his bed-chamber riven down the wall. Gave him 50 c. and wrote my name again in the visitors' book.

November 26.   Decided to take the boat at 2.30.   Evening darkened as we sailed towards Naples. A fierce red sunset between black clouds. Vesuvius veiled. Beautiful view of the Piano di Sorrento—its peculiar shape, cliffs, etc. A cold wind, but sea calm.

Thursday, November 29.   Decided to leave for Rome by the 10.40 to-night.

Found myself with a ticket for Rome. Carriage full. I was too late to get a corner, so of course did not rest the whole night. Some good fellows and amusing. One lad, lithe and good-looking, amused us particularly. First he played some airs on a little wooden whistle; then he stowed himself away on the top of the rack for luggage, and slept there comfortably ; and, getting up, he said comically once or twice, " Farò un poco di gimnastica! " Not a Neapolitan from his language.

As often as he woke, he tickled me greatly by shouting to his companion " Bosco! Bosco! " A good, frank lad I think. Another phrase, used by another passenger, struck me through the strangeness of its sound; he said he was going, not to Rome, but to "la penultima stazione." All night long, a hundred times one or other was using the phrase "a Roma." It rang in my ears strangely enough. Century after century has this name "Roma" been used, and pronounced doubtless in much the same way. An odd and dangerous thing was the examination of tickets whilst the train was at full speed—the collector going along from door to door outside. At about 7 Rome was reached. It was too dark to see anything before the aqueducts.

Friday, November 30. In spite of intense weariness could not resist the Forum and Colosseum in the afternoon. The astonishing difference between Rome and Naples. They are not the same nation. Here no noise, no pestering to buy, etc.— all grave and quiet and dignified.

Saturday, December 1. A day of wandering. To the Pincian and enjoyed the view. Then to the Pantheon, copied the inscription on the tomb of Raphael and Annibale Carracci who lie separated only by a chapel. Had dinner and walked up to the Capitol. I walked right on to the Porta di San Paolo, getting clear ideas of the topography of the hills. Then entered the Protestant Cemetery and walked up to Shelley's grave, which is right at the top under the Aurelian Wall.

The old cemetery is quite distinct, at a few paces distance; you just pass through a wooden gate, then over a field, then through a locked door, which leads you over the deep trench (walled on both sides) which surrounds the little graveyard. The key of the door I found, by guardian's directions, in a hole in the wall. Very few graves here. A few pines and cypresses and some roses in bloom. Keats' grave just by the entrance; the marble slab with his bust is placed against a wall close at hand.

The inscription on the other slab to Keats is become at present all but illegible, the black of half the letters quite gone.

Next to it on the same plot of ground, which is all enclosed with iron rails and a thick low hedge of some common shrub which I ought to know the name of, lies Severn. Over Keats, from left hand corner, grows a laurel—now with black berries. Severn's inscription:

TO THE MEMORY OF

JOSEPH SEVERN

Devoted friend and death-bed companion

of

JOHN KEATS

Whom he lived to see numbered among
The Immortal Poets of England.
An Artist eminent for his representations
Of Italian life and nature.
British Consul at Rome from 1861 to 1872
And Officer of the Crown of Italy
In recognition of his services to

FREEDOM AND HUMANITY

Died 3 August 1879 aged 85

The only difference between appearance of the two stones is, that Severn has a pallet instead of the lyre. A very small stone by the foot of this grave is to the child Arthur Severn, of whom it is mentioned that Wordsworth was present at his baptism in Rome.

Leaving the cemetery I walked on to the Monte Testaccio, and looked long at the view. The origin of the hill is obvious, as you walk up it—everywhere potsherds. I noticed that the size of St. Peter's dome can only be appreciated from some distance; from here it seemed immense, looming above horizon; this morning from the Pincian, rather small. With delight, distinguished Mt. Soracte in the N.W.

December 2. Capitoline Museum. The splendid majesty of that great sea-god (I think the shell in his hand proves him of the sea, and not river, as Baedeker believes) in the Cortile! Calm rest in blessed sunshine, in an enchanted land. The interesting little case of ivory stili in Room VII. The Venus of Praxiteles revolves on its pedestal—a very sensible arrangement, standing as it does in a niche; busts of Euripides; again my delight, as at Naples. That one numbered 42 has, I notice, a singular resemblance to Tennyson.

December 3. I suppose it is in great measure due to my improved health, and the great amount of exercise I take, that I have had moments of strange peace lately. If I awake in the night, I lie thinking of only the pleasantest things, and experience a strange revival of some of the feelings of my boyhood—the peculiar love of art, etc.

December 4. To St. Pietro in Vincoli, and gazed long at Michelangelo's *Moses.* Thence to the Colosseum and walked about it for an hour. On to the Forum, where I made the acquaintance of an American, a good sort of fellow, without education. He began by addressing me: " Well, can you locate it ? " Unable to speak a word of any language but English, he was getting along in strange fashion, of course being swindled everywhere. We walked about the Forum, then had lunch, then turned southwards to the Porta San Sebastiano, and out on to the Appian Way, as far as the tomb of Cecilia Metellus. I overtired myself and got back in extreme exhaustion. For all that, went to the Biblioteca, just because I had ordered the book, and at 10 o'clock got home in state of utter deadness.

December 8. Most of the day spent in Forum and Colosseum. The latter irritates me. I can't understand the arrangements, and have access to no good book. The guide-books are futile. Again and again I try to distinguish clearly the various rows of seats, and cannot determine their exact position.

The weather is still brilliant ; I notice the blueness of sky far more than in Naples. I suppose because I always see it from between houses.

Grubbed about the Temple of Julius Caesar, and from the basement picked up some bits of pottery which must be very old, seeing that the digging out of the basement only has exposed them.

Also found a number of curious snails, and brought away.

Walked through the Velabrum, to the site of the Forum

Boarium. Turned aside to look at the Cloaca Maxima. Saw the church called Bocca della Verità : to round Temple called of Vesta, and the Temple of Fortuna Virilis, with its fine columns and basements. The Ponte Rotto is stopped; a new bridge seems to be building there. The whole locality in state of ruin—indeed that applies to the greater part of modern Rome just now ; everywhere new streets are being made.

As I ascend homewards from the Forum, I always hear singing in my head:

Dum Capitolium
Scandet cum tacita virgine pontifex.

After dinner, home and read Horace's First Epistle. At 9 o'clock went out to see, for the first time, the aspect of Rome at night. It being the " Immaculate Conception," there was flaring illumination on the top of the Church of Trinità de' Monti, up between the turrets. The effect from the Via de' Condotti was very striking; the lights seemed to shine on the summit of an impossibly high building. The main streets all but empty. The electric light is frequent (four lamps gleam around the Column of Augustus) but one doesn't see whom they are for. In search of a little life I went into the Café Venezia, and had coffee ; few people there, and those not at all enlivened by some music that was going on.

December 9. To the Kircher Museum and found very little there that interested me. Away speedily to the Palazzo de' Conservatori. Here found rich matter. The well-preserved half length of Commodus is interesting; for my own part I am not sorry that all the best marble statues have lost their polish, to judge from the effect on this one.

The Wolf of the Capitol; good to see this with one's eyes. The Boy extracting thorn; is this the original of all the existing duplicates ?

Found some good things in the Pinacoteca. Sala I. *A Holy Family, attributed to Giorgione.* Very striking, the Mother has a large illuminated Bible open before her, and with one hand she

points to a text she has just found.   Her look of awe of the
Child shows that the text has some reference to the Messiah,
and perhaps to his fate.   The Child is raised towards her by
Joseph, and it stretches its arms to her.   The colouring rich,
the grouping admirable.   Especially fine, the Virgin's attitude.

Sala II.   *Portrait of Michelangelo*, supposed to be by himself.   Seems to be the original of the engraving I have at
home.   If so, the expression is blander here; has an awakened
look, almost of happiness.

Sala IV.   *Veronese's Europa*.   What a distance between
this treatment of the subject and that we find in antiques!
To begin with the picture combines three different times.   The
main group at left of canvas, shows Europa just seating herself
on a bull, the animal is kissing her foot.   Loves fly in the
air; to the right of that she is seen riding away, her maidens
beside her.   And lastly, in the distance, the bull is swimming
with her over the sea, the maidens crying out.   An odd feature
is, that two animals, on the left a dog, and on the right a cow,
are looking on with clearly expressed astonishment.   I can see
that the grouping and colouring are fine, but the picture is one
of those that gives me no real pleasure.   It would be so, even
if that repugnant blending of these actions were not there.
In such a subject one wants more simplicity, in fact one wants
the antique.

Guercino's St. Petronilla.   I don't know the story.   The
saint is being raised out of her tomb, to be shown to her lover,
who stands by.   A grand picture I think, of enormous size,
occupying all one end of the Hall.   More than I thought
Guercino capable of.

Guido's Sebastian.   Here is the culmination of Sebastianish
sweetness.   Take his head alone and it belongs to a very
charming girl.

The Sale dei Conservatori were open, I am glad to see.

Went to the Palatine and by degrees got an idea of the plan
of the Palaces.   It was a good idea to set up a board with
appropriate quotations from Latin authors.   In the gardens
between the Palace of Caligula and that of Tiberius, large pink

roses are in bloom, and several trees heavy with oranges. Warm sunshine. From the hilltop, I remarked well the situation of the Circus Maximus. Of the seven hills, the Capitoline, Palatine, Aventine and Quirinal are still well distinguishable ; the others scarcely rise as distinct hills. Of course the Janiculus is plain enough.

The Romans of to-day are a very orderly people, but they have a bad habit of scribbling their names on objects of interest. Some statues and busts are completely disfigured with pencilling.

Happened to read in Murray, Byron's stanza on the Palatine. What poor stuff it is! And I am afraid the same applies to the greater part of *Childe Harolde*. I seldom see a quotation but it strikes me as feeble.

Thence to the Pincian, to hear the band and see the sun set. There is absolutely no rowdy element in public gatherings here, though the working classes are well represented. The Romans are generally grave and always rather silent. I looked for beautiful faces and could find hardly any. Some pretty ones but these with a tendency to be coarse and stupid. Now and then a very pure contour, and these generally of grave expression. The picturesque costumes of the nurses carrying babies; much white, and brilliant head-dresses. The head-dress of plain black lace common in lower classes. The elegant soldiery represented; but they look best in their mantelli at night.

Monday, December 10. To the Vatican for the first time, and spent the morning in merely *orienteering* myself. Impossible to look at anything, what with the excitement of being on such ground and the agitation which invariably disturbs me amid unfamiliar surroundings.

The impression I brought away was, that it is a good thing only *old* men are elected Pope. A young man, finding himself in possession of such a palace, would surely go mad.

December 11. There are no street organs in Rome, and by the bye, there were none in Paris. I regret it. In Naples the monotony of tunes was astonishing but I preferred that to none. An interesting feature of the by streets are the splendid teams of oxen bringing in loads of straw, etc. from the country. These fine beasts, with their immense horns, always make me think of the antique. Such animals Virgil saw, and Homer, I suppose. The oxen at Naples were of larger size, marvellous beasts, but they haven't the same long horns.

On my way to Vatican, crossed the Bridge at Ripetta. All the district on the other side, but that in the Castle St. Angelo, marked in the map as occupied by the Villa Salonge and Villa Altovili, is now being built upon, and great square ugly barrack-like houses are rising thick. Indeed modern Rome is extremely ugly.

For an hour gave good attention to the *Last Judgment* and the *ceiling*. How it enrages one to see the coarse drapery that has been daubed on to some of the finest figures—thus defeating M. A.'s very purpose, for they are always figures seen in some strange position, with wonderful foreshortenings! In revenge, one chuckles over the portrait of Messer Biagio di Asena, with his ass's ears.

When I began to examine the painting at about 9.30 the light was poor, with difficulty I made out details; between 10 and 11 everything was much clearer, and that seems to be the best time.

I suppose few people notice the face of Satan (is it not?), which looks out from the cave at the bottom. A terrible face with white eyes and white teeth; throwing upwards a fearful look of rage and hatred.

What impressed me most to-day was the left hand bottom group, the dead rising from their graves. It is awful beyond words, to see those skeletons re-assuming flesh. Some but half transformed, indescribable things between corruption and life. In the foreground at the bottom is a fearful face, half putrid, just waking from death with a sort of nameless horror in its look. Then the man who just turns in his grave. The awed hope on some of the faces.

I turned to the ceiling. What are the exquisite figures seated on the beams that divide the nine spaces? I don't find them mentioned either in Murray or Baedeker. One of them,

on the last beam but one at further end, is obliterated all but
hand and foot.   The guardian told me it was the result of the
explosion of the powder magazine at St. Angelo.   The ruin
seems to have been whitewashed over.

Off to Sybils ; I suppose the Delphic is my favourite.   By
the bye it would be very difficult to decide whether the archi-
tectural shaping of the roof were actual or merely painted.
The illusion constantly troubles me.   All the pictures of
the ceiling have to be seen with one's face towards the
Last Judgment.

What defence can any one contrive for the monstrous practice
of putting fine pictures on high ceilings, or on any ceilings at
all ?

Went to the Loggia.   Yes, I like these Bible pictures better
than anything else of Raphael's that I know.   They fill me
with keenest joy.   The clear colouring, the sweet idyllic treatment, the exquisite landscape; it is the Bible made into a fairy
tale, of the most touching kind.   That lovely picture of Jacob
with his flock, meeting Rachel and Leah at the well.   Those
that have suffered most by damp are naturally the squares on the
outer side all along.   But most are nobly preserved, and the
colours fernlike in their freshness.   What a sweet and gentle
idealism there is here.   They bring back to me the early long-
ings of the days when I copied several of them from outline
engravings that father possessed.

Had lunch and went round the Museum.   Went carefully
through a few halls.

December 12.   *The Sala Rotunda.*   All round are glorious busts.
If the eye suddenly falls on that of Antinous from a little distance,
one no longer wonders that so many likenesses of the man were
made; a divine profile.   Two Jupiters, that called of Otricoli
and the Jupiter Serapis.   The former the more majestic; the
latter remarkable for a divine placidity.   The former has one
deep line across his forehead ; one might almost attribute to him
something of his care of rule, and something of pity for mankind.   The Serapis is above care of all kinds, a sublime and
passionless reverie holds him; the face is unutterably bland.

There is a bust representing Epimenides asleep? Why? Epicurus is remarkable for the large nose. From the Belvedere window there was a glorious view to-day. Much snow to be seen on the further Apennines. The colour of the hills recalling Naples. Just in front of the window, on the balcony, is a fine old dial, with the names of the winds in Greek and Latin all round it.

Galleria delle Statue. The two seated statues of Poseilippos and Menandros. One sees that it was the custom to throw large cushions across the marble Greek chairs. Baedeker says that these two were long worshipped as saints at San Lorenzo in Panisperna. One chuckles to think of it.

Friday, December 14. Went to the Vatican. The Chapel for an hour, studying the prophets and sybils; then to the Loggia where my delight increases. By the bye, the painting of these frescoes was done by pupils, Giulio Romano, etc.; but, of course, the designs are Raphael's. Wonderful how the pupils in those days could be trusted to carry out a master's ideas. I think the " Abraham and Melchizedek " is about the finest of all for colour, perhaps also for grouping; the fine effect of the large jars in front. " Joseph telling his Dream " is exquisite; the grouping splendid.

Back home by 1 o'clock and passed afternoon in reading Poynter's *Italian Painting.*

To his sister Margaret :

ROMA
December 17 1888.

To you the letter this time, no doubt you will kindly send it on for perusal at Broadway. Herewith I enclose some New Year cards. I have got something else for little Enid [his niece] to remember that I was in the City of Rome during the first month of her existence. Chi sa ? as we say here. Who knows ? By the time that she can understand it, perhaps I myself shall be nothing but a memory.

L.G.G.   R

Where am I to begin, in telling you about Rome ? In the first few days I was in despair; it seemed to me that I should never see anything, so difficult was it to make a beginning in this inexhaustible world. However, I have seen and studied a great deal, and already the end of my stay draws near. A year would be utterly inadequate and I can give only a month, but I hope to come again, and more than once.

The change in passing from Naples to Rome is inexpressible. One is no longer in the same country, no longer among the same people. Then, there are the indescribable Italian tints on the Alban and the Sabine hills, but to see them you must climb to some high place; the streets of modern Rome are monotonous and wearisome to an incredible degree, and there is absolutely no picturesqueness in the common life of the people. Rome is very silent. Never a street organ—not one ; never a man crying his wares. To be sure it makes it much pleasanter to walk about than in Naples. There you can't go a yard without being importuned on one account or another. Here you are never addressed. The people are grave, decent, sober; very good-natured, but also, it seems, very dull. No, it is not the same nation as in South Italy.

The roads in the neighbourhood of the town have just one piece of picturesque life to show—and that is the splendid yoke of oxen, that draw the carts from the Campagna; magnificent beasts these, though scarcely as large as the Neapolitan ones. Whenever a team passes me I stop to look at them with delight ; they always bring to my mind antique statues and bas-reliefs. They have enormous horns and plod along with a stately dignity which is not to be described. Such oxen Homer had in mind, and Virgil. A ring is put through their noses and a rope attached to this goes up over their foreheads and between their horns serving to guide them. Ah, if you could see these splendid beasts!

The first week I gave to the old part of the city—the Forum, the Colosseum, etc.—and to a few of the galleries in the private palaces. The Borghese, Babarini, Corsini, etc. These palaces are very generously thrown open to the public on certain days in the week; the number of such private collections is very great, and I cannot hope to see them all. One or two of the palaces are gorgeous; the most interesting to me is the Farnesina which is open only on the 1st and 15th of every month.   Last Saturday was the 15th and I rushed there, for the palace contains some of the very finest of Raphael's frescoes.

For several days I studied the Forum conscientiously.   In the course of centuries, what with ruin and traffic, the ground has risen to a height of some 15 feet above the old level, so that the Forum, as it is more dug out and exposed, lies like a deep valley among the modern highways.   There you may wander at will, and without payment from 10 o'clock to sunset.

The ruins are very fragmentary but nearly all have been identified and one walks among places that have been familiar to one's imagination since Harrison's Back Lane School [Wakefield].   The paving of the Via Sacra is still preserved in many places, and on these very stones the old Romans took their daily walks, and everywhere are ruts worn by old Roman wheels —like in Pompeii.

The most interesting spot to me is a pile of rubble on which there once stood a temple, and it was the temple of Julius Caesar, built by Augustus.   On the spot the body of Caesar was burnt ; on this spot Mark Anthony delivered his great oration, and here it was that Tiberius spoke the funeral speech over Augustus.   These are undoubted facts and one has the strangest feelings in standing by such a place.   Of the temple here and there just a few columns remain.   But I have got some good photographs and I hope we shall talk it over before long.

Of the Colosseum little can be said.   It is terrific.   To stand on one of those broken stair-cases, and to think that here, actually here, a Roman crowd once rushed up to see gladiators fight, and Christians devoured by wild beasts, is as strange an experience as life can give.   I went there a few evenings ago to see it by moonlight.   The impression was awesome—almost too much to endure.

The seven hills are clearly distinguishable from any high

spot, as, for instance, from the Janiculum, on the other side of
the Tiber, where is the Church of San Pietro in Montorio,
said to be built on the spot where Peter was crucified and
commanding an admirable view.   Nearest are the Capitoline,
Palatine, and Aventine Hills; the outer semi-circle is the
Quirinal, Viminal, Esquiline and Cælian.   The Palatine is not
inhabited, it is covered with ruins of the palaces of the Caesars.
Impossible to give you an idea of these ruins.   The walls that
remain are huge, but they are not a thousandth part of the old
buildings ; and, moreover, they are only the brick skeleton; all
their clothing of marble is gone.   All gone but just a few
scraps of exquisite carving, a few bits of columns, a few square
feet of coloured marble pavement, just enough to show you that
the splendour of these places surpassed all imagination.   I
thought I had formed an idea of ancient Rome but I had
done nothing of the kind.   I had not a notion of such
magnificence.   What paltry houses our modern towns consist
of in comparison!

In one of the palaces on the Palatine you see what used to be
the judgment hall of the Emperors.   It is a vast space with a
semi-circular tribunal at one end, where the Emperor sat.
There are a few scraps of the variegated marble floor remaining
and even a little bit of a beautiful marble trellis that divided the
tribunal from the hall.   Stand there, and think of the poor
creatures who have trembled on that spot of ground, in face of
Caesar Augustus!   At one moment I burst out laughing, at
another I felt miserable and uncomfortable.

Here and there one sees bits of the very oldest wall, the wall
which enclosed Rome when its site was only the Palatine—the
Rome of the Kings.   A wall built of huge blocks of tufa without
mortar, what a wall!   And doubtless much more than 2,000
years old.

Till the second week, I did not dare to think of the Vatican,
for I knew that if I once got there I should have to go day after
day, and be tormented with the thought that there are so many
things in old Rome that I had not yet seen.   But at last the
time came.   The Vatican has 8 grand staircases, 200 small

ones, and 4,422 rooms! Well, fortunately one has not to see
it all; only two little corners are open to the public. One
contains the paintings of Michelangelo and Raphael, with a
general picture gallery; the other (which you reach after a walk
of nearly a mile), contains the incomparable galleries of sculpture.
You have to obtain tickets of admission from the Pope's Major-
domo, but it is a mere formality. Unfortunately, here too one
has to give gratuities, sometimes as many as *five* in a morning's
walk through the rooms. The Italians are shameless in such
matters.

After getting my card of admission, I went up to the Scala
Regia—a sublime staircase—and at length, very tired, found
myself before a dark little door on which was written " Cappella
Sistina." I knocked and was admitted. I was in the Sistine
Chapel amid the greatest works in painting that the world can
shew. That first morning I saw nothing; impossible to take in
more than the situation of the place and to stare like an idiot
at walls and ceilings. You know that the one end wall is
covered with Michelangelo's " Last Judgment," and that the
ceiling is painted in the most incredible way, also by Michelangelo. The second morning I began to study, and at the end
of a week I had got a faint idea of what was to be seen in that
one chapel. The " Last Judgment " alone would require
months of observation; and the ceiling even more, you have to
exhaust yourself and half break your neck in studying it. That
idiotic practice of putting great works on the ceiling of a high
room! Why, I can't even distinguish the figures without my
opera glass! I shan't attempt to describe what is to be seen
there, some day we must talk about it. It crushes one in its
stupendous excellence.

You know that my enthusiasm for painting is not slight,
yet I think I derive even more pleasure from sculpture. In the
museums of the Vatican I walk about in a state of exultation,
waving my arms and *shouting* in a suppressed voice.

The weather this last week has been bitterly cold, and, of
course, there is no means of making a fire in my room and no
fireplace. In some of the museums there are braziers, with

burning charcoal, but they are of little use.   Ten days ago when
I was on the Palatine I found a garden full of large pink roses;
yesterday when I went there again I found the frost had killed
them all, or nearly all.   However, to-day the weather has
changed again, and it has been like summer.

What a walk I have had!   I went first of all to see a celebrated modern church—St. Paul's outside the Walls.   I
think this the most magnificent I have seen except St. Peter's.
You can walk on coloured marbles which reflect the rows of
enormous marble columns, and the ceiling is one mass of gilded
ornament.   Well, from there I cut across the country into the
" Via Appia."   It was, as you know, the main highway of the
Romans southwards, and about 50 years ago it was cleared of
the obstruction of the middle ages.   Mile after mile on each side
are the ruins of Roman tombs, whilst to the left hand, away on
the Campagna, you see the vast old aqueducts, some of which
still supply Rome with water.

A glorious walk!   At the distance of a couple of miles from
the city, it is so still that you can hear the sheep nibbling the
grass.   A vast plain of uncultivated land stretches on either
side.   Far away are the Sabine and the Alban Hills and beyond
them the peaks of the Apennines gleaming with snow.   It is a
wonderful thing to walk along the road, where generations of
Romans have gone about their pleasure and their business, and
to look at the vast ruins of tombs—robbed of their marble
clothing—on this side and that.   Now and then one finds a
legible inscription.   One I copied, and the translation is this:
" This monument is erected to Marcus Caecilius.   Stranger,
I am grateful when you sit down by my resting-place.   May
you prosper in business and in health, and may your sleep be
without care ! "   The Latin spelling is very antique; it was
written at least 2,000 years ago.

Wherever you go it is the same.   Everywhere the wonderful
antiquity haunts you.   The Roman life and literature becomes
real in a way hitherto inconceivable.   I must begin to study it
all over again; I must go to school again and for the rest of my
life.   Ah, if only I could have come here years ago!

Horace begins one of his poems with saying " Do you see how Soracte stands there covered with white snow ? " And almost every day I see that mountain Soracte in the far distance, though not as yet with snow on it. I shouted with delight the first time I recognised it.

The Tiber is a strange river. Horace calls it " flavus," which means " təwny," and to this day it is the exact colour of it. It is deep yellow, and, when the sun shines on it, seems almost solid; this comes from its mixture with the earth from which it flows. Its breadth is about that of the Calder [Wake-field] ; I must confess that the Calder is every bit as picturesque— at all events within the city. Still there is the Tiber, and the most interesting river in the world.

A word about St. Peter's. Of course I cannot describe it. One has to go there several times before one gets an idea of the size of it. That idea is best got, I think, by watching the men who sweep the marble floor. They have enormous besoms and their work is something like having to sweep Trafalgar Square. They seem to make no progress at all, when in reality they are getting on as fast as possible. The dome can only be appreciated from a considerable distance, when it is compared with multitudinous other domes. As, for instance, from the Pincian Hill, at the foot of which I live. The top of the hill is laid out with gardens, and is the fashionable resort of wealthy Rome. Here, every evening at sunset, you see multitudes of carriages, a sort of Rotten Row. The view is glorious, and the dome of St Peter's in the distance, stands up, right on the horizon. There a band plays several evenings a week, and a good band. It is delightful to walk there and see the sun set. If you remember *The Newcomes* well, you will know all about the Pincian.

I eat at purely Italian cook-shops and manage it very cheaply. This is where I gain over the ordinary foreigners who are obliged, whether by prejudice, or, more often by ignorance of Italian, to go to dear places where French is spoken. The other day I met an unfortunate American who was crazy when I took him to an Italian Restaurant, and gave him an excellent

dinner for little more than a franc; he had been paying three
times as much for a worse meal at his hotel.

Well, I have told you nothing. I can't help it. If we
live, I shall see you at the end of February, and then there
will be some talking.

Diary :

December 14. Woke early this morning and enjoyed
wonderful happiness of mind. It occurs to me, is not this
partly due to the fact that I spend my days solely in the consideration of beautiful things, wholly undisturbed by base
necessities and considerations? In any case the experience is
most remarkable.

December 19. To-day I have been to Veii. I had thought
it too far for a walk, but managed it, with a good deal of
weariness at the end. Took the train to Ponte Molle and
thence tramped up into the Campagna by the Via Cassia.
From the 6th milestone the road is paved like the streets of
Rome, with small diamonds of lava, bordered with diamonds of
larger size; on either side is a broad walk unpaved.

Not far after La Storta, which used to be the last relay
before Rome—the road parts; left hand to Bracciano, right to
Viterbo. I followed the latter, and, at a short distance, by the
first road off to the right, was led to Isola Farnese. This is
supposed to have been the Arx of Veii. In middle ages was a
stronghold.

I spoke to the priest who was walking up and down the
street; the shabbiest priest I have yet seen, and evidently quite
uneducated. He found a guide for me to the ruins, which are
on the property of a farmer, who keeps a key to the painted tomb
—called here "La Grotta." A lad set out with me, and we
had a long difficult walk, impossible to find the way alone;
wild tracks over brushwood and moor and hill. Saw the
Ponte Sodo. The stream believed to be the Cremera, the
Columbarium and the Tomb. The last very interesting.

The guide lit a candle which was insufficient, but I just

made out the paintings on the walls and the fine great Etruscan vases, which have been left just as when the tomb was found. On the tufa walls the chisel marks are distinct.   Brought away a bit of tufa from inside.

I find in Murray that during late years nearly all the ruins of Veii have been destroyed; there used to be traces of walls and gates, etc. ; now nothing but what I have mentioned.   Still I noticed that all over the fields lay scraps of pottery and brick and cut stone; I suppose they must all be remains of one period or another.

December 21.   Note from Walter Grahame, in which he tells me that Mrs. Woods has printed a volume of poems for private circulation, and that her sister Miss Bradley has a copy for me.

This morning a second visit to the Borghese Gallery, taking Poynter's little *Italian Painting* with me, and seriously studying the first three rooms.

In afternoon to the Vatican Museum.   Lounged with delight in my favourite Sala Rotonda.   Leaving the Museum, turned into St. Peter's and was in time to hear Vespers sung in the Choir-chapel.

December 24.   Proved an exquisite afternoon, clouded, but with soft rays of sunlight, and warm.   Climbed some stairs on the S.E. end of Colosseum, and sat there looking over the arch of Constantine, whilst soldiers were drilling on the ground just below me.   The Colosseum is a ruin, but soldiers and slaughter still thrive.   Went down into the *Mamertine Prisons*—a terrible place.   Stairs have been made down into the lower hole, to which originally only the round hole in the upper floor led.   The upper prison made into an oratory; in that below is a spring shown as having miraculously arisen when Peter and Paul were here. Thought of Jugurtha, of the Catilinarian conspirators. Thence to San Giovanni in Laterano and examined the church which pleased me.   The façade is beautiful and the view from it one of the most charming I know in Rome.   Better still from the steps which go up to the so-called Triclinium Leo III. just opposite. In front the Sabine and Alban Hills, with just a tip of the Volscian between. In the foreground the fine arcaded city wall, with the gate of San Giovanni and the older Roman gate hidden by trees. Beyond the walls the long stretch of the Aqua Claudia. The faint sunlight gave a singular white gleam to the top of the Sabine Hills; I thought at first there was snow on them. Walked across by the Via Merulana to Santa Maria Maggiore, and thence all the way down the Esquiline, by the Via Urbana, Via Baccina, and Via Bonella to the Forum. This part of Rome thickly populated with working class ; the streets to-day one continuous market ; reminded me of Naples a little. A good deal of merriment going on as always in Rome, much good temper.

Saw for the first time the three remaining columns of the Temple of Mars Ultor, which stood on the Forum of Augustus. It makes one's heart sink to look at these remnants of glorious buildings, wedged into mean streets.

Tuesday, December 25, *Christmas Day.* Bright sunshine the first thing, but soon darkened, and at 10 o'clock a severe thunderstorm. I was then in St. Peter's, where I remained from 9.30 to 12 hearing service after service in the Cappella del Coro. Masses were going on in nearly all the chapels. Again a strange effect produced by listening for a long time to these resonant voices chanting their psalms, etc., and watching the richly clad priests go about their wonderful ritual. At one moment contempt for them all, at another reverence, seeing that they represent a system which was once so powerful and embodies so much human intellect.

By the bye, it must be a great undertaking to learn the routine of these offices.

Friday, December 28. In morning to St. Peter's, ascended the Cupola, going right up to the ball, where I didn't feel at all comfortable. Of course glorious view though misty. Saw the full extent of the Vatican and its gardens: much snow on Apennines. Then a farewell hour on the Sistine Chapel, where there were a great number of people. Again admired the exquisite beauty of those figures between the pictures of the ceiling. Let no man say that Michelangelo is always rugged!

Walked on to the Lateran Museum which I had always postponed.

December 30. *Florence.* Good night's rest—an unknown thing to me in a new place. To-day fine but cloudy, and a little sun. It being Sunday, resolved to reconnoitre as many of the galleries as possible; thus saving expense. I am never able really to see the pictures at a first visit. Went to the Uffizi, the Pitti, the Museo of the Bargello, and the Belle Arti. Something like despair is the result; it is cruel to have my opportunities of study curtailed by having to pay a lira each visit. Familiarized myself with the outside of the chief buildings. Unfortunately the Campanile has got scaffolding near the top, which spoils the aspect.

Delightfully impressed by first view of Florence. A wearying day, but I am nothing like as tired after it as I should have been three months ago.

December 31. At 11 o'clock (p.m.) wandered out into the streets to see the end of the old year. In the Piazza del Duomo a male soprano singing to a guitar.

Finally was tempted into the Ristorante Etruria and had a supper of cignale—in vast discomfort, owing to the place being full of Italians in exuberant spirits who were supping at table d'hôte. It made me feel wretched. At midnight they all began to shout and stamp and ring bells—a terrific uproar. I rushed out into the streets.

To his sister Ellen :

FIRENZE,
December 31, 1888.

It is the last day of the year and I cannot better spend some part of the evening than in writing to all in England an account of the last fortnight. I always feel the painful unsatisfactoriness

of these letters. They might as well be pages copied from
the guide-book, so insufficiently do they express all that I daily
learn and enjoy. But I have no time for more. I hope to
tell you about things better before long.

Since that one week of cold weather in Rome things have
returned to their normal state, and the days are very mild—at
times decidedly warm. The only drawback is frequent rain.
Rainclouds often make the sky of Italy every bit as dull as that
of England. And, in Florence, at this time of year, there
prevails a sort of autumnal mist, which spoils the views from the
hills. What those views are, there is no imagining. I have
been up to-day to a height on the south of the city, where is
the Church of San Miniato. Great heavens! The view of
the Arno Valley from that height!

The journey from Rome was pleasant; it only took from
1.30 p.m. to 8.30 p.m. So that I had the first half in daylight.
The most striking thing I saw was this—about half an hour
after leaving Rome, I looked out of the window, and saw in
the far distance, right on the horizon, a great and wonderful
Dome, splendidly outlined against the sky. It was St. Peter's.
Not a trace of the city to be seen, but only that wonderful
Dome (to the top of which, by the bye, I had ascended on the
previous day—up into the very ball on which stands the Cross),
seeming to stand alone in the midst of the desert Campagna!
It must be a most impressive sight for those who approach
Rome for the first time by this route.

Alas, it had already become dark when the train passed all
along the shore of Lake Trasimenus. I would have given a
sovereign to see it. I heard the rumbling of the train over a
stretch of viaduct—but that was all.

Modern Rome is an insufferable place. To live there at
present is just the same as occupying a house which is in the
hands of carpenters, upholsterers and builders. Not a street
where there is not extensive pulling down and rebuilding going
on. All the ways are inches thick in mud. Of picturesqueness
in the town itself there is nothing whatever. But, thank
goodness, the old Rome still remains, indeed is constantly

being increased by excavations, and no words can express the interest of it. It is a great and wonderful thing to me that Rome is no longer a name. The Forum I know well as I know 7K [Cornwall Residences]; I have walked daily upon the Via Sacra; I have made glorious tramps along the Via Appia, out towards Alba Longa; I have seen every aspect of the Colosseum; I have tracked out all the ruins of the Caesars' Palaces on the Palatine. All these things are realities to me, and, as long as I keep my memory, no one can rob me of them. Day after day I climbed the sacred Capitoline, and from it I saw the same hills that Cicero and Virgil and Horace saw. The Tiber is an old friend—my life is richer a thousand times —aye a million times—than six months ago. I am no longer ignorant of the best things the world contains. It only now remains for me to go to Greece, then I shall have all the ground-work of education. The education itself must be the work of my life.

I have got a book full of notes on the galleries. Day after day I write an endless list of observations. Some day I must read them to you.

Italian is, of course, a tolerably familiar language to me. But for that knowledge, it is terrible to think of the money I must have spent. How I pity the poor people I see dragged about by guides speaking broken English! I am, in such matters, quite independent.

Many and many an hour I spent at the Vatican. I am bringing back some priceless photographs of pictures and statuary. Magnificent photographs obtainable here for 5d. a-piece, twice cabinet size.

I told you on a postcard that I had spent a day at Veii, or rather in the spot where Veii once was. All that remains is a few bits of stone structure, and one most interesting tomb, discovered only a few years ago. This tomb has been left just as it was found; you go in with a candle, and inside are a number of splendid Etruscan vases; on the walls are strange grotesque paintings, perhaps done more than two thousand five hundred years ago. Save these poor relics, not a scrap left of what was once a great and flourishing city! It is in the middle of the Campagna, and close by is a miserable little village, which in summer is desolated with malaria. The shepherds who live there go about wrapped in undressed goat skins, a strange sight. No one could possibly find the site of Veii alone; I had to take a guide, and it was a very laborious day. I stood there in the midst of the desert, and thought and thought till I could think no longer.

You have probably seen from the newspapers that Gladstone has taken a villa at Posillipo for the winter. My window at Naples used to look right into Posillipo, and I follow with much interest all the accounts in the Italian papers of his doings. Here (at Rome also) I regularly get the " Corrière di Napoli " which is about the only readable " daily " published in this country; it is like an old friend to me now. Of course it makes comical mistakes ; on Gladstone's arrival, it had an enthusiastic leading article, which began—" Sir Guglielmo Gladstone." Then, next day, it referred to him several times as " Sir Gladstone." I shall bring home several copies of this newspaper for the amusement of you all.

I am making a few miserable sketches of places and things that take my fancy. They are abominable beyond description, but perhaps they will help you to see some of the glorious things which are now familiar to me.

To-day I have been tempted into a wild piece of extravagance, but the thing was quite irresistible. Walking along the street which skirts the Arno, I came to a bookseller's with English books in the window, and then—what do you think ?—I saw a whole series of the American reprints of Ruskin's works. Now the American prices for these books vary from sixpence to a shilling a volume—incredible as it sounds; here they were priced at from a shilling to half-a-crown. Without a thought of expense I rushed into the shop, and seized on four volumes—one *Mornings in Florence*, another *St. Mark's Rest*, which is a guide to Venice.

Many a time, in spite of all the glories of Northern Italy, I look back to the South with a sense of something lost. At

Naples I was just in time for the last days of autumn, and the
impression produced by that season of glorious weather, of
fruit time and luxury in general, will always remain. The
South of Italy is a land of incredible fertility. It seems
impossible that anyone there can suffer from want. The
" Corrière " describes every day the appearance of the Naples
streets at this Christmastime. Every shop is bursting with
things to eat and drink; every street and lane and alley over-
flows with good things. I must see that country in its glory,
in the height of springtime, and when every thing is just ripe
in autumn. They tell me there is no picturing the colours of
that landscape when all the leafage is flourishing, and when
the sunlight is at its best. A man I talked to in Capri threw
up his arms in despair at his inability to describe the gorgeous
colours of a summer sunset over the bay of Naples. Everything glows and flames with splendour. Ah, and the delightful air of happiness and enjoyment of life which you find
everywhere. Everywhere music, singing, laughing, shouting,
quarrelling. I cannot tell you how I miss these Neapolitan
organs. Here, as in Rome, never a note of music; in that
respect it is very disappointing, for Italy. How well I can
hear the tune that was played by the organs the very first
night that I walked about the streets of Naples! How warm
it was! How brightly the shops were lighted! What life
this, all along the Via Roma!

This seems ungrateful, for, after all, this, where I now am,
is the country of Art. The explanation is simple. Here, as
in Rome, I often suffer a little from loneliness; in Naples I
never did so, owing to the fact that the joyousness of life about
me always made a kind of society. There was always a feeling
of sympathy in the people about me. Since then I have often
wished to have someone to speak to. In the train, when I
saw that magnificent view of St. Peter's, I could no longer
contain myself, and I turned to an Italian, who, with a good old
woman, his mother, was travelling in the same carriage. " Si
vede San Pietro benissimo da qui ! " I exclaimed to him.
And both he and his mother came to the window to look.

On the whole I like the Italians much.   They have plenty
of failings, and can, at times, be intolerable; but beyond all
comparison they are better than the French.   There is a
genuine good-nature in them which constantly shows itself.
The Italian officials are, at all times, polite and eager to assist;
whereas the Frenchman in office, is, for the most part, a
detestable creature.   I shall never forget the gentlemanliness
of the custodian at Paestum, and I have known many others
like him.   The faults which mark the Italians are those of
poverty, and you notice this most of all in the South, the faults
induced by ages of slavery.   They have got into their heads
that all foreigners are rolling in money and consequently they
do their best to get a share of it.   The impudence of the worst
of them is beyond belief.   When I was at Camaldoli, I asked a
fellow to guide me to the monastery.   The distance was about
a hundred yards, but I could not find the way alone.   " How
much do you ask ? " I said.   And the reply, very coolly given,
was " Ten francs! "   Whereupon I burst into obstreperous
laughter, and speedily found a guide who took me to the place
for threepence!

January 1, 1889.   " Oggi è festa ! "   The English do not
know what that means, but we hear it very often in Italy.
This evening the streets are crowded with people, and, as I
write, the bells of the great cathedral are sounding freely.
" Oggi è festa ! " and in a double sense.   I wonder what kind
of weather you have had to-day ?   Here it has been
brilliant summer as England never sees.   I have spent the day
at Fiesole.   The view from it of the Valley of the Arno is
unthinkable by man.   There I saw roses in full bloom in open
gardens !   And the sky—no invented colour has ever painted
that sky.   I wish you could see the effect of cypress-trees
standing out against it !   For three hours I sat there, reading
and dozing, and the warmth of the air was delicious.   Until
1 o'clock a soft haze veiled the city of Florence; then it rose
in light feathery clouds and every building was discernible.

To his brother :

January 2, 1889.

To be sure Florence does not appeal to me as much as Rome, or even as Naples. Christian art has not the unspeakable charm that I find in the Pagan relics and memories. Florence is the city of the Renaissance, but after all the Renaissance was only a shadow of the great times, and like a shadow it has passed away. There is nothing here that impresses me like the poorest of Rome's antiquities.

But there is unspeakable natural beauty. Tongue of man cannot describe the view from the heights on either side of Florence. Fiesole is glorious and no wonder old Landor established himself there. By the bye, I want you to tell me whether your *Life of Landor* contains any indication whereby I could discover his villa. Please let me know if it does. Baedeker, being a German, of course says nothing about it. Dickens found the place when he was here. I remember from Forster.

Diary :

January 13. In afternoon to Uffizi where I examined the Venetian schools.

January 15. A day spent in the house, thinking of the novel I must write when I get back home. No very good results.

Gissing was frequently ill during his stay in Florence, partly on account of the very cold weather of which he complains continually.

To his sister Ellen :

January 22, 1889.

They write and tell me the fogs in London have been terrific. I am very glad to have missed them, but I have very often missed, in another sense, the English fireplaces. It can

be terribly cold in Italy.   I wonder whether your house can
be made warm.   For my own part I get more and more
incapable of enduring cold and I fancy I shall always have to
flee from it.   You would scarcely believe that I shut up
Golden Treasury the other day because my eye—inopportunely
—fell on the words " Along the *cool* sequestered vale, etc."
It spoiled the whole poem for me.   Of course this is grotesque,
but absolutely truthful.

I have given up the idea of letting 7K for this summer,
but shall try and get rid of it by the winter following.   I shall
have to set to work at once on my return to England.   I
wonder whether you will all be at Wakefield.   A fearsome
journey I shall have from Milan to Antwerp, and then over
the North Sea or German Ocean.   Slow trains, and probably
depths of snow.   At all events I shall get a glimpse of the high
Alps.

To the same :

Firenze,
January 28, 1889.

Your much desired letter has put me into excellent spirits.
Moreover I rejoice to say that after a spell of very severe
weather, yesterday was like the beginning of summer.   And
the same continues to-day.   The sky is so blue that if you gaze
at it for a moment it makes everything black before your eyes.
Last night the rising of the full moon was one of the most
wonderful sights!   With difficulty I could look at it, it was
so brilliant—but they say that in Venice it is yet more
wonderful.

I saw last Saturday's *Athenaeum* at the " Biblioteca Nazion-
ale " yesterday, and find that *The Nether World* is advertised
already for March, so they will have to be quick.

Old Gladstone is enjoying himself rarely at Naples.   The
newspapers make much of him.   It would make you laugh
heartily if you could read the comical extravagances of these
Italian writers.   At Pompeii the other day he was offered a
cup of tea and the reporter says he took it with " squisilissima

affabilità." But that is nothing. I am bringing back some specimen newspapers and hope to read you extracts.

I must end, but you shall soon hear again.

To the same :

Venezia,
February 5, 1889.

Here is a picture for you:

I open my window at a quarter to eight this morning. Dark below me and dark in either direction are the waters of the Grand Canal, which ebbs and flows (for the sea here has tides) against the walls of the house in which I live. Dark, but for one unsteady patch of glistening silver—the reflection of the seven days' old moon, up there amid fleecy clouds in the south-west sky. Just opposite stand dimly defined the great Church of S. Maria della Salute, with its vast dome and its campanile. The silence would be absolute, but for the constant gentle splash of an oar, as the gondolas with a light on their prows, steal this way and that. Next to our house is the little landing stage of a ferry from one side to the other of the Canal ; looking down I see half a dozen gondolas lying side by side, and presently one of them moves out, with a passenger, across the dark gulf. The voice of the boatman, even when he speaks in ordinary tone, sounds very loud.

I hear the bells of S. Mark's beginning to toll eight. Then suddenly comes a great echoing boom, that of the gun at San Giorgio, which fires at this hour every night.

Now I am waiting for something. I look away past S. Maria, and presently see a gondola with four red lamps coming silently hitherwards. It draws near to our side and moors itself just in front of a large hotel, two houses distant. I listen intently. There is a soft touching of violins, and the deep rich note of a violoncello. Then suddenly begins a prelude of music, and in a minute is followed by an outburst of singing voices, a chorus, and their song is the " Addio a Napoli." When their song is finished there is clapping of hands from the windows of the houses. But stop, for now I am listening still more earnestly. Again a soft prelude, then one voice only begins to sing, a woman's voice, exquisitely rich and true—this is "street music," but such a voice I have never heard anywhere but in great concert halls, never.

The concert lasts for half an hour, it seems only a few minutes, there is reply to applause and remonstrance, a voice from the boat laughingly calls out "Basta per stasera!" and the four red lamps—the gondola itself invisible—float away towards the Adriatic.

February 7. I must tell you about my journey from Florence. The part to Bologna was most remarkable. You will see from the map that the railway has to go right over the Apennines. It ascends by a winding mountain pass, and the highest point is reached at a place called Pracchia, 1,854 ft. above level of the sea. Before reaching this there are twenty-two tunnels. From Pracchia you descend by the valley of the river Reno, and there are twenty-three more tunnels before Pistoia is reached, making fifty-four in all. The scenery, whenever you get a glimpse of it, is magnificent. The high peaks were thick in snow. There are little villages everywhere, and at the stations stood strange-looking people, gazing curiously at the train. These villages are *conglomerates* of houses some twenty being built all in a heap, as if to prop each other up. The mountains are very rocky and bare; the numerous mountain streams were frozen, and made dazzling white streaks.

Bologna is a wonderful old town. All the streets have broad arcades on both sides, so that people here never need carry umbrellas. There is a leaning tower, indeed it leans frightfully; I shouldn't care to live under it. Bologna has always been renowned for its good cheer, and such fat shops I never saw, wonderful kinds of butter and cheese; cakes incredible! An uproarious place, too; I scarcely got any sleep for the row in the street all night.

Excellent music in many of the cafés, and, indeed, a few organs in the streets.

I got an hour next morning to look in at the picture gallery and saw Raphael's "Saint Cecilia." A glorious picture! I wish I could have stayed longer.

The day proved cold and dull, and very suitable to the country. For miles and miles, as you know, the land has not a hillock. It is mostly planted with rows of vines, between which is grown rice and other grains. We crossed the river Po, a vast muddy river, and actually *above the level* of the plain. Had a dreary view of Ferrara and of Padua, where at last hills appeared. Shelley's "Euganian Hills"—strange conical heights of volcanic formation, like gigantic pyramids far off. Then came the approach to Venice. It was not exactly what I had expected. Very much like the viaduct over Morecambe Bay at low tide.

It rained a little as I came out of the station and found myself on the side of the Grand Canal, at the gondola "stand." I got in with all my traps, and we set off by a most winding course, all small by-canals to the Palazzo Swift. How this house got its name, I know not. My landlady, a good talkative woman, a native of Bologna, makes me very comfortable indeed. I found the place in my Baedeker, who, as always, has proved trustworthy. Blessed be Baedeker!

The dialect of the people is very difficult; indeed, in its pure form, unintelligible to me. And even those people who do not speak the pure dialect have very strange pronunciations. The difference between city and city in the matter of language is remarkable. The first evening here, at dinner, I asked for an apple, calling it, as always, *una mela,* and the waiter absolutely didn't know what I meant. A gentleman bent over and told me the word here was *pomo.* But to think that the other word was absolutely unintelligible.

All day long, in front of my window, splendid white seagulls wheel about and scream, fishing in the canal! One morning it was wild weather, with rain and snow mingled, and the whistling of the wind was precisely as one hears it on board ship in the open sea.

Here is a story. I was sitting at a table in front of a café on the Piazza the other day and a shoe-black came up and began bothering me. " What's the good ? " I cried at last, " it'll rain again directly." " No, no signore," he replied. " I guarantee that it won't rain. If it rains, I'll give you back your money ! " I burst out laughing and let him clean the boots.

February 8. The wind has once more ceased to blow, and to-day has been perfect. The sky a cloudless blue, and a soft autumnal sort of mist all round the horizon. Warm, warm.

Venice and its lagoons are protected from the sea by certain long, narrow islands running from north to south. That nearest Venice is called *Lido*, and thither I went to-day by steamboat. The view of the city on the way is magnificent. Landing on the inner side of the island, I walked at once right across it, and very soon came in view of the open Adriatic, a grand unbroken expanse of bluest sea. Then I walked down the length of the island, a distance of some five miles. At first there is a very fine beach, wide sands, and instead of pebbles there are *shells*. Such an abundance of shells I never saw. I made a great collection, a few very beautiful. Where the beach ends there begins a sort of huge terrace, formed of great rugged blocks of stone heaped up, to make a barrier against the sea.

Walking here in perfect solitude, I found my old associations once more. Here again is a Greek sea. Looking south-east, I knew that over there was fought the battle of Actium, and that a little further away was the land of Hellas.

Here I am, of course busy with the Venetian School of Painting ; Titian and Tintoretto and the rest of them. As for architecture, Venice, as you know, is unrivalled in the modern world, but, unfortunately I care little for any architecture save that of the Greeks and Romans. A pity this ; I feel it is a narrowness of sympathy. But there is no good in pretending interest where you do not really have it. To enjoy myself among buildings, I must be at Paestum. Ah, that glorious Paestum! The old temples of sunny-golden travertine.

The Temples that heard the voice of Greeks! Shall I ever stand there again, and see the far off strip of the Mediterranean, and the rising Valley of the Apennines, and watch the oxen ploughing through the ruins of two thousand years ago? No, whatever my opportunities I shall never spend much time in the Italy of the North. I have seen it, and it is well; but the South is what I shall always long for. Rome, of course, glorious Rome, and all that lies beyond. Next I must see Sicily, where there are finer Greek ruins even than those of Paestum. One of the aims of my life now is to read Thucydides and Theocritus in Sicily.

I am excogitating my next book [*The Emancipated*] and think I have got the outline of something good. I hope to be able to begin upon it as soon as ever I get back. I expect it will be high time.

Diary :

February 10. The snow still on the roofs, but a fine day and warm. Morning at the Accademia. I have tried to interest myself in the S. Ursula series of Carpaccio but cannot. It is some defect in me, doubtless, but the pictures make absolutely no appeal to me. I cannot feel poetry in them. An interesting realism here and there strikes me, but not in sufficient degree to hold my attention. On the other hand, I was greatly interested by two Giovanni Bellini's; one a Madonna with St. George and St. Paul; the other a Madonna between Magdalene and S. Catherine. They are in the Renier Collection. The faces of all are dispassionately meditative. The colouring is beautiful, very warm; the drapery light in a wonderful degree. In these two pictures the figures are half-lengths. I suppose my lack of interest in Carpaccio partly arises from utter carelessness about the subjects—for he is a *subject* painter. The Bellinis may mean anything and simply respond to one's ideals.

Wednesday, February 13. Hurricane all night. This morning our ground floor is quite under water. The Piazza almost the same; water of some kind rushing up through holes.

At high tide the sea more than level with the Piazzetta. A furious wind and bitterly cold; a little snow. Grew calmer towards evening ; feeble sun-set.

Thursday, February 14. Sunny but colder than ever. In the morning first of all to San Zaccaria, and looked at G. Bellini's " Santa Conversazione." It is hung absurdly high; always something wrong with pictures in churches. Then to San Sebastian and saw or tried to see Veronese's work : it profited me little.

A poor unfortunate sacristan. Finding that he spoke hoarsely and breathed hard, I said that I feared that he had caught a cold this bad weather. " No," he replied, with a smile, " I've had it for many years; and cough too." Not many more to come for him, fortunately. I gave him half a franc, and afterwards much wished I had given a whole one. Perhaps shall see him again. He was good and patient, poor fellow.

Saturday, February 16. The most wonderful change in the weather. Not a cloud all day. At 11 went to Lido and sat on the shore till 4 o'clock, under a black-blue sky and hot sun. A splendid view of the Alps, behind Venice. They spread over about 90 degrees of horizon. Thought much of new book.

February 19. At 1.30 in the night two Germans took possession of the room next to mine, and for half an hour talked and laughed at the top of their voices, now in German, now in Italian, with like fluency. Austrians perhaps. Every word audible in my room. They got up at 7 this morning, and shouted and stamped about without the slightest considera-tion for the rest of the house. This is absolutely characteristic of Germans. I know now that they are not calumniated where such grossness is attributed to them. The English rough would be more considerate, but at the same time he would not exclaim about the beauty of the sun-rise, as these fellows did.

In the morning to the Scuola di San Rocco. I know not why I have delayed this visit so long. Cleaning and restoration going on but I enjoyed the pictures more than any I have yet seen in Venice. The custodian upstairs spoke to me of what " Il Professor Roskin " had written on his works.

In afternoon went to look at Tintoret's house. It stands in the Fondamente dei Mori, just to the E. of the Campo dei Mori. A fine old front; inscription and bust. The first floor has pointed windows, with carving; the neighbourhood a very poor one; I noticed that there are still *dyers* about here.

February 26.   Left Venice by the 9.15 train—a dull and cold morning.   Stopped at Milan, too ill to enjoy anything— caught 7.30 train.

February 27.   View of Como, but very gloomy and cold. A magnificent broad and flat vale stretching from the head of Lago Maggiore to Bellinzona.   An indescribable line of railway—train toils up very slowly to the great St. Gotthard tunnel.   Perpetual changes in the magnificent views.

Lucerne a big ugly town; scarcely saw the lake.   The Righi in view.   Decided not to stop at Basel, but to take the train there and go straight on for Brussels.

February 28.   Can scarcely tell how I spent the day, waiting for boat-train.   Walked about the hilly streets, and thought of Charlotte Brontë.

VI

RETURN FROM ITALY TO SETTLEMENT AT EXETER (1889-1891)

Diary :

March 1.   London at 9 o'clock; snowing and streets thick with slush.

March 2.   By the 1.30 to Wakefield.

March 6.   Returned to London.

March 24.   In morning to studio of Alfred Hartley in Chelsea.   I found Hudson sitting.   Hudson, the man I have wished to see for two or three years.   Very striking face; gentle and sympathetic manner.

Spent the evening over the description with which Chapter I of my new novel begins—several hours writing some 20 lines, a terrible business.   But the ground is broken, I think I can get ahead now.

March 26.   No writing, but a long hard evening of mental work.   Found I was not quite ready with details enough for going on.   A rich flow of them this evening.

March 30.   In great trouble about details of my story, but towards evening got it clear.   Read a good deal of Landor —wrote nothing.

April 2.   At 3 o'clock sat down to Chapter II and by 9.30 had written only 2½ pages.   Fearful labour and worked myself into a headache.   The first since I left England last October.

April 6.   Got to work at 3 o'clock and wrote till 11.   Had to go back to beginning of Chapter II and did 4½ pages. Also re-wrote last page of Chapter I.

April 16.   Worked from 3 to 10 and did a little more than 4 pages, but then only a re-writing of what I had done in Chapter IV.   To-morrow I get ahead again; have improved all I have re-written.

To his sister Ellen :

7 K,
April 24, 1889.

Yes, it is long since I wrote, but I have been *acharné* at work.   You will rejoice to hear that I positively approach the end of the first volume and am tolerably pleased with the thing so far.   It is delightful to live over again the Neapolitan days in this manner.   Last night I was at Pompeii with a crowd of most curious people.   You will laugh over them before long, I hope.

As to *The Nether World*, it is not easy for me to realise the horror it seems to excite in you.   Of course I am not in the habit of thinking of it in that way; to me the first thing is vigour of artistic treatment, and your words seem to imply that you appreciated that.   My acquaintances in general seem to think it is the best work I have yet done.   Roberts sat down to the book at 7 p.m. and finished it at 3.30 a.m., says he could not lay it down.   Reviews I shall, of course, not see, except the *Spectator* and that may not come for half a year.   I don't think they can treat the book slightingly.

I am in great health and spirits.   Every morning, rain or shine, I take a walk of an hour and a half; here is one advantage of being free from teaching.   I generally write from 3.30 to 10.30 p.m. or so.

If only I can hold on through the summer in the present state of mind and body, it will be the most remarkable year I have yet passed.   Beyond doubt that five months of rest have done me vast good.

I was looking over an old diary the other day, and made out, to my own astonishment, the following historical statement:

Between July 1885 and March 1886 I wrote three novels : *Isabel Clarendon, A Life's Morning* and *Demos.* I also read through the *Divina Commedia* and supported myself by teaching!

My reading at present is *The Frogs of Aristophanes,* Cicero's letters, *The Tatler* and *Boswell.* You, I suppose, toil in pretty much the usual way.

I was glad to hear how much smoother the Latin got. Tell me if ever you want any book or help of any kind.

Goodness knows when we shall again see each other. But at this rate I ought to have finished the book by the end of July.

Mother's letter pleased me much, my love to her.

Diary :

April 28. A very unsatisfactory day. Nothing done, nothing really read only some mooning over *Boswell.* An hour's walk at mid-day. These long breaks in my writing suit me very ill. Dull day till evening, heaviness upon me. Never am well when I break off my work.

May 1. Got to work at 3 o'clock and wrote till 10. Re-wrote Chapter I. except the first page. This perpetual re-writing seems to be a necessity of my method. I always go at it with stubborn vigour.

May 7. Read some of Woolner's *My Beautiful Lady.* The mental labour over story is at present so great that I cannot attend to any serious reading. Worked from 3.30 to 9.30 and did five pages, being the third chapter.

From May 25 to August 19 of this year Gissing stayed with his mother and sisters in Wakefield, in very poor health, and suffering much from depression. On August 20 he went to Guernsey with his sister Margaret.

Writing to his brother on *August* 3 he says:—Am at the middle of Volume III. of my new book, which I think will be called *The Emancipated.*

To his sister Ellen :

HOTEL DU GOUFFRE, GUERNSEY,
August 29, 1889.

A few lines on the eve of departure for Sark. You already know that we have abandoned our Brittany project.

But we have done very well here and I think a fortnight in Sark will complete the holiday. I went over to the island myself yesterday and after a great deal of hunting under a sun which blazed from a cloudless sky, found very good lodgings. But they were literally the only ones untaken in the island. There are two hotels, but every room is full; and the little houses that take lodgers are all occupied. Sark contains altogether some thirty houses. A wonderful place—two points only where a landing can be effected; elsewhere, the coast is perpendicular granite, with abundant caverns, abysses, arches, and the like.

I grieve that you are having such unspeakable weather. Yesterday and to-day have with us been marvellous—from sunrise to sunset not one speck of cloud visible in the heavens— literal fact. Naturally it has been very hot, but in many places one gets a delightful breeze from the sea; but, of course, every breeze is a sea breeze. The beauty of the place seen under such conditions is very great. It is a feast of colour. The granite rocks—the orange lichen—the brilliantly green ivy and ferns—the purple heather—the fuchsias and endless flowers of which I know not the name—yes, one is no longer in Britannic climes, here.

Our boat goes at 9.30 to-morrow morning, and the voyage is only of one hour; probably the sea will be without a ripple and blue indescribably.

I read old Ovid and to do so under such a sky half brings back the indescribable feeling of being in Italy.

To his brother :

September 11, 1889.

On Saturday morning we shall leave here at 8 o'clock and reach Guernsey in time to catch the boat from Jersey to Southampton.   If all goes well, 10.30 that night will see us in London again.

Small as Sark is, we shall scarcely have been able to see the best things during our fortnight; a month would be none too much.

It is a marvellous and beautiful island ;   inland there are exquisite lanes and valleys, where no one would suspect their existence.   I have seen nothing whatever that is not picturesque. In places the sheer cliffs are hung with the thickest ivy; the ferns are magnificent everywhere.   Our cottage is all but concealed with a giant geranium, growing up the walls, and to the roof—now in full flower; the same house has myrtles and fuchsias and ivy in profusion about it.   I am very glad to have been here.   The caves are such as I never saw.   A perilous place everywhere for those who like to be incautious. The tides and the precipices make dangers that have incessantly to be guarded against.

To his sister Ellen :

7K,
September 29, 1889.

Yesterday I went down to Chiddingfold in Surrey; it is a few miles beyond Godalming, and very near the borders of Hampshire.

More beautiful country cannot be found in England.   The Downs were a profound blue against the cloudy sky, and the rich foliage had a marvellous variety and intensity of colour. One tree I saw on which every leaf was the most brilliant scarlet; I think I never saw such a hue on trees.   And the village of Chiddingfold is, I think, quite as beautiful and ancient as Broadway [Worcestershire].

I suppose there really is no part of England more richly wooded and more tempting to people who want absolute quietness.

The journey from London takes an hour and a half.

An odd thing, I found that Miss Sichel occupies a little house together with a Miss Ritchie, sister-in-law of Mrs. Ritchie.

I lunched there, had a long walk with them; a vast amount of talk, and was back in London to dinner at 7.

To his brother :

September 30, 1889.

I suffer wretchedly from a cough. What my own plans are for the winter I cannot decide. I should like to go to Athens, but it would be expensive. On the other hand, I cannot stay here through the black months. Naples wouldn't cost much.

On October 3 *in his diary he says :*

Have grown tired of noting the monotonous and ignoble days. My solitude is a wearisome topic.

October 7. Did nothing. Thought nothing.

October 10. A bright and mild day. In morning worked out my plan of new book, to be called, I think, *The Head Mistress.* Afternoon with Roberts to Hartley's studio, where met a lot of men. Thence to the studio of Lee, the sculptor. Some very interesting work.

To his brother :

October 9, 1889.

When the book [*The Emancipated*] will be published I don't exactly know, but I think before the end of the year, they have put 1889 on the title page, at all events. I fancy it will give a good deal of offence, for the satire is rather savage in places, especially that directed against religious formalism. At

Agbrigg [Wakefield] the book will not be liked, but I cannot help that; it is quite impossible to restrict one's literary activity with a view to the sensibilities of one's friends. Just that has brought English fiction to its present pass. The better I become known, of course, the freer hand I shall have, and it is by no means my intention to neglect this advantage.

To his sister Ellen :

7K,
October 10, 1889.

To-day comes the first of the winter fogs; yesterday was mild and sunny. Strange how one's difficulty in bearing adverse conditions is increased when such endurance is not absolutely necessary. In past years I have gone through the London winter as a matter of course, now it begins to be intolerable.

My plan is to go by rail to Marseilles—perhaps stopping a day in Paris—and there to take a steamer for the Piraeus, the port of Athens. The boat will probably call at Naples.

I am studying a little modern Greek. At the hotels French is spoken, but a knowledge of Greek would, of course, reduce expenses.

To his sister Margaret :

October 10, 1889.

An odd story about a cat. I was at D.'s the other evening, and saw a very large cat on the rug. On my observing it I was told that the creature was in the habit of " sitting up " at meal times, and begging like a dog. But something stranger than this. At the beginning of the summer, the D.'s did away with their kitchen fire, and substituted a gas-fire. This very much displeased the cat, and in a day or two she disappeared. All the summer she remained away. The people often saw her in the distance, but could not tempt her to approach; she was always in good case, and evidently lived somewhere near.

Now a day or two after the kitchen fire had been resumed, the cat presented herself in the calmest way, resumed all her old habits and seems to be established for the winter.

I am getting on with the proofs.   It is possible they may be done before the end of November.   As soon as possible, I shall start for Athens.

Alfred Hartley, the painter, thinks of going to Sark for November.

I had a great party here the other evening.   Roberts, Hudson and Hartley.   Great was the talk, portentous the tobacco-smoke; huge the laughter; boundless the scorn of critics and the public.

To-morrow night Hudson entertains Roberts and myself— Hartley has a dinner at the Grosvenor Gallery, and can't come unfortunately.

To his sister Ellen :

October 20, 1889.

The weather is terrible, though occasionally there comes a gleam of sun.   I know not how I could get on through the whole winter here, yet I am perpetually having it forced upon me that it is brutal of course to go abroad.   I dare not speak of the matter to ——, for he always droops his head and grows wretched, if not angry.   B. writes in a melancholy strain about his inability to go anywhere.   The fact of the matter is, I am beginning to feel that it is a disagreeable thing to have any measure of success, when those about one do not share in it.   Yet have I not gone through enough misery ?   Who has experienced more—other things being equal ?   In what should I benefit other people if I stayed here and moped through these ghastly months of English winter ?

" Well, well," said —— the other day, " you will wake up on a sunny morning in Athens and chuckle to yourself when you think of us poor wretches here ! "

Unfortunately it is more likely to depress me, such thought.

I am beginning to understand that it is not always heartless-ness that makes a successful man shun the unsuccessful; it may be sheer inability to bear the strain upon his sympathies. I should have twice the vigour if I were surrounded by people whom success made cheerful. Half my time I am groaning uselessly on others' account.

I have decided to go by sea to the Piraeus from Marseilles, but whether by the Messageries Maritimes—which goes through the straits of Bonifacio and Messina—or by a coasting vessel, I don't yet know.

If I manage to make some expedition every year, I shall know something of Europe soon—what ? Well, that is my way of making life endurable. Other people have domestic interests and so are helped along; if my life is to be a lonely one, I must travel much; that I begin to see clearly.

Have an eye to conversational French, for the Parisian expedition.

I am working much at *The Head Mistress* and think I can make a strong book of it.

To his sister Ellen :

7K,
November 3, 1889.

There go the last of the proofs. It is a strange uncomfortable book [*The Emancipated*], few will like it and very few indeed understand it; but on the whole it pleases me.

I shall let you have postcards from Paris, Marseilles and Athens—and possibly from Genoa, for I think of going by a boat that will call there, if not also at other places. It will be a long time before you get a letter from Athens, your own letters will take at least five days.

It rejoices me that a 6s. edition of *The Nether World* is announced. I wonder whether they will send me a copy.

I know few things delight you more than a new book of poetry; I shall post you before I go the poems of P. B. Marston. I don't think them in any sense great; he derives from Swinburne, and Rossetti; but the man's life-story, told in the preface, is dolorous almost beyond anything of the kind I have read.

Please tell mother I was delighted with her letter.

Curious thing, all last night I was talking Italian in dreams. I had a long discussion with a railway official in Rome, explaining to him that I had had a ticket for Naples but had given it up at Rome by mistake; when I woke up he was hunting for it, in a lot of pigeon-holes.

The Head Mistress is thoroughly prepared, even to the names. After that will come a tremendously savage book, the scene once more in London. Not, however, among work people but among the poor and wretched educated. It will probably be called *Revolt*.

To his mother :

Opposite Corsica,
November 15, 1889.

My first letter shall be addressed to you, and you can let it pass on to the girls and to Harbottle [in Northumberland where his brother Algernon was staying].

I reached Marseilles in the normal way, and the boat started next morning. From there to Genoa the sea was rather rough, a high wind blew, and it was cold. But at Genoa itself the weather became perfect and just like it was on the Mediterranean last year. We had to stop a whole day to unload and load. I went into the town and saw a little of it, in company with French-speaking Greeks. It is Italy once more and I felt in great spirits as I rambled in the splendid sunshine.

This morning at 8 o'clock we started again, and now it is nearly 7 in the evening—we are drawing past Corsica. To-morrow I hope to have at least a distant view of Naples; it will grieve me to look at Vesuvius from far off. This evening there was a magnificent sunset of purple and flaming gold, the island of Elba was just ahead of it. This morning we passed in view of the Bay of Spezzia, where Shelley was drowned.

The scenery seems to me as wonderful as ever, and it is just as impossible to give you an idea of it. The Gulf of Genoa is magnificent—I think the most splendid scene I know after the Bay of Naples. The Maritime Alps had a sprinkling of snow, which at sunrise was a most marvellous rose-pink, such a colour as I never before saw. Unfortunately we passed Cannes, Nice and Monaco in the night, but the sail up the centre of the Gulf of Genoa with the vast amphitheatre of mountains in front, is never to be forgotten.

November 16. With much difficulty I distinguished the faint outline of old Vesuvius on the horizon, we were too far from land to see anything more of the coast. I should like to have gone nearer; however, I strained my eyes and saw the old mountain sending forth his clouds of smoke. A very warm day, the sea still perfectly calm. Wonderful conversations on all sorts of subjects with my fellow-passengers; one of them is going to Constantinople, and then to Angora—where the *cats* come from.

November 17. A grand day so that I could not long sit in the full sun. Went up on to the deck at half-past three in the morning; we were passing just by the Island of Stromboli, a volcano always in activity. Every few minutes there was an eruption which made the clouds up above the mountains a deep crimson; the last quarter of the moon was shining so brilliantly that I could scarcely look at it. Virgil makes the island the home of Aeolus.

At eight o'clock we had entered the straits of Messina. It was indescribably beautiful. On the left the wild mountains of Catalina; on the right the hills of Sicily, very barren and of a wonderful colour in the morning sun.

Here and there one saw the broad tracks of mountain torrents, which are now quite dry, but in rainy seasons, of course, become violent streams rushing to the sea; they look like vast high roads and are often walled in on both sides. It took us about an hour to pass the straits. Even then we could not see Etna on account of mist in the upper air. But when I came up on deck again after breakfast—there—right in front, was the magnificent mountain, its summit gleaming with snow. I never yet saw any mountain which so impressed me with a sense of its hugeness; all the other great

mountains of Sicily and Calabria were paltry hills in comparison.

Scarcely any smoke issued from it.

So we sailed south-east; out into the Ionian Sea. At mid-
day Etna was invisible, for the heat raised mists. But at
sunset, when we had travelled a very great distance, behold the
horizon cleared up and there was Etna still, perfectly clear
rising in solitary majesty, high above the horizon—
never to be forgotten.

November 18. The Ionian Sea is almost always rough.
In the middle of the night I woke up and found the ship tossing
about. The same this morning, a grand sea, covered with
great foaming waves. It does not trouble me in the least,
I eat heartily and enjoy myself. No land is yet in sight—I
often wonder how M. would get on with this diet. Everything *drips* with butter and oil. Imagine it on a rough sea!

About 11 o'clock this morning we first descried the hills of
Greece! Rapidly we drew near and at 8 o'clock a glorious
scene was before us. The morning was gloomy, but now a
huge storm-cloud was driven over towards Africa by the
north wind, and east-ward the sky was blue and sunny over
Greece.

As the sun descended, the effects of light became wholly
indescribable. It is no use to say that such things are like a
vision: no one ever *had* a vision like what this is in reality.
It is more marvellous than south Italy! The mountains seem
translucent; all the coast is incredibly barren and desolate—no
sign of habitation—but the light transforms it to indescribable
loveliness. The sun set behind clouds, and the light on the
mountains gradually vanished, upwards, upwards, until only a
few peaks glowed with exquisite rose-colour.

We are now just off Cape Matapan, the most southerly point
of Europe. But unhappily it is dark, or we should see the
island Cythera. By seven o'clock in the morning, we shall
be in the harbour of Piraeus.

To-morrow will be the ninth day that I have been travelling
—it is a long journey but I have enjoyed it much. Since I

left London I have not spoken a word of English and am not likely to, for many a week.

Write to me "*Poste Restante, Athens, Greece,*" and let me know that all goes well.

Three years ago, it seemed to me a wildly extravagant hope that I should ever see Greece, but here I am! Ah! It does me good this travel. My Greek acquaintance on board has been pressing me to go to Constantinople but I cannot afford it.

Well I think I shall never spend another winter in England. I had rather live in the south on 2d. a day, here life is worth living; I am well and hopeful—whereas in England neither.

Much love to all. I shall post this on reaching Athens, but it will take a long time to get to you.

To his brother:

HÔTEL DE LA COURONNE,
ATHENS,
November 29, 1889.

It seems that letters take even more than a week to pass between here and England. In fact, for purposes of communication, one might as well be in America. The Greeks always talk of " going to Europe," and indeed this is not Europe, but the East. It will be very long before Greece gets rid of its Orientalism. All the quick and easy traffic is with Constantinople and Asia Minor. The public markets are called bazaars. The extraordinary costumes worn by the lower classes suggest oriental barbarism. But I am getting rather anxious to hear from England. I wonder whether you have yet received from Agbrigg the letter I posted on landing; send a postcard if you can. But it must be at once, for I shall only be here a month altogether (living is dear), and about the 19th December I shall sail for Naples. Between the 10th and the 19th December you may address " Poste Restante, Napoli."

You know, by the bye, that the old calendar is in use here.

To-day the date is 17th November, 12 days behind European time.

The weather is that of an English midsummer, varied by tremendous gales.   Every few days the wind blows terrifically, but seldom with coldness.   When there is no wind, the sun becomes almost intolerable in open spaces.   I have tried to read placards in the streets, but cannot; my eyes ache immediately, and dazzle with the glare.   In walking, the rays smite upon one's back, as if from a furnace.   The sky is magnificent; a deeper blue, I think, than I ever saw in Italy.

In addition to this, you must understand the extraordinary physical condition of the soil in this part of Attica.   Owing to the lack of water (the Kephisos and Ilissos are streams of a foot in breadth, disappearing altogether long before they can reach the sea; and there is seldom heavy rain), the ground is incredibly arid.   In Athens itself, with the exception of a few carefully watered trees and shrubs, there is literally not a speck of verdure to be seen!   Take the large open space in front of the royal palace, where anywhere else would be a lawn; it is— I speak literally—as bare as the high road, a mere expanse of what seems to be waste building ground.   And everywhere the same.   The result of this is, that you live in a cloud of dust.   It is the duty of a waiter at every hotel to dust the boots and trousers of all who enter.   You have not walked ten yards before your boots are white in mid-street.   Anything so extraordinary as this barrenness I never conceived, though I had read of it as a feature of Athens.

You might imagine that this would destroy all picturesqueness.   So it would—in the north.   But here everything is transfigured by the sun.   These vast deserts and dustheaps become unspeakably beautiful when seen from a little distance: they are coloured wonderfully, and their forms keep changing in the strangest way.   Impossible to judge of distances here. One hour Mount Hymettus seems twenty miles away, the next you feel disposed to climb it as an after-dinner amusement —every stone is defined from base to summit.   The sunsets are of unspeakable splendour.   When you stand with your back to the west and look towards the Acropolis, it glows a rich amber; temples, bulwarks and rock are all of precisely the same hue, as if the whole were but one construction.   The marble slopes of Pentelicon become violet and purple and all manner of nameless tints.   Impossible for you to imagine what I mean.   Impossible for any painter to render such scenes.

From the Acropolis itself there is of course a view of which one can never grow weary.   A plain stretches for about four miles to the sea, and there lies the town and harbour of Piraeus (with mill chimneys, I grieve to say).   The Attic Gulf extends for a great distance between our mountains and those of Argolis; in the midst of it lies the island of Aegina, rising to a splendid peak.   To the right of Piraeus you see the island of Salamis, also very mountainous, and between it and the land is the spot where the battle was fought, all perfectly plain to sight.

Looking further round towards the north, you have first the mountains of Corinth, then of Megaris, then at last the great range of Parnes (with snow upon it) which closes the Attic Plain.   Westward is the marble Pentelicon, and southwest, very near, the rugged Hymettus, where the famous bees still make their honey, as in the classic days.

The Attic Plain itself is largely planted with olives and fig trees.   There are also extensive currant bushes.   Along the roads grow huge agaves (aloes) and cactuses.   Just now the trees have a fine autumnal colour—except of course the olives, which keep for ever their grey-green.

I walked the other day to Salamis, and stood on the spot where Xerxes set up his throne to behold the battle.   It was a hot and perfectly calm day; the sea scarcely lapped upon the craggy shore.   I suppose not a detail of the landscape has changed since B.C. 480, and there is only one modern building in sight to disturb the impression.

Acropolis is, of course, the centre of interest.   I spend many hours in studying it.   It is maddening to think that up to two centuries ago the Parthenon was entire—you remember it

was destroyed by the explosion of a powder magazine, when the
Venetians were fighting against the Turks.   The more I see
of these Greek and Roman civilizations, the more powerless I
feel myself to imagine what the cities were like in their prime.
The universality of marvellous arts astounds one.   The
museums are of almost purely archæological interest.   All the
fine statues have long ago been distributed over Europe.
Besides the Acropolis, there are only half a dozen ruins to be
seen (excepting the temple of Theseus, which is the best
preserved building of the kind in existence), and it takes only
two or three days to examine everything in an ordinary way.
But of course the interest is in the locality.   It is heightened
by the fact that there are so many hills about here whence you
have views of great extent; and every visible inch of ground
has its association.

The spoken language is exceedingly difficult to understand,
owing to peculiarities of pronunciation and accent; still I have
got just enough of it to buy, and ask ordinary questions.   The
newspapers I can read without much difficulty; the Greeks are
doing their best to reform the written tongue on the classical
models.   At first it seems very strange to walk about and see
Greek capital letters everywhere.   Sometimes the trans-
literation of foreign names into Greek has a highly comical
effect.   For instance, over the offices of Cook (the tour man)
is written :

Θ KOUK KAI VIOS
(Th. Cook & Son).

In fact, I shall no longer consider Greek as a dead language,
for in discourse for half an hour I scarcely use a word that
wouldn't have been understood by Xenophon.   At this
moment, I hear newsboys shouting the morning papers, and
one of them is ῾Η ᾿Ακρόπολις.

In this hotel, which is a large and good one, I am the only
foreigner at present.   The waiters can speak a few words of
French and Italian.   A restaurant is attached to the establishment, and one eats *à la carte*; very extraordinary dishes I eat,

too, occasionally. Everything swims in oil. The ordinary wine of the country is made intolerable by being strongly flavoured with resin; the Greeks like it. Fortunately I have found a white wine that I can enjoy. Coffee is served very curiously. They bring you a tiny cup in which is coffee, together with the grounds; before drinking, you let it settle and cool; then there are only *two* sips (it is already sweetened, of course no milk), but such coffee I never tasted. This is the Turkish method. Such a cup costs three halfpence. As for tobacco, everyone smokes cigarettes.

As I was eating the other day, the waiter brought a newspaper and offered it. To my amazement it was the *Newcastle Weekly Chronicle*. I cannot understand why, but it seems that they receive this regularly, with other foreign papers. Certainly it contains a great deal of fine confused reading; but how on earth they came to know of it here I can't imagine.

The common people very frequently speak a little Italian, not French. I suppose the necessities of commerce have brought this about. The people on the whole, as far as I have seen them, do not recommend themselves to me. There is no politeness in them, for one thing; one thinks regretfully of the smooth grace with which you are cheated in Italy. To be sure, living is simpler here; you are allowed to go about without being pestered by people; coachmen never try to attract your attention. But there is a general want of liveliness. I vastly prefer the scoundrelly and annoying Neapolitan. The Greeks seem to have curiously harsh voices; their language has even a disagreeable sound, which I cannot believe was of old the case. They are all bent on money-making, and are, on the whole, grossly uneducated—if not unintelligent. Of course this would especially be accounted for by centuries of slavery.

My evenings I spend in reading Greek, chiefly Aristophanes, who is above all the poets associated with Athens. Of course a vast amount of light is thrown upon him by my experience here. No one can hope really to appreciate the Romans and Greeks who has not seen Italy and Greece.

In the meantime, you have probably finished your book ; I hope to hear from you about it.   Perhaps you and Katie are already gone to Agbrigg.   If so, I hope this letter will be sent after you.   When you have read it please pass it on to Agbrigg in any case.

It is to be hoped that all goes well with you.   My love to Katie and Enid.   I fear you never see the sun, and will not for many months.

I shall not be able to stay long at Naples.   But I look forward to it; it is like a home to me.   Here there is no music unfortunately, or next to none.   The Neapolitans alone know how to make life melodious.

ATHENS,
December 16, 1889.

MY DEAR MOTHER,

I write to you again this time, as it is probable that when this letter arrives there will be a family gathering at Agbrigg, and all can read it together.   It is my last day here and most unfortunately I cannot go about the town, for there is a violent, cold wind which has now lasted for four days.   In fact it is a mistake to come to Greece in winter.   We have had seven or eight days since I have been here, which were more wonderful than any summer day in England, but the rest of the time has been very far from comfortable; it is never cold—you don't feel the want of a fire (and, of course couldn't have one if you did), but the fierce winds are so frequent and last so long; it will be vastly better at Naples.

Two acquaintances I have made here, that of a young Greek who speaks French, and that of a Scotchman—a most amusing man of whom I must tell you some day.   At the age of fifty he has come out here from Glasgow (having never left England before) to be accountant for a new railway line, leaving his wife and family who will come out in a few months.   He speaks not a word of any language but his own (the railway is being made by an English company), but already is in great spirits about this country and talks seriously of " becoming a

Greek." If he ever learns to speak two sentences of Greek I shall be greatly surprised, for he is quite uneducated and very dense in the matter of languages. For all that, one of the best hearted and most child-like men I have ever met. He comes to have meals here in this hotel, and the food is a perpetual source of astonishment to him. When I am not there to guide him, he chooses a dish at random on the bill of fare, with strange results.

The other man—a Greek—took me, one day, to one of the ordinary classes at the University. They were reading a play of Sophocles, very much as we do in England, and I enjoyed it much.

There have been a few magnificent sunsets. One of them was rendered extraordinary by the fact that, at the same time, there was a perfect rainbow circling over the whole of Athens, from the foot of one mountain to that of another; the colours of the hills were unimaginable.

Athens is about four miles from the sea-shore. Its port as you know is the Piraeus, which, I grieve to say, is a busy manufacturing town, with fuming chimneys. Along the coast, a mile or so from Piraeus, is a village called Phaleron, and here the Athenians go in the summer to bathe. I was there one glorious day—hot and cloudless; the sea had scarcely a ripple and the beach invited one to take a bathe—-all smooth sand.

From every part of the great plain in which Athens is situated, you see the Acropolis and its temples rising magnificently above the modern houses; from many miles away, the gleaming marble columns of the Parthenon are always visible. That one sight is more than enough, even when you have travelled so far; there is nothing like it in the world.

I have twice been at Salamis and stood where Xerxes placed his throne to watch the battle. And one day I walked to Eleusis, the finest walk I have had. Further excursions I have not attempted ; partly because, in the absence of railways, the expense was too great, partly because of the uncertain weather.

To illustrate the lack of water from which this part of Greece suffers, I will mention that when I was at Phaleron, I saw a boy carefully scooping up into a big bottle the contents of a rain pool.   It was too valuable to be wasted.

I am sorry to say that the photographs are rather poor. I can't understand why.   I have bought only half a dozen. For Madge and Nelly I have chosen two different views of the Acropolis.   But one cannot bring presents from Athens like from Italy, there is really nothing interesting to buy.

The Museums contain a great quantity of interesting fragments, but there are no splendid statues; all those have long ago been carried off to Italy and Paris and London.   And, of course, the town does not possess a single painting of any kind.   To enjoy a stay here thoroughly, one must be able to live in the open air, for it is the country itself, the scenery, etc., that interests one.

Every town and village has its historical associations and poetical value; but the modern life is, as far as I can judge, very uninteresting indeed.   It is altogether different from Italy; there both old and new are delightful.   For anyone who has not had a classical education, it would be folly to come to Greece.

By railway to-morrow I shall go through Corinth to Patras.

The boat leaves Patras at 10 at night, and this is most unfortunate because it will be dark when we pass "Stony Ithaka."   I don't know whether the girls remember that this was the island of Odysseus.   I would have given much to see it.   We call at Corfu next day, said to be one of the most beautiful islands in existence.

I shall not post this till I reach Naples, so that it will tell of my arrival.   What day that will be I don't know.   I think it takes two days to reach Brindisi, and then a day of railway across Italy.

All good wishes for Christmas, and the New Year.   My Christmas will be spent in the midst of wonderful Neapolitan uproar.   They are very strong in bagpipes there at that season

—anything that will make a noise. The principal street is turned into an open air bazaar. Ah, how I shall enjoy it!

With much love, dear mother, and to all assembled at Agbrigg.

GEORGE.

To his sisters :

December 19, 1889.

I continue this letter under extraordinary circumstances.

First for the journey from Athens to Patras. It was a vile day—a terrific wind blowing; at Corinth one could scarcely put one's head out of the window. They are just finishing the Canal which is to cut across the Isthmus of Corinth. The railway goes over it, and when in the middle of the bridge, you look along the trench (which is terrifically deep), out to the sea at both ends. It was very interesting to see this.

On leaving Corinth the railway goes along the north coast of the Peloponnesus. Opposite is Mount Helicon, and afterwards Mount Parnassus. Both were thickly covered with olive woods and currant grounds—miles and miles of currant bushes. They are quite little trees with thick trunks—perhaps four feet high. At sunset, the snow on the great mountains turned, as it always does, a beautiful rose colour.

Arrived at Patras, I dined and went on board. Boat started at 10 o'clock.

Next morning I went upon deck at sunrise; we were just opposite the Ambracian Gulf, where the battle of Actium was fought. In the distance, behind us, lay the Ionian Islands. To the north rose the great snowy mountains of Epirus (Albania is the modern name, but it has no meaning). At 11 o'clock we reached Corfu. Look at the map and you will see that the town is on the inner side of the island. A magnificent bay with great mountains in every direction.

We waited here till 5 in the evening. I should like to have gone on land but the expense was too much, I have to avoid all such extra payments as much as possible. So I spent the day on deck, reading Sophocles. A glorious day, so hot that when I took my watch out, I found the sun had baked it. Well, as soon as we had left Corfu, the wind rose again (I am getting utterly tired of hearing it roaring), and the sea became very rough. This morning I went on deck and saw land just ahead. But on speaking to someone, I found it was not Italy but Turkey! About midnight the captain got afraid and actually turned back—when we possibly must have been half way to Brindisi. This enraged me, for the sea was not really rough at all in comparison with what one is accustomed to in the north.

We have entered a great bay and are anchored here; goodness knows how long we shall stop. On the top of the hill on the shore is a town which they tell me is called Avellona. Unfortunately I have no map of the Turkish coast. Please try to find this place, to the north of Corfu; a great bay with one island at the mouth of it. A boat has been ashore with men to try and dispatch a telegram. Also a boat of natives has come off to us, offering to take anyone ashore who wishes to go. But the captain says these people are not to be trusted; they might purposely keep you till it was too late to catch the steamer again.

A cloudless—quite cloudless—sky, and hot sun; but still I hear the wind roaring, so I sit on deck and read Sophocles, or think of a letter of Cicero's in which he speaks of being detained by adverse winds on entering from Greece to Italy. Goodness knows when I shall get to Naples. It is fortunate that the fare I have paid includes food.

I find that the passengers all consider the captain's conduct absurd, but the stewardess tells me that the ship has not sufficient ballast, and is only safe in the very calmest weather. A nice state of things! Fortunately it only takes six hours to cross the Adriatic from here to Brindisi.

There is a great babel of languages on board; Greek, French, Italian, German, English—it is characteristic that the French are the only ones who speak nothing but their own language. We have a Queen's messenger among the passengers, a very aristocratic young man!

The ship's boat has returned, and has brought a quantity of provisions, very necessary, for there is nothing to eat on board. Curious Turkish bread, brown and half baked. We learn that meat in these parts costs 4d. for 2 *lbs!* Again it has been a cloudless day and there is a beautiful sunset.

I walk about the deck in this purple glimmer and hear the waves breaking upon the shore.

Friday, December 20.

As the wind had fallen we weighed anchor at 1 a.m. I felt that the sea was calm, so slept without disturbance. At sunrise we were at Brindisi. This part of Italy is perfectly flat; in the harbour you see nothing but the surrounding houses. Here *Virgil* died on returning from Greece. At 9.25 a train for Naples. It follows a very interesting line, round the great Bay of Taranto; you will see it on the map; first to Taranto, then to Metaponto, then striking north to Salerno and Naples.

A cloudless day; here in Italy the weather has been glorious. A contrast to Greece.

Naples at 10.30 p.m.—a long journey—carriage full of shouting Neapolitans, of course.

8 Vico Brancaccio,
Saturday, December 21.

Ha, ha! Sunlight and warmth and uproar and palm trees and wine and fruit—Napoli, Napoli! How glorious it is to be here! I have a beautiful room looking over Posillipo.

To my utter astonishment, letters have already been sent to this address from Poste Restante. Would you believe it? They must positively have kept the address ever since last year; this is astounding activity for this part of the world.

The weather is specially favourable. A great number of visitors here, they tell me. Oh, how I enjoy walking about the streets! The Via Roma is lined with Christmas stalls. Curiously they have the habit here of playing bagpipes at Christmas—the players come down from the mountains. Of course they don't allow you to sleep at night—an extraordinary row!

Letter received.   Hope you have all mine.   Many thanks for notice of *Nether World*—was astounded to hear of Browning's death; well, well, he was very old.   I wonder if he will be buried at Venice or at Florence ?

To his sister Ellen :

NAPOLI,
January 7, 1890.

It seems that the so-called " influenza " has reached Naples, but in its mildest form ; it does not make me anxious, but of course I shall be careful; I think it is safer to face it here than in London.   I wonder whether it troubles you at all in Yorkshire.

The weather after being very unsettled has become glorious again.   Three days ago we had one of the worst storms known here for many years.   For *thirty-six* hours it thundered and lightened almost incessantly, and rain!   I never heard anything like it, torrents and torrents.   In one part of Naples the roads were blocked for days by the masses of debris swept down from the higher streets and roads.   As you climbed the narrower streets, it was just like wading against a mountain stream, about up to the ankles.

Christmas was extraordinary.   In spite of the prohibition of the police, all night long there was ceaseless explosion of bombs and fireworks, a dozen of people were taken injured to the hospital.   From all the windows people burned coloured Bengal lights, and, of course, the fire dropped on to your head as you walked below.   The food eaten at the season consists almost exclusively of giant eels and broccoli ; no one dreams of going to bed that night.

But a most miserable and indeed incredible thing has happened.   Just at Christmas the town authorities issued an order that henceforth the organs were forbidden to play in Naples.   For days I could not believe it.   It has most seriously diminished my pleasure here.   Well, and that is how one thing after another disappears from Italy.   It is lamentable.

I have decided to return to England by sea, for I want to see Gibraltar and shall be glad of an experience of the Bay of Biscay in winter weather.   I shall take one of the Orient Line boats ; they call here on returning from Australia and go straight to London.

I am again getting eager to be at work, as I always do after rest and change.   We shall see if the next doesn't turn out something noticeable.

Well, I must go out and enjoy the sunshine.   Last night was full moon—a cloudless deep blue sky, scarcely the sound of a breaker to be heard.   I walked for a long time by the sea-wall (which extends for some three miles) and felt glad to be here.   It is probable that the fine weather will continue. Old Vesuvius shows that the scirocco has ceased to blow.

To his brother :

January 22, 1890.

I, this moment, receive your letter and rejoice vastly at the news it contains.

I am groaning at the pecuniary necessity of returning to England just on the verge of Italian spring.   Already there are green peas here in full bloom; among the golden fruit, burdened orange and lemon trees, flowers begin to abound. But things are rather wretched here, owing first of all to the "influenza" which has ruined the season, and then to the death of the King's brother.   Theatres and museums closed, streets melancholy, it is not like Naples.

S. has been over here spending a week with me.   Together we explored old Naples—the most wonderful and fearful place in Europe.   Day by day it is vanishing.   I shall always rejoice that I saw it.   Some 1,500 men are at work destroying and rebuilding.   You cannot imagine what old Naples is like; descriptions are useless though I shall try my hand some day. London is, of course, vaster ; but the squalor of Naples never ceases to be amazingly picturesque.

The middle ages still survive in many a whole street and

square—inconceivable, the quarters where cholera was worst in '37 and '84. I begin to understand a good deal of the dialect, fortunately.

One day we went out to Pozzuoli, Baiae, Cape Misenum, and lastly to Cumae, the first Greek settlement in Italy, now a desolate shore, with the hill on which stood the Acropolis, but scarcely a ruin left. Hard by is a great wood of evergreen oaks, where are many wild boars. For impressiveness, the scene comes after Paestum, I think.

I have made the acquaintance of a few Italians. One of them is a *notaro* (notary), who has a brother, a judge in Salerno.

The sun has set over Posillipo, and the Ave Maria is sounding from all the churches. I think with dread of Marylebone—I shall sail about the 6th February; and shall probably reach England about the 15th.

I shall be glad to see Gibraltar and get a glimpse of Africa. But I don't want to travel about much just now. I wish it were possible to stay here in peace.

To his sister Ellen :

7K,
March 2, 1890.

I am just now in good health and fair working spirits. Anxious to get to my book.

Ten years hence I shall perhaps be able to have a home like other wealthy people. Yes, but I don't think it will be in England. Well, we will talk about this some day perhaps.

I think longingly of Naples. Well, at the end of the autumn I want to go to Germany, perhaps for half a year, just to make myself perfect in the spoken language, and then it will, I hope, be southwards again.

The weather is terrible. Snow and slush and fog!

Best love to you now and always.

On board the " Orient " were several parrots brought from their native homes. They stood in cages on the deck and made queer noises. Looked like old Polly [an old parrot at his home in Wakefield].

Diary :

March 15. A week of thinking over new story. It is not to be *The Head Mistress*; materials for that will lie over. To-day actually got to work and did the first two pages. Thank heaven!

To his brother :
March 16, 1890.

I have made a beginning of the next book—rather a mill-grinding business, this, of book after book.

Everything points to the likelihood of my practically leaving England for a long time. London is too solitary for me; I can stand it no longer. Little by little, the subjects of my books will probably change a good deal; in fact, the process has already begun, as you will see in *The Emancipated.*

Very decent weather for London just now. Of course, one never sees the sky, but a sunny haze hangs about the streets for a few hours daily. Ah, but what is Naples now! Long before I left, the almond trees were everywhere in full blossom—a mass of pinky-white, without a trace of leaf on the boughs. By this, the vines will have begun to bud, and all the country ways will be covered with spring flowers.

To his sister Ellen :
7K,
March 16, 1890.

I have made a beginning of my new book and must work vigorously. Tell Madge that a good deal of it will be in Guernsey and Sark. After all, those are splendid places. I retain a very pleasant memory of them. The sky was all but as blue as that of Italy, the atmosphere delightful.

I shall be tempted to go there again, only that I am utterly weary of my present mode of life and can think of nothing but how to change it. England is a failure with me; twelve years of hopeless struggle have convinced me that I must look for a home on the Continent.

I cannot get on with English society, the thing is proved.

I hope you still feel better.   I have explained to Madge all the arrangements for our journey [to Paris].   Going by Dieppe way the railway journey in France is both shorter and more interesting than the other way.   We shall go through Rouen in the light of early morning.   At all events you will see Paris in a very different way from that of ordinary tourists— that I can assure you.

In April, Gissing was in Paris with his sisters and returned with them to Agbrigg near Wakefield for three months, continuing his writing there, but with much difficulty, owing to ill-health and depression, as the following jottings from the Diary show.

June 29.   Last night at eleven o'clock came to a conclusion which I had not foreseen by more than an hour. Absolutely determined to abandon my story and commence a new one, for which an idea suddenly flashed upon me.   The result was an immense relief.   I have still perhaps time to write a book before the end of August, that is, if I can put my heart into it.

June 30.   Rain all day, in morning began my new novel, and by evening did five pages which ought to be my daily quantum.   Heavens!   The relief I feel and not much fear in the prospect of toil, either.   No one could deny my courage. I had half finished the other novel.

July 4.   In morning did three pages.   In afternoon a rush of inspiration.   Decided to re-write from beginning these last days' work, to rename all my characters, and to call the book *Storm-Birds*.   Wrote one and a half pages of Chapter I.

July 30.   No sleep at night.   No work to-day.   Misery.

August 4.   Utter wretchedness, until evening, then a blessed change came and I was able to think of my story once more.

August 7. Abandoned work again and shall not resume till I go to London.

August 19. Left Wakefield for Worcester and thence to Bredon, where Alg. met me.

August 21. Reached London about 5.30. Feeling very shaky and hopeless.

August 23. Made a beginning of a new novel, a jumble of the various ones I have been engaged on all the summer. Wrote three pages, but in evening saw that they were no good. Am on the very verge of despair and suffering more than ever in my whole life. My brain seems powerless and tied up.

August 25. Began yet once more my novel, to be called *Hilda Wolff*. Did six pages, mostly re-writing.

August 30. A very fine day, feeling better, did six pages, which makes thirty-one this week. If I do thirty a week I am satisfied.

Monday, September 15. Complete breakdown again. Am at end of Volume I. but feel it won't do. Have no pleasure in it. Wandered about in despair.

Wednesday, September 17. Began a new story, which, at present, I call *Victor Yule*. Wrote from 3 to 11 and did a little more than three pages.

Thursday, September 18. Curious that I feel in good spirits about this new story. I seem to have hit the possible vein again once more.

Friday, September 19. Wrote from 3 to 9.30 doing five pages. No reading of any kind now-a-days. A bad, bad time with me; the wasting of my life in bitterness.

Friday, September 26. Dull day. Worked hard but did only about three pages.

Saturday, September 28. Fine, hot; in afternoon with E. to Richmond; thence walked to Kew and had tea there. Exquisite sunset beyond the river from Kew Bridge; rich dusky scarlet and no clouds. Opposite, the rising of a full red moon, a wonderful sight.

Wednesday, October 1. A fresh beginning once more. It will be *New Grub Street* after all.

Monday, October 6. Re-commenced *New Grub Street*.

In October (date not given), he wrote to his brother :

I rejoice to tell you that things are going greatly better with me. This last week I have written *half a volume*, and now I begin to hope that I shall finish my book much before the end of the year. I think I told you it is to be called *New Grub Street*. No, I don't think it will be possible to share your house. For one thing I am bound to be in London because I must work hard at getting together some new material. Then again, I can't stand my solitary life any longer and it must not surprise you if you suddenly hear that I am going to be married again. [Gissing was not married until February of 1891.]

Diary :

December 6. In morning re-wrote the page of Reardon's death and so finished *New Grub Street*.

On the same day a postcard to his brother with the single word " Finished."

In the course of a letter to his sister he says :

7K,
December 26, 1890.

I have decided to go to Exeter and there take up my abode for a year or two. If the expense is not too great, I shall have

all my furniture moved down there ; I think it would not cost
so much as buying new.

I am waiting in miserable expectation for news from the
publishers. Can take no single step until I hear.

Diary :

January 7, 1891. Letter from Smith & Elder. They
think *New Grub Street* " clever and original " but fear it is
too gloomy. Offer £150 [for copyright]. I wrote at once
accepting (eheu!).

To his sister Ellen :

24 PROSPECT PARK, EXETER.
January 20, 1891.

I am afraid it is long since I gave you a direct report of
how things go with me.   Happily I am able at length to write
in my own orderly room—everything finished.   It has been
a considerable expense, and, of course, has given me a violent
cold, this removal, but I think it was not unwisely done.   As
soon as the weather ceases to be arctic, I shall enjoy a few
weeks of walking about this delightful country, before settling
down to my new book.

The situation could not be better.   The house is in the
highest part of Exeter, not a quarter of an hour's walk from the
heart of the city, yet within sight of absolute rurality.   No
shops in the neighbourhood.

I took a walk the other day through wonderful hilly lanes
to a village called Stoke Cannon.

By the beginning of March, I hope to make tentative
beginnings at my new book, for I am determined to have no
repetition of last year's fearful experiences.

Of course I shall have no society here.   My ambition now
is to make my name known, whilst personally I remain unseen
and unheard of.   In a time when every man of any shadow of
distinction does his best to keep always in the sight of the public,
one may reasonably find solace in the thought of winning

reputation whilst remaining in quiet corners. We shall have to see whether I can keep my mind active without the help of congenial minds. I have the feeling of being deserted by all who ought to be my companions: but then these miseries are useful in giving a peculiar originality to my work.

I know you would be pleased if you could see this room in which I am writing.

VII

EXETER TO RETURN FROM THE IONIAN SEA (1891-1898)

To his brother :

EXETER,
January 24, 1891.

I am glad to hear of your intentions south-ward, for it means that we shall be able to see you before long.   Between Exeter and Bristol the fast trains only stop once, at Taunton, and the journey into Gloucestershire would be a small matter.

It is now raining, but warm.   People here think that the winter is over.

On Thursday I walked to Dawlish, 12 miles, down the right bank of the Exe.   A beautiful sea coast, strange in appearance owing to the red sandstone cliffs.   But on the opposite side of the estuary, 5 miles east of Exmouth, is a little place called Budleigh Salterton, said to be of marvellous beauty, and thither I must walk soon.   It lies in a little combe described as thick with myrtles.   From Exmouth, one goes if need be, by omnibus, for the railway does not extend in that direction.

I have just been seeking particulars about the Devon and Exeter Institution.   It seems to be an admirable establishment, much like the London library.   They have 25,000 volumes of sterling universal literature, and reading room with all current ephemerides.   One has to be elected by the committee and then to pay £3 3s. a year.   I must try to compass this. The institution has existed since 1813.

To the same :

Yesterday I went to Budleigh Salterton.   It is a delightful place; I hope to be there more often.   Wonderfully sheltered and much richness of vegetation.   The furze along the roads is in full yellow bloom; perhaps that is the same with you. Hard by is a farm called Hayes Barton, where Raleigh was born, and Coleridge's country lies in the valley of the Otter, which flows into the sea just beyond Budleigh.

To the same :

One delightful feature of this country is the abundance of pines and firs and non-deciduous trees in general.   Everywhere there are splendid pines along the roads and lanes.   Then every village is thick with laurels, and other evergreens of which I know not the names.   Alas, I would pay a man 5s. per day to accompany me about and name to me the trees and shrubs.

I have discovered a village called Brampford Speke on the Exe, which I seriously think is the most perfect I ever saw. One imagines that some lord of the manor must exert himself to keep it in a picturesque state.

The whole of the Exe valley is wonderful; perfect English rurality, with much variation of level.   The prevalence of red sandstone has sent me to geology; I have got Lyell out of the free library, and am working at him.

Title for a novel.   I saw in Smith's second hand catalogue *Under Your Very Boots!*

New Grub Street goes through the proofs, and I am astonished to find how well it reads.   There are savage truths in it.

To the same :

February 27, 1891.

In a week or so I hope to be at my new book. In any case, the summer is the only available time for work; I cannot write when I am frozen ; and never yet have I inhabited a room which could be warmed by a fire—never. I doubt whether *any* room is ever of even temperature, and that a tolerable one in winter.

I have discovered the warmest place in the United Kingdom. Murray says that it is Salcombe, down by Start Point. The mean winter temperature is only two degrees inferior to that of Florence; this is astonishing.

And the scenery all about is very grand. Thither I go for a day or two before long. Happily no railway reaches it. The approach is by coach and steamer.

Diary :

March 23. Did two pages morning and two evening. Getting on admirably. Got Masson's *Life of De Quincey.*

To his brother :

EXETER,
March 26, 1891.

Herewith I send the passage of Virgil—the whole of it, with a free translation—done chiefly for my own amusement. It is noticeable that his idealisation conflicts with the general tone of the Georgics, which is distinctly practical and rather tends to the expression of hardship.

I shall be glad to hear that you are on your way to the new abode. The difficulties must be considerable, I fear.

All goes well with us. I am working steadily from day to day, and have done about a quarter of my first volume. Wild spring weather at present, grand clouds over brilliant sky.

I am going through a good many of the " Men of Letters "

series; they are well-written books most of them. The one whose style has strongly pleased me is Mark Pattison ; his Milton is admirably written.

Yes, yes, this business of writing English is a hard enough job. At the end of a lifetime one will perhaps manage a page that is decently grammatical and fairly harmonious.

I am in good health and spirits and work more easily than for a long time.

Diary :

March 27. Am trying to make my handwriting larger ; *New Grub Street* is microscopic. The difficulty is that I shan't be able to calculate quantity so well.

March 28. In morning, thought only. Afternoon beautiful walk to Brampford Speke. Saw the first primrose.

March 29. Reading XXIV. *Odyssey.*

March 30. Began a complete reading of *Chaucer*, in the Aldine.

April 2. Note from Frederick Dollman asking me to be interviewed for the *Pall Mall.* Wrote telling him I lived at Exeter, and that in any case, I had nothing to tell the public.

April 15. Smith & Elder have sent me reviews of *New Grub Street* in the *Scotsman* and *Daily Graphic.* Wrote to stop this horror.

Worked well morning and evening, doing four and a half pages.

April 17. Letter from mother praising *New Grub Street* highly. Afternoon to Pinhoe, found white violets.

On April 12 *to his brother :*

EXETER.

I am going in for a little herb-gathering, but find desperate difficulty in identifying plants. However, I yesterday noted (in flower), coltsfoot, dog-violet, primrose, wood sorrel, wild strawberry, celandine ; wall pennywort is very abundant about here. The ferns puzzle me greatly; I can only distinguish bracken, hart's-tongue, and common polypodium.

To his sister Ellen :

EXETER,
April 29, 1891.

This letter of yours contains criticism; laudatory, to be sure, but with discrimination. You appear to have taken in very much of my meaning—more than most readers will. I rejoice that you like the book. Writing it, I believed it trash, for it was wrung page by page, from a sluggish and tormented brain.

Strange ! I find, however, that the reviews are going to take your attitude with regard to it. Bertz thinks it my maturest and most interesting book. It astonished me that mother should care so much about it—and then again, Edith declares it the most pleasing book she ever read. So it seems to contain something which appeals to a great variety of readers.

As for your comments on the philosophical tone of the book, well, it is too late for me to change my views of the universe. I do not dogmatise, remember; my ideas are negative, and on the whole I confine myself to giving pictures of life as it looks to my observation of it. The outlook, certainly, is not very cheerful; impossible for me to see the world in a rosy light.

At the best it looks to me, only not intolerable. As for human aspirations, I know not their meaning, and can conceive no credible explanation—even as I am unable to understand what is called the instinct of animals. The problem does not trouble me, either. I have reached the stage at which one is content to be ignorant. The world is to me mere phenomenon (which literally means that which *appears*) and I study it as I do a work of art—but without reflecting on its origin.

I have finished Volume I. of *Godwin Peak* [*Born in Exile*], and to-morrow morning we start for a three days' holiday at Budleigh Salterton some 15 miles away. The weather is sunny and warm ; it ought to be pleasant on the sea-shore. Reports of influenza in Yorkshire make me uneasy now and then about you and those at Wakefield. I hope you all escape that noisome epidemic.

My own health is admirable; for years I have not been so well. I botanise for a couple of hours every afternoon. Primroses are very abundant about here, and still more so the wild strawberry. It enrages me that I cannot identify many flowers. But for the first time I have seen the blackthorn and learnt its distinction from mayblossom.

We make no acquaintances, and seem very unlikely ever to do so. The people in the house do not at all suit us and we merely keep on civil terms with them. Intellectual converse is, of course, wholly out of the question.

I hope you will return in good health. Don't trouble to write, save when you have leisure and the disposition.

To his brother :

Exeter,
May 21, 1891.

Happily *New Grub Street* has excited more attention than any other of my books. There have been not only good reviews, but positive articles on the subject.

The *Saturday* had one, rather caustic, opposing my view of literature out at elbows, and then next week it printed a highly favourable notice of the book as a novel. In the same paper, I see myself, for the first time, mentioned in a list of novelists, men who are " likely to be successful in America," in an article on a topic which has nothing to do with me.

The *Illustrated London News* had a whole column. In the *Daily News* not long ago, *New Grub Street* was casually referred to in a leader.

Now this kind of thing ought to increase one's market value. If not, when is the increase to begin ?

My book will probably be done by end of July. Then I want to write something shorter.

I am very glad you are all improved in health ; may the benefit endure! I wish I could see and talk with you of things in general. In this way one's life flits past, and we have seen very little of each other. Surely that may some day be remedied.

I feel the want of *new* books, as you have always done. One cannot do without a glance at the day's literature. Especially I need French novels.

By the bye, at Exmouth station the other day at Smith's library shelf I saw *A Village Hampden.* I rejoice to see you in these parts; beyond doubt you have plenty of readers.

To his sister Ellen :

EXETER,
June 1, 1891.

It must be a good thing that your High School toil is over; with the hot weather coming on, that was certainly too much for you.

Yesterday (a fine day for a wonder just now) we went by train to Teignmouth (associated in my mind with Keats), and walked thence to Dawlish. Wonderfully beautiful country, but the sea-shore at these places is quite ruined by modernism; it is tame at best, and sea walls, etc., make it rather depressing. Inland one has far more enjoyment—delightful lanes, fields and woods.

I was reading in the *Daily News* to-day an article on French novelists; seven or eight of the best of them were spoken of as living in the midst of luxuries, enjoying a very large income. The explanation of that is, that a really good French writer addresses not only his own countryfolk, but the best people in all other countries as well. Now the public for anything but " popular " work in England is decidedly small, and English literature is very little read in other countries, as we have a name, especially in fiction, for producing weak stuff.

Most interesting life of Browning by Mrs. Sutherland Orr, just out. Wish I could get hold of it. But no library subscription, no anything else.

To the same :

EXETER,
June 21, 1891.

At last we have summer.   The heat is overpowering but
the sky magnificent.   Instead of waiting till the end of July,
we have decided to go to Ilfracombe a fortnight to-morrow.
I shall then have half my last volume to write.   If decent
lodgings are procurable we shall stay at least a month.   Of
course, you shall have address as soon as we get there.

The country is very rich with foliage and flowers, yesterday
we brought home an armful of enormous foxgloves.   I
gathered, too, a single spray of briar, scarcely more than a foot
long, on which were *forty-eight* rosebuds, and it looks as if
nearly all would come out.   Surely this was extraordinary.

Things go very well with us, except that there is no possibility of associating with the people downstairs, who are
extremely selfish and vulgar beyond belief.

Give my love to mother.   Would it be quite impossible for
her to come to Ilfracombe early in August?   I suppose the
journey would be too serious ?   Yet it is no distance after
Bristol.

To his brother :

EXETER,
June 26, 1891.

I hope you are hard at work at the deal table.   The heat
is oppressive here, but you have probably a less relaxing
atmosphere.

We had decided to go to Ilfracombe, but I have altered this
plan.   An article I lately read in the *Daily Graphic* has
decided me to try *Clevedon* in Somerset, which is said to be
perfect from a health restoring point of view.   At Clevedon,
you remember, Coleridge once lived, and in the church is
buried Arthur Hallam.

How I wish you still had your year's holiday to take and
could come to Clevedon!   We shall be tolerably near you there.

I received yesterday from Mrs. Frederic Harrison, two magnificent photographs, one of herself, and one of Mr. Harrison. The former, really a work of art, larger than cabinet size, she had inscribed to my wife.

I want to find some country place where it would be possible to take a small house for a year or so, some few months hence. Now it is not impossible that Clevedon may be suitable, though there comes the library difficulty.

We hope to leave on Monday week. I shall not quite have finished my book, but the first fortnight at the sea-side will probably see the end of it.

Foxgloves are in splendid bloom about here, and the hedges full of roses and honeysuckle.

On July 23, to the same :

I am glad you get on so well with the new book. My own has been finished since last Friday. I have sent it to Smith & Elder and have asked £250 for English and American copyright. But I don't suppose I shall get it.

Yesterday we went over to Cheddar. I was simply astonished at the scenery. There is a pass through the Mendips of real grandeur; limestone cliffs occasionally 450 feet high, and these for more than a mile on either hand. One is strongly reminded of Cumberland. Furious wind and rain had to be struggled against. Some very fine stalactite caves.

On Monday we shall leave Clevedon, and go to a little sea-port called Watchet, on Brigewater Bay. I think it will be out of the reach of Bristol cheap trippers. But with Clevedon itself I am anything but disappointed. The shore is not good, but the inland scenery is most delightfully varied. I was never in more rustic surroundings than one reaches by half an hour's walk in any direction. And the air is very inspiriting.

I should verily like to take a house somewhere in your neighbourhood, but I fear the remoteness from reading rooms and libraries would be destruction to me. I am so perpetually in need of works of *reference* on the most unlikely subjects. The house must, I think, be taken in Exeter. But I am not at ease in that part of England; intellectually it is very dull. I shouldn't be surprised if some northern manufacturing town attracted me.

Diary :

August 29, 1891. A week of horrors. Weather wretched, ceaseless rain. On Tuesday got the moving over; left 24 Prospect Park with profound thanksgiving. On Wednesday morning came letter from Watt, saying that Chatto & Windus will only give £120 for the British rights; he has passed the MS. on to Longman.

To his brother :

1 St. Leonard's Terrace, Exeter.
August 31, 1891.

Heaven be thankit. I am at last established in a house of my own. And a very satisfactory house indeed. The neighbourhood is beautiful; not easily to be matched, I should think, in English suburbs. We are a mass of garden, flowers and leafage in every direction; a view from every window of the house is one of unspoilt grace. Inside, every convenience.

To-morrow I sit down to work once more. My study is small but very quiet.

To the same :

September 19, 1891.

Am reading (for the first time), Carlyle's *Cromwell*. Carlyle as a mere prophet is now (humour aside), little palatable to me. But as a historian he remains delightful. I hope to buy the four volumes of his life, some day, in Longman's Silver Library. One of the best and most entertaining biographies in existence, all twaddling clamour notwithstanding.

Daudet is said to be wretchedly ill, allowed only half an hour's writing per diem. I fear we have read the last of him; an extinction of the delight of nations, if ever there was one.

Harrison has been soundly abused for his lecture on
" Woman " the other day, maintaining the law of domesticity,
etc.　In my new book I am tackling that topic.

Remembrances to your household.　Hope you get on
steadily, as I think your reputation certainly does.

Diary :

September 26.　Letter from Lawrence & Bullen, the new
publishers, saying that they are told that I am engaged on a
one volume story, and offering to publish it for me at 6s., giving
me 1s. on each copy; also willing to pay £100 on account.

The *Illustrated London News* of to-day, in an article called
" London in Fiction," has this passage: " In such a book no
inconsiderable part would be played by the Temple, which has
been the happy hunting ground of so many of our novelists,
from Sir Walter Scott to Mr. George Gissing."　The mention
is good, but I have never made use of the Temple.

October 20.　Rain all day.　When will it cease?　Worked
well, doing three pages in the morning and two in the evening.
Am working with extraordinary ease just now.　Means vastly
improved health, I suppose.

To his brother:

EXETER,
November 24, 1891.

Greetings from us both on your birthday.　I suppose your
age is one and thirty, is it not ?　Plenty of time yet to do a great
deal of work before forty, at which age so many people have
begun.　All good wishes.

I am writing short stories to make up a future volume.　One
I finished last week, " A Casual Acquaintance "; and I am
now engaged on " A Victim of Circumstances."　Several more
are in my mind.

A hard frost.　Coming down to my bath this morning,
I found the plug frozen to the bottom; and my wet footmarks
on the floor were soon slippery with ice.

To the same :

January 22, 1892.

We have had a most difficult time of it during the last few weeks.   Edith when just able to walk was seized with influenza. We had to send the child away, and I was lucky in finding some really trustworthy people out at a little village called Brampford Speke, four miles from Exeter.   There he remains thriving on milk warm from the cow.

To the same :

February 16, 1892.

We are back from our week's holiday at Penzance.   It is wonderfully warm down there; a fire was needless.   Two glorious days we had, the rest was heavily clouded, ordinary Cornish weather.   We didn't get to Land's End but had a day at St. Just and another at St. Ives.   The latter a delightful place, the most picturesque spot I have seen in England.   I should like to stay there several weeks in summer weather.

I don't know whether to send you a copy of *Denzil Quarrier*. It isn't worth much, but you can have one if you like.

I gave a good month's work to the MS. of *Godwin Peak* and greatly bettered it.

The name is to be *Born in Exile*.

To the same :

Exeter,
March 6, 1892.

I have received specimens of the German translation of *New Grub Street*—most conscientiously done.   It really delights me to think that I am read day after day in Buda-Pest.   The title, however, is inadequate : " Ein Mann des Tages."   The translator tells me she will find a better one when the novel comes out as a book.

The infant flourishes astonishingly.   Has got over his vaccination, and already clutches at objects and wants to crawl.

To his sister Ellen :

EXETER,
March 14, 1892.

No, I didn't expect you to like " D. Q." [*Denzil Quarrier*], yet it is very favourably reviewed.   The *Times* of Saturday has a good notice.   The *Saturday Review* amid much laudation remarked " perhaps this author succeeds better with a bolder subject."   That, to you, will sound strange.

The book is, in fact, a strong defence of conventionality, and most people seem to understand that.   But, alas, you will not like my future work, least of all *Born in Exile*, the proofs of which I am now correcting.   It is very unfortunate but of course I must work in the direction which I feel to be, for me, the true one.   Doubtless you understand that.

The new spirit in fiction is pretty sure to repel you, yet never cease to reflect that there are a great many people, of substantially your own way of thinking, who welcome a new movement as a vast improvement upon the old worn out processes.   I shall be very curious to see what the *Guardian* says about " D. Q."   It is always very complimentary to me.

Edith has just spent four days out at Brampford Speke with little Gubsey [his pet name for his eldest boy Walter].   He has got over his vaccination and seems very strong.   In about a month's time will probably come home.   He is in short clothes, and kicks so strongly that it is difficult to hold him for long. I wish you could see him, but when can that come to pass ?

I am just beginning a new book.   Must finish it before the end of the summer.

By the bye, a little story of mine, which I think you will like, has just been accepted by *Blackwood's Magazine* ; it is called a " Victim of Circumstances."   The scene is laid at Glastonbury.

Very fine summer weather with us just now, but continuous frost.

Do you suffer for want of coal ?   I fear we shall live through great troubles yet, owing to the social revolution that is in progress.   You will have understood, in part, my attitude to this revolution. We cannot resist it, but I throw in what weight I may have on the side of those who believe in an aristocracy of *brains*, as against the brute domination of the quarter-educated mob.

To his brother :

June 19, 1892.

My own plan for the future stands somehow thus:—When the infant is quite out of arms, I hope to take a house either at St. Alban's, or Hatfield or Barnet, so as to be quite near to London and yet away from the baleful atmosphere. That might, perchance, be a definite and final settlement, if all goes well. I shall not be able to dispense with immediate study of London for very much longer. My health, I think, has profited considerably by this sojourn amid the fields.

The weather seems to be improving again. We have had some good walks, and Madge [his sister] has become much sunburnt. Yesterday we spent at Budleigh Salterton, and returned with a great quantity of yellow iris, growing thickly in the marshy meadows about there.

Diary :

July 1, 1892.   On looking back I see that this novel I have now begun is the *seventh* attempt since my last was finished. Each time a new subject. Something wrong here.

October 4.   Finished the last chapter, shall call the book *The Odd Women.* I have written it very quickly but the writing has been as severe a struggle as ever I knew. Not an hour when I was really at peace in mind. A bitter struggle.

October 5.   News that Tennyson is on his death-bed. Walk in the afternoon on to the hills below Wonford. Mild air, windless. Sky thickly strewed with manifold cloud-shapes, some of rain; bright blue between. Golden sunlight on the trees, making their autumn foliage a rich brown. An exquisite afternoon, and, later, rose full moon ; one of the most brilliant I have ever seen.

October 6. Fine but showery, warm. Went to reading-room for news of Tennyson. Morning papers only report that he was sinking. In afternoon noticed, in Eland's window, a card with "Works of Late Lord Tennyson." He died at half-past one in the night. A gloriously peaceful death, the room full of that moonlight which we had here. Not long before death, he asked for a Shakespeare and turned for a few minutes to "Cymbeline." Once or twice he smiled at those about him.

October 22. Had a fairly enjoyable week [at Weymouth], though little Gubsey makes it impossible to more than pace the sea-front.

WILLERSEY, GLOUCESTERSHIRE,
October 30, 1892.

Exquisite day. Climbed the hill with Alg. amid clear sunshine. Looked down on the plain covered with mist; Bredon and the Malvern summits standing out precisely like islands from a sea. No wind, and warm. Colours of trees this autumn are very fine, owing to long dry summer. The beeches are a magnificent russet; the leaves a rich yellow (beautiful with sun through them); hawthorn warm; wayfaring tree frequent, with its noble leaves; maple, bright yellow. At nine in the evening when mist was thick, Alg. and I again went up the hill to hear the owls crying. There were several of them, answering each other far and near. "Tu—tu—whoo—oo!" is the general cry. Some voices deeper and more tremulous than others as if with age.

To his brother :

November 28, 1892.

At Birmingham I happened to see in the *New Review* an article by Gosse on Tennyson, wherein he threw scorn upon the journalistic assumption that Tennyson was enjoyed by the multitude. This delighted me and I sent Gosse a note to say so. Yesterday came a reply " I greatly value the letter which you have had the kindness to send me.   It confirms in the most authoritative manner an impression I had formed more by intuition than by experience.

May I venture to say with how much interest and sympathy I follow your career and read your powerful and mournful studies of life.   With sincere thanks for your valued letter."

I hope you are getting into smoother water.

To the same :

Exeter,

Christmas Day, 1892.

Hearty good wishes to you, and to Katie and to Enid for the New Year!

We draw strangely near to a new century—I count greatly on January 1, 1900: a bottle of good Burgundy must be secured for that day.

Did you ever come across *The Recreations of a Country Parson* (A. K. H. Boyd).   It really is very pleasant reading—somewhat in the style of *Dreamthorp*.

I am thoroughly well at work on a new book, scene in Birmingham.   Must manage two this next year.

You speak of projects for a fixed abode.   For my own part, I am seriously inclined, at Michaelmas of next year, to make a move to suburbs of Birmingham, at all events for a year or two. Those Midlands interest me and the free libraries are so excellent. Music, too, is obtainable, of good quality, on reasonable terms.

For yourself, I suppose, the far north would really be most congenial.   There must be a good deal of intellectual life in Newcastle, and, you may depend upon it—as reflection will assure you—that it is a good thing for an author to be clearly associated with some *locality*.   But, of course, you would reflect maturely on such a definite movement.

A week or two ago I brought out and read a great batch of dear old Will's [his brother's] letters.   They struck me as remarkable, not only by their revelation of a character rarely surpassed, I should think, for delicate unselfishness, but judged as mere writing.   One or two of them seem to me as good as letters written by men of the epistolary time—really models of such composition.   Eheu, eheu!

Your short book must be well nigh finished.

To his sister Ellen :

EXETER,
December 30, 1892.

I have indeed been wretchedly remiss in the matter of writing to you.   I hardly know why.   Letter-writing is, I suppose, so uncongenial to me that I practise a great deal of dilatoriness whenever the thought of it comes up.

One must, undoubtedly, set apart an hour or two in the day for mere amusement of one kind or another—an amusement quite unlike our ordinary concerns.   I don't do it myself, for the time and opportunity are not to be had; but I should be better for it.   At all events, don't sit up late at night.   Sufficiency of early sleep is a great point.

You will, I am sure, enjoy your holidays.   Ah, how I envy this going about among people.   Never to speak with a soul outside one's own household is very trying.

I have an idea that it might be well to change my abode, for a year or two, to Birmingham.   A new book [*In the Year of Jubilee*] I am engaged upon, deals with that region, and I think I might make further use of it.

We went to hear the " Elijah," but it was very poorly done. Curious that the people of Exeter will not support anything good in drama or music.

The little lad goes on very well.   He can very nearly walk. He knows the meaning of a great many words and evidently observes everything that goes on ; this morning, for instance, he picked up a comb in the bedroom, and at once attempted comically enough *to comb his little pate.*   Hair he has scarcely any.   He gives us very little trouble now o' nights.   He is delighted with his squirrel ; we have taught him to handle it with peculiar gentleness and he coos over it. A book with pictures makes him chortle delightedly.

Diary :

December 31. The year 1892 on the whole profitless. Marked by domestic misery and discomfort. The one piece of work, *The Odd Women*, scribbled in six weeks as the autumn drew to an end ; and I have no high opinion of it. Have read next to nothing; classical studies utterly neglected.

This, and the following extracts, are from letters to his brother :

EXETER,
January 29, 1893.

It is long since I had news of you; surely the weather of Jersey has improved, for here we have had warmth and sunshine the last week or more.

Your proofs, I suppose, have been arriving ; we shall appear about the same time, for I have just got through proofs and reviews of *The Odd Women*—a great task, for I made many alterations.

In addition to this work, I have also written Volume I. of my new novel, and a short story called " A Minstrel of the Byways."

By the end of March, if all goes well, I shall have finished the book. That will probably allow me to do a second book this year.

The little chap grows and flourishes. He makes an attempt at three words : book, brush and crust, which take the form of Boo, Bar, and Cur.

A book he seizes with a cry of delight; I have much ado to keep him from demanding all the lower shelves; he points at pictures and chuckles. His other mania is to get hold of a brush and scrub the floor.

About our removal. Everything is uncertain. I have recently been made to think of London again by the announcement that a great public library is shortly to be opened in

Brixton.   One of Tate's gifts.   They say it will be by far the
best local library in London.   Now that part, South Brixton
close to Clapham, is a high and healthy position, with tram and
train to every part of the town.   Really, I don't know what to
do.   I simply must not go anywhere if there is not a good
reading room at hand, as, in my personal isolation, I am so
greatly dependent for material and suggestion on the daily and
weekly papers.

Have you any idea about returning ?   I want, if possible, to
come north in the early summer, and, of course, we ought to
see you.

February 28, 1893.

The weather has been rather doleful this last week, and will
have added to your burden.   But I hope you have the sunshine
this morning, as here.   The ceaseless trouble about money all
around one, has made me strike a rather clearer note on socialistic
matter in my new book.   The name I propose is *Gods of Iron*—
meaning machinery, which is no longer a servant but a tyrannous
oppressor of mankind.   One way or another this frantic social
struggle must be eased.   I have a few people who work their
way to an idea on the subject that the intellect of the country
must proclaim for Collectivism, but by no means for democracy
unrestrained.

March 25.   Edmund Gosse is going to print, as an appendix
to a new book of his, a letter from me on the estimate in which
poetry is held by the lower classes.   It came out of the correspondence of which I told you.

Hudson has sent me his *Idle Days in Patagonia*—a beautiful
book.

April 11.

Mother, we hope, is coming to us shortly for a fortnight.

On the whole, I fear that I have wasted two years here in
Devon.   It is obviously in London that my material lies, and
I must work hard to recover lost ground.   But, of course, I
keep up courage: that is the *sine quâ non.*

We are having a bad time with the little man's teething. Doctor coming in, no sleep at night, etc. Love to you all. Sursum corda, that's all one can say.

April 23. I am very glad to hear that you go ahead in such good spirits. We had heavy rain in the past night; things much brighter this morning in consequence. Strange that the swallows and martins have not yet shown themselves here. Laburnums are in full bloom, and the may, white and pink, is out in the garden.

A pestilent idiot in Germany (meteorologist of some repute), has been prophesying European earthquakes of the most serious nature. The papers have given much attention to it. I feel a personal animosity against such a man. As if we had not trouble and misery enough, public and private, without such suggestions ; pretty sure to be nothing but a false alarm.

May 16. Mother has been with us since Saturday, and all goes well. On Friday we shall all go together to Burnham (Somerset), that mother may have a breath of the sea air before going home, and that her backward journey may be shortened.

I have arranged to take the upper part of a house in Brixton; if you are really going to London could you get a lodging in the same neighbourhood ?

Diary :

June 13. Letter through Lawrence & Bullen from a member of the Athenaeum Club who addresses me on ground of admiration, and invites me for a Saturday to Monday at his country house near Tonbridge. Must, of course, refuse.

To his brother :

The day before yesterday, I had a card of invitation from the Lord Mayor to dine at the Mansion House on July 1st to meet representatives of art and literature. Of course refused.

Diary:

June 20.   Getting the house stript.   A dreary outlook, packing, etc.

June 23.   All the things away by 1.30.   London by a quarter to eight and put up at an hotel.

June 27.   Toiling like a slave, with moments of wretched discouragement.   By night got something like order.

To his brother :

76 BURTON ROAD,
BRIXTON,
July 12, 1893.

I am doing my best to get to work, in the new circumstances, but it is very difficult.   The struggle of life gets harder as one goes on, instead of being lightened.   It would be a strange sensation to look forward with easy confidence for a year or two.

Diary :

July 29.   Got up at 3.30 a.m. to explore the city; idea for my short story.   Went to Waterloo to see the 5.50 newspaper train off.   Home to breakfast at 8.   Then to work as usual.

To his brother :

BRIXTON,
October 22, 1893.

I am labouring at a novel, did I mention it ? ,   To be called *Miss Lord of Camberwell.*   But the coming on of winter weighs upon my mind, and already I begin to suffer from coughs and colds.   Indeed I wish it were possible for me to come over for a day or two, but the sinking of my funds forbids anything of the kind; I must press on as hard as possible.

In leisure moments I am re-reading Froude's *Life of Carlyle,* which I still think one of the few excellent biographies in the language.   But it is plain that the worst form of pecuniary difficulty never afflicted Carlyle; the miseries of his early life are subjective. Why he was not altogether more prosperous in later years, I can't understand. With such an immense popularity he never became rich, or anything like it.

Astonishing how little that is worth reporting happens to one, week after week, and month after month. I rarely see anyone. So many pages are dismissed daily and that's all.

I wonder how Enid gets on. Of course she will soon be able to read. The boy here will be two years old in a month or so, incredible flight of time.

By the bye, T. tells me that several times of late there have been trade enquiries for copies of *The Unclassed*. Of course it is unobtainable save second hand, and the book seems to have grown extremely rare. The latest to enquire is a man at Nottingham. Sometimes they advertise for it in the *Publishers' Circular*.

Kindest remembrances to all about you.

It would do me good to walk from Willersey to Broadway, and smell the moist fields.

To his sister Ellen :

December 31, 1893.

The geographical question is a very difficult one, and I do not know of any small book which is of much use for your purpose. But let me give a few hints on the matter, which are the result of my experience and reflection. (1) Never let geography be learnt from a book alone, but *always* from the map. Let map be constantly *drawn* by pupils.

(2) Absolutely no learning by *rote*. It is useless. No profit in saying off lists of capes, bays, etc.

(3) Take one country—or continent—at a time and spend weeks over it. Talk with pupils of imaginary journeys, from England, and in the country itself. Get a Bradshaw and make use of the list of steamboat voyages at the end. *Insist on clear ideas of distances.* Make it understood how long a steamer takes to cross the Atlantic, for instance. (This you will find

in Whitaker's Almanack, stated at the end of his information about each foreign country.)

(4) Do not separate geography from history. No use in learning about *places*, merely as places.

(5) Get a book of travels concerning the country in hand. Read these and *talk* about what you learn therefrom. Your ideas will be much clearer and more interesting than any to be gathered from professed treatises on geography. Apropos of this, buy a cheap edition of Lady Brassey's *Voyage in a Sunbeam* and use it for a quarter of a year as class book. Infinitely better than any dry manual.

Tell me if these suggestions are of any use.

For the sake of the little boy's health, the family spent from the beginning of February, 1894, to April of the same year, at St. Leonards-on-Sea and Eastbourne.

Diary :

February 7. Reached St. Leonards at 1.18. A comical mistake on arrival. The landlady met me with a grave face, and said she couldn't take in a " cat." " Cat ? who talked about a cat ? " And then it struck me, yesterday I sent her a postcard, saying that " the cot " had been dispatched, and might arrive before we did!

February 8. Glorious day, sunny and warm. In morning with fearful effort got to work and did one page. Of course had to destroy it in the evening but did three more.

February 10. Strong wind, high sea; fine. Wrote in better spirits four pages.

February 19, *to his brother :*

Here we are in a sad state again. The boy is once more in bed with bronchitis. It is a cheerless outlook. I am afraid I shall have a hard struggle to get the novel done in the time allowed.

If I could sleep at night, I might work well in the day time, for it is wonderfully warm here, in spite of an east wind and the thermometer at freezing. But fires have to be kept up all night, and poultices made, and the little man lies gasping for breath. Dreary business.

And in a letter to the same on March 25, written from East-bourne, he says :

It is obvious that St. Leonard's was entirely the wrong place for the boy. Since coming here we have had a shrewd east wind every day, and the result is that he skips like a lamb. He has absolutely ceased to snore and gasp in his sleep. The air is grand; I have been walking over the downs to forgotten little hamlets that date from Saxon times; wonderful places, and all the time I feel a lightness unknown elsewhere.

Diary :

April 13. In the evening finished *my interminable novel* [*In the Year of Jubilee*].

After much domestic discomfort, Gissing decided to give up the house at Brixton and store furniture for a time. All went down to Clevedon on June 2 and remained there until August. From there they went to Dorking.

To his sister Ellen :

CLEVEDON, SOMERSET,
June 4, 1894.

You will be surprised at my sudden change of purpose—but such surprises have often befallen you. The vile weather made it impossible to think of the east coast, and, as we were obliged to get away at any cost, both on the boy's account and because my work had hopelessly come to an end, I suddenly resolved on trying Clevedon. We were fortunate enough to get the same lodgings as when we were last here. Much cleanliness and good temper.

Whilst thinking of the east coast, I went down into Suffolk to look at Southwold, a little seaside place. It did not please me but I made another use of the journey. The junction for Southwold is Halesworth, father's birthplace, and there I spent two or three hours.

It will amuse you to hear that I started on that Suffolk expedition at 3.30 a.m. I walked to Liverpool Street Station (4½ miles), breakfasted there. Left by the 5.10 train and was at Southwold about 10 o'clock. I got back to Brixton at 7 in the evening. It was a day of furious winds and hailstorms. I had no overcoat, nay not even an umbrella.

To-day it pours with rain, and a hot south wind is blowing. If all goes well I hope to begin work to-morrow. But I feel by no means in a mood for it.

To his brother :

CLEVEDON,
June 17, 1894.

Heaven be praised, another week or so will bring me to the end. [Writing *Eve's Ransom* to come out serially in the *Illustrated London News.*]

I feel in a very low state, and the atmosphere of this place does not help me. The house lies low; we ought to be upon the hill. Work is martyrdom.

Of course, I shall come over before long ; we shall be here till the end of August.

To the same :

August 4, 1894.

Yesterday I had a most delightful walk from Cheddar to Wells, along the lower slope of the Mendips, about 8 miles. It is exquisite country, and if ever I am able to build a small house, I think it will be somewhere in that region. Wells itself is ideally situated, amid the hills which break away from the windy Mendips to the great Somerset level. A peaceful village, little more; and at a turn of the street you come upon that glorious Cathedral, set amid surely the most beautiful Close that exists; the entrance at each corner through archways of grey crumbling stone. Anything like the Bishop's Palace I never saw. It is surrounded by a wall and a moat: the wall embattled and loop-holed, overgrown with ivy, and in places with peach and apricot; the entrance a drawbridge and portcullis; and the moat very wide, supplied with water that rushes into it foaming and roaring from St. Andrew's well, a great spring coming somehow from the hidden depths of the Mendips. Swans and ducks swim about on the olive-green water. Close by is a walk shadowed by huge, dense elms, and all around are lawns, meadows, hills, rising to woodland and heath. A marvellous spot, civilized with the culture of centuries, yet quite unlike the trimness of other cathedral towns.

You are quite right in what you say about Hardy. He is not a realist; his books are fantasias on the rural theme: his strength is his humour and imagination.

George Eliot's rare conscientiousness appears on every page of the book you mention. Of course the truthfulness of her country folk has never been surpassed.

Diary :

August 27. Left Clevedon by the 8.30 train; got to London 12.25. In search of an abode for us all.

August 30. White mist early; it cleared, and there followed a blazing day, throughout which I travelled and tramped many a weary mile. I went by train to Dorking and looked for rooms, where, at length, took two rooms.

September 4. Went to Epsom and there at length found a house that pleases me—Eversley, Worple Road. Chalk and gravel. Decided to take house on yearly tenancy.

September 17. Went early to London. Then to see Bullen. Thence to Shorter who told me that, owing to Fred

Barnard's breakdown, the publication of my novel is unavoidably postponed to January. He asked me for some more short stories, and promised cheque for *Eve's Ransom* at once. Accepted his invitation to dine with him and meet Dr. Robertson Nicoll, at Devonshire Club.

To his sister Ellen :

EPSOM,
September 26, 1894.

Many thanks for your letter. We are getting settled. We have found a servant who can positively cook a joint and boil a potato. It is incredible.

I have now to get to work on short stories as hard as I can. They want several more for the *English Illustrated*. I think all goes well.

The boy is in great spirits, and seems better here than at any of the other places where we have lived. He grows apace and talks incessantly.

To his brother:

EPSOM,
May 30, 1895.

To-morrow I go down to Aldeburgh, whence I proceed to Yarmouth, just to see whether that or any place near it would do for our summer holiday. In this hot summer, as it bids fair to be, one must needs go to the east coast.

This place has been hideous for the last few days [on account of the Races]. All traffic on the railway disorganised, no getting anywhere, fields and lanes filled with verminous ruffians, the night hideous with yells and fireworks. Happily it takes place but once a year.

The boy keeps in admirable health ; living, of course, in the open air. I too, am fairly well, but don't get through much work: in fine weather I begin to find it a struggle.

To his sister Ellen :

Epsom,
June 9, 1895.

The holiday at Aldeburgh was vastly enjoyable. Our party consisted of Grant Allen, Shorter, L. F. Austin, a literary solicitor named Whale, and Sir Benjamin Ward-Richardson, the great authority on hygiene. Clodd has a very nice house close upon the shore. In his sailing boat we went about on the river Alde and got huge appetites. I have not eaten so heartily since boyhood.

On leaving Clodd I went to Yarmouth and stayed for a day. At Gorleston, a suburb of Yarmouth, I found a suitable place for our holiday this year; splendid sands and a great deal of shipping. If all is well, we shall go there for three weeks towards the end of July.

I am overwhelmed with work. Shorter, using the occasion to do a stroke of business, got me to promise him six more stories for the *English Illustrated*, and twenty papers for the *Sketch*—all the rest of this year I shall have to work very hard.

To his brother :

June 9, 1895.

I have a letter from Hudson. He has been spending ten weeks in the west of England, and stayed for a whole fortnight at Wells, which he agrees with me in thinking the most country town within the four seas.

So you are coming to London for a few days. If it is any convenience to you to sleep here, pray say so; we could easily manage it.

Diary :

July 2, 1895.

Invitation from Shorter to be his guest at the dinner of the Omar Khayyám Club at Burford Bridge Hotel, on Saturday of next week. George Meredith to be there—accepted. Made a new vigorous start; story to be called *The Paying Guest*.

July 4.   Went to Weybridge, and drove to Dorney House.
Found the T.'s excellent people.   After lunch we went on the
river, and in pouring rain visited Matthew Arnold's grave at
Laleham.

July 13.   Went to Boxhill (to Omar Khayyám Dinner).
Before dinner a few of us walked up the hill.   Present at the
dinner were Clodd, Hardy, Henry Norman, Cook, Cust,
Robertson Nicoll, Shorter, Max Pemberton, L. F. Austin,
George Whale, Forestier the artist, Edmund Gosse, Theodore
Watts, William Sharp and many others whom I knew not.
As soon as dinner was over, Meredith entered; we all stood up
and received him with applause.   Clodd began the speeches by
a toast to Meredith, who briefly replied.   He said it was the
first time in his life he had publicly spoken—strange fact.
Then Austin gave " The Guests " in a capital speech.   Hardy
replied very shortly, just mentioning that twenty-six years had
passed since he first met Meredith, which was in a back room
of Chapman & Hall's.   Then my name was shouted, and there
was nothing for it.   I told the story of Meredith's accepting
The Unclassed for Chapman, and my interview with him, when
I didn't know who he was.   Cust then spoke, and Cook.

Meredith grievously aged; very deaf and shaky, but mind
clear as ever.   As he came round the tables on entering, someone
mentioned my name to him, and he said " Mr. Gissing!   Ah,
where is Mr. Gissing ? "   And we shook hands.   Then he sat
at the top of the table, talking with Clodd and Watts.   On going
I went to shake hands with him, and he asked me to go to his
house one day.   With Hardy I talked a little and he asked me to
write to him.

August 28.   Very hot.   In afternoon boy and I made our
first expedition alone together.   We went up to town, and to
the National Gallery.   The boy recognised the portrait of
Turner, " The death of the Stag," and other pictures, which
he knows from our books of photographs.

Time of great domestic misery.   No servant heard of yet,
and of course no work possible.

September 3. In afternoon went over to Boxhill and called on Meredith. Found him sitting in a little drawing room, unoccupied, smoking cigarette. Very soon came in his daughter and her husband, who were driving past, they invited me to call any Sunday (house near Leatherhead). When they went Meredith led me out into the garden, which lies beautifully on the slope of the hill, and, high above, his chalet. In the chalet only two rooms ; splendid view southward. The writing room has bookcases all round the walls. Had talk of simple matters. Pleaded for imagination in the novel ; "must be fruit for the reader to take away." After an hour or so, Lady Lawrence called, and I took my leave, with invitation to dine next week. I am pleased and proud to be thus received by the old man. He walks with signs of severe lameness in left leg. He mentioned the journalism for *Saturday Review* in old days; hated it for the trouble it gave him. Said he had a miserably hard time in his youth. Thinks he will now rest—write no more.

To his brother :

EPSOM,
September 8, 1895.

I am right glad that you have finished the book. It has been a really hard bit of work.

The change you look forward to is, I have no doubt, quite necessary. I only hope you won't have a very hard winter to face up yonder; for any illness in the family would, of course, stand grievously in the way of work. As for servant difficulties, I have exhausted all possible utterances. The matter becomes a very grave one, and I am sure that in a few more years great numbers of people will find it necessary to do without servants altogether; a state of things which has largely come to pass in the United States.

How domestic life is to go on I don't quite see. I suppose it will be reduced to the simplest elements. We shall have to live in very bare houses and eat only the plainest food.

I have an invitation from Hardy to stay a day or two with him at the end of this week. As our east coast holiday was so wretched I am going to take Edith and the boy down to Weymouth and join them for a few days when I leave Hardy. All this idling is very unsatisfactory, and even rather alarming. But I shall have to work very hard when the sun has gone.

Diary :

September 12. At 4 o'clock went over to Boxhill, and stayed to dine with Meredith; he very cordial. His son with wife and baby boy arrived just before dinner. Among the books lying about I noted Kennedy's *Agamemnon* (present from Cotter Morrison); *Mommsen* (in original); *The Memories of Barras*, Léon Daudet's latest novel. William Watson's last volume (from author).

Meredith has never been to Rome, though so familiar with North Italy.

He says he knew " Sir Willoughby Patterne " in the flesh.

To his sister Ellen :

November 15, 1895.

I have dreary things to tell of. A week ago we thought the boy had scarlet fever. It has proved, however, to be some form of blood poisoning. He is just up again and will soon be all right I hope. But his tonsils give the poor little chap trouble. I am toiling to finish some short stories for the *English Illustrated*. In January begins a series called "Great Men in Little Worlds" which will run month by month to the end of September.

Did you see Fred Barnard's beautiful illustrations to *The Fate of Humphrey Snell* ?—a favourite story of mine—symbolical of much, as Carlyle says.

Some people I know very slightly have just sent a present of giant grapes and a fine fowl.

Diary :

December 25, 1895. Last night had several strange dreams. I met dear old Willie somewhere and he told me he had just

come from Continental travels, and he had been in Rome.
He looked well and cheery.   Oddest of all, we conversed in
German, and I remember correcting myself in a false past
participle.   Then I dreamed that I had cancer, though unaware
of its situation.   Friends gravely assured me of it, and recommended operations and I was much perturbed.   Then I was
saying to someone that there was only one bit of Byron I could
repeat with strong feeling, and it was the stanza beginning
" O Rome, my country, city of the soul."   I repeated the
following line which I forget.   Queer thing is I don't remember
to have thought of this passage of verse.

Letter from Davidson, saying he sends me his new volume,
and asking me to lunch next Saturday.

To his brother :

December 30, 1895.

I have put an end to all short-story writing for the present.
It is now two years since I had a novel ready for publication,
and if I do not put aside everything else I fear no new book will
ever be done.

To the same:

Epsom,
March 3, 1896.

My public progress is terribly balanced by private misfortunes
and miseries.   Last night, on coming home late from London,
I found there had been a gas explosion in the house.   No one
hurt, except a workman, but endless damage.   Two ceilings
blown down; the drawing-room buried under a desert of plaster;
bedroom only just saved from a fire which would have burnt
the house down, wicker chairs and bedding ruined.

The workman who came yesterday to test the pipes, found
a bad leak, and went to it *with a candle.*

Edith and the children [his younger son Alfred being now
three months old] must go into lodgings while the house is
repaired.   Impossible to dream of work, and will be for a long,
long, time.

The following is the first letter to his son Walter (four years old), who had gone to live for a time with his aunts in Wakefield.

EPSOM,
May 2, 1896.

MY DEAR WALTER,

I shall write to you every Saturday, so that you may always expect a letter on Sunday morning.

I wonder how you like your school. The letter you wrote to mother was very nicely done. Try to be patient and to learn all the things that a good boy ought to know.

I think of you very often, always the first thing in the morning, and when you are going to bed at night. Think of me too, dear little son, and say good-night to me.

I hope Brownie [the cat] keeps quite well.

The weather is rather colder again just now, but we shall very soon have the beautiful summer and then you will have nice walks with grandmother.

I am writing day after day, and writing a big book; so we are both of us very busy, I and you.

Give my love to grandmother and to Aunt Margaret and Aunt Nellie. And very very much love to you, dear little boy, from old father.

BOOK-WRITER.

Diary :

May 12. In afternoon went to Box Hill to see Meredith. Found the Meynells and their children staying there. Had tea and came home. Meredith bright and good. He is revising his works for the Library Edition, and says he is " slashing " at them—probably a great mistake.

EPSOM,
May 15, 1896.

DEAR LITTLE BOY,

Another week of splendid weather; but everything is getting dried up, and the roads are deep in dust. We begin to want rain badly.

On Tuesday I went over to Box Hill, and had tea with George Meredith in his beautiful garden, and I enjoyed it very much, and I am to go to dinner with him before long.   When you grow up and are able to read books, you will be glad to talk to me about George Meredith, and what he looked like, and what he said.

I was glad to hear that you are able to find a few flowers. Try not to forget those that you had learnt.   The best way will be to look now and then all through the pictures in your plant book, and read the names where you do not know them.

And now much love to you, dear laddie, and give my love to all at Wakefield.   It makes me very happy to know that you are so good and getting on so well.   Think of old father.

To the same :

June 6, 1896.

To-night I have to go to London to eat a great dinner. I shall be sitting down to it just after you have gone to bed, and in the middle of all the people I shall think of my dear little son at Wakefield.

To his brother :

May 20, 1896.

In looking over the *Journal of Botany* yesterday, for 1889, I was much pleased to find father's name in a " Biographical Index of British Botanists."   Pretty full particulars were given:—place and date of birth, date of death, place of burial, business, books published.

To the same :

EPSOM,
June 19, 1896.

I have been wondering how things go with you.   I have managed to do a little work.   I think about one third or more of my book is written, not finished, for it will need close revision.

Next week I am disturbed. The disturbance begins, indeed, to-morrow, when I go to Marlow for the Omar Khayyám dinner, and shall not get back till Sunday afternoon. On Thursday I dine at the Savoy Hotel with the editor of *Cosmopolis*, and on Saturday I go to Weybridge to visit some acquaintances.

Do you move from home before the autumn ? It is very grievous that we see so little of each other; it ought not to be. Well, in literature there is hardly such a thing as holiday; no sooner is one bit of writing finished than the mind has to renew its toil in preparation for the next. Enviable are men of business, who leave their affairs behind them.

We get, I fear, a very small margin of satisfaction out of life. One keeps hoping that years will bring improvement, but cares and responsibilities increase as one gets older.

Diary :

June 20. Went to Marlow for the Omar Khayyám dinner. New acquaintances. J. M. Barrie, Maarten Maartens, Dr. Walter Leaf and Harold Frederic. Barrie and I next each other at dinner.

Our joke late at night. We bought pots and pans from a cheap jack in the market-place, and presented them to Shorter, who is to be married in a few weeks.

George Whale took me to see the cottage where Shelley lived; an inscription is over it.

June 21. Had breakfast at 7.30. Frederic and Whale coming down to keep me company, and going to station with me. Got to London about 10 o'clock. No train to Epsom till 1.20. Went to see Hudson and spent time pleasantly.

To his brother :

EPSOM,
June 23, 1896.

I saw Hudson on Sunday, for the first time since he was at Willersey. He speaks of his visit to you with great delight— poor fellow, he is in bad health.

Diary :

June 25. Went up to the " Cosmopolis " dinner at the Savoy, a great assembly. New acquaintances·: Bryce, Justin McCarthy, Nisbet Bain (who sat next to me), Zangwill. Saw Andrew Lang for the first time, but no speech with him. Zangwill decidedly a good fellow as I have always felt from his books. Met Frederic Harrison after lapse of six or seven years.

June 29. In evening got once more to my book, and wrote one and a half pages. Read a little Ovid and Horace. Ah, if I had but the energy to give but half an hour daily to Greek and Latin !

July 3. To town, to lunch with Gosse at the National Club, Whitehall Gardens. Present: Austin Dobson, Andrew Lang, young Edward C. Fitzgerald (who has just published his feats on the New Zealand mountains), and Mr. Bateman (head of Commercial Department of the Board of Trade), an American named Armour, and Hamo Thornycroft the sculptor.

November 20. Great difficulty in getting a red rose for the Omar dinner, held at Frascati's. There, my guest, John Davidson met me at 7 o'clock. Sixty-two diners altogether. New acquaintances made: W. E. Norris, Mackail (author of *History of Latin Literature*), H. G. Wells, and Conan Doyle.

Left with George Whale and went home with him to Blackheath.

November 26. A letter from H. G. Wells, asking me to go and see him at Worcester Park.

November 30. Did only half a page. I work with extraordinary difficulty and slowness now-a-days. Shall I ever get done ? More than thirty pages still.

December 10. My boy Walter is five years old to-day.

December 18. Yesterday morning there was a shock of earthquake, all across England, at about 5.30.

Wrote one page and finished *The Whirlpool*.

December 29.   Went to Dr. Beaumont about my cough. He made an examination and says that there is a weak point in right lung.   This may be a grave matter, or it may not.   But I am to paint with iodine and take syrup of hypophosphites.

January 1, 1897.   Having seen in paper that Meredith had just undergone an operation of some kind, I walked over to Box Hill in the afternoon to make enquiry.   Found he was at his son's house in London.   The servant said the operation was for his deafness.

January 5.   Letter from Shorter, asking for "bright little love story" for the *Illustrated London News*.   Told him I couldn't do it.

January 9.   Days too miserable to chronicle.
Weather foggy and rainy.   Went to British Museum, and there chanced to meet Joseph Anderson.   On my way back home, looked in at Wells's, Worcester Park, and stayed till midnight.

January 19.   Invitation from the Royal Societies Club for evening of February 5, to meet Dr. Nansen.   Shall go.   Editor of *Westminster Gazette* asks my contribution to a discussion on "Reviewing."

In February of this year, on account of lung trouble, Gissing was advised by his doctor to go to South Devon, where he spent three months.   During his stay he did much reading in preparation for his historical novel *Veranilda*, which he was engaged upon up to the time of his death.   Some of the following extracts from the *Diary* show the number of books he read on the subject, and the care he bestowed on every detail.

Diary :

June 2.   . . . . Meanwhile [during his time in Devon] *The Whirlpool* was published and sold better than any of my books hitherto.   By the end of May the first edition of 2,000 copies was finished.

My reading was concerned with the Ostragothic rule in Italy.   In the first volume of Gregorovius I got hold of a good idea for a historical novel, and worked it out.   I obtained from London the works of Cassiodorus, and read very carefully the twelve books, noting good material.   Got also Manso's *Geschichte des Ost. goth. Reiches*, and read it twice; studied carefully Burn's *Ancient Rome*.   Read a good deal of Dickens for the little book I am to write.   On morning of departure, I received from Miss McCarthy a copy of the new volume of her father's *History of Our Own Times*.

On June 1.   Went up to see the doctor.   He says I am decidedly better, and that I must now choose a suitable place of abode—high and dry.

Enthusiastic letter from Barrie about *The Whirlpool*.

June 3.   Reading Gibbon on Justinian.

June 7.   Went to keep appointment with W. Rothenstein, at his studio, Glebe Place, Chelsea.   He made two drawings of me ; one sitting, the other standing—latter I liked best.   Max Beerbohm came in, and had lunch with us.

June 8.   Sent the boy his silver mug, the gift of Dr. Zakrzewska and Miss Sprague, which has lain here since its arrival from America.   Thinking out my story *The Town Traveller*.

June 9.   Wrote nearly three pages.   Good beginning.

June 10.   Re-wrote last half-page and did two more. Reading Lanciani's *Ancient Rome*.

June 12.   Wrote three pages.   Getting ahead very quickly.

June 13.   Finished Lanciani, and read greater part of third volume of Hodgkin.

June 16.   Reading Hare's *Russia* and Lanciani's *Pagan and Christian Rome*.

June 19.   Began Middleton's *Ancient Rome*.

June 25. Reading Dyer's *City of Rome.*

June 27. Read Brandes' book on *Russia.*

June 28. Reading Volume I. of Milman's *Latin Christianity.*

July 10. To Marlow for the Omar dinner. Barrie a new member, but did not come. New acquaintances : Prof. Walter Raleigh of Liverpool, who told me I had met him years ago at Miss Crum's, but I had forgotten it,—Alfred East, and Sir Henry Craik. Also met Sir George Robertson of Chitral, whom I had casually met once at the " Cheshire Cheese," when he was lunching with McCormick.

July 11. Left Marlow at 8.20 and called on Hudson, who is far from well. Lunch with him ; then to Worcester Park, to dine with Wells. Home by 11.

July 14. Finished *The Town Traveller.*

July 15. Reading Leroy-Beaulieu's *The Empire of the Tsars.*

July 18. Began Beugnot *Hist. de la Déstruction du Paganisme.*

July 22. In evening to Blackheath to dine with Whale. Guests: Sidney Lee, Clodd, Shorter, West, and Wheatley the philologist.

Lee told me of an oldish literary hack, who one day came to him in great discouragement, and said he should abandon literature. It turned out that he had been reading *New Grub Street.*

Having decided to go abroad in September of this year, Gissing stored his books and furniture. In preparation for his journey he paid short visits to Willersey and Wakefield.

Diary :

September 17.   I got to Honeybourne by 10 o'clock, and drove to Willersey—worn out.

September 18.   Very gloomy and cold.   Much talk.

September 20.   Left Willersey at 10 o'clock.   Got to Wakefield at 6 p.m.   All well.   Enid staying here.   Little man very glad to see me—sweet and affectionate.   Much talk till late in the evening.

September 21.   Left Wakefield.

September 22.   Left by the 11 o'clock from Charing Cross. Smooth passage.   Straight on by the Laon line for Basle.

To his sister Ellen :

MILAN,
September 24, 1897.

Arrived last night (Thursday) at 8 o'clock, tired but not too much.   From London to the top of S. Gotthard an unbroken leaden sky, with some rain; as soon as the pass was crossed, glorious sunshine, which continues to-day.

Too hot for ordinary clothing.   Am going on to Siena.
In great health and spirits.

Oh, the glorious sunshine!   I write in front of the great cathedral.   Next from Siena.

To the same :

SIENA,
September 27, 1897.

Am in very comfortable quarters, and getting to work.   You shall soon hear more news.   Never a cloud in sky, day or night, but heat tremendous, though Siena is 1,000 feet above the sea. My window wide open, goat bells tinkling in the street below; when I look out I see the great marble cathedral glistening against the blue sky.   Close by me the house of S. Catherine who lived 500 years ago.

To his brother :

Siena,
October 12, 1897.

I rejoice to tell you that I have written more than a third of my *Dickens*. I do 2,000 words every day (it is slower work than fiction), and I think the result will be rather good. Of course it is unfortunate that I should have to do this *here*; I so much want to attend to other things. But I hope to have finished very early in November, and then I shall go straight to Naples, leaving Rome till my return.

I write from 9 to 12, and from 2 to 6, which, of course, leaves me very little time for sight-seeing, as I dare not go out after dark lest I should get cold. But in truth there is nothing of very great interest in Siena. I like the town for its picturesqueness and quietness, but only stay here to get my work done.

This book on Dickens has put it into my mind that I should like to do a corresponding one on Tennyson. But I have such a variety of work before me. My appetite is excellent. Here you know we are 1,000 ft. above the sea; in the winter it is really cold, and already the north wind begins to feel chilly. It must be very healthy indeed, so high and dry. The streets are kept remarkably clean. It is here that the best Italian is supposed to be spoken. Certainly one is struck by the delicate pronunciation of the common folk.

I only wish it were possible for you to send me some honest English tobacco. Of course you cannot, it is forbidden. But the Italian for pipes is miserable stuff. Together with *salt* it is a government monopoly—which means much.

To the same :

November 14, 1897.

The scirocco is blowing to-day, and it leaves one little strength for anything. On Tuesday I leave for my Calabrian journey. Best address till you hear again will be : Poste restante,

Catanzaro, Calabria Ulteriore. I go by steamer from here
to a little port on the Calabrian coast. The British consul
here has given me notes of introduction to several people in
Calabria, so I think I shall get on very well.

I look forward to doing some solid work when I get settled
at Rome in January. My book, it seems, is out—the collection
of short stories [*Human Odds and Ends*]. I shall send cards
from several old world places. The Worcestershire fields only
gain by being viewed from this distance, and in such contrasts.

COTRONE,
November 26, 1897.

DEAR LITTLE BOY,

I must write this letter small, but grandmother will
read it to you. Did you remember that the 22nd of November
was my birthday ? I shall not forget yours on the 10th of
December, but shall let you have a letter as near that day as
possible.

I hope you follow my travels on the map. I stayed five days
at Taranto then went by train to Metaponto, where there is a
beautiful ruin of an old Greek temple. Then I came on again
by train—the railway goes all round the shores of the Gulf of
Taranto—and now am staying at a place called Cotrone, which
used to be a great Greek city called Croton. You see, the
name is not much altered. You will wonder perhaps what the
Greeks are doing in Italy. When the people got too many
for their own country, Greece, they came over the sea in ships,
and made themselves a new country here ; and the towns they
built were so splendid that this part of Italy came to be called
Greater Greece. Now there is nothing left but a few stones
to show where these places were. But the country is very
beautiful, and I enjoy seeing it very much.

Cotrone is a very strange little town. All day long herds of
goats are wandering about the streets. There is no cow's
milk to be had, and all the butter and cheese are made of goats'
milk. And the extraordinary thing is that when they bring

you butter, it is not on a plate, but in the rind of an old cheese. There is hardly any water to be had in the place. I never drink a drop, it is so dangerous; but in my bedroom is a green earthenware bottle of so-called drinking water, carefully corked.

To-day I have visited some splendid lemon and orange orchards. You would like to see those trees covered with fruit, they are very beautiful. And everywhere grows the *cactus*, sometimes twice as high as I am; and great beautiful palm trees. The geraniums here are not little plants, but great bushes, almost trees.

At night I see stars that we cannot see in England; because this is so far south.

I am afraid you have cold weather now. Here I always sit with the windows open, and very often I can hardly bear the sun as I walk. I suppose it is very much the same here all through the winter, but people think it very cold, and go about in enormous top coats, with fur collars turned up. In summer the heat must be terrible.

I shall be very anxious for letters by the time I get to Catanzaro, which will not be very long now. It seems ages since I left England and even a long, long time since I was quietly working at Siena.

There is a remnant of a Greek temple near here—just one great column, 26 feet high, which stands on the end of the promontory south of Cotrone; I can see it from here, though it is 6 miles away. To get to it, I shall have to hire a boat and land at the foot of the promontory, and climb up the cliffs. It was once one of the greatest buildings in the world. But a long time ago people pulled it down, and used the stones to make the harbour of Cotrone.

I think I shall go as far south as Reggio, which is just opposite to Sicily, and then back again to Rome. From Reggio I shall have a fine view of Mount Etna. But I don't think I shall go across into Sicily this time.

I hope you are all well, and I constantly think of you.

Much love, dear little man, from

FATHER.

While at Cotrone Gissing had a sharp attack of fever and congestion of the lungs; though the inn at which he was staying was miserably uncomfortable in every way, he found the people very kind during his illness.   He notes later in the *Diary* :

December 1.   The people here, though horribly uncouth, are showing themselves very kind.   Two or three of them come together into the room, to look at me and sympathize.   The padrona and her servant are alike in the habit of perpetually moaning and groaning.   They go about muttering " Ah, Signore!   Ah, Cristo! " for no reason in particular.   This evening they quarrelled in the kitchen, and the servant—a middle-aged woman—stout and very black-eyed, a pure savage —came to tell me in her terrible dialect all about the *guai*— lamenting that she should be so used after having *tanto lavorato,* and saying that her relatives were all *freddi morti.*   I thought at first she was railing at *me*, for giving trouble, but saw her drift at last.

Twice a day comes the newspaper lad, leaving me *La Tribuna* (which reaches here at 10 p.m. too late for reading that night), and in afternoon the *Don Chisciotte*.   He tells me to-day he has a bit of fever and has taken quinine.   Then there is the bright little imp of a lad (about 10 years old) who acts as chambermaid. He enters, doffs his cap, asks how I am, and then says " Mi permettate di fare un po' di pulizia, signore ? "

The food is very bad, I can hardly swallow anything.   Only goats' milk to be had ; I take an egg in it.   Boiled chicken nothing but rags, so much broth taken out of it.

December 2.   Much better.   Able to eat a little.   Had a roasted pigeon, not bad.   The chicken broth is tolerable.   But the execrable wine, with its taste of the chemist's shop!   Got up for a couple of hours.

December 4.   Storm all night and all to-day.   Able to get up, and eat in dining room ; but atmospheric conditions make things miserable enough.   Doctor called for the last time, and gave me prescription for a " cure " of the right lung.

The wretchedness of the people in this wild weather, with pelting rain and furious howling scirocco. Objects wretchedly huddled in great capes lurking under the portico opposite my window, and struggling to cross the road. Drearier scene I never knew. Sky a mass of grey cloud till about 4.30, then suddenly appeared a shimmering of pink cloudlet in a blue space, the beginning of calm, I hope.

December 5. Wind furious all night, this morning sun, but wind still blowing. To-night, I am told, two ships were wrecked in port; one full of pigs which are scattered all about the shore. No men lost.

I feel inwardly well, but terribly shaky. Shall not regain strength till I get into a better atmosphere.

In afternoon wind fell, and sky clouded over. Very doubtful for to-morrow, but I think I shall go in any case; this place becomes intolerable. Went out for five minutes.

December 6. Fine and calm. Got away from terrible Cotrone, by the 1.56 train, which, of course, started twenty minutes late. The slow, methodical railway official, coming into carriages, looked round, murmuring to self "Non mania niente." At Cotrone, they warned me to the end against Catanzaro—so cold and windy.

Pleasant journey along valley of Esaro—mostly a dry channel. Hills on either side, sometimes grassy, much agriculture. Olives generally amid the ploughed fields. Then a tunnel before descent began towards Catanzaro. Two or three broadish rivers—the banks, as usual, a sort of jungle, very picturesque.

Shepherds, with sheep and goats, idling on the plain by the shore. Very blue sea; white breakers tossing up on shore—result of gale. The lonely shepherds recalling old time.

Towards Catanzaro, inland mountains very beautiful. Plump rosy man got in at station and puzzled me by his healthy appearance; found he was a type of Catanzaro. At entrance to the valley, splendid orange orchards—a wonderful sight with the setting sun blazing on them. Full moon rising. Tinted clouds on Sila. The upward valley a line to Catanzaro. Arrived at 6 o'clock and, after much delay, went up to town, in the post cart. Winding ascent of half an hour.

To his sister Ellen :

CATANZARO,
December 7, 1897.

Twenty-three letters awaiting me here, and a mass of proofs to correct. Extraordinary town this, on the top of a mountain, with precipices on each side. Half an hour's drive (by winding road), from railway station. Delighted to hear that all is well. Have all sorts of good news of literary matters.

Shall go from here to Squillace, thence to Reggio, and then direct to dear old Roma. It is very plain that I must get to work again. I have materials for a good little book. [This came out under the title of *By the Ionian Sea.*]

December 8. Beautiful day. At 10 o'clock went with my card of introduction to call on the English vice-consul. Found him unable to speak a word of English. He took me to the public gardens (beautiful, over-looking ravine on east side), then to the Duomo, and the Church of the Immacolata, where there was a great crowd ; and to-day is the festa of the Immacolata—" as much thought of here," said the vice-consul, "as Christmas " ; a lively orchestra of string music, playing loudly in a gallery of the church. Early this morning I heard bagpipes, and they have been sounding all day. Picturesque costumes of contadine, the same I saw at Cosenza. A very few instances of the Calabrian hat, which is falling out of use. Plenty of fine, even heroic faces, among peasantry. And all so healthy. It delights me to see the healthy, happy children here. Even a beggar, crawling on all fours on pavement, has a ruddy face. No uproar in spite of crowds, people grave and dignified.

The vice-consul took me lastly to a chemist's shop, furnished with desks, etc., of finely carved wood, imitated from sixteenth century work, really a magnificent display. Outside, at street corner, they have a *mostra*, in wrought iron, a sort of griffin, work such as one sees at Siena. Shop full of peasants, the chemist pointing to a group, called them *Greci*. They come from a village near, and still speak a sort of Greek. They carry babies and other burdens on back, not in front.

At another shop the vice-consul gave me two silk handker-chiefs of Catanzaro manufacture.

To his sister Ellen :

December 11, 1897.

This is the end of my journey in Calabria. I am at the *toe* of Italy, and as I walk by the sea-shore, I see Sicily opposite, with Mount Etna rising into the clouds, covered with snow. Follow on the map as usual. I went from Catanzaro to Squillace and spent a day there. Bad weather and such a horrible, miserable, filthy little inn that I *durst* not stop the night, much as I wished to.

To-morrow I shall take the train for Naples. It leaves here at 7 in the evening and gets to Naples at 7 next morning. There I shall spend one or two days, then on to Rome.

I hope to work quietly for a month or two.

Diary :

December 14. Left Naples by 8.30 train. A beautiful morning, but soon clouded ; and, on arriving at Cassino, found myself in thick, cold mist, which hid everything. Went to an hotel in the town. Towards 2 o'clock the mist began to rise, so I ordered a donkey, and with a lad for a guide started up to the monastery. Wonderful ascent of about one and a half hours. Received at entrance by a monastic porter, who took my card to the Prior. In a few minutes the Prior received me; very courteous. I told him I was getting materials for a historical novel [*Veranilda*], and he listened with interest. Told me he had been in England this last summer; but, of course, speaks no English.

After showing me a few of the treasures of the library, he passed me over to the sacristan, who showed me all the little chapels, forming the original monastery (interesting modern frescoes), and then the church. A wonderfully simple man, telling his stories of old times with perfect intelligence yet with the *naïveté* of a child. His delight in the treasures of the monastery and in the mosaics and the marbles, and, above all, in the glorious wood-carving of the choir. Such work as that (walnut wood, seventeenth century) I never saw. The exquisite foliage, the saints there amid, and the " putti " on the seats of the choir! My guide kept repeating " Quanto lavoravano allora! Si divertivano, lavorando! "

The porphyry pillar, in middle of court, in which stood statue of Apollo; and the pillars from the temple, round outer court of church. It grew dark whilst we were in the church. Guide lit a taper to keep showing me the beautiful carving. Silence, and dark, and smell of incense, and glorious work all around.

Then I was conducted to my room, curious oil lamp. Comfortably furnished but no looking-glass; told, to my alarm, that supper would not be till a quarter to eight. The glorious landscape from the little window. Sea of mist of the valley of the Garigliano, mountain top rising above. Lights of Cassino just visible, a profound depth. Lights of the train starting for Rome. Lingering sunset over towards Gaeta, where there is, in clear weather, a glimpse of sea.

The supper has been frugal with a vengeance. A plate of lentil porridge with bits of meal in it; a slice of cold brawn; and an apple—decanter of wine, of course. I grow old, this lenten fare does not suit me. Three other guests in the cold, bare room; Italians, besides servants, seated at another table. Now to bed. The great corridor at night, with two or three hanging lamps—gloomy and echoing to every step—the light of the middle ages.

My window here looks over the Liris Valley. The mist still lying everywhere below, but the stars above are very bright. One short row of lights shows the town of Cassino.

December 15.   All round the monastery lies cultivated land, kitchen gardens, and ploughed fields.   The trees are oak, ilex and olive.   The oaks covered with russet foliage.   Not far away is the bare cloud-capped height of Monte Cavio, over-looking the monastery.

The geography is this.   A spur of hills running westward ends over Valley of Liris in a high hill with two crests.   On the higher and broader stands the monastery, wooded all round; on the lower, bare and stony, once stood a Temple of Venus. Below both heights is a steep crag, which once had Temple of Janus, and where now is castle—about half the height of monastery.   Characteristic of hill is the rocky surface—great rocks everywhere protruding.

In the monastery is a regular post and telegraph office.

Walked about this morning, after cup of coffee and slice of bread.   The Grand Terrace in front of church, over-looking Liris Valley—very broad, with great mountains beyond.   Round the atrium are granite columns, belonging to old Temple of Apollo.   The bronze doors of church have thirty-six panels, en-graved (once in silver) with possessions of monastery in eleventh century.   Met the Prior and took leave of him.   Donkey ready for me at 9.30.   Morning dull, but not much mist.   Snow on heights eastward.   The old road (carriage road made in 1885).

Went to my inn again, ate, and walked about for three hours. Inspected the amphitheatre, and sketched it.   Best view of monastery with castle below it, from the bridge over Rapido, at north end of town.   The Rapido a swift and full little river, tinged faint blue with lime.   The amphitheatre covered outside with *opus reticulatum* ; the work looks very fine from distance, but the stones are really of anything but regular diamond shape; often very irregular indeed.

Same work inside, only a long top.   Inside a mere mound of grassy earth.   The remains of five entrances visible; only one is used.

Beautiful costumes of women; bright shawl, orange stripe on red brown.   They say there is no work to be had, and constant emigration.

" C'è miseria! "   But the people look wonderfully healthy, children too.   The toil, the toil, of that old world!   Think of building on these great heights.   The old hilly roads mere human Calvaries.

The commonest word in Italian conversation is " mangiare " heard incessantly.

Left Cassino by 5.20.   In Rome at 8.30.   The three Americans in train.   " How long do you think of staying here ? "   " To-day's Wednesday, how does Saturday morning strike you ? "   " So long ? "   " How does Friday strike you ? We've got to see Rome."   " Well, that gives us one clear day."

To his brother :

December 15.

This comes to you from Monte Cassino.   I have passed the night in the greater monastery (founded by Benedict 529). Mother of all the Benedictine foundations.   Glorious beyond description—ascended the mountain (1,500 feet) on a donkey (one and a half hours).   The nocturnal hours vastly impressive. Weather bad, no sun and much mist.   To-night I arrive in Rome, and rest from my much travelling.   What a talk some day!

To his sister Margaret :

ROMA,
December 18, 1897.

Comfortably settled; by straining out of my window I can just see the Colosseum.   I hope to work here till May.   Have several introductions.   Endless correspondence as usual. Strangers have begun to write me birthday letters.

Wonderful night in the monastery of Monte Cassino. Do read about it.

Good news about little Alfred.   Hope little man with you is well.

To his sister Ellen:

Roma,
January 23, 1898.

My experience is that people with a weak chest should *not* come to Italy.   I believe that many a one has lost money and life, who would have saved both by simply going to South Devon or the Isle of Wight.   Italy is a splendid country for the young and the strong.   For invalids it offers little comfort and many dangers; to send Keats to Rome was the height of folly.   It resulted from ignorance, of course, but might have been a deliberate plan for shortening his life.

By the bye, Keats' rooms, in the Piazza di Spagna, are now occupied by a medical man.   A tablet on the front tells people that here Keats died.   So, in the Corso, a tablet on a house front tells one that here Shelley wrote the " Cenci " and " Prometheus Unbound."   Another proclaims the residence of Goethe.   These tablets abound in Italy.

VIII

THE CROWN OF LIFE TO THE END
(1898-1903)

Gissing left Rome on April 14, 1898, and travelled to England through Germany, spending four days at Potsdam with his friend Edouard Bertz.   On his return to England he settled down at Dorking, where he took a house in July of this year.

Diary :

July 15, 1898.   Made a beginning of *The Crown of Life.*

August 10.   Made beginning of *Preface to Pickwick.*

November 13.   In morning Clodd and I walked over to Box Hill to see Meredith.   He, far from well, sat with the typewritten copy of the dramatization of *The Egoist* on his knees, in which he has little faith.

Early in 1899 Gissing finished *The Crown of Life*, and, after a severe attack of influenza followed by pleurisy, left England, spending some time in Paris; it was here that he began *By the Ionian Sea*.   During the summer he and his wife travelled about in different parts of France and Switzerland.   This proved of considerable benefit to his health.

From this date, by the kind permission of Miss C. E. Collet, certain letters, written by Gissing to her, are introduced.

To Miss C. E. Collet :

PARIS,
December 29, 1899.

The best of good wishes for the New Year. It is an evil time enough at present, goodness knows, and one has need to hope for brighter things. But I limit my wishes to individuals. Nations being masses, are brutally stupid, and all one can hope is that any given mass will not bring too heavy a curse on the rest of the world.

My agent cheers me with his prophecies that no books will be read in England for long enough to come. That *my* books will not be read is a pretty safe forecast; but, on the whole, I imagine that booksellers are not much affected by the war. I see that this and the other novelists have been making their hundred thousand copies lately. It must be a strange feeling, to see one's book really going off like that. Twenty years ago I hoped for it, now I hope no more.

However, I am writing now a book called *Among the Prophets*, which deals with new religions and crazes of various kinds. I could make it good if I had the time; but it must needs be done very quickly.

You do not see *The Academy*, I daresay. On December 16 some unknown person wrote about me, therein, to the extent of several columns, to answer the question why I don't sell. It was rather more intelligently done than usual, but like everybody's writing on this subject, showed an imperfect knowledge of my later work.

PARIS,
December 29, 1899.

MY DEAR WALTER,

Your letter pleased me very much. I am glad indeed that you get to write so well.

So you have been having snow. I hear that there has been a great deal of snow in Italy and even in Sicily, where it scarcely ever falls. I remember once seeing snow at Naples. For a few hours, Mount Vesuvius was white from top to bottom, but it very soon vanished. Here, there has been no snow at all but a very hard frost for about five days.

What book have you been reading lately ? I suppose you *do* read books by yourself now, do you not ? I don't want you to spend a great deal of time in reading, for, of course you have your lessons to do, and walks to take, and games to play, and friends to visit. But you always ought to have a book on hand for quiet times.

I suppose you sometimes hear people talk of the war which is going on. You must understand (as aunties no doubt will tell you), that *War* is a horrible thing which ought to be left to savages—a thing to be ashamed of and not to glory in. It is wicked and dreadful for the people of one country to go and kill those of another. Never suppose that victories in war are things to be proud of. It is disgraceful to talk much about them. Some day people will be astonished that such things could be done. What we ought to be proud of is peace and kindness—not fighting and hatred.

You are getting old enough now to understand these things, and that is why I speak of them.

Give my love to all, dear boy, and think often of your affectionate father.

GEE-GEE.

A very very happy New Year to you, and to all!

To his sister Ellen :

PARIS,
January 2, 1900.

I feel so sorry for you, going through that villainous influenza. The weakness that follows is very wretched, and it lasts so long. Do try to keep up heart, dear girl. This abominable winter will come to an end before very long, and never will the sunshine have been more welcome.

I work and work, not of course in very good spirits. Just as I was hoping to earn a little more money comes this scoundrelly war, and the ruin of the book trade. It's a dreary outlook for the next year or two.

I hope you are now able to read a little. How on earth do people get through illnesses who don't care for books? In a book one can, at all events, forget one's self for a time.

Think of me when I had my illness at Cotrone! Nothing whatever to read except an Italian newspaper, which arrived at 10 o'clock every night. The boy who brought the papers from the railway station used to tramp straight into my bedroom, and hold a little conversation. Once he disappeared for three days, and I was told that he was down with fever.

Everybody has fever at Cotrone.

It seems strange to remember that I have been in such places. Sitting here, I often let my memory wander about the south of Europe.

I see spots in Greece, on the coast of Albania, in Calabria, and see them so vividly! But how much more I should have enjoyed my travels if I had been free from anxiety. Ceaseless torment about money, and other things. And so it will be to the end.

Try to keep cheerful, all of you, through this bad time.

Diary :

February 14, 1900. For two months and a half have ceased to chronicle. A week ago I finished my novel *Among the Prophets*—yesterday and to-day wrote the preface to *Sketches by Boz*. Feeling much depressed by the South African war, with its hateful motives and ceaseless disasters. Reading very little; my novel is poor stuff, I wish I could afford to destroy it; but I am sore pressed for money.

February 19. Finished all my Dickens prefaces—*Christmas Books* being the last.

April 21. On April 2nd I left Paris, to pass a month or so

in England—spent the night at Clodd's.   Next day to Wakefield—mother just recovering from bad influenza.   Stayed at
Wakefield nine days.   Then to Lincoln where I spent five
days and took many notes.   Then to St. Neots.   Went over
to Huntingdon; saw Cromwell's house and Hinchinbrook from
outside.   Returned to London.

May 1.   After a couple of days at Sandgate, with Wells,
I travelled to Newhaven, spent the night there, and to-day
crossed to France—found all well at home.

To Miss Collet :

PARIS,
May 21, 1900.

As for Mafeking, why, of course I am as glad as anyone else
that the place is relieved.   I fear I have not made clear to you
that my quarrel is not with *England*, but with the people who
are doing their best to change, and perhaps destroy, that English
civilisation which, on the whole, is the most promising the world
has yet seen.   Do you really approve of the spirit which has for
immediate result those outbreaks of brutal lawlessness throughout
our country—a country hitherto renowned for its sober pursuit
of the just ideal ?   I do not pretend to have studied the merits
of the case between Briton and Boer, but I am only too sure that
a just and great cause has rarely declared itself in blind violence
against all who venture to criticize it.   This reckless breaking
with the fine English tradition is a sad proof of what evil can
be wrought by inculcating the spirit of vulgar pride and savage
defiance.   I am sick at heart when I read of these things and
when I picture to myself what we English should think and say
of any other nation which so disgraced itself.   I entreat you,
dear Miss Collet, to reflect on this sign of the times and not to
allow yourself to be carried away by a natural patriotism, which,
just now, may lead one into sheer betrayal of one's country's
better hope.

No, no, don't write about war-matters again, but about
yourself and your real life.   For remember you are a force on

the side of civilisation, and to hear of your natural activity
encourages me; whereas the other things—oh, how they weigh
me down with fear and loathing.

Diary :

May 25.   Having let the flat, we left Paris for St. Honoré
les Bains where we have taken the Villa des Roses for the whole
summer.

May 28.   Made a beginning of *The Coming Man* [*Our
Friend the Charlatan*].

May 30.   Better work, I think, than I have done since
New Grub Street.   This place suits me well.   I have a little
bedroom for study, with view of trees and hill.   Blessed
tranquillity without and within the house.

St. Honoré les Bains,
June 17, 1900.

Dear Boy Walter,

I see from the newspapers that you had winter at the
beginning of June and now are being killed with heat.   Here
the weather has been steadily summerlike, sometimes just a
little too hot to be pleasant.

I wish you could see this house.   It is surrounded by a
beautiful garden, full of rose-trees.   It stands at the end of a
village which is on the first slope of a range of hills, not high,
but covered with woods and of graceful outline.   People come
here to drink medicinal waters, as at Harrogate and Buxton,
you know; the waters were known to the old Romans, who
drank them nearly two thousand years ago.   One of the
sources is called Caesar's spring.

I have not time to walk much, but the country delights me.
It is wonderfully like England, and I see all the old flowers—
foxgloves, honeysuckle, rockrose, yellow rattle and numberless
more.   The trees are very fine, great woods of oak and chest-
nut and beech, where one can wander as one likes—only there

are plenty of snakes. Here the acacia grows wild, and, a week ago, all the country was white and perfumed with its blossom.

Several strange sounds would amuse you. All day long the *field-crickets* make a loud chirping; and wherever there is a pond the *frogs* deafen one with their croaking. Then, at night, the *toads* make a noise just like a boy blowing a penny trumpet— you can hear it a mile away. A great deal of broom grows here and there, making yellow patches on the landscape.

I am working better than for a long time. The air suits me, I sleep well and I can write nearly seven hours daily, in spite of the heat.

I hope you also are working well, dear boy. Another term will soon come to an end. I shall be very glad to have a good report of you. Be sure that I think of you constantly.

Always your loving father.

To Miss Collet :

St. Honoré les Bains,
July 8, 1900.

The summer goes on and I should lament over it, but that I am working more steadily and to better purpose than for several years. This place is delightful.

You will be alarmed to hear that I have decided to put aside the book I wrote last winter [*Among the Prophets*]. It never satisfied me, and this I am now doing is so vastly better that I should be ashamed to let the other see the light. I must re-cast and re-write it presently. Of course, this has been rather a serious step to take, but, in the end, it will prove the more profitable in every sense of the word. What I am now writing is to be called *The Coming Man*. Of course it is satire, but I think tolerably entertaining. It is about half done.

The barbarisation of the world goes merrily on. No doubt there will be continuous warfare for many a long year to come. It sickens me to read the newspapers ; I turn as much as possible to the old poets.

And a few months later to the same:

Who knows what fantastic horrors lie in wait for the world. It is at least a century and a half since civilisation was in so bad a state.

Diary :

July 10.   To my great surprise, a note from Ouida from Lucca, praising *By the Ionian Sea* and wondering how I understood the dialects!

To Miss Collet :

October 24, 1900.

I have not wasted my time here.   First I wrote a novel, *The Coming Man* ; then I executed a project that had been in my head for some ten years and which took the form at last of this :

AN AUTHOR AT GRASS.

Extracts from the Private Papers

of

HENRY RYECROFT.

EDITED BY GEORGE GISSING.

It consists of the informal diary of a fifty-year old Grub Street toiler, who, having come in for a legacy of £300 a year, goes down to a cottage on the Mendips, and there passes his last years of life, in great happiness.   A strange miscellany, this book, but, as a bit of English, the best I have yet done, I fancy.

On settling in Paris, I got to work on another novel which is shaping itself.   Plainly what I have to do is to publish, publish, publish.   People begin to forget me, and the outlook is not bright just now.   Happily my energy does not fail. At present I am in particularly good health.

On November 2, to the same :

Another thing worrying me now is the obvious necessity of bringing my books over to Paris. I must enter upon a hateful correspondence with furniture removers. This business will mean weeks of enforced idleness and disorder and consequent misery. Heaven be thanked that I worked well through the summer.

Diary :

December 25. I suppose the first Christmas Day in my life in which I worked. Began *A Vanquished Roman* after long labour at the scheme, and did more than a page.

To Miss Collet :

December 27, 1900.

I am beginning my historical novel (*Italy in the Sixth Century*), of which I spoke to you long ago. I have made a laborious study of the period, and feel able to treat it; a month's toil has resulted in a detailed plan of the book, but whether circumstances will allow me to write it, I cannot say. To break new ground, I think, is my only chance. I wonder whether it would be well, if the book gets written, to publish it anonymously ? What do you think ? The difficulty is that I should get very little money upon it in that case ; and money is, of course, my first need.

This book was eventually published as *Veranilda*.

Diary :

January 23, 1901. A long interruption. A fortnight ago my books arrived from Dorking, all safe. But the dampness of the books gave me a bad cold, from which I am only just recovering Hope to get to work again soon but am still very weak.

PARIS,
January 23, 1901.

My Dear Walter,

News comes this morning that the Queen is dead.   I must
send you a line, for when you are a man you will remember the
death of Queen Victoria, and this letter which your father
wrote you.   There will now once more be a King of England,
let us hope he will do his duty as well as Queen Victoria did.
Kings and Queens have not so much power now as they used to
have in the olden days, but they can still do a great deal of harm,
if they are foolish or wicked.   Queen Victoria always acted
for the good of her country, and it is because the English people
know she did so, that they grieve for her death.   I am very
much afraid her life was shortened by the miserable war in
South Africa, which she seems never to have approved.   It is
a sorrowful thing that her long reign, so full of good things, was
not allowed to end in quietness, as she hoped.

You will hear all about the coronation of King Edward,
and it will help you to understand your English History all the
better.   If the time of year permitted I should be tempted to
come to England, to see something of what will go on in London ;
but in the winter I dare not travel, for my cough is rather bad,
and whenever I get a cold the results are very troublesome.
So I shall have to be satisfied with reading the newspapers.
Much love to you, my dear boy, thank you very much for your
last letter.   I hope you are working well.

Your affectionate father.

PARIS,
January 23, 1901.

My Dear Mother,

We hear that the Queen died at half-past six last evening.
It is impossible not to be affected by this news, for Queen
Victoria has been a part of all our lives, and now that she is
gone the world is greatly changed.   Strange to think that when
I was born Victoria had already reigned for twenty years, and
that I am already beginning to feel old at the time of her death.

I am afraid there can be no doubt that the war has killed her. In one way, it is probably a very good thing that the change has come, for the state of public affairs is very serious, and under a new reign necessary reforms may be more easily made.

This morning there is almost a London fog in Paris; I can hardly see to write. The most wretched month of the year is now before us, but after that comes the hope of spring, and winter will once more be forgotten.

You are well, I hope. Much love, dear mother, to you and to the girls, from George.

To Miss Collet :

PARIS,
February 17, 1901.

The most elaborate preparations are being made for *By the Ionian Sea*. It is to be illustrated with full page pictures *in colour*, as well as with engravings in the text (these from my own sketches). The volume, I imagine, will be costly. I am immensely gratified by all this.

Meanwhile, I am advancing slowly, but I think well, with *The Vanquished Roman*. It will be the first really honest piece of work I have offered to my readers, for it represents the preparatory labour of years, and is written without pressure. I hope to finish it by the end of the summer.

I am in a much better state of mind since I got all my books about me, and some of my own furniture; work is vastly easier. I cough rather badly, and am taking cod liver oil, but I hope the end of this terrible weather will help me. On the whole, I feel pretty well.

To the same :

May 2, 1901.

I have been to see a much recommended doctor. He finds a moist spot on lung, with bad emphysema and chronic bronchitis. He advises a return to St. Honoré at end of May, or else some mountain retreat thoroughly sheltered from winds. We cannot yet decide what to do; so many things have to be considered.

This time, I fear, the situation is rather grave. I must make the best fight I can. My great trouble is that I am possessed by a ceaseless longing for movement and above all (of course) for the sea, which is absolutely forbidden. Before seeing C. (the doctor), we had arranged for me to run down to the coast of Normandy. It will be difficult to live here in idleness during this month of sunshine; but I must give the doctor a fair trial. And my book just half finished!

There is here a break of twelve months in the Diary, but Gissing's entry in April, 1902, explains his movements and therefore is introduced here:

Soon after the last entry I went to England, chiefly to sit for my portrait for "Literature." My wife went with me and we stayed with the Wells at Sandgate. As I seemed to be getting good, I stayed on for a month.

Hick persuaded me into seeing a specialist who took a discouraging view of my chest disease, and advised a sanatorium. I went to Dr. Jane Walker's newly opened sanatorium at Nayland and stayed there till August. Then I joined my wife and her mother at a villa at Couhard, Autun, where we remained for a month or two. Place very damp and did me much harm. After that we were guests at Tazières till the end of November. I then went up to Paris and saw the doctor who shook his head and advised the winter at Arcachon. To Arcachon I went.

To his sister Ellen :

NAYLAND,
SUFFOLK,
June 25, 1901.

This place is very beautiful, and one sees at once that the " open air and over-feeding cure " does all that is claimed for it. One lives, day and night, in free air—no window ever shut, and all are casement. The feeding is stupendous—makes one feel ill at first.

The house (specially built for a sanatorium) is about 4 miles from a railway station.   Very beautiful country—the district painted by Constable in his last pictures.

I have not yet written to Walter, for I find it difficult to do anything at all, and the enforced idleness depresses me rather.

I mentioned that Wells and I went over to Rye, and spent a night at Henry James'.   He has a lovely old Georgian house, superbly furnished, looking over the shore to Winchelsea. Talked much of his acquaintance with Tourguéneff—interesting story.

Is mother well, and Margaret ?   Don't be uneasy about me. It is overstrain, that's all; the lung trouble not serious.   I am putting on weight vigorously.

Love to all of you.

To the same :

East Anglian Sanatorium,
July 6, 1901.

I shall come to Wakefield on the 26th just to see you. About a week later I shall have to go back to France, where I am going to spend the rest of the summer at Autun, not far from St. Honoré.   But I shall have to travel very quietly, for I am not strong.

To his brother :

Autun, France,
August, 1901.

Sanatorium has done much good, but health still cause of anxiety.

I fear it is hot with you now.   Here we are at a good height and get breezes in spite of powerful sun.   Shall be here till October 15.   Do not yet know arrangements for the winter; there is talk of a sanatorium in the high Alps.   Can work only two hours a day, a wretched stint.   This is an old city of churches and monasteries, very beautifully situated.   It is in Burgundy, but, alas, I may not drink a glass of wine!

Love to all of you ; some day, I hope, I shall see you once more.

To his sister Ellen :

AUTUN, FRANCE,
September, 1901.

I am feeling much better, and have greatly increased in weight.   It cannot yet be decided where I shall pass the winter.   Happily I am able to do some work here.

I rejoice that you know the Alps!   Fins-haut is a wonderful place—I see it now—the great gorge of the Trient, and the huge summits above.

To the same :

ARCACHON,
GIRONDE, FRANCE,
December 8, 1901.

After a good deal of miserable experiment and consultation, I seem to have got at the truth about my lungs.   I am threatened with gradual hardening of all the surface, which, if it went on, would of course stop all breathing, and so extinguish me.

A good doctor assures me that, at present, the climate of the north might have fatal results, and that, unless some great change takes place, I ought to live in the north only during the warmest months.   My case seems to be rather a singular one, and puzzles doctors a good deal.   I keep in good flesh and look very well indeed, but I cannot walk a mile, and pant terribly if I have to go upstairs.   I tell you all this lest you should think that I am exaggerating precautions, and going to needless expense.

I am in a very good boarding house, nearly all the day has to be passed in a lounge chair in the garden.   The air is not warm just now but the sun shines brilliantly.   The part of Arcachon called " Ville d'hiver " is situated amid a pine forest.   Birds sing in the trees, and all day one hears the roaring of the Atlantic as it breaks on the shore a few miles away.

The doctor here is very encouraging, and sees no reason why my lungs should not get into, at all events, a much improved state.

I have no fever—sleep well, and have an excellent appetite. The cough will evidently be less troublesome here than at Fourchanbault.

To the same :

ARCACHON,
December 26, 1901.

On Christmas Eve, I found on my table a lot of splendid roses and white lilac and with them a visiting card on which was written " From two admirers of the genius of Mr. George Gissing." It is a certain Mr. Williamson, who is staying with his wife at the great hotel here, and who had seen about me in the newspapers. The Arcachon paper had a paragraph about me headed " Etranger de distinction." Of course I called on the Williamsons. They said they recognized me from my portrait. Well, well, and one can't make money enough to live quietly !

To his brother :

December 28.

I am very glad to have your two letters, especially as they seem to breathe an air of relief, such as I have not yet known in your writing for a long time.

Your own health and that of all about you is in itself an inestimable blessing; one piece of advice thereanent, let me urge upon you (if it be necessary), never neglect the slightest cold. My present miserable state results—immediately—from paying no heed to a cold I caught in England in the spring of 1900. At the moment I was in greatly improved health ; since, I have steadily declined, until my difficulty of breathing has caused such physical weakness that, to all practical purposes, I cannot walk at all. The emphysema is, I fancy, more serious than the ordinary complaint which I have, for, with the difficulty of breathing, all the functions become disorganised. It seems to me extraordinary that only two years ago I climbed mountains. I am constantly dreaming over my old walks; I could not now go from Willersey to Broadway and back without exhaustion and fever—a dolorous state of things.

So you had an evening with old Hudson. I do hope his friends will not allow him to end his life in the workhouse.

This place would interest you. Along the flat sea-border from Bordeaux to the Pyrenees, wind and sea have, from time immemorial, heaped up several ranges of immense sandhills, more than a hundred feet high, and these are covered with a forest of great pines—a forest which stretches over more than 80 miles along the coast. Between two ranges of these hills is built the "winter town" of Arcachon—which consists of some hundreds of villas, each apart in its garden; no streets, no shops. Near by, on the shore of the great inlet which the sea makes at this point, is the other Arcachon, the "summer town" with its bathing places, shops, etc. Our position in the forest is an absolute security against wind. There is a good deal of rain, but cold very seldom, and occasionally a few days of summer sunshine at the worst of the year. The odour of the pines is said to be good for one; the sandy soil, of course, absorbs moisture at once. Constantly one hears the sound of the ocean breakers; they are ten miles away, but sometimes roar as if they were close at hand. The disadvantage is that there is no view: but the universal green of the trees keeps the mind from gloom.

I am living in a *pension* where there are only French people; we make a family of eight in all, most of us ill. In the garden is a shelter, open on the side facing the south, and here, on *chaises longues*, we sit all day, writing, reading, talking. The post is good; only twenty-four hours from London and four deliveries daily. English people used to come here a good deal, they have now deserted it for Pau, a much more attractive place.

A thing of mine called *An Author at Grass* [*The Private Papers of Henry Ryecroft*], which you are pretty sure to like, and which I finished this last summer, is to come out serially in the *Fortnightly*.

On the *chaise longue* I am getting on with an abridged edition of Forster's *Dickens* for Chapman & Hall.

Heartiest good wishes to you all. Don't let the children forget me.

To Miss Collet :

January 31, 1902.

The weather here is very bad. This is the second day of thin snow. I get no worse, but cannot hope for solid improvement till the spring. One thing I must say to you about the climate; it is good but most distinctly less good than that of South Devon—of which I have had experience in three winters; there is less sunshine and severer cold. If I get good here I should do better in Devon. And this encourages me with the prospect that some day my exile may come to an end.

To his brother :

Arcachon,
March 14, 1902.

I have weathered the winter, and begin to feel that Arcachon has done me substantial good. I am now able to walk a couple of miles without fatigue, or anything but good results. Appetite keen, not much cough. But the emphysema still troubles me much; I cannot climb the slightest hill without painful effort. I fear no great improvement in this respect is to be hoped for.

The doctors urge upon me that, to get really strong again, I could not do better than continue to live for a year or two in the S.W. of France. It is possible, therefore, that we shall do so; we are thinking of St. Jean de Luz, a place just at the foot of the Pyrenees below Biarritz. I fear it would be the merest folly for me to think of coming to England this year—even if I could easily afford the journey. Of course I don't like this long absence from the good old island, but I must have regard first of all to health. Wind and cold are things which at once have a grave effect on me, and if I were seriously attacked once more, I could not reasonably hope to pull through.

It is a blessed thing that you keep so well and vigorous, and that all your household are like unto you. I do earnestly hope that your path may be smoother before long; it has been a terribly long and hard fight. Give my love to K. and to the girls and boys. Shall I ever hope to see them again, I wonder ? The days of easy hopefulness are past. I no more reckon on the gifts of the future.

Spring is warm and bright with us now. In the pine forest there is not much verdure, but the gardens show mimosas and almond trees in bloom ; and on the ground I note such old friends as the celandine and the chick-weed ! Every night there is fine hooting of owls among the pines. I wonder where they nest; for there are no hollow trees and no suitable buildings.

Your book is out I see—I hope it may go well.

April 5 to the same :

I make slow, and only slow, progress of late. At the end of this month I shall go to Paris, there to decide what the next move is to be. A wearisome life, this homeless wandering.

There is good news from Falmouth; little Alfred is vastly enjoying the change to country life, and I dare say will soon profit much by it.

Perhaps you are already gone to the north ; if not, love to all those about you. It is long since I saw you all. I wonder whether I shall be able to make the journey *next* year ?

Diary :

April 7. Yesterday chanced to open the first volume of my *Diary* and found it such strange and moving reading, that I have gone on, hour after hour. Who knows whether I may not still live a few years; and if so, I shall be sorry not to have a continuous record of my life. So I resolve to begin journalising once more, after all but a year of intermission.

Not much work done this last year. However, at Autun I revised and lengthened *An Author at Grass*—I wrote a *David Copperfield* preface for a new American edition, and an article *Dickens in Memory* for a special number of *Literature* ;—then I undertook for Chapman & Hall an abridgement of Forster's *Dickens,* and got it finished by January of this year. At Arcachon have also written a couple of short stories, *Miss Rodney's Leisure,* and *Christopherson. Our Friend the Charlatan* and *By the Ionian Sea* came out in May of last year, and were brilliantly reviewed. Not much sale though, I think, for either—the old story.

April 8. Troubled all the winter by insomnia. A couple of days ago tried spending the morning down by the shore, instead of on the *chaise longue,* as always; result six hours of good sleep which continues. Mr. Radcliffe (English clergyman of Arcachon), called in morning during my absence, and left me the *Spectator.*

April 10. Grey sky, a little rain. In afternoon to the shore. Reading idly in *Country Month by Month*—a book which often makes me *ache* with thoughts of England.

April 14. Decided that we go for a year or so to the *pays basque.* We shall leave Paris (I hope for ever) in June. A piece of good news is that *La Rue des Meur-de-faim* [*New Grub Street*], is accepted for volume publication by the *Revue Blanche* people.

To Miss Collet :

April 16, 1902.

I must tell you what arrangements we have made for the rest of the year—after unspeakable hesitation and fear and difficulty of every sort. We shall warehouse our furniture and take a chalet for a year at St. Jean de Luz, at the foot of the Pyrenees. The climate there will, it is hoped, be advantageous to me, and it is sufficiently temperate to allow of one's living there both winter and summer. Arcachon has not suited me very well, but chiefly, I think, because the place is un-beautiful and rather depressing. At St. Jean one has a glorious shore and the mountains in view.

I do not know whether you see Miss Orme. After quite infinite kindness on the part of her and her sister, little Alfred is at home in a farm house near Falmouth, and seems to be enjoying great happiness.

I believe the first part of *The Author at Grass* will appear in the May *Fortnightly*. This little book is more to me than anything else I have written. It has grown in my mind for nearly ten years, and more than two years have gone to the actual writing.

I have just undertaken to review for *The Times* the new *Life of Dickens* which Kitton is about to publish. If I live a few more years, I may hope to have earned in a quarter of a century the reputation which twenty authors of to-day have achieved by the publication of a couple of volumes.

To his sister Ellen :

ARCACHON,
April 17, 1902.

I rejoice that your winter seems to be over. If only I could be with you at Leyburn! You will find it breezy there, but beautiful country.

Yesterday a very fine day, I joined a party to go for a long drive through the forest to a point of the sea-shore some twelve miles away. The road was very hard for the horses, as of course there is nothing but sand, and often very hilly. All that part of the forest which has been *planted*, though the trees are very fine, is uninteresting comparatively; yet often very beautiful owing to the glorious masses of broom and gorse in full bloom.

Much better is the true forest of immemorial date; here the undergrowth consists largely of great old hawthorns (already in flower), and there is much bracken. Wild boars are said to abound, but they do not show themselves. At this season, the foresters (who live in little huts far away from each other), are busy getting the resin from the pines. They cut a long strip of the bark and attach to the naked trunk a pot (like a flower pot) into which slowly trickles the resin, day by day. From this is made turpentine. The scent of the forest is

delicious just now, what with the flowering of the pines and
the flow of resin.

Very huge, absolute mountains, are the sand banks along the
shore, and it is curious to note how the sand constantly gains—
whole acres of pines here and there being buried up to the middle
of the trunk.   We came out at length on to the strand, and there
was the old Atlantic, sending in his long, heavy rollers—nothing
between here and America.

I have decided to take a little house at St. Jean de Luz, a
very beautiful seaside place at the foot of the Pyrenees, close to
Bayonne, in the country of the Basques.   The climate is good
both summer and winter, and I hope it may help me, for indeed
I must get to work!

The result of Arcachon is not *remarkable*, but progress there
is, and I have not lost hope.   It is possible that a summer and
winter at St. Jean de Luz may do much for me.

Diary :

April 18.   Mr. Radcliffe brought me a batch of Black-
woods, which occupied the day.

April 24.   With great gladness said good-bye to Arcachon,
took the 7.42 a.m. train, and reached St. Jean de Luz at mid-
day.   To the Pension Larréa quaint, decent house.   Greatly
delighted with first view of town and neighbourhood.   On the
journey the first view of the great breakers rolling in at Bidart,
very fine; in afternoon walked about a good deal, and without
fatigue.   Very fine day—the country a mass of spring flowers.
After dull winter among the pines, the mountain and shore
refresh my eyes.

April 26.   Can get no sleep yet.   A nightingale sings all
night behind the house.

To his sister Ellen :

St. Jean de Luz,
May 6, 1902.

Impossible to thank you sufficiently for all the care and thought and tact which you and Margaret have expended on the matter of Walter's school.   Let me say at once that I think your suggestion admirable.

I think I shall manage to get a house here, but it is very troublesome as rents for furnished houses are, of course, high, and I must find one well sheltered from cold winds and with a bit of garden.

The country is very delightful and I fancy the climate will suit me well.   Can you believe that in the ten days I have been here I have gained more than three lbs.   And that, too, without much sleep.

Last night we had a slight shock of earthquake—the rarest thing here.   I was dozing, when, suddenly, amid the perfect quiet, there came what seemed an extraordinary rush of wind *through* the house, shaking not only doors and windows, but the very walls.   I never thought of earthquakes, until I heard people talking about it in the morning.

Diary :

May 8.   Feeling vast improvement of health.

May 20.   Had meant to leave to-day (for Paris).   Decided to wait two days more.

May 21.   Sun shines, but very cold north wind (in night terrific rain).   In morning walked a little: the rest of the day did not venture to go out.   Having nothing to read and nothing to do, passed the day in utter idleness—heaven knows, indeed, how the hours have gone by.   And how often in my life have I spent such a day as this—blank, wearisome, wasted!   A sort of destiny of idleness and wasted time seems to oppress a great part of my life.   Each time a day such as this comes, I make a resolve that it shall never happen again.   But circumstances are too strong for me.   Indeed, the only way in which I could avoid this miserable folly of barren hours, would be to live always in reach of a large library—the impossible thing for me, now and ever.

May 22.   Left St. Jean de Luz by 1.44 train.

July 1.   A month of disorder and weariness.   Having decided to take a cheap flat as *pied à terre* at Paris.   On Saturday last did the removal.   Weather hot, but I bore the toil better than I expected.

July 2.   Travelled from Paris by the 9.29 a.m. and reach St. Jean de Luz at 9.52 at night.   Easy journey.   Found all in good readiness at Ciboure.

July 10.   Got to work upon my new novel *Will Warburton.*

July 13.   See from *Athenaeum* that Hudson has received a Government pension.   Greatly rejoiced.   Received from him the *Spanish Dictionary and Grammar* he has bought for me.   In afternoon went all through the *Spanish Grammar,* and in evening read a page of *Don Quixote*—in the little four volume edition I bought years ago, looking forward to a day when I might learn Spanish.

CIBOURE,
July 27, 1902.

MY DEAR MOTHER,

It is time that I gave you some account of my doings here.   The weather has been very unsettled, never very hot, but on the whole it is very pleasant indeed, and I feel the climate is doing me decided good.   It is not at all the climate of Italy, but very much like that of Devonshire, except that there is no mist.

The frequent rain keeps everything very green and the flowers are just the same as in the south of England.   Of course some things ripen here that do not with us; for instance, there are grapes and figs in abundance and large fields of Indian corn.   But in many a lane you might fancy yourself in Devon, seeing the hartstongue ferns and all sorts of familiar plants.

I write from 9 to 12 every morning.   In the afternoon I go and lie down on the sea-shore and breathe all the air I can. In the evening I learn Spanish.   It will amuse you to hear that already I have read several chapters of *Don Quixote*.   All my life I have wanted to do this, and now at last I have found the time.   It is a great satisfaction to me.   I hope to go through the whole book before the end of the year.

Let me know exactly when you leave Wakefield.   Happily you will not be troubled by any change in my address for a long time.   I hope to stay quietly here till next summer and then, if all goes well, to pay a visit to England.   Indeed it seems a long, long time since I saw you.   But I was really afraid to come this year, especially when the weather was so bad.   Let us hope there will not be another summer of this sort.

I shall be anxious to hear of Walter's preparation for the new school, but, of course, I leave everything in the girls' hands with perfect confidence.

I wish you could see the beautiful view of the Pyrenees that is before my window.   Every day at 12 o'clock, there passes a train called the Southern Express, which goes from Seville to Paris.   I should like to see a little of Spain, but it would never be to me what Italy is.

Much love, dear mother,

Ever affectionately, Yours,

GEORGE.

To his brother :

St. Jean de Luz,
July 27, 1902.

Here I am, between the Pyrenees and the sea.   This Basque people is very interesting.   Strange to hear them talking a language older than any other in Europe, and of absolutely unknown origin.   It is *agglutinative*—in that akin to Chinese. Most of them speak French as well (in Spain, of course, Spanish), but there seems no decay of their own tongue.

When last you wrote to me, you talked of going northwards.
I wonder whether you took that holiday.

By the bye, you know, I suppose, that Hudson has a pension?
I learnt it only from the *Athenaeum,* and wrote to congratulate
him.   I don't know what the sum is, but he tells me he is
"a rich man."   I rejoice heartily.

Walter leaves Ilkley and goes to Holt Grammar School
(Norfolk).   Little Alfred is rejoicing in farm-life at Mabe,
near Falmouth; has learnt to milk cows.   So I hope he will
soon be strong and well.

Diary :

August 11.   Got to work again, after a week, on my novel,
and did half a page.   Been reading in my " Latin Anthologia "
lately.   Done seventeen chapters of *Don Quixote,* which I now
read very easily.

August 18.   By early train to Irun over the Spanish border.
Thence by train to Fuenterabbia: very picturesque the pro-
jecting roofs in carved wood, draperied balconies, etc.   Old
ivy-covered castle of Charles V.   Some old dwelling houses
falling into ruin.

September 20.   Up very early to catch 6 o'clock train to
Bayonne, going to St. Jean Pied de Port.   But at station found
that time of train had been changed to 5.30.   Decided to go to
Sare, and just caught the diligence.   Very fine, warm, autumn
day.   At Sare had déjeuner at primitive hotel.   Ham and eggs,
the only good dish obtainable in the mountains.   Called on
Mr. Webster, long English Chaplain at St. Jean de Luz.   Has
given life to study of Basque, speaks of his ruined health, but
looks very well.   Said he knew me well by name; had not read
my books, but always read the notices of them.

Sare, little village with several very large houses, lies in a great
basin, hills all round, itself on a hill.

To his sister Ellen :

October 18, 1902.

I am well again but have to be very careful.   By the bye, my bronchitis, says the doctor, comes simply from being too much *on the shore of the sea.*   In England, there is a disposition to think sea air good for everybody, and in all circumstances; but French doctors—whom I find in general remarkably good —are much more cautious in this matter.   Henceforth I have to take my walks inland.   Indeed I am much better in every way, since I ceased to go to the shore.

Diary :

November 1.   Third part of *Author at Grass* appears in *Fortnightly.*   Have corrected all proofs of the volume for Constable, to appear early in the year.   Am writing *Will Warburton* which, after more than fifty pages finished, I had to begin all over again about a fortnight ago.   Do only one page a day.   Think of the old days, when I have done as many as ten !

November 8.   Left in carriage at 8.30 in morning, with the G.'s for an excursion into Spain.

After this date, the daily record of his life was abandoned.

To Miss Collet :

St. Jean de Luz,
December 24, 1902.

How it is with you, I don't know; as for me, I have not yet got accustomed to writing 1902 at the head of my letters, and behold one must begin 1903!   This year has passed in ailing idleness, and therefore has gone like a month.

In the days gone by, I used to imagine for my later life all the evils of poverty; what I never foresaw was inability to write through failure of health.   Here have I been pottering at a novel since mid-summer, and it is not yet half done, owing to constant breaking down.   This is a cheerless state of things. If a few months hence, I really do get to the end of my work, I shall feel better, and more hopeful.   At present I am trying to speak out of the middle of a wool-bag, and naturally little to say that is worth anyone's hearing.

We have made a good many acquaintances, one or two of them very pleasant people. But of course my inability to do any serious work takes away from any kind of enjoyment.

I hope my *Ryecroft* will be out as a volume early in the year. Of course you shall have a copy. On the whole I suspect it is the best thing I have done, or am likely to do; the thing most likely to last when all my other futile work has followed my futile life.

Well, one thing I have done this year—that is, I have learned to read Spanish, and gone through *Don Quixote*—a book unique in the literature of the world. Do you know that the first part of it was published when Cervantes was fifty-eight years old, and the second *ten years later?* I know nothing more marvellous than the production of work such as this when a writer was nearly seventy years old—for he was writing on it till the year of his death. Since boyhood I have had this ambition.

Read Conrad's new book. He is the strongest writer—in every sense of the word—at present publishing in English. Marvellous writing! The other men are mere scribblers in comparison. That a foreigner should write like this, is one of the miracles of literature.

In the course of a letter to his sister Ellen :

CIBOURE,
ST. JEAN DE LUZ.
January 11, 1903.

I think I am better; at all events I walk more easily, and can take much more exercise. For a week the weather has been like summer, no need for fires, and brilliant skies.

The other day I went to see the brother of Mrs. Browning, old Mr. Alfred Barrett. He is eighty-three years old, and shaky, but quite able to talk.

To the same :

St. Jean de Luz,
March 21, 1903.

I don't know whether you have heard that *Ryecroft* is just announced in a *third edition !* Even here, in the English colony, the book is being universally read. I hope you all liked it, if indeed you had time to read it, which is not certain, overwhelmed as you are.

Splendid weather here. I have finished a novel, called *Will Warburton*, which I hope will be disposed of on good terms.

Now, I have another in mind.

I shall stay here till June, and then go into the Pyrenees for the hot months. As for next winter, perhaps it will be wise to return here. There seems to be no doubt that my health is slowly improving. But very slowly, and any sort of imprudence would undo all the good. Of course the success of *Ryecroft* helps to keep me cheerful and hopeful.

I wonder how you all are. It seems very long since I had news.

My love to mother and Margaret.

To his sister Margaret :

Ciboure,
St. Jean de Luz,
March 25, 1903.

I cannot remember whether it was to you or to Nellie that I wrote last. Unfortunately I have had nothing cheerful to write about. At the beginning of the year I had an attack of sciatica, and it is only just now going away—all these months I have been a cripple, often scarcely able to walk across the room. I can now get out, and, with a good deal of suffering, walk for half an hour.

The lungs are, I believe, slightly better. At all events I cough very little, and breathe more easily; but I keep very thin.

I am now taking a dozen raw eggs every day, with a good deal of milk, and I think I feel the benefit of this.

At the end of June I leave the sea-side and go for four months to a place in the Pyrenees called St. Jean Pied de Port, where I have taken rooms.   It will be hot, but they tell me that I must have a change from the sea air.   Switzerland would be better, but we cannot get so far.   At St. Jean Pied de Port life is at all events cheap.

I have had more than fifty letters from strangers about *Ryecroft* and from every part of England.   They tell me that it has been the subject of conversation in every London drawing-room.   And see the result in cash!   Of course people who know nothing of such matters think I am drawing large sums of money.

To his sister Ellen :

Ispoure,
St. Jean Pied de Port, B.P.,
April 12, 1903.

Surely this cycle of wretched summers will soon come to an end.   Yet the newspaper reminds me that 1879 was worse than this.   I don't remember it, I was then toiling in London, and often starving—aye but I was young and well and strong, and nothing mattered.

I rejoice to tell you that, by the end of this month, I shall have finished *half* of *Veranilda*.   I believe it will be a strong book dramatically, and at the same time a very faithful picture of the times.   It interests me greatly.   I shall be very anxious indeed to know what you all think of it.

Health vastly improved.   Great appetite—of course I cannot breathe properly—and so cannot walk much—but there is a slight advance even in that.

Please give my love to Walter.   Don't let him trouble to write until he has really something that he wishes to say.

It is excellent news that mother has benefited so much by her holiday, in spite of the evil weather.   My love to her.

Tell her that people still write to me now and then about *Ryecroft*.

I wonder when I shall see you all again. Next summer, perhaps. There ought to be a sufficiency of cash before then. Tell Margaret not to pursue vegetarianism if she feels her strength decline!

Three weeks ago I had a four days' excursion into Spain. Saw the famous Roncesvalles and the old, old town of Pamplona. I got on better with colloquial Spanish than I had expected.

Oh, the strange barbarism of the Spanish villages! Pure middle ages.

St. Jean Pied de Port,
August 2, 1903.

My Dear Mother,

At last I am able to say that I feel greatly improved in health. All my sciatica has gone, which tormented me for six months, and I feel better in every way. During the last few weeks I have done a good lot of work and without the slightest fatigue. If this state of things goes on, I shall be quite a new man at the end of the summer.

In England I know you are having a wretchedly wet summer, and I grieve over it on your account. Even here, the weather is extraordinary for this time of year; never very warm, and never unclouded for more than a day or two. Rain and mist very frequent. However this suits me very much better than great heat. I evidently made a mistake in staying so long at the sea-side; the sea air, I am afraid, never does me good for more than a month at a time.

I wonder what your holiday plans are; no doubt I shall hear before long, and I shall hear very soon about Walter.

The best news comes to me about little Alfred. He enormously enjoys the life of the farm near Falmouth, and has begun to do well at his day school.

Much love to you, dear mother,

Ever affectionately,
George.

To his sister Ellen :

ST. JEAN PIED DE PORT, B.P.,
November 11, 1903.

This is an excellent letter of yours and it does me good. I am convinced that, with your school, you and Margaret are conferring a great boon on Wakefield, and, little as such work is recognised, *some* recognition of it will eventually come. It rejoices me to know that you are more and more interested in the labour of your lives; but that is the certain test of all labour worth anything. The story of your old pupil in the cricket field is very significant.

I am glad to tell you that I have done about two-thirds of *Veranilda*; when it will be finished, I dare not say, for, with the beginning of winter have come the usual troubles—illness and discomfort—and I have just lost a week. It *might* be finished before the end of January. I am just now in the monastery of St. Benedict, and very difficult it is to make such a man talk.

Well, I suppose you will read it some day.

By the bye, if ever you need a good History of the Church, from the beginning up to the Reformation (*not* inclusive), a very cheap and thorough book has just been published (Relig. Tract Society), by Dr. S. Green, price 6s. It treats all the heresies, and so on, very well, and has very useful chronological tables—a volume of more than 600 pages.

You are quite right about the disastrous effect of too much wealth. I have grave fears that England is being ruined by this—this, and excessive poverty.

I am delighted to hear of your health. Splendid, mother's daily drives!

My best love to all of you,
Ever affectionately,
GEORGE.

But *Veranilda*, in preparation for which so many years of close study had been spent, was destined never to be finished.

It was written during the last severe struggle with ill health, in spite of which it contains some of Gissing's most powerful writing. Had the author lived longer we might have possessed several more works of this class ; for the old world of sordid realism had passed out of his life, and a new era had begun, in which his mind, tired of dwelling upon the evils of our corrupt civilisation, had turned for refreshment to ancient days.

It is significant that a historical romance of this kind should have been his last work, for, needless to say, he had loved the Classics all his life, and was an accomplished scholar, as well as a born teacher.

He fell seriously ill early in December 1903; and, in spite of careful nursing, died of pneumonia on the 28th of the same month, in his forty-seventh year.

He was buried in the English Cemetery at St. Jean de Luz.

APPENDIX A

The following is an extract from a letter written to Gissing's sisters, shortly after his death, by the Rev. Theodore Cooper, the English Chaplain at St. Jean de Luz, with whom Gissing had had much friendly intercourse the winter before :

I had been rather overdone and sleeping badly, so that on Christmas Eve I meant to have a bit of idleness. After I had been to Church, I went home intending to start for a round of golf and found Mrs. Gissing's telegram, " Prière venir—état déséspéré." There was no train till 12 so I had plenty of time to arrange. . . . . I got to St. Jean Pied de Port at 3 and went straight to Ispoure; Mrs. Gissing said he was rather better. I asked " Did he know I was coming ? " She said, " No, but you may walk straight in." I went up to the bed and said, " Mr. Gissing do you remember Mr. Cooper ? " He put out his hand and said heartily " I am very glad to see you." And all that afternoon and evening, except for about two hours' absence, we had very pleasant talk; and next morning also.

So much passed in those three or four days that I find it a little difficult to remember the order of events, but I could not have been with him more than a quarter of an hour (perhaps it was just after I came), when he said very earnestly, " I am dying, Mr. Cooper, and I want you to do something for me; Wells is coming, has perhaps started; I want you to persuade him to bring me home to England, to see an English doctor." I replied " You can see an English doctor without going so far." " Where ? Who ? " He was rather excited. " Dr. Malpas from Biarritz, who is a great friend of mine, and has, I may say, been the means of saving my life more than once, during fourteen years that he has been my doctor." He begged

397

me to go at once and telegraph for him. This I did but he was unable, through delay of telegram, to come till the next day. After dining early I came back to set Mrs. Gissing free, and we talked of many things; of his books, with which I was familiar; of my early life, in some little ways, I knew, like his; of *Henry Ryecroft*.

I said, " It struck me that in it you took a larger and softer view of life." He said, " That is true," and added, " but I did not put my innermost thought into *Henry Ryecroft*." Other things were said between us which showed how much we were in sympathy. . . .

As we parted he said, " I shall look forward to seeing your face in the morning." I went up at eight in the morning (Christmas Day), and found he had had a good calm night. As I went to the bedside he stretched out his hand and said aloud, " A man was sent from God unto me." I had much nice quiet talk then; he said (for he was suffering), " Tell me something interesting or amusing to distract me from this pain." So I chatted away telling him of things I knew, about the country—some of my little adventures. He had been reading Spanish, I knew, in the winter, and I reminded him of the Spanish proverb *El sol sal para todos* (the sun comes forth for all).

*　　　*　　　*　　　*　　　*　　　*

He was not so well, and I was sent for after lunch about 12. Then the French doctor came, and was fairly content; but he seemed to lose consciousness; at 3 Doctor Malpas arrived and by the same train Mr. Wells. Doctor Malpas thought it better for Mr. Wells not to see him till next day. He said there was hope, but a very grave case. He said he might die in the night.

About 7 I went up. Later he got worse. When the doctor had gone, saying he might linger on till morning, I went and stood by his bed. After a few minutes he opened his eyes suddenly, thrust out his hand and grasped mine firmly, murmuring " Patience, patience " (with the French accent). I leaned over him and said " My friend, you are going home."

Distinct and clear came the words " God's will be done." He was still holding my hand and I gave him the blessing, " Unto God's gracious mercy and protection I commit thee." Then he loosed my hand and relapsed into unconsciousness.

At 11 p.m. I left, being unable to stay.

He never was able to speak to me again nor I to him.

Sunday came, and at 11 came an English nurse from St. Jean de Luz.

I felt then I must leave, and after some rest at home, could return. My wife and I left at 4.30 with Mr. Wells. I slept at Combo about 30 miles away. On Monday morning I wired for news; reply came that he was dying. I drove back and found he had died about an hour and a half before. I stayed that night; Mr. Roberts arrived next morning; I left at 11.40 (for St. Jean de Luz), and he followed with the remains at 4.30. Your brother had a devoted wife: she was unsparing of herself. I fancy her life and spirit helped him much.

I had some argument with your brother in the winter, and a few nice talks about books, etc., and he gave me some for our library. I liked him before—much; in that sick room I felt very near to him and understood how his friends loved him. . . .

APPENDIX B

Extract from *The Times* of December 29, 1903 :

We regret to announce the death of Mr. George Gissing, the novelist, which took place yesterday near St. Jean de Luz on the Franco-Spanish frontier.

Mr. Gissing, who was born in 1857, and educated at Owens College, Manchester, published his first [1] novel *The Unclassed* in 1884; but it was not till two years later that any considerable amount of attention was attracted to his name (or rather to his work, for *Demos* was published anonymously), by what may justly be regarded as the first of a remarkable series of studies of modern life in some of its least comfortable aspects. There were traces in *The Unclassed* of a borrowed idealization; *Demos* was entirely characteristic of its author. Briefly speaking, Mr. Gissing's literary outfit may be said to have consisted in a sadness of outlook on modern life that practically reached hopelessness—a determination to tell what he believed to be the truth and nothing else, and an insight into character and tendencies which enabled him to realize that determination. A good classical scholar and a man of the highest literary ideals, he cared little or nothing for what the average reading public thought of his work. In his monograph on Dickens (one of the few short studies of authors which have proved really successful, and the very one which at first sight would have seemed to be doomed to failure), he says of Dickens's point of view:—" To write a novel in a spirit of antagonism to all but a very few of his country-men would have seemed to him a sort of practical ' bull ' ; is it not the law of novel-writing, first and foremost, that one shall aim at pleasing as many people as possible ? "

[1] This was his second novel. The first was *Workers in the Dawn*.

That was precisely what Mr. Gissing cared about least of all;
like Balzac, he wished to picture the truth of life, and, like
Balzac, he achieved his end by the patient enumeration of small
and accurate details, noting them down in a style that rarely
aimed at beauty and was distinguished only by the lucidity of
his thought, and an occasional sharpness of expression, achieving
his effects rather by a cumulative method, as it were, of proof
than by any dramatic moments, any moments of exaltation, or
any appeal to the pity or charity of his readers.   The result was
a series of books which, if they cannot justly be called great
work, were at least the work of a very able and conscientious
literary artist, whose purity and solidity may win him a better
chance of being read a hundred years hence than many writers
of greater grace and more deliberately sought charm.   *Demos*
examined Socialism; *Thyrza*, life in factories; *The Nether World*,
poverty and crime; *New Grub Street*, the life of the literary
hack; *The Odd Women*, the " superfluous " woman; *In the Year
of Jubilee* is chiefly remarkable for its studies of the ill-tempered
women whom he shows Dickens to have been such a master
in portraying.   All these books show a dislike and a despair of
modern life which amounted almost to hatred, if hatred were
compatible with the amount of thought and study he devoted
to the subject.   But that the obsession was hardly less is proved
by words he wrote *in propria persona*.   The last sentence of
his book of travels, *By the Ionian Sea*, is a sigh that he might
wander endlessly amid the silence of the ancient world, " To-
day and all its sounds forgotten ": and again, in the same
volume, he declared that his intellectual desire was to " escape
life as I know it and dream myself into that old world which
was the imaginative delight of my boyhood."   His pessimism,
then, if it deserves the name, was no wilful maundering, and his
" realism " no prurient probing into unsavoury things for the
fun of it.   He saw life in a grey light, and following the law
of his being, represented it in a grey light, never allowing his
pity for the sufferers to interfere with his conviction that their
sufferings were the results of the operation of law.   And later
in his career, his novels began to show signs that a brighter,

more humorous view of things (no one without a keen sense of humour could have written as he did of Dickens), was dawning in him.   And a temperament that is obsessed by the sadness of modern life need not be a temperament without joys.   Mr. Gissing's joys in life were very real, and his last [1] published book—in many respects the best he ever wrote—*The Private Papers of Henry Ryecroft*, was that which gave them their chief expression.   If it is impossible to say of a book of this kind that this or that in it is autobiographical, it is equally impossible to deny that the general scope of it cannot be anything else; and these " Private Papers " give us more than a glimpse into a retiring, sensitive nature, happy to be at last free of the noise and squalor of active life in town, free to revel in country sights and sounds, pure air, simple food, and the classics of literature, though still with no very ardent personal affection for the writer's fellow men.   It was the first of Mr. Gissing's books in which all the varied fancy and delicate charm that were in him had free play; that it was the last he was to write means the too early loss of one who valued his artistic conscience above popularity, and his purpose above his immediate reward.

[1] *Will Warburton* and *Veranilda* were published after his death.

APPENDIX C

His sister Ellen writes the following reminiscences:

My brother George was ten years older than I, and I first remember him as a big schoolboy, when I myself was a very little girl. From my earliest recollection, however, he is connected in my mind with books and learning; and I remember being conscious of a burning desire in him that the rest of us should be learning too.

My mother used to tell us how, once, when he was a small boy, he insisted on rushing off to school with a sharp herring bone in his throat, for fear of missing his first lesson. He would not allow the trouble to be attended to, until school was over. Also, that when he was eight years old, the elderly lady who kept a small school in Wakefield to which he had been sent, came and said that she had taught him all she could, and begged that he might be sent on to another school, as she felt that his time was being wasted.

I see him best, when he was, I suppose, about sixteen—a tall boy with dark auburn hair, high white brow and eyes slightly short-sighted so that the lids had to be drawn together when looking at any distant object. I remember that his hand was peculiarly soft to touch, with rather square finger ends; and that he shewed a marked gentleness of manner in expressing what he would like one to do, lest any offence should be taken at his wish. This over-sensitiveness to what others were feeling or thinking, was, all through life, a very strong characteristic, and one that greatly added to the strain of his life. I remember how, in later years, even so slight a thing as an order to be given to the woman who kept his flat, would loom before him as a gigantic difficulty, lest she should be offended at the change of plan.

But, needless to say, George did not find it necessary to spare the feelings of his brothers, when all were boys together; for he had scathing words to denounce their boyish pursuits and love of adventurous literature. There are still preserved clever caricatures of them, which he drew when he was fourteen (they being a year or two younger), with verses deriding their way of spending their time.

As I look back I realise in him an especially strong bond of family affection. I remember well that whatever holiday or excursion was planned, his favourite expression was, " Let us go in a body "; he always had a particular dislike of anyone being left out. In his earlier days it was impossible for him to be attracted to people outside his own family, unless he could admire their intellectual gifts. For power of intellect he had an overwhelming veneration, which, but for his sensitiveness to the feelings of others, might have made him hard and indifferent.

Among the things which impressed themselves most strongly upon me as I grew older was my brother's great gift for teaching; not only had he the power of making clear the most intricate subjects, but he had also, I see vividly in looking back, infinite patience in explaining difficulties. I remember well, when he was with us for a short time and giving me help with Latin, how I was astonished that he could give the same explanation time after time, without the least sign of impatience.

To travel with him was always a delightful thing, because he knew all the interesting places, usually overlooked, and could at all times be appealed to for explanations, or historical details. As I said before, he was ten years my senior, and nothing would have surprised me more than to find that I had asked him a question to which he could not give a full and complete answer.

Yet, in spite of all, a note of depression was the most strongly marked of all his characteristics. One always felt that his enjoyment, and the eagerness which he threw into all that interested him, would be followed, for they always were, by a sinking of spirit. A cloud of depression so often fell upon him. Well I remember, when he was with us for a month or two at a time, busy upon some novel, the sight of his face on his joining us in the evening. If the work had not gone well that day, the dejected look and the deeply lined forehead gave him almost a haggard appearance. It was impossible to think that he was the same person, who, perhaps only the day before, had been quite boisterous in his merriment, and had given vivid descriptions of some amusing incident he had seen. But in all things he went to extremes; he loved, for instance, to exaggerate up to the point when the laughter of his listeners showed that they were no longer taking him seriously.

It is impossible to think of anyone more affected by the weather than was my brother. If all the references in his letters and diary to weather had been included, the size of the book would certainly have been greatly increased. Want of sunshine would plunge him into a deeper gloom at once.

He was devoted to animals of all sorts, and many were the strange names he gave to pet cats which he managed to keep at different times in his rooms in London, " Grimmy Shaw " being the most renowned. For these pets, whom he treated as companions, he would give himself any amount of trouble and inconvenience.

Of music he was particularly fond, and always regretted that he knew nothing about it; or to use his own violent expression that he was " brutally ignorant " of the subject. He would try hard, when at home, to understand some of the classical composers, to whom he felt drawn.

In his later visits, when responsibilities weighed heavily upon him and his health was poor, he lost a good deal of that ardent flow of talk and energy with which he used to describe his travels ; but even then the old enthusiasm showed itself occasionally when touching on some favourite topic, especially when there was any reference to Rome, or other place of classical interest.

He was particularly devoted to his children, and would spare no pains or trouble in planning for them. His one anxiety was that they should be in robust and happy surroundings, and that, if it were possible, they should be spared that strain on nerve and brain, which love of learning and want of relaxation had brought upon himself, and from which he had suffered so much.

The last glimpse of my brother comes to me vividly. It was the day on which we saw him off to London from the Wakefield station, in August 1901, at the end of his last visit to England. He had improved in health and was going back to France quite hopefully, trusting to carry out some of his plans for work. I remember that, as we walked up and down in the station, our talk was cut short by a porter who hurried him into a relief train for Kings Cross, in which he said there would be more comfortable travel. So the wave of the hand, and cheery smile for his boy Walter and for ourselves, who were standing on the platform, proved to be our last farewell.

APPENDIX D

CHRONOLOGICAL LIST OF WORKS.

1880. "Workers in the Dawn."
1884. "The Unclassed."
1886. "Isabel Clarendon."
1886. "Demos."
1887. "Thyrza."
1888. "A Life's Morning."
1889. "The Nether World."
1890. "The Emancipated."
1891. "New Grub Street."
1892. "Born in Exile."
1892. "Denzil Quarrier."
1893. "The Odd Women."
1894. "In the Year of Jubilee."
1895. "The Paying Guest."
1895. "Sleeping Fires."
1895. "Eve's Ransom."
1897. "The Whirlpool."
1898. "Human Odds and Ends."   (Stories and Sketches.)
1898. "The Town Traveller."
1898. "Charles Dickens : A Critical Study."
1899. "The Crown of Life."
1901. "Our Friend the Charlatan."
1901. "By the Ionian Sea."
1903. "Forster's Life of Dickens " (abridged).
1903. "The Private Papers of Henry Ryecroft."
1904. "Veranilda."
1905. "Will Warburton."
1906. "The House of Cobwebs."

INDEX